THE FOREGROUND OF

AMERICAN FICTION

BY

HARRY HARTWICK

GORDIAN PRESS
NEW YORK
1967

Originally Published 1934
Reprinted 1967

Library of Congress Catalogue Card Number: 67-30703

Published by GORDIAN PRESS
With the Permission of American Book Company

TO
ANTIC

The effort of all history is to begin with the fact and to end with the symbol.

LESSING

*

FOREWORD

*

It is a truism that the traditions of the past can be fruit-
fully grafted on the present only when one understands
what the present represents. But how is one to gain an
understanding of the multifarious aspects of American life
today and the currents of thought which underlie our activity? In one of Mark Twain's serious essays he concludes
that such an understanding comes only after "years and
years of unconscious absorption; years and years of inter-
course with the life concerned; of living it, indeed; sharing
personally in its shames and prides, its joys and griefs, its
loves and hates, its proprieties and reverses, its shows and
shabbinesses, its deep patriotisms, its whirlwinds of political
passions, its adorations — of flag, and heroic dead, and the
glory of the national name. Observation? Of what real
value is it? One learns peoples through the heart, not the
eyes or the intellect. There is only one expert who is
qualified to examine the souls and the life of a people and
make a valuable report — the native novelist." And there
is no better index to the American mind during the last
forty years than the American novel.

As a means, then, of securing a cross-section of our
national mind during this period, Mr. Hartwick, formerly
a member of the staff of The School of Letters at the State
University of Iowa, has provided us with this rationale
of recent fiction. During the last forty years, what forces
and fashions, literary creeds, technical experiments, folk-
ways, scientific discoveries, and social trends have been
reflected in the American novel? What light does such a

study cast on the ideals of living in America and the results of these ideals in terms of human satisfaction? To what extent have the various literary creeds resulted in a literary art of universal appeal and enduring beauty? These are a few of the questions Mr. Hartwick has tried to answer. The American novel has just traversed one of the most fertile and animated periods of its history; and now that its revolutions have begun to display signs of hardening into conventions, the time seems ripe for a trial balance, for an evaluation of causes and results, and for a serious estimate of its ethical and esthetic achievements.

Mr. Hartwick's purpose has been to explain the novels of our recent past not as products of any one cultural force, but in relation to their whole social, economic, religious, philosophic, and literary environment. For instance, he does not interpret the novel solely in terms of an economic class-struggle, as many recent critics have tended to do. He is aware of the complexity and diversity of the factors involved, and he has approached his problem inductively, without narrow pre-conceived conclusions. His book is accordingly both a picture and an idea, a pandectic view of American fiction during this century; it begins with facts and ends with symbols. The facts are the novels themselves and their authors; the symbols are the ideas they represent.

This volume is designed to be both complete and provocative; for Mr. Hartwick has made an effort not merely to describe but to detach the wheat from the chaff. His book should therefore be useful to anyone who reads contemporary American fiction, whether for pleasure or with a critical eye; and readers will be especially grateful to him for enlivening the subject with a refreshingly crisp and vivid style, as well as with wit and penetration.

The Foreground of American Fiction helps us to see the novel against a background of those forces and ideas of which it is a product. Mr. Hartwick has pointed out the fundamental alignments in our fiction of the last forty years, though the categories have not been drawn too rigidly. As a glance at the table of contents will indicate, the book is organized with reference to four general philosophic tendencies. Part One, entitled "The Noble Savage," deals with the manner in which Crane, Norris, London, Dreiser, Anderson, Hemingway, and Faulkner have developed the naturalistic superman's quest of the primitive, the strong, and the ruthless. Part Two, entitled "Beyond Life," deals with the desire of such men as Cabell and Hergesheimer to escape from an unpleasant reality into a paradise of beauty. Part Three, entitled "New Worlds for Old," deals with the social revolt of such novelists as Sinclair Lewis, Upton Sinclair, and Dos Passos, whose desire is to create a new social order looking toward either socialism or anarchy. Part Four, entitled "Laws as Wings," deals with Howells, James, Edith Wharton, and Willa Cather, and their Emersonian quest of beauty as the by-product of spiritual health, self-control, decorum, and the golden mean. Though I see most hope in the tendencies represented by the latter group, I have as general editor made no attempt to dissuade Mr. Hartwick from his conviction that more is to be hoped from the tendencies of the naturalists, though he admits that their present degraded practice has reached a *cul de sac*. He seems to me to have dealt fairly with each of the four tendencies, to have relived each group's vision of life with sympathy and objectivity.

No doubt I cannot escape being a prejudiced witness, but I insist on saying that I do not know where one will find a more lively, penetrating, and comprehensive survey of the recent American novel, as it reflects the American mind, than this which has been given us by Mr. Hartwick.

HARRY HAYDEN CLARK

MADISON, WISCONSIN
May 15, 1934

*

ACKNOWLEDGMENTS

*

The following books and articles are those from which brief quotations have been borrowed for this discussion. I have tried to reach all of the copyright holders; and when this effort has met with success, as it has in practically every instance, permission to reprint has been courteously granted.

AMERICAN LITERATURE MAGAZINE. Walter Fuller Taylor's "William Dean Howells and the Economic Novel."

SHERWOOD ANDERSON. *Dark Laughter* (Boni & Liveright, 1925), *Marching Men* (John Lane Company, 1917), *Perhaps Women* (Horace Liveright, 1931), *Sherwood Anderson's Notebook* (Boni & Liveright, 1926), *Mid-American Chants* (John Lane Company, 1918), *Poor White* (B. W. Huebsch, 1920), *Many Marriages* (B. W. Huebsch, 1923), *A Story Teller's Story* (B. W. Huebsch, 1924), *Windy McPherson's Son* (B. W. Huebsch, 1922).

D. APPLETON-CENTURY COMPANY. Edith Wharton's *The Gods Arrive, The Children, Hudson River Bracketed, New Year's Day*, and *Twilight Sleep;* T. K. Whipple's *Spokesmen;* Jack London's *John Barleycorn;* Fred Lewis Pattee's *American Literature Since 1870.*

THE ATLANTIC MONTHLY. Edith Wharton's "Confessions of a Novelist."

GEORGIA LORING BAMFORD. *The Mystery of Jack London.*

BOBBS-MERRILL COMPANY. Herbert Quick's *The Hawkeye.*

BRANDT & BRANDT. John Dos Passos' *Manhattan Transfer* and *Orient Express.*

BRUCE HUMPHRIES, INC. Gertrude Stein's *Geography and Plays*, copyright 1922, by the Four Seas Company and used by permission of Bruce Humphries, Inc.

JAMES BRANCH CABELL. "In Respect to Joseph Hergesheimer."

GRACE ISABEL COLBRON. "Jack London."

COVICI, FRIEDE. E. E. Cummings' *Eimi.*

COWARD-MCCANN. Thornton Wilder's *The Angel That Troubled the Waters.*

viii

ACKNOWLEDGMENTS ix

CURRENT HISTORY MAGAZINE. Lewis Mumford's " The America of Sinclair Lewis."

BENJAMIN DE CASSERES. " Portraits en Brochette."

THE DIAL PUBLISHING COMPANY. Wilson Follett's " Factualist Versus Impressionist," and Alyse Gregory's " Sherwood Anderson."

DODD, MEAD & COMPANY. Anatole France's *The Garden of Epicurus*, and Rupert Brooke's *Collected Poems*.

DOUBLEDAY, DORAN AND COMPANY. Mildred Howells' *Life in Letters of William Dean Howells* (copyright, 1926); Aldous Huxley's *Do What You Will* (copyright, 1928); Sinclair Lewis's *Ann Vickers* (copyright, 1933); Gorham B. Munson's *Style and Form in American Prose* (copyright, 1929); Franklin Walker's *Frank Norris* (copyright, 1932); Frank Norris's *A Man's Woman* (copyright, 1902), *Moran of the Lady Letty* (copyright, 1902), *The Octopus* (copyright, 1901), *The Pit* (copyright, 1903), *The Responsibilities of the Novelist* (copyright, 1903), *Vandover and the Brute* (copyright, 1924), and *McTeague* (copyright, 1899); John Macy's *The Spirit of American Literature* (copyright, 1913); Joseph Collins' *Taking the Literary Pulse* (copyright, 1924); Floyd Dell's *Intellectual Vagabondage* (copyright, 1926); John Dos Passos' *One Man's Initiation — 1917* (copyright, 1917, 1922), *A Pushcart at the Curb* (copyright, 1922), *Rosinante to the Road Again* (copyright, 1922), and *Streets of Night* (copyright, 1923); Arthur Davison Ficke's *Selected Poems* (copyright, 1926).

DUFFIELD & GREEN. Maurice Samuel's *Whatever Gods*.

E. P. DUTTON & COMPANY. Van Wyck Brooks' *Emerson and Others*.

THEODORE DREISER. *A Book About Myself* (Boni & Liveright, copyright 1922), *The Financier* (Boni & Liveright, copyright 1912), *Hey Rub-a-Dub-Dub* (Boni & Liveright, copyright 1920), *Jennie Gerhardt* (Horace Liveright, copyright 1911), *A Hoosier Holiday* (John Lane Company, copyright 1916). Also " Statements of Belief."

ENCYCLOPÆDIA BRITANNICA. M. Ginsberg's " Social Philosophy."

JOHN FARRAR. *The Literary Spotlight* and " Sex Psychology in Modern Fiction."

FARRAR & RINEHART. Norman Foerster's *Humanism and America* and *Toward Standards;* Samuel D. Schmalhausen's *Our Neurotic Age*.

WILSON FOLLETT. " The Simplicity of Henry James."

FUNK & WAGNALLS COMPANY. Horatio Krans' " Henry James."

HAMLIN GARLAND. *Crumbling Idols*.

C. HARTLEY GRATTAN. " Jack London " and " Howells: Ten Years After."

HARCOURT, BRACE AND COMPANY. Hugh I'Anson Fausset's *The Proving of Psyche;* Nathan Asch's *The Office;* John Dos Passos' *1919;* Elizabeth A. Drew's *The Modern Novel;* Ramon Fernandez' *Messages;* Joseph Wood Krutch's *The Modern Temper;* Sinclair Lewis's *Arrowsmith, Babbitt, Dodsworth, The Trail of the Hawk, Elmer Gantry, The Job, Main Street, The Man Who Knew Coolidge, Our Mr. Wrenn,* and *Addresses by Erik Axel Karlfeldt and Sinclair Lewis, On the Occasion of the Award of the Nobel Prize;* Vernon Louis Parrington's *Main Currents in American Thought;* Harold E. Stearns' *Civilization in the United States.*

HARPER & BROTHERS. Frederick Lewis Allen's *Only Yesterday,* James H. Bossard's *Man and His World,* Ralph W. Sockman's *Morals of Tomorrow,* Mark Twain's *What Is Man?* Glenway Wescott's *The Apple of the Eye,* Ludwig Lewisohn's *Expression in America.*

HARRISON SMITH AND ROBERT HAAS. Dorothy Dudley's *Forgotten Frontiers;* William Faulkner's *Sanctuary, The Sound and the Fury,* and *A Green Bough.*

HARVARD UNIVERSITY PRESS. Oscar Firkins' *William Dean Howells.*

JOSEPH HERGESHEIMER. "James Branch Cabell."

GRANVILLE HICKS. "The Past and Future of William Faulkner."

HENRY HOLT AND COMPANY. Henri Bergson's *Creative Evolution,* Helen T. and Wilson Follett's *Some Modern Novelists,* Stuart Pratt Sherman's *On Contemporary Literature,* J. C. Squire's *Contemporary American Authors,* J. E. Spingarn's *Creative Criticism,* Rebecca West's *Henry James.*

HOUGHTON MIFFLIN COMPANY. Pelham Edgar's *Henry James, Man and Author;* Irving Babbitt's *Literature and the American College* and *Rousseau and Romanticism;* Willa Cather's *The Song of the Lark;* Havelock Ellis's *Fountain of Life;* William Dean Howells' *The Minister's Charge, A Modern Instance, The Rise of Silas Lapham,* and *Their Wedding Journey;* Henry James's *The Europeans;* Paul Elmer More's *Shelburne Essays,* Seventh and Eighth Series; John Herman Randall's *The Making of the Modern Mind;* Meredith Nicolson's *A Hoosier Chronicle.* By permission of, and arrangement with, Houghton Mifflin Company.

MILDRED HOWELLS. *Life in Letters of William Dean Howells;* William Dean Howells' *The Minister's Charge, A Modern Instance, The Rise of Silas Lapham, Their Wedding Journey, An Imperative Duty, Annie Kilburn, Criticism and Fiction, A Hazard of New Fortunes, Literature and Life, My Literary Passions,* and *The World of Chance.*

FORD MADOX HUEFFER (Ford Madox Ford). "On Impressionism."

GLENN HUGHES. V. F. Calverton's *American Literature at the Crossroads,* Benjamin De Casseres' *The Superman in America,* Joseph T. Shipley's *The Literary Isms.*

ACKNOWLEDGMENTS xi

ALFRED A. KNOPF. Thomas Beer's *Stephen Crane;* Willa Cather's *A Lost Lady, My Mortal Enemy,* and *Youth and the Bright Medusa; The Borzoi, 1920;* Wilson Follett's *The Work of Stephen Crane;* Joseph Hergesheimer's *The Lay Anthony, Tampico, The Three Black Pennys,* and *From an Old House;* H. L. Mencken's *Prejudices: First Series;* Elizabeth Sergeant's *Fire Under the Andes;* George Jean Nathan and H. L. Mencken's *The American Credo;* Carl Van Doren's *The Roving Critic* and *Many Minds.* Reprinted by permission of, and special arrangement with, Alfred A. Knopf, Inc., authorized publishers.

LADIES' HOME JOURNAL. Edith Wharton's " A Backward Glance."

CARROLL LATROBE. " Willa Sibert Cather."

SINCLAIR LEWIS. " Self-Conscious America."

LIVERIGHT PUBLISHING CORPORATION. William Faulkner's *Mosquitoes* and *Soldiers' Pay;* Evelyn Scott's *The Narrow House.*

THE LIVING AGE. Edith Wharton's " The Criticism of Fiction."

CHARMIAN LONDON. Jack London's *A Daughter of the Snows, The Sea-Wolf,* " Rods and Gunnels," and *The Works of Jack London,* VII (Review of Reviews Company, 1917).

LONGMANS, GREEN & COMPANY. William James's *A Pluralistic Universe* and *Pragmatism;* Carl Snyder's *The World Machine.*

THE MACMILLAN COMPANY. Charles and Mary Beard's *The Rise of American Civilization,* Durant Drake's *The New Morality,* A. S. Eddington's *The Nature of the Physical World,* Harold Underwood Faulkner's *The Quest for Social Justice,* Hamlin Garland's *Roadside Meetings,* Henry James's *Hawthorne* and *Partial Portraits,* Friedrich Nietzsche's *Complete Works,* Edwin Arlington Robinson's *The Man Against the Sky,* A. M. Simons' *Social Forces in American History,* Preston William Slossen's *The Great Crusade and After, 1914–1928,* Carl Van Doren's *The American Novel* and *Contemporary American Novelists.* By permission of The Macmillan Company, publishers.

EDWIN MARKHAM. *The Man With the Hoe.*

ROBERT M. McBRIDE & COMPANY. James Branch Cabell's *Beyond Life, The Cream of the Jest, Straws and Prayer-Books,* and *These Restless Heads;* Robert Morss Lovett's *Edith Wharton;* René Rapin's *Willa Cather;* Burton Rascoe's *Theodore Dreiser.*

PAUL ELMER MORE. " A Revival of Humanism."

EDWIN MUIR. *We Moderns* (published in England by George Allen & Unwin, and in America by Alfred A. Knopf).

THE NATION. Maxwell Bodenheim's " Psychoanalysis and American Fiction," V. F. Calverton's " The Upton Sinclair Enigma," Willa Cather's " Nebraska: The End of the First Cycle," Clifton Fadiman's " Ernest Hemingway " and " Sherwood Anderson," C. Hartley Grattan's " The Calm Within the Cyclone," Henry Hazlitt's " Panorama " and " Salvation for the Modern Soul," Joseph Wood Krutch's " New Morals for Old: Modern Love and Modern Fiction," Sinclair Lewis's " Main Street's Been Paved! " and " Mr. Lorimer and Me."

NEW OUTLOOK. L. R. Dickenson's " Smyth County Items."

THE NEW REPUBLIC. E. Preston Dargan's " Jack London in Chancery," Robert Littell's " Notes on Hemingway," George Soule's " Realism as Confession," Louis Weinberg's " Current Impressionism."

THE NEW YORKER. Janet Flanner's " Dearest Edith."

NEW YORK HERALD TRIBUNE. An Interview with Louis Bromfield.

THE NORTH AMERICAN REVIEW. Lloyd Morris's " Willa Cather."

W. W. NORTON & COMPANY. Bertrand Russell's *The Scientific Outlook* and *Mysticism and Logic.*

VINCENT O'SULLIVAN. *H. L. Mencken* (Alfred A. Knopf, 1920).

OVERLAND MONTHLY. Calvin B. Houck's " Jack London's Philosophy of Life," and Louis Wann's " The ' Revolt from the Village ' in American Fiction."

OXFORD UNIVERSITY PRESS. Thomas M. Parrott and Willard Thorp's *Poetry of the Transition.*

G. P. PUTNAM'S SONS. *The Cambridge History of American Literature,* III.

RANDOM HOUSE. James Joyce's *Ulysses.*

RAY LONG & RICHARD R. SMITH. Grant C. Knight's *American Literature and Culture.*

THE SATURDAY REVIEW OF LITERATURE. Henry Seidel Canby's " Something About Fig Leaves," Willa Cather's " Shadows on the Rock: A Letter," Katherine F. Gerould's " Stream of Consciousness," and an untitled contribution by Don Marquis.

CHARLES SCRIBNER'S SONS. W. C. Brownell's *American Prose Masters;* V. F. Calverton's *The Liberation of American Literature;* Max Eastman's *The Literary Mind;* Ernest Hemingway's *Death in the Afternoon, A Farewell to Arms,* and *The Sun Also Rises;* Henry James's *The Sacred Fount, The American, The Awkward Age, Daisy Miller, The Portrait of a Lady, The Princess Casamassima, Roderick Hudson,* and *The Spoils of Poynton;* Percy

ACKNOWLEDGMENTS xiii

Lubbock's *The Letters of Henry James;* Meredith Nicolson's *The Valley of Democracy;* George Santayana's *Little Essays;* Mark Sullivan's *Our Times,* IV; Edmund Wilson's *Axel's Castle;* Edith Wharton's *The Custom of the Country, Ethan Frome, The Fruit of the Tree,* and *The Writing of Fiction.*

THE SEWANEE REVIEW. George E. DeMille's " The Infallible Dean," Edward Niles Hooker's " Something About Cabell," and Leon Kelley's " America and Mr. Hergesheimer."

UPTON SINCLAIR. " A Home Colony," *The Book of Life, The Brass Check, Mammonart, Manassas, The Millenium, Money Writes, The Metropolis, The Profits of Religion, They Call Me Carpenter, American Outpost, Mountain City,* and *Oil!*

MARSHALL J. SMITH. " Faulkner of Mississippi."

FREDERICK A. STOKES COMPANY. Louis Bromfield's *Twenty-Four Hours.*

ALAN REYNOLDS THOMPSON'S. " Sanctuary: A Review " and " Farewell to Achilles."

THE UNIVERSITY OF CHICAGO PRESS. Percy H. Boynton's *Some Contemporary Americans,* and Robert E. Park and Ernest W. Burgess's *Introduction to the Science of Sociology.*

WILCOX & FOLLETT COMPANY. Percy H. Boynton's *The Challenge of Modern Criticism.*

ELIZABETH WYCKOFF. " Dorothy Canfield: *A Neglected Best-Seller.*"

THE YALE REVIEW. André Gide's " Henry James," William Lyon Phelps' " William Dean Howells," and Edith Wharton's " The Great American Novel."

I also wish to extend my thanks to C. Hartley Grattan for several clarifying judgments in regard to the social fiction of today; to Harry Hayden Clark of the University of Wisconsin for his Preface and friendly assistance in every stage of the book's growth; and to Frank Luther Mott, Director of the School of Journalism at the University of Iowa, whose keen interest in American literature was the first to encourage my own.

H. H.

NEW YORK CITY
May 25, 1934

*

CONTENTS

*

* THE NOBLE SAVAGE

*Man is the work of Nature: he exists in Nature: he is sub-
mitted to her laws: he cannot deliver himself from them; nor
can he step beyond them even in thought. . . . Instead,
therefore, of seeking out of the world he inhabits for beings who
can procure him a happiness denied to him by Nature, let man
study this Nature, let him learn her laws, contemplate her
energies, observe the immutable rules by which she acts: —
let him apply these discoveries to his own felicity and submit
in silence to her mandates, which nothing can alter.*

HOLBACH

*

WHAT'S O'CLOCK?

*

BACK TO NATURE   *Laissez faire* is the litmus paper of
modern thought; and from his tendency to glorify or stig-
matize this concept, the philosophical bias of every recent
American novelist may be judged. Reduced to lowest
terms, it means: *Let Nature take its course, and obey the instincts
that Nature has presented to man for his guidance. Ideals of
human conduct are only the toys of an ignorant and puny biped, his
naive interpretations of a scheme too big and dark for him to
decipher. Nature alone knows what is best for man, having
created him. Therefore he must resign himself to its leadership,
to impulse rather than wisdom, in order not to go astray.*

The father of this doctrine is science, and its three revolutionary premises have been drawn from the laboratory.
(1) *Nature is a machine that runs by itself, without the interference
of any divinity.* It embraces everything, and reserves no
place for God, the soul, or immortality. When Dante, in
the fourteenth century, scribbled Amen to his *Divina
Commedia* and the Middle Ages, this earth was still an absolute monarchy, with God its intimate and puissant King.
But during the Renaissance and after, Galileo, Kepler,
Copernicus, and Newton pushed back the outskirts of the
universe, and in doing so, destroyed heaven. Nowhere
could the new telescope spy God. He had vanished, save
as an explanation of how man came into being; and since
Darwin, even this sole remaining function has been wrested
from Him. His dominion over the plant and animal kingdoms has been usurped by the law of evolution, just as the
law of gravitation drove Him out of the sky. "The anthro-

3

pomorphic notion of a deliberate architect and ruler of the world has gone forever," and "the 'eternal, iron laws of nature' have taken his place." [1]   Prior to 1500 almost everyone sang "God's in His heaven." Today many people are convinced that He is extinct.

Once he decreed the fall of every sparrow and counted the hairs upon every head; a little later he became merely the original source of the laws of nature, and even today there are thousands who, unable to bear the thought of losing him completely, still fancy that they can distinguish the uncertain outlines of a misty figure.   But the rôle which he plays grows less and less, and man is left more and more alone in a universe to which he is completely alien.[2]

Religion has surrendered to mathematics; and instead of God, "authorities seem to be agreed that at, or nearly at, the root of everything in the physical world lies the mystic formula $qp - pq = ih/2\pi$." [3]

Immortality, too, has been thrown into doubt; for science now tells us that our cosmos is suffering an entropic decline in energy, slowly fatal to all life; that man is the product of causes which had "no prevision of the end they were achieving; that his origin, his growth, his hopes and fears, his loves and his beliefs, are but the outcome of accidental collocations of atoms; that no fire, no heroism, no intensity of thought and feeling, can preserve an individual life beyond the grave; that all the labors of the ages, all the devotion, all the inspiration, all the noonday brightness of human genius, are destined to extinction in the vast death of the solar system, and that the whole temple of Man's achievement must inevitably be buried beneath the débris of a universe in ruins." [4]

[1] Haeckel, Ernst, *The Riddle of the Universe* (1900), p. 261.
[2] Krutch, Joseph Wood, *The Modern Temper* (1929), pp. 9–10.
[3] Eddington, A. S., *The Nature of the Physical World* (1929), p. 207.   By permission of The Macmillan Company, publishers.
[4] Russell, Bertrand, *Selected Papers of Bertrand Russell* (1927), p. 3.

THIS SIMIAN WORLD As the frontiers of space have widened, man's importance has shrunk, until Einstein's universe is said to be 585,900,000,000,000,000,000,000 miles in circumference, and we mammals have been reduced to the size of bacteria on the epidermis of a huge apple. Man's ancestry has also been impugned, and to scientists he has become only an ape "grown rusty at climbing." "The theory of biologists before Darwin was that there is laid up in Heaven an ideal cat and an ideal dog, and so on; and that actual cats and dogs are more or less imperfect copies of these celestial types. Each species corresponds to a different idea in the divine mind, and therefore there could be no transition from one species to another." [5] But since Darwin's *Origin of Species* (1859), many of us have come to believe that life derived by osmosis from a granule of colloidal slime, and crawled up through lower plants and animals before flowering (as we like to think) in the genus *homo sapiens*. Man, science implies, is not a mundane angel produced by God in His own image, not "a gift from the beginning, but a laborious conquest which is achieved little by little through the evolution of organisms and of human societies." [6]

(2) *This machine of Nature is a kind of "cream separator." It brings the strong to the top and exterminates the weak, thus rendering society purer and more durable.* Evolution, it is said, works by "survival of the fittest," and for men to introduce pity into this scheme only serves to perpetuate those who, because they are too feeble to live without help, deserve to die. They are weeds in the garden; and left to its own devices Nature will pluck them out for us. According to Malthus in his *Essay on Population* (1798), the world's population tends to increase geometrically, while its food supply increases arithmetically, with the result that those weaklings who cannot exact their share must perish, or at

---

[5] Russell, Bertrand, *The Scientific Outlook* (1931), p. 42.
[6] Needham, Joseph (ed.), *Science, Religion and Reality* (1925), p. 182.

least resign the comforts of life to those who are more powerful. Today there are some 250,000 species of plants and 500,000 of animals that have survived because they were able to adapt themselves to changing environments, and husky enough to seize from others without letting others seize from them. By this process of "natural selection," then, Nature sees to it that only those live who are "fit" to live.

Evolution views man as competing, not against the powers of darkness (as religion warned us), but against other men. Life has been transformed into a desperate struggle for essentials and luxuries.

Everything in nature, living or not living, exists and develops at the expense of some other thing, living or not living. The plant borrows from the soil; the soil from the rocks and the atmosphere; men and animals take from the plants and from each other the elements which they in death return to the soil, the atmosphere, and the plants. Year after year, century after century, eon after eon, the mighty, immeasurable, ceaseless round of elements goes on, in the stupendous process of chemical change, which marks the eternal life of matter.[7]

Those who are not endowed with sufficient pith and perspicacity become the victims of those who are. Even the idea that evolution must at least signify a trend toward better things, though popular for a time, has since been discarded; and now the only progress recognized by science is that of an organism from homogeneity to heterogeneity. "Society never advances. It recedes as fast on one side as it gains on the other. It undergoes continual changes; it is barbarous, it is civilized, it is christianized, it is rich, it is scientific; but this change is not amelioration." [8]

Spencer believed that evolution stood for progress; and it is this much of science that our present socialistic novel

---

[7] Park, Robert E., and Ernest W. Burgess, *Introduction to the Science of Sociology* (1927), p. 521.

[8] Emerson, Ralph Waldo, *The Complete Works of Ralph Waldo Emerson* (1903), II, 84.

has retained. But as the nineteenth century neared its end, the concepts of Spencer gave way in the province of scientific philosophy to those of the German biologist, Ernst Haeckel; and this change soon reflected a deep gloom into the minds of educated people. Evolution, to Haeckel, did not mean improvement; everything had turned to flux and chance. The old laws of Nature still held, but they moved toward no purpose as they had in Spencer; the latter had found a place for good and bad, whereas Haeckel did not. Even the hope of a future had now been taken from men by science.

Purpose had disappeared from the grim face of the material universe, and they found themselves in the coils of a determinism that was more likely to prove malignant than benevolent. The idea of progress slipped quietly from their minds, and in its stead was only a meaningless and purposeless flux of things.[9]

DETERMINISM Nor has science left us an independent mind. The soul has been pictured as a myth, and man exposed as a rude mixture of charcoal, water, nitrogen, sulphur, oxygen, phosphorus, arsenic, and mineral salts, worth about eighty cents. Matter alone remains, composed of waltzing protons and electrons, like a vibrating pocket of gnats in the air. The rest, as some would have it, is mere opinion.

To judge from his later *Descent of Man* (1871), Darwin himself believed that human beings were gifted with free will; and Spencer and Huxley, who developed the ideas of Darwin, also inclined to this faith. But while one group of astronomers and geologists were attempting to prove with telescope and spade that there was no place in the universe for God to hide, another family of scientists had been turning the microscope on man to demonstrate that there were no crevices in him where a mind or soul could secrete itself. These investigators rose through Descartes, Locke, Boyle, Holbach, and La Mettrie to a climax in

[9] Parrington, Vernon Louis, *Main Currents in American Thought* (1930). III, 202–203.

Haeckel, whose famous *Riddle of the Universe* was translated into English in 1900.

Haeckel and his fellow determinists based the mysteries of thought on chemistry and physical components of the body. They believed, in the words of a modern novelist, that

Men were simply insects of the most insignificant sort being driven by a tyrannical power along paths which had nothing to do with their own wills. Nature did not concern itself with their happiness nor with what became of them once they had accomplished what she meant them to accomplish. It did not matter to Nature whether they were faithful and monogamous or unfaithful and as promiscuous as guinea pigs, because, of course, Nature was not concerned with moral peccadillos. Romance and morality and sentiment were simply excrescences constructed through thousands of years all about the main question in order to disguise it and save the ego and vanity of men.[10]

Recent physicists, after the example of Newton, describe the universe as a majestic engine, and biology sees man as a helpless automaton, operated by instincts and reflexes. Just as "Copernicus abolished the primacy of man's planet in the universe, Darwin abolished the primacy of man within his planet, and materialistic psychology abolished the primacy of mind within the man."[11] "The heart is a pump," one writer alleges, "and the blood vessels an intricate system of irrigation. The lungs are bellows, worked automatically from a centre at the base of the brain. The muscles are pulleys and the bones are cranes. The eye is a telescope, the ear an inverted megaphone. The kidneys are filters, the liver is a sugar factory, the stomach a vat for fermenting food, the thirty feet of coiled piping of the intestines the vital still where strength, warmth, courage, good feelings and bad, and all our out-

---

[10] Bromfield, Louis, *Twenty-Four Hours* (1930), p. 455. By courtesy of the Frederick A. Stokes Company.

[11] Joad, C. E. M., *Guide to Modern Thought* (1933), p. 40.

look upon life are brewed." [12]   Man has become a tangle of nerve circuits, an electrical slot contrivance. Drop in a stimulus through one of his sensory organs, eye, tongue, ear, nose, or skin, and it will release a cluster of habitual responses, which force him to react in an invariable way, at the dictation of whatever desire happens to be strongest in him at the moment. "Consciousness, thought, and speculation — are functions of the ganglionic cells of the cortex of the brain," [13] said Haeckel, and "The human will has no more freedom than that of the higher animals, from which it differs only in degree, not in kind." [14]

Life, according to the determinist, is a string of firecrackers exploding down its length until the last fizzling hiss announces that our world has blown itself out. Each event is a tiny burst of energy ignited by its predecessor. "Mental events are caused by preceding cerebral events; all cerebral events are subject to the law of cause and effect, and are caused, therefore, by preceding bodily events or by external stimuli to which they are responses; the preceding bodily events are in their turn caused either by preceding bodily events or by external stimuli. Along these lines we travel backward until we reach the first events in the history of the organism, which are the result of its initial inheritance or of its external environment. In so far as they are the result of inheritance," they can be traced back to the evolutionary processes which made the organism what it is. "The chain of causation from a happening in the external world to a thought in mind is, therefore, complete." [15]   And everything being explained by the natural law of cause and effect, God, the soul, and free will have made their exit. What was once termed "mind" has been relegated, with the rest of the universe, to "matter."

[12] Snyder, Carl, *The World Machine* (1907), p. 32.
[13] Haeckel, Ernst, *op. cit.*, p. 17.
[14] *Ibid.*, p. 131.
[15] Joad, C. E. M., *op. cit.*, p. 39.

Science (with the aid of reason) has demonstrated the invalidity of reason. Mind is now represented as a simple correlation between stimulus and response, a reflex over which we have no control. That is to say, it is determined by the body, which is in turn determined by its surroundings; or as Mark Twain put it:

Whatsoever a man is, is due to his *make*, and to the *influences* brought to bear upon it by his heredities, his habitat, his associations. He is moved, directed, COMMANDED, by *exterior* influences — solely. He *originates* nothing, not even a thought. . . . A man's brain is so constructed that *it can originate nothing whatever.* It can only use material obtained *outside.* It is merely a machine; and it works automatically, not by will-power. *It has no command over itself, its owner has no command over it.*[16]

MORALS À LA MODE   (3) *Because Nature is a mere "cream separator," it does not take any account of human ethics.* As a machine, it can have none of its own; and so man, who is geared to Nature, cannot be held responsible for *his* behavior. Evolution, as a theory, has been carried over into the sphere of morals. Fixed and established standards of conduct (sanctified by tradition) are nowadays frowned upon as the attempts of a past or passing generation to lay its dead or dying hand upon the present. After Darwin's *Origin of Species* came Spencer's *Synthetic Philosophy*, which contained a generalized application of Darwinism to society and culture; and today the feeling has ripened that there are no eternally valid conventions. A belief holds good, we say, only in reference to its original background. Men and their environments change; conscience varies with them, to flatter and keep in step with their revised desires; and a value retains its legitimacy only as long as the cultural situation of which it is a product and expression. Social forces, attitudes, opinions, wishes, sentiments, and patterns of faith are, like men, in a constant flux and

---

[16] Twain, Mark, *What Is Man?* (1917), pp. 5–7.

"struggle for existence." When they can no longer be of service to us, there ensues a conflict with more serviceable codes and finally an accommodation to a new intellectual order or equilibrium. Ideas, as well as men, are born, grow, mature, and even die. "The great lesson to be derived from a study of the customs of various peoples is that there is no absolute standard of rightness. The standard used in judging the rightness of mores is itself part of a set of mores. There is scarcely a crime that has not somewhere at some time been considered a virtue. Murder of the aged, cannibalism, infanticide, polygamy, prostitution, thieving, and human sacrifice all have received the approval of custom. The most rigid mores may be quite lacking in rational justification and become in time objects of ridicule, just as the costumes and proprieties of medieval chivalry would provoke amusement if seriously displayed on the streets of a large modern city. When we realize that people are Republicans, Socialists, Catholics, atheists, polygamists, head hunters, and cannibals because of the culture in which they are reared, we become more tolerant of views that differ from our own. Personalities and customs foreign to our own are not necessarily due to innate depravity and stupidity, but are rather the products of cultures which cannot be fairly judged by standards which we have derived from our own particular and perhaps inferior culture." [17]

"Against the static conceptions which characterized medieval thinking is the modern idea of a dynamic and ever changing universe. The concept of change is fundamental to all of our modern interpretations. We see everything in a state of becoming. That which has been yields to that which is, to be replaced in turn by that which will be — this, applicable from electron to solar system and from amoeba to man, is the cornerstone of contemporary interpretation." [18]

[17] Bossard, James H. S. (ed.), *Man and His World* (1932), p. 409.
[18] *Ibid.*, p. 23.

Each journeys steadily beyond the desires and the ways of thinking which at any present moment were his. There is no passion which endures, no desire which stays fervent, and no comrade who remains near to the eternal journeyer. He may not hope to touch permanence anywhere. Not even in his own being may he look to find permanence, for that being alters unceasingly, alike in its physical body and in spirit and in needs and in intelligence. As the shape of a cloud is altered in its drifting, so do your virtues and your beliefs take momentary form and then melt away acquiescently into some other shaping in the while that you journey; and so must all men change at every instant in their noisy journey through a continuous changing until the supreme change has created its quiet carrion.[19]

Measured by the leaves of rock that comprise its surface, our planet's geologic eras correspond in number and significance to the four ages of man. Paring off these horizontal rinds of earth, we discover first the Cenozoic, upon which we live today, then the Mesozoic, Paleozoic, and oldest of all, the Archeozoic; just as, turning back the clock of history, we retreat through the temporal ages of modern, medieval, ancient, and prehistoric. Each crust of earth, in its turn, gives birth to characteristic species of flora and fauna, only to have them stamped out by the next crust, like withered flowers between the pages of a book. And in the same way, past faiths and institutions of mankind have become mere worm tracks in the strata of time. Conventions fade out invisibly with the loam that nurtured them; loyalties expire in a few years, and are buried under newer ones. Even the "vital lie" of man's unity has been replaced by a more recent fiction, which regards man as a diverse organism. Freud and others see the individual, not as a single consistent being with one set of beliefs and one outlook upon life, but as a private universe, harboring several different personalities who take turns at ruling him. Thus it has become usual to think of man as

[19] Cabell, Branch, *These Restless Heads* (1932), pp. 216–217.

"a colony of separate individuals, of whom now one and now another consciously lives with the life that animates the whole organism and directs its destinies," [20] instead of as a unit functioning with one set of ideals from cradle to cemetery.

CRUMBLING IDOLS   This, in general, is the reading of Nature upon which *laissez faire* and a great deal of modern literature have been founded.   True, the latest discoveries of science have overflown this tightly woven interpretation. Yet most writers still base their philosophies upon it, and even Einstein retains his faith in determinism (though his researches have helped to bring Nature as a perfect machine into doubt).   There is a "cultural lag" in man; his brain can invent things that his emotions cannot immediately accept.   Fiction, which appeals to man's heart, always trails behind science, which is a product of his restless mind; and as a result, our present novel springs from concepts already being abandoned by physiology and physics.   In spite of science's new and almost *mystical* reinterpretation of the cosmos, fiction in America today continues to sprout from the very *realistic* universe of Newton and Spencer.   For in relation to social changes, art is always a delayed echo.[21]

By 1900 rumors of this "realistic universe" had winged the Atlantic to the United States, where physical science had heretofore run mostly to inventions.   During the last forty years of the nineteenth century, over 600,000 patents had been issued in this country.   But even in pure science we could boast of several investigators whose contributions had won them a European reputation, men like Samuel P. Langley in solar physics, Lewis H. Morgan in ethnology, James D. Dana in geology, Simon Newcomb in astronomy, and Josiah Willard Gibbs in chemistry.   Darwin himself

[20] Huxley, Aldous, *Do What You Will* (1929), pp. 257–258.
[21] *Cf.* Santayana, George, *Little Essays* (1921), pp. 112–113.

placed a high value upon the judgment of Asa Gray, the Harvard botanist, and declared that "the two most striking reviews" of his *Origin of Species* had appeared in America.

Championed by Gray, the doctrine of evolution soon became a topic of vehement controversy on these shores, and found an appreciative public. Spencer's *First Principles* (1862) had a faster sale in the United States than in England. Before 1882 Huxley, Tyndall, and Spencer had lectured in this country; and E. L. Youmans, who established the *Popular Science Monthly* in 1872, was able to raise $7,000 here to help Spencer publish his *Synthetic Philosophy*. Courses in scientific thought were being given at Harvard and Cornell by the end of the century, and colleges were beginning to finance laboratories. John Fiske was Spencer's disciple in America; and in his *Outlines of Cosmic Philosophy* (1874) he took up the battle for evolution where Gray had left off. In the work of Charles S. Peirce, Josiah Royce, William James, and John Dewey, there had been formulated a new coupling of science to ethics, known as "pragmatism," which identified goodness with usefulness (as Spencer had linked it to "survival"), and laid the foundation of modern reform movements. But it was chiefly in the field of American theology that evolution had plowed its deepest furrow.

The candles at the altar were smoking down; nor could such reactions as Annie Besant's "Theosophy," the sudden growth of Catholicism, and Mary Baker Eddy's "Christian Science" stem the rising tide of disbelief. Dissensions broke out in various congregations, and by 1905 had fractured them into 157 religious sects. Churchmen made vain attempts to reconcile the Bible with Darwin (as Thomas Aquinas had tried to merge Aristotle and Scripture during the Middle Ages). Ministers who leaned toward considering the Bible, not as a divine revelation, but as mere literature, were arraigned and suspended. Treatises denying the Bible's inspiration appeared, based on the evidence mustered by Darwin. In Europe the authority of the Gospels had been questioned by David Friedrich Strauss's *The Old Faith and the New* (1872) and Ernest Renan's *Life of Jesus* (1863); while in America, Robert Green Ingersoll and William Cowper Brann, editor of *The Iconoclast*, were leveling arrows of wit at traditional Christianity. From an "Imitation of Christ" we had shifted to an "Imitation of Nature."

PURITAN TO IMPURITAN The Puritan influence in morals had entered upon its wane, to be superseded (as the conservative element in this country) by a philistinism born of our new mercantile culture. For instance, drunkenness and idleness had come to be looked upon, not so much as sins against God, as conditions that were "bad for business." Jonathan Edwards had lost out to Benjamin Franklin. But even business could not interrupt our drift toward ethical bankruptcy. With the passing of religion, morals had been deprived of their former source; and in spite of pragmatism's contention that science should be directed only toward humanitarian ends, great "captains of industry" were reading into Spencer's "survival of the fittest" an excuse for their exploitation of weaker men or classes. Atheism had sprung up in the wake of Haeckel. Reverence for inherited usages had declined, and hedonism (the pursuit of pleasure) had taken its place. Because if science did not recognize any distinction between good and evil, if life was a perpetual clash of forces in which the strongest always won out, and if there was to be no punishment beyond the grave, it stood to reason that one should take his pleasure where he found it. Indeed, supposing man to be a helpless mote of dust "tied to the wheel of things," how could he be expected to do otherwise than follow wherever his instincts of hunger and sex drove him? A simple amoebic reaction toward joy and away from pain,

Spencer had declared, would pilot a man naturally into "right" behavior. *Laissez faire.*

This growth of hedonism in America was curiously marked, during the nineties, by the vogue of Omar Khayyám's *Rubaiyat.* For years this poem haunted the newspapers and magazines of our country, after its translation from the Persian by Edward Fitzgerald in 1859 (*Anno Darwini*). It was illustrated by various painters (one of them Elihu Vedder), and quoted in every drawing room.

> Come, fill the Cup, and in the Fire of Spring
> The Winter Garment of Repentance fling:
>   The Bird of Time has but a little way
> To fly — and Lo! the Bird is on the Wing.
>
> Ah, fill the Cup: — what boots it to repeat
> How Time is slipping underneath our Feet:
>   Unborn To-morrow and dead Yesterday,
> Why fret about them if To-day be sweet!

EAT, DRINK, AND BE MERRY   Honesty, industry, and abstinence, the blessed trinity of McGuffey's *Readers,* the Bible, and Horatio Alger, have in large measure given way to a new trinity of wine, women, and song. Our twentieth-century slogans have become, "The world well lost for love," "let joy be unrefined," *sauvez qui peut,* "judge not lest ye be judged," "to err is human," "everybody's doing it," and "if you can't be good be careful." The simple moral system of *Pilgrim's Progress* has vanished. Man's old treasury of accepted wisdom has been set aside by an epicurean philosophy of "eat, drink, and be merry." The Ten Commandments have been swallowed by an eleventh, which reads, "Do as you please." Finding ourselves in a shattered, materialistic world, we have decided (in the words of George Meredith) to "eat our pot of honey on the grave." [22]   Moral curfews are out of style. "Not the fruit of experience," we say, echoing Walter

[22] Meredith, George, *Modern Love* (1895), p. 33.

Pater, "but experience itself, is the end. A counted number of pulses only is given to us of a variegated, dramatic life. How may we see in them all that is to be seen in them by the finest senses? How shall we pass most swiftly from point to point, and be present always at the focus where the greatest number of vital forces unite in their purest energy? To burn always with this hard, gem-like flame, to maintain this ecstasy, is success in life." [23] There is a vanishing sense of guilt in our modern world, caused perhaps by the disappearance of God. Who among us, now that God has perished, is to say what is good or bad? A suspicion has developed that no single code of abstract morality can be devised that will cover all deeds; and so we have taken to supplying a new and entirely personal system for each emergency, while sin is on its holiday.

Once we thought life didn't matter, wasn't anything but a preparation for eternity: a vale of tears — with a sunny paradise, very strange and full of songs, all ready for the worthy. That's all over. We've found out we're only cells; they break up when we die. We've found out that we're animals, just animals that remember more and worry more. So life is the only thing that does matter. A few years, thirty or forty or fifty years, hungry years; then we end up here, under the grass; and we're going to have a good time.[24]

UMBILICAL TO EARTH   Naturalism (the philosophy of *laissez faire*) "implies that Nature considers man just another of her creatures and ignores his claim to be akin to the angels. Our strongest animal impulses are most fundamental to life's continuance and are therefore most to be trusted." [25] The naturalist lets Nature take its course, accepts the universe of science, and cares only for things "as they are," rather than for things "as they have

[23] Pater, Walter, *The Renaissance* (1900), p. 236.
[24] Wescott, Glenway, *The Apple of the Eye* (1924), pp. 134–135.
[25] Parrott, Thomas Marc, and Willard Thorp, *Poetry of the Transition* (1932), p. xxviii.

been," or "should be." "What is," he agrees with Pope, "is right." Nature is a vast contrivance of wheels within wheels; man is a "piece of fate" caught in the machinery of Nature; and love is ultimately a product of the same forces that control gravitation. The world is a jungle, where men grapple with one another for life and its accessories, murder (and are in turn murdered), fly after pleasure, and resign themselves with stoic calm to whatever pain they cannot elude. Man's only duty is to discharge his energies and die, at the same time expressing his individuality as best he can. Naturalism deserts conventional ethics (which magnetize people into the strict patterns of popular opinion and social health) to espouse the neuter tempests of Nature and the winds of impulse. It regards men, not as divided into good and evil, but into strong and weak; conceives everything to be "true in its own time, place, circumstance, and untrue outside of its own place, time, circumstance"; [26] and has no moral axe to grind. People, insists the naturalist, "always deceive themselves by abandoning experience to follow imaginary systems. Man is the work of Nature: he exists in Nature: he is submitted to her laws: he cannot deliver himself from them." [27] He is a poor instrument "for converting stimuli into reactions." [28]

Life is "a perpetual gushing forth of novelties," as Bergson has said. Nothing is good or bad; it is only unique. The naturalist is convinced that man is an animal, governed by his visceral impulses and desires; that his mind is a slavish echo of these bodily tropisms, and his soul an empty legend; that he is shaped and limited by factors beyond his jurisdiction; that only Nature, with its blind spasms of caprice, is real; and that men should court the

[26] Lawrence, D. H., "Morality and the Novel," *The Golden Book* (February, 1926), III, 249.
[27] Holbach, Paul H. T., *The System of Nature* (1868), I, 11.
[28] London, Jack, *John Barleycorn* (1913), p. 327.

simple atavistic behavior of children and savages, who have not yet been corrupted by ideas. Things, from his point of view, never progress; they merely change. "Life is a horizontal fall," and humanity always has the same quantum of folly to squander. The prime thing is to avoid ethical bookkeeping; for man is a ledger that will not balance, and "Morality is a cerebral weakness." Of pity, reason, self-control, and human sympathy, the naturalist is very skeptical. Such abstractions hold no meaning for him. He has decided to enjoy each thing for its own sake, and not for the sake of future or spiritual rewards. He has come to prefer the earth to heaven, to desire art for art's sake and passion for the sake of passion. With Jack London he says, "The ultimate word is I LIKE."

Nothing remains for him, save Nature and its "struggle for existence." A helpless bundle of molecules, nerves, and glands, he must take his chances with the rest of matter, live minute by minute, and capitulate to every prompting (good or bad), without attempting or being able to modify it. Frequently he leads a vegetable existence, founded upon pure intensity and the superlative. "The sin I impute to each frustrate ghost," he hears Browning intone, with approval,

> Is — the unlit lamp and the ungirt loin,
> Though the end in sight was a vice, I say.[29]

Past stanzas of his life are forgotten in the present, and he sheds remorse like a snake's skin, guided by a barnyard philosophy of conduct. But at last, pushed out of the fray by new and younger opponents, he "breaks, grows old, is blown about the winds of the world, and fades from brains of living men, and dies." [30] As for immortality, so prized by the medieval mind, there endures only the doubtful

[29] Browning, Robert, *The Complete Poetic and Dramatic Works of Robert Browning* (1895), p. 286.
[30] Brooke, Rupert, *The Collected Poems of Rupert Brooke* (1915), p. 122.

prospect of rising into life again through the roots of some flower, or of being eaten as a stalk of wheat by posterity.

In this chameleon world from which God, its previous yardstick, has been removed, life can be neither good nor evil in any moral sense. To many it is an unfriendly universe, ruled by "the blind dicings of fate," where we are forced to dig our own graves and water the seeds of our eventual demise. Permanence has departed, and all promise of glory. Impressions stream in through his senses, and compel the naturalist to flow along with them. Self-restraint has made way in him for self-defense; and no longer under ethical obligations to his neighbors or God, he soon finds himself drifting upon a river of sensations, untamed, and content to live accidentally in an accidental world.

*

THE RED BADGE OF NATURE

*

PHOENIX   Our nineteenth-century novel blazed out on a funeral pyre of historical romance, kindled by the Spanish-American War, Anthony Hope's *Prisoner of Zenda* (1894), Rider Haggard's *She* (1887), and Stevenson's *Kidnapped* (1886).   It left behind it such embers of euphemism as George Barr McCutcheon's *Graustark* (1901), S. Weir Mitchell's *Hugh Wynne* (1897), James Lane Allen's *The Choir Invisible* (1897), Charles Major's *When Knighthood Was in Flower* (1898), Mary E. Wilkins Freeman's *The Heart's Highway* (1900), Maurice Thompson's *Alice of Old Vincennes* (1900), F. Hopkinson Smith's *Colonel Carter of Cartersville* (1891), Mary Johnston's *To Have and To Hold* (1899), Thomas Nelson Page's *Red Rock* (1898), Richard Harding Davis's *Soldiers of Fortune* (1897), Paul Leicester Ford's *Janice Meredith* (1899), and John Fox's *The Little Shepherd of Kingdom Come* (1903).   But from these ashes of counterfeit passion arose Stephen Crane, to herald a new cycle of American prose.   He might be termed, in a way, the earliest naturalistic author of this period, the first to peck himself out of the shell.

THE DARK HOURS   Crane, the son of a clergyman, was born November 1, 1871, in Newark; but his family afterwards moved to various other cities in New Jersey, among them, Paterson and Asbury Park.   Because of delicate health, he was forced to delay his education a few years, before entering Pennington Seminary and the Hudson River Institute at Claverack, New York.   Later on he weathered two seasons at Lafayette and a year at Syracuse, a mediocre student devoted to athletics, poker, fraternity activities, and any books not related to his courses.

With his older brother Townley, Crane had already operated a news bureau in Asbury Park for several eastern papers; and so after leaving college, his first thought was to locate a reporter's assignment on New York's famous "Park Row." Unsuccessful in this, he had to accept work in a mercantile house. But not for long. He found a year's employment with the New York *Tribune*, spent a brief period on the Newark *Morning Times*, and ended up back in New York writing free lance articles, ready, as he told Hamlin Garland, to sell his literary future "for twenty-three dollars in cash."

His journalistic experiences, though, had provided him with material for a lame, febrile novel entitled *Maggie: A Girl of the Streets* (1892), the story of a degenerate Irish family trapped in the tenements of lower Manhattan. Beside this sour narrative the work of contemporary fictionists took on the aspect of "pink valentines," an epithet that Crane once applied to a volume by F. Hopkinson Smith. Its principal character, Maggie Johnson (who anticipates the weak heroines of Dreiser) is tempted into the arms of an animalistic bartender, by dreams of finery and the desire to escape her drunken mother. Then finding herself quickly deserted, she tries in vain to become a prostitute, and at last commits suicide. All of which helps to explain the book's failure.

To the reading public of 1892 *Maggie* gave an attack of indigestion, with its "fallen angel," its freckling of "damns," its reference to social evils, its roman candle similes, and its Bowery "slanguage," which Edward W. Townsend was soon to use again in his *Chimmie Fadden* (1895). In fact when Crane took the sketch to Richard W. Gilder of the *Century*, he was urged, after that editor had spent "a bad evening" with it, to lay the thing aside. For any book

that involved Maggie's younger brother could scarcely
expect to ravish an audience brought up on Frances Hodg-
son Burnett's *Little Lord Fauntleroy* (1886).[1] But Crane
hopefully borrowed a thousand dollars to issue it himself
under the pseudonym of Johnston Smith, and had the
pleasure of watching it drop strangled from the press.
Years later he used the returned copies to build a fire.

WAR, REAL AND IMAGINARY   Fame, however, was near at
hand. After reading *La Débâcle* (1892), Zola's tragedy of
the Franco-Prussian War (and finding that it left much to
be desired), he accepted the dare of a friend to write a
better novel if he could, and chose as his subject our own
Civil War, which during the 1890's was still a source of
anecdotal and economic interest to many people, including
Frank Norris, who planned a trilogy of Gettysburg, though
he did not live to pen it. He sat down, focused his
clairvoyant fancy, and in ten days wrote *The Red Badge of
Courage*, that clinical study of a recruit in the Battle of Chan-
cellorsville. Never having witnessed a military engagement, he was obliged to draw his information from history
books, the "yarns" of veterans, football, and the memoirs
of ex-soldiers being printed at that time in *Harper's* and the
Century. Yet the result was instant renown. *The Red
Badge* is said to have created even more of a sensation than
Whitman's *Leaves of Grass*.

THE TESTING GROUND   Crane, thus far, had been living
among poor art students on the East Side of New York,
who "slept on the floor, dined off buns and sardines, and
painted on towels or wrapping paper for lack of canvas." [2]
But with the friendly aid of Garland and William Dean
Howells, whose attention had been attracted to Crane by
Maggie, he was able to find a publisher for *The Red Badge*

---

[1] When Crane read it in 1894, he almost ran a temperature.
[2] Garland, Hamlin, *Roadside Meetings* (1930), p. 192. By permission of
The Macmillan Company, publishers.

of Courage, take a trip to the Southwest, and market a number of rejected manuscripts.

As author of *The Red Badge*, he suddenly found himself in demand as a war correspondent; and in 1896 he sailed for Cuba. Mysteriously shipwrecked in the Gulf Stream (by Spaniards, as rumor had it), he barely managed to reach land, wandered for days through the swamps of Florida, and bending this ordeal to his own ends, wrote it up in "The Open Boat." The next year he left to cover a Balkan disturbance, fell sick, and on his way home, lingered a while in England, making friends and writing, until in 1898, the Maine disaster sent him flying down to Cuba again for the New York *World* and the *Westminster Gazette*.[3] When the war ended, he came back to America, but soon returned to England (and the wife he had married in Athens). He died at a Bavarian resort in 1900, of tuberculosis, having made himself "a testing ground for all sensations of living." "What I discovered very early in our acquaintance," mourned his friend Joseph Conrad, "was that Crane had not the face of a lucky man." [4]

FOURTH ESTATE   Since 1900 the profession of journalism has achieved a special glamour for novelists, as evidenced by such books as Henry Justin Smith's *Deadlines* (1922), Meyer Levin's *Reporter* (1929), and Ben Ames Williams' *Splendor* (1927), though in Crane's own day it was just beginning to reap its adventurous reputation from the exploits of men like Richard Harding Davis (in the reportorial field), S. S. McClure (the editor), and others. Crane himself spent most of his life in this work, and appeared to enjoy it. But he was a touchy person, unable to abide injustice in silence; and as a result he found himself unsuited to journalistic routine, which required conformance to duty and

[3] See Seitz, Don C., "Stephen Crane: War Correspondent," *The Bookman* (February, 1933), LXXVI, 137–140.
[4] In his Introduction to Thomas Beer's *Stephen Crane* (1923), p. 10.

public taste. Early in his career, these quixotic habits cost him his job with the *Tribune*, for burlesquing the bourgeois ardor of labor groups on their picnics and parades. During the war with Spain he sent back from Cuba reports of regimental cowardice that got him, as he expressed it, "wonderfully disliked." And on still another occasion, he embroiled himself in more trouble by trying to shield a harlot from the New York police. Indeed he seems even to have been touched with a kind of hysteria, or sense of impending fate, that led him to flirt deliberately with misfortune; and his last works are marked by the pathos of haste, as if he could see death over his shoulder, drawing swiftly near.

A MOVING BOX Crane's fiction plainly reflects the naturalistic concept of man as a helpless animal, driven by instinct and imprisoned in a web of forces entirely deaf to the hopes or purposes of humanity. Nowhere do we find this more clearly indicated than in "The Open Boat," his story of four shipwrecked men trying to beach their dinghy upon a rocky strip of Florida coast. On the shore there was a windmill, "a giant, standing with its back to the plight of the ants. It represented in a degree, to the correspondent, the serenity of nature amid the struggles of the individual — nature in the wind, and nature in the vision of men. She did not seem cruel to him then, nor beneficent, nor treacherous, nor wise. But she was indifferent, flatly indifferent." [5]

The Red Badge of Courage embodies this same theme. Its tumbling clouds of smoke and gunfire blow Henry Fleming, the youthful private, up and down the battle field, first in blind panic and then in wild bravery, like some tortured beast, divorced from intelligence and free will.

[5] Follett, Wilson (ed.), *The Work of Stephen Crane* (1925–1926), **XII**, 55–56.

He saw instantly that it would be impossible for him to escape from the regiment. It enclosed him. And there were iron laws of tradition and law on four sides. He was in a moving box.[6]

Crazed with fear, he runs away during a Confederate attack, loses his regiment, and finally discovers that it has met the charge and held the line. He wanders over the field, stricken with shame, meets a wounded friend, and sees him die in a ghastly "rendezvous with death" (which may have inspired Alan Seegar's poem). "A dull, animal-like rebellion against his fellows, war in the abstract, and fate grew within him."[7] Yet a moment later he finds, as an excuse for his cowardice, that everything in Nature operates upon the principle of self-preservation.

He threw a pine cone at a jovial squirrel, and he ran with chattering fear. High in a tree-top he stopped and, poking his head cautiously from behind a branch, looked down with an air of trepidation.
The youth felt triumphant at this exhibition. There was the law, he said. Nature had given him a sign. The squirrel, immediately upon recognizing danger, had taken to his legs without ado. He did not stand stolidly baring his furry belly to the missile, and die with an upward glance at the sympathetic heavens. On the contrary, he had fled as fast as his legs could carry him; and he was but an ordinary squirrel, too — doubtless no philosopher of his race. The youth wended, feeling that Nature was of his mind. She reinforced his argument with proofs that lived where the sun shone.[8]

Hours pass, and the private roves on, afraid to return to his brigade, until after he is struck on the head in a chance skirmish with another frightened member of his own troop. Then he picks his way back to camp in the dark, and allows his comrades to suppose that his injury has been caused by a bullet. But in succeeding encounters with the enemy he proves himself a man of maniacal valor, and

---

[6] Follett, Wilson (ed.), *op. cit.*, I, 48.
[7] *Ibid.*, I, 81.   [8] *Ibid.*, I, 82–83.

reaches the conclusion that the chief thing is to resign himself to his fate, to participate in Darwin's "survival of the fittest," to play "follow the leader" with Nature, and to confront this mad, implacable world with "intestinal fortitude" and a brave smile; in one word, to become a stoic.

He felt a quiet manhood, non-assertive but of sturdy and strong blood. He knew that he would no more quail before his guides, wherever they should point. He had been to touch the great death, and found that, after all, it was but the great death. He was a man.[9]

Armed with this new code of *laissez faire*, Henry Fleming moves on. Crane does not slay him during the war, for we meet him again in "The Lynx" and "The Veteran," where he dies trying to save a cow from a burning barn, a fighter to the end. Like Frank Norris and Jack London, Crane admired the man of action, the brawler, the trailmaker, and "men with the bark on." Hence these are the types he chose for his heroes.

Crane rings another change upon his theory of man's subservience to Nature in "The Blue Hotel," the tale of a Swede who thinks he is marked out by fate for destruction, and so brings on by his own fears the tangled circumstances that finally lead to his death at the hands of a gambler in a Nebraska saloon. Neither the Swede nor the gambler, insists Crane, was responsible; they were merely the victims of Nature's machinery. As another character in the story remarks, after the disaster:

We are all in it! This poor gambler isn't even a noun. He is a kind of an adverb. Every sin is the result of a collaboration. We, five of us, have collaborated in the murder of this Swede. Usually there are from a dozen to forty women really involved in every murder, but in this case it seems to be only five men — you, I, Johnnie, old Scully; and that fool of an unfortunate gambler came merely as a culmination, the apex of a human movement, and gets all the punishment.[10]

[9] *Ibid.*, I, 199.   [10] *Ibid.*, X, 131–132.

To Crane the individual was only one of those "lice which were caused to cling to a whirling, fire-smitten, ice-locked, disease-stricken, space-lost bulb." [11] The dead would appear to be well out of it. But the corpse of the Swede, alone in the saloon, ventures no denial or assent, "its eyes fixed upon a dreadful legend that dwelt atop of the cash-machine: 'This registers the amount of your purchase.'" [12]

MORALITY PLAY   From a military point of view, *The Red Badge of Courage* represents the change that has come over warfare since knights engaged in strife with opponents they could see and touch. No whistling death came arching down upon King Richard the Lion-Hearted from guns sixty miles away. Man was a free creature (or so he placidly imagined), not bound to take part in a "struggle for existence," whether he wanted to or not. He had not yet decided to adopt the doctrine of *laissez faire* and "let Nature take its course" with him; in his scheme of things, there were no such arbitrary currents, no such blind forces as those that swept Crane's luckless recruit up and down the field in impotent bewilderment, at the complete mercy of Nature.

Yet the comparison becomes even more significant if, for this theater of war, we substitute the theater of life, which in medieval times housed grand opera. Men in that period looked upon the universe as a small theater, built in one stroke by God about the year 4004 B.C., and never changed. The properties, curtains, backdrops, wings, furniture, and costumes on the stage meant nothing. In fact the play itself mattered little; it was not a drama to be enjoyed in the acting. What counted was its sequel in heaven, for which it was only a prologue.

The stars were mere lights around the balcony where God the Author sat, carefully watching; and down in the

---

[11] Follett, Wilson (ed.), *op. cit.*, X, 124.
[12] *Ibid.*, X, 130.

orchestra pit lurked Satan. On the stage, men and women acted out a play, in which they wrestled with temptations, to win or lose. If they won, they were allowed to go up and sit with God when their lines were spoken; if they lost, they were jerked down into the stifling pit by Satan's hook. But man was still "master of his fate" and "captain of his soul." This life on earth was only an interlude, a state of probation, to test him. His eyes were open; he had the Bible to tell him what was good and what evil; he was the darling of God, who had given him the Scriptures to guide him in his search for heaven; his will was at liberty.

The scenery was colorless and unreal: castles, manorial estates, dirty towns, and churches. And the players were monks, ladies in "stiff, brocaded gowns," heretics, and noblemen. (Peasants were also there, but they were not allowed in any of the principal rôles.) The prompter was a saint, or holy priest, who directed the cast from a Bible held in his hand, while the actors went through the gestures of their parts, in bursts of chivalry, sublimated love, and cruelty. Should the play lose its course, God dispatched an angel down to the prompter, who took the miracle sent him and straightened out the plot with it. Or else God, as a polite warning, flung down a bolt of lightning or a comet. Meanwhile, in the pit, Satan continued to warm his hands at a large fire, leering over the footlights and sending his own bad spirits, like bats, to interrupt the plot.

Behind every development in this drama, no matter how curious or trivial, moved the hand of God. There was felt to be a reason for everything, even if man could not understand it. No one gave way to doubt, except a few lonesome heretics; and no one tried to inquire too closely into the play's meaning. Much more important than the things of this world were their symbolic references to salvation. Every circumstance, lighted up by this happy ending, inherited an order and proportion; discordant facts were denied admission. God and His Script(ures) were perfect, from whence it followed that His theater must be perfect, too. It was only natural that infidels should become objects of popular and clerical hatred. Man's ideal was that of saintliness, and his dream, immortality. Feudalism, the catalogues of the schoolmen, the hierarchy of the Church, the hermit's chastity, exertions of faith, rituals, and the knight's vows were all part of a yearning toward a massive synthesis of life, in "imitation of Christ." For the sake of achieving heaven when he died, man gladly consented to sacrifice his present joys.

From this medieval distinction between God and Satan, heaven and hell, or good and evil, emerged the dualistic theory that man himself was composed of two warring elements, a body and a soul. The body was vicious, the soul virtuous; the body was contaminated by its love of earthly pleasures, the soul spent its time in dreaming of God, or trying to pierce the surface of things to their "meaning." If the soul remained inviolate to temptation and undefiled by the body, it would endure forever, while the body, like other material objects, died and rotted away into dust. The soul was a spirit whose true home was heaven; the body a mere prison of flesh in which it was sent to dwell for a space by God. Man, of course, was at liberty to place either one above the other in his conduct, but since the Bible told him that God preferred the soul, he ran a grave risk of going to hell if he chose to favor the body instead. Thus the natural life of man, with its worldly vices, became something to be avoided, to be forsaken for higher things of the soul, for a union with God after death. To the Middle Ages the earth was a vale of tears and sin, and life just a "dress rehearsal" for the real play which would take place in heaven following Judgment Day.

ENTER SCIENCE   But about 1500 a new character strides out of the wings. Glancing at the program, we discover that his name is Science. In one hand he bears a telescope. When he looks through it one way, he can see the stars; and when he gazes in the other end, he can see atoms. Then suddenly, with a strange magic, he enlarges the old theater of medieval times to an infinite size. The walls topple backward, and God and the Devil both disappear. The other characters are hurled into confusion, the scenery begins to move about, and in front of the theater is placed a new sign, which reads, *Closed for Repairs. To open soon under a different management, with the modern play: Whirl is King, or Paradise Lost.*

For the modern drama of science is not a play in the sense that our medieval prologue to heaven was. It is not a morality play, concerned with man's heroic struggle against sin, and his translation to glory after death. The old drama had a plot, a story to it, based upon man's choice between God and Satan, body and soul; it also had a beginning, a middle, and an end. But our contemporary play is more like vaudeville, in its absolute lack of plot. According to science, life does not build up to anything, since Nature has no values or sense of direction. Existence is a series of brief sketches, acted with violence and novelty, but leading to nothing. There is no continuity, no story, only the ceaseless parade of anonymous characters who walk in and out of the play without cues or meaning, after the kaleidoscopic fashion of events in a tabloid newspaper. It is a mongrel flux of atoms, tossed about by storms of Nature, rising and fading in beautiful but senseless circles. Deprived of free will, the actors are mere seeds on the winds of Nature that blow through the old drafty theater. Up in the balcony God has vanished. There is no light there. Even the Devil has deserted the orchestra pit; and on the stage, the farce of life continues without end or purpose.

The old style hero, too, has disappeared from literature in the wake of these changes, and his place has been taken by such automatons as Henry Fleming, hopeless figures driven about by their instincts and the fluid undertows of Nature. Naturalism, with its emphasis upon the physiological forces that rule this modern and scientific world of the twentieth century, has reduced the hero in fiction to an animal, to a savage dwarf, to nil.[13]

THE CHILD OF NATURE   Crane's treatment of children is also enlightening, as a further index to the modern mind. His affection for them led him to include children in almost every one of his sketches, and even to write an entire book about them, which he entitled *Whilomville Stories* (1900). During his stay in England he became very fond of Conrad's son, and used to sit by the hour, studying him in silence; for he tended to sympathize with the naturalistic argument that children, animals, and savages (because they are untainted by civilization) must be nearer to the secrets of Nature. This is the idea of "the noble savage" which, ever since Jean Jacques Rousseau enunciated it in the eighteenth century, has governed a wide section of our thought, and buttressed with emotion the scientific foundations of *laissez faire*. It is the same thing that Havelock Ellis had in mind when he said, "Animals living in nature are everywhere beautiful; it is only among men that ugliness flourishes. Savages, nearly everywhere, are gracious and harmonious; it is only among the civilised that harshness and discord are permitted to prevail." [14]   And it is identical with Whitman's statement that

I think I could turn and live with animals, they are so placid and self-contained.
I stand and look at them long and long.
They do not sweat and whine about their condition,
They do not lie awake in the dark and weep for their sins,

---

[13] *Cf.* Thompson, Alan Reynolds, "Farewell to Achilles," *The Bookman* (January, 1930), LXX, 465–471.
[14] Ellis, Havelock, *Fountain of Life* (1930), p. 11.

They do not make me sick discussing their duty to God.
Not one is dissatisfied, not one is demented with the mania of
    owning things,
Not one kneels to another, nor to his kind that lived thousands
    of years ago,
Not one is respectable or unhappy over the whole earth.[15]

How this belief in youth's special relation to Nature is
employed by Crane, we may observe in the way he plays his
men of action, stained with experience, against the innocent insight of children, as in "Death and the Child,"
where a small boy, loitering near a battlefield in Greece,
comes upon an exhausted deserter.

The child heard a rattle of loose stones on the hillside, and,
facing the sound, saw, a moment later, a man drag himself up
to the crest of the hill and fall panting.   Forgetting his mother
and his hunger, filled with calm interest, the child walked forward, and stood over the heaving form.   His eyes, too, were
now large and inscrutably wise and sad like those of the animal
in the house.

After a silence, he spoke inquisitively: " Are you a man?"

Peza rolled over quickly, and gazed up into the fearless and
cherubic countenance. He did not attempt to reply. He
breathed as if life was about to leave his body. He was covered
with dust; his face had been cut in some way, and his cheek
was ribboned with blood. All the spick of his former appearance had vanished in a general dishevelment, in which he
resembled a creature that has been flung to and fro, up and
down, by cliffs and prairies during an earthquake. He rolled
his eyes glassily at the child.

They remained thus until the child repeated his words: "Are
you a man?"

Peza gasped in the manner of a fish. Palsied, windless, and
abject, he confronted the primitive courage, the sovereign child,
the brother of the mountains, the sky, and the sea, and he knew
that the definition of his misery could be written on a wee grass-
blade.[16]

[15] Whitman, Walt, *Leaves of Grass*, I, 71–72.
[16] Follett, Wilson (ed.), *op. cit.*, XII, 268.

VERS LIBRE   Because he was an enemy to the moralizing that afflicted his age, it is hard to trace Crane's philosophy. "I like," he protested, "my art straight."   Yet his poems, a handful of free verse in *The Black Riders* (1895) and *War Is Kind* (1899), tell us considerable.   Freighted with symbolism, cryptic, and unrhymed, they resemble translations from the Chinese (but this was a treasury of inspiration that Crane did not draw upon as his contemporaries, Whistler and Lafcadio Hearn, drew upon Japanese art and literature).   If his poems were stimulated at all, it must have been by the verses of Emily Dickinson, which have influenced modern poetry to a great degree.   Of Crane's own effect upon recent vers librists, perhaps the most that can safely be said is that he " imitated them in advance."

His poems speak of God with definite suspicion and view the world as a place where men must fight for their lives.   Since God's departure before the new broom of science, no "friend behind phenomena" remains.   No motive lingers in the gyrations of Nature.

> A man said to the universe:
> "Sir, I exist!"
> "However," replied the universe,
> "The fact has not created in me
> A sense of obligation." [17]

The world itself is depicted in Crane's poetry as a ship, built for no ethical reason by the hand of chance.

> So that, forever rudderless, it went upon the seas
> Going ridiculous voyages,
> Making quaint progress,
> Turning as with serious purpose
> Before stupid winds.[18]

IMPRESSIONISM   In 1874 the French painter, Monet, labeled one of his canvases "Sunrise — An Impression," and

[17] Follett, Wilson (ed.), *op. cit.*, VI, 131.   [18] *Ibid.*, VI, 38.

provoked a controversy that has not yet subsided. Many artists, in his wake, discarded the old practice of "telling a story" in their pictures, and began producing those compositions "that show you in one corner a pair of stays, in another a bit of the foyer of a music hall, in another a fragment of early morning landscape, and in the middle a pair of eyes, the whole bearing the title of 'A Night Out.'"[19]

Novelists like Crane and Conrad, as well as poets like Mallarmé, were beginning to do the same thing in literature, where the technique consisted of reducing prose or verse to a procession of images. In Crane, for instance, we discover these examples:

The guns squatted in a row like savage chiefs. They argued with abrupt violence. It was a grim pow-wow.[20]

The red sun was pasted in the sky like a wafer.[21]

Canton-flannel gulls flew near and far. Sometimes they sat down on the sea, near patches of brown seaweed that rolled over the waves with a movement like carpets on a line in a gale.[22]

The swing doors, snapping to and fro like ravenous lips, made gratified smacks as the saloon gorged itself with plump men.[23]

Crane's principal biographer, Thomas Beer, provides us with a fifth illustration of this method when he says, "a tug put up a parasol of curly smoke."[24] Joseph Hergesheimer, who was especially struck by Crane's "wafer" line at the age of fifteen, contributes "Would Adeline and he, Bradier wondered, be shot together, would they, cut in half by the same stream of lead, fall together on red hinges."[25] And many other samples are to be found in such novels as James Huneker's *Painted Veils* (1920), Paul Rosenfeld's *Boy in the Sun* (1928), Nelson Antrim

[19] Hueffer, Ford Madox, "On Impressionism," *Poetry and Drama* (December, 1914), II, 175.

[20] Follett, Wilson (ed.), *op. cit.*, I, 69.   [21] *Ibid.*, I, 98.

[22] *Ibid.*, XII, 33.   [23] *Ibid.*, XI, 22.

[24] Beer, Thomas, *Sandoval* (1924), p. 218.

[25] Hergesheimer, Joseph, *Tampico* (1926), p. 200.

Crawford's *Unhappy Wind* (1930), and Gloria Goddard's *Backyard* (1926).

"Any piece of Impressionism, whether it be prose, or verse, or painting, or sculpture, is the record of the impression of a moment." [26] It is a sequence of pictures, visual, aural, olfactory, or tactile (one type of which is precisely represented in *God's Man* (1929), a novel by Lynd Ward, composed entirely of woodcuts). Impressionism is *decadent* art, as differentiated from *classic* art. "It is simply a further development of a classic style, a further specialization, the homogeneous, in Spencerian phraseology, having become heterogeneous. The first is beautiful because the parts are subordinated to the whole [as advocated by Aristotle]; the second is beautiful because the whole is subordinated to the parts." [27]

The effect of an impressionistic tale or poem is not conveyed in outline, but in spasmodic spots, an extreme specimen of which may be studied in this quotation from *The Office* (1925), by Nathan Asch.

tik-tik-tik-tik-tik-tik-tik-tik-tik-tik-tik-tik-tik-tik

money five per cent
money five per cent
Kranz tell Mister Zuckor
yes sir

check for Doran
wait a minute
comparisons
God damn you shut up
check for Doran
right six four three seven point two four five seven two 0 0 point
    six two

---

[26] Hueffer, Ford Madox, "On Impressionism," *Poetry and Drama* (December, 1914), II, 174.

[27] Ellis, Havelock, in his Introduction to J. K. Huysmans' *Against the Grain* (1931), p. 23.

check for Doran
call money five per cent
call money five per cent right
I met a little kid last night a pippin some dancer too
do anything
check for Doran
hey if you can't shut up I'll shut you up
eight five seven point 0 nine seven four eight three six point 0 0
took her to the movies and mushed up some kid I tell you
I suppose that's all you ever do mush
check for Doran [28]

Impressionism is a sensory kodaking, a confused mosaic of details, a rivulet of hyphenated photographs, which the reader himself must fuse into some eventual relationship. Its character is well expressed in Proust's "intermittances of the heart" and "discontinuities of the mind." Experience becomes a series of "intense moments"; plot loses in importance; and from an interest in the larger aspects of his product, the author turns to an interest in "the bright, particular word." At one time the fundamental integer of composition was thought to be the paragraph; but since Crane's day it has focused down to the sentence, and in such experimentalists as Gertrude Stein, to the syllable. Sentences have tended to grow shorter (and even elliptical), as in Ernest Hemingway's, "I thought I had paid for everything. Not like the woman pays and pays and pays. No idea of retribution or punishment. Just exchange of values. You gave up something and got something else. Or you worked for something." [29] And paragraphs, too, are leaning in the direction of greater brevity.

When I had been with the woman all night I left in the early morning. The sun was shining brightly. In the streets children were playing.

[28] Asch, Nathan, *The Office* (1925), pp. 18–19.
[29] Hemingway, Ernest, *The Sun Also Rises* (1929), p. 153.

That day I got drunk and in the afternoon went into a park. Seeing a child with its mother I followed.

At last I ran to the child and falling on my knees tried to apologize.

It was not understood.   People thought me insane.   Kneeling before the child I muttered a few words about life, the sources of life and how they were befouled.

The mother being frightened, screamed — the child stared at me.

I escaped through bushes and running a long way got into a street car. [30]

The movement toward this "telegraphic" style may be in part due to the fact that so many of our modern writers have served their literary apprenticeship in journalism, which puts a premium on sententiousness; in this age of speed, the public demands its mental diet in capsule form. But impressionism, above all, traces back to the deep changes wrought upon our twentieth-century mind by science, whose principle is that of analysis, or the refraction of large units into smaller ones for the purpose of study and classification.   Science has been entitled "conceptual shorthand," [31] and by the same token, impressionism may be called "perceptual shorthand."   From its vision of man as a "stream of consciousness," or group of unassorted chemical reactions to an environment, science has promoted a universal disintegration of wholes into parts; and impressionism should be viewed as only one of its many symptoms.   Others are:

(1) the tabloid, a simplified type of newspaper, designed for facile consumption; and such magazines as the *Literary Digest* or *Reader's Digest*, which contain synopses of longer articles.

(2) the amazing vogue of the short story, and more recently, the short short story.   *Liberty* even publishes with its stories an estimate of the time that will be required to read them.

---

[30] Anderson, Sherwood, *Sherwood Anderson's Notebook* (1926), pp. 60–61.
[31] Pearson, Karl, *The Grammar of Science* (1900), p. 504.

(3) the moving picture, in which a scene is first chopped up into millions of tiny snapshots, and then reunited by swiftly "flickering" them before the eye.

(4) the effect of this "flicker" technique upon present day novelists like John Dos Passos, Jules Romains, Alfred Döblin, Leane Zugsmith, and George Anthony Weller.

(5) the increasing specialization evident in every province of modern culture.

(6) the growth of sectionalism within countries, and of nationalism among them.

(7) the breakdown of life into a hedonistic series of pleasant events, chosen without regard for standards of morality, duty, or consistency, and contributing to America's annual bill of over two billion dollars for luxuries.

(8) the substitution of a "pluralistic universe" by science for the old religious unity of Dante's world. Says William James, of this new conception: "Things are 'with' one another in many ways, but nothing includes everything, or dominates over everything. The word 'and' trails along after every sentence.[32]

Just as science has leveled the world until one thing is no more important than another (or better), and just as God no longer remains for many novelists as the climax of human aspiration, so impressionism voids every accent. It is in line with the destruction of rank throughout modern life, as opposed to the medieval hierarchy in which some things were considered more important than others, and each had its fixed place. Democracy, impressionism, and relativity in morals are all yoked together, and follow in the track of science.

We move in an age of impressionistic living. All is atmosphere and movement. There are relatively few hard contours, all is a matter of environment. There are few fundamental bed-rock traditions or deeply rooted faiths. Most things are enveloped in the vibrating atmosphere of doubt — light, the rationalists call it. In our social life, in our industrial life, in our political and in our very religious life, all is changed. In place of the

[32] James, William, *A Pluralistic Universe* (1909), p. 321.

old social castes we still have a constant shifting of social planes. The mechanic travels from city to city, from trade to trade. Creed follows creed, party follows party, and in the confused panorama of varying policies, a policy well drawn and classic in proportion is hardly to be expected.

To this mode of living and thinking, science, which through the industrial revolution had contributed so much to the building up of the new social order, now adds still further kaleidoscopic variety. The railroad, the telephone, the telegraph, the linotype machine, the steamship, the phonograph and "the movies," all contribute to the rush of changing impressions, to the bewildering multiplicity of effects. What time is there for revery, imagination or principle in the life of the modern city dweller? His newspaper furnishes numberless thrills each hour. His library is a storehouse of electric sensations and impressions. His very excursions and vacations are not given to idling or to play. They are arranged on compact tourist schedules. Torn between a thousand sensations he grows sensation-sated. To hold his interest the impressionist statesman, churchman, play producer, manufacturer, and publisher each vie with one another in providing new sensations and fresh thrills.

The dominance of impressionism in our art is the outcome of this life. The motive of this aesthetic creed is not expression or the search for beauty, it is curiosity. The interest of life is in each moment; of nature, in its slightest quivering tone; of humanity, in the least gesture of its meanest citizen.[33]

What we call "Impressionism as a technique is a means of recording the transitory nature of phenomena and the fluidity of motion. As a principle it is based on a philosophy of change. As painters, as writers, as musicians, impressionists are not so much men of strong convictions and deep words as they are craftsmen recording the flitting sensations of an ever changing world. The chief interest of impressionism is the ephemeral." [34] It stands for anarchy and the erasure of emphasis from life, and bears to

[33] Weinberg, Louis, "Current Impressionism," *The New Republic* (March 6, 1915), II, 124.

[34] *Ibid.*

older styles in prose and morals the same relation that "free verse" does to poetry with established rhythms and meters. It represents the collapse of consistency in thought and literature, and abolishes every form of tradition or precedence. It sees the universe, with Bertrand Russell, as "all spots and jumps, without unity, without continuity, without coherence or orderliness or any of the other properties that governesses love." [35]   "*Life*," it contends, "*does not proceed by the association and addition of elements, but by dissociation and division.*" [36]   Borrowing the words of a prominent contemporary philosopher, we might define it as an attempt "to solidify into discontinuous images the fluid continuity of the real." [37]   Experience, it insists, should be broken into fragments, each fragment to be respected for its own sake, each passing moment or passion to be welcomed individually and squeezed dry before it can escape us.   In the field of ethics it takes the shape of Crane's declaration that

> There is nothing save opinion,
> And opinion be damned.[38]

just as it harmonizes, in literary criticism, with his pronouncement that "One need respect nothing in art, except one's own opinion."

According to one English critic, Edward Garnett, *The Red Badge of Courage* is "a series of episodic scenes," [39] and Crane "the chief impressionist" of his day.[40]   His sentences jerk themselves out breathlessly, and there is a conscious, almost smart, felicity of phrasing about them.   Crane's pages bleed with exquisite miniatures and startling images (a comparison rendered apt by his taste for red).   Over

---

[35] Russell, Bertrand, *The Scientific Outlook* (1931), p. 95.
[36] Bergson, Henri, *Creative Evolution* (1911), p. 89.
[37] *Ibid.*, p. 302.
[38] Follett, Wilson (ed.), *op. cit.*, VI, 81.
[39] Garnett, Edward, *Friday Nights* (1922), p. 208.
[40] *Ibid.*, p. 209.

the surface of existence darts his eye, picking out details and whipping them up into welts of fire. But while he could lay the bricks, one by one, he lacked the architectonic touch, a larger sense of the whole ; he did not know how to build up connective tissues. Consequently his work is a mass of fragments, sunshine dancing on the bayonet points of a marching regiment; and whenever he tried a long novel, as he did in *The Third Violet* (1897), *Active Service* (1899), and his unfinished *The O'Ruddy* (1903), he played himself false. Even his letters are often no more than bits of slang, joined by rows of dots. "He had, so to speak, no literary small talk; he could not manage what the musicians call passage work. His superlative skill lay in the handling of isolated situations; he knew exactly how to depict them with dazzling brilliance, and he knew, too, how to analyze them with penetrating insight, but beyond that he was rather at a loss: he lacked the pedestrian talent for linking one situation to another." [41]

How far Crane was influenced in his impressionism, it is hard to say. The spirit of his age, of course, must have guided him to some extent. He was probably not inspired by the French school of impressionistic poetry, whose leader, Mallarmé, he fondly imagined to be an Irishman! But Mallarmé and his group did create antecedents for the poetical cult of Imagism, which emerged about 1908, and included such writers as T. E. Hulme, F. S. Flint, H. D. (Hilda Doolittle), Ezra Pound, William Carlos Williams, Richard Aldington, Amy Lowell, and John Gould Fletcher, whose aim was to "concentrate their thought in a dominant image." [42]

It is also hard to decide whether Crane caught any of his verbal pointillism from modern theories of painting. He did live among artists when he first went to New York, in

[41] Mencken, H. L., in his Introduction to Follett, Wilson (ed.), *op. cit.*, X, xii.
[42] Aldington, Richard, *The Imagists* (1915), p. 71.

the Art Students' League building on 23rd Street; his novel, *The Third Violet*, was written around an impressionistic painter named Hawker; and Monet's dispute had reached this country before 1893, in the columns of *Scribner's*. Yet the true explanation of Crane's stylistic sharp-shooting was probably his hypersensitivity to objects and colors, which left him as elaborately alive as an exposed nerve, and may have been heightened by the disease that eventually killed him.

Nor is it any easier to name other authors who might have influenced him, either in theme or technique, because of the fact that his reading experience was so limited. His appetite for adventure may have been prompted, to an extent, by the popularity of Kipling, whose *Plain Tales from the Hills* came out in 1887; and Crane, who thought Tolstoy "the supreme living writer of our time," is suspected of having drawn some of his inspiration for *The Red Badge* from *Sebastopol* (1855), though he fervently denied that Tolstoy or anyone else had aided him. He said, "I like what I know of Anatole France, Henry James, George Moore, and several others. I deeply admire some short stories by Mr. Bierce, Mr. Kipling, and Mr. White." [43] Thomas Hardy (whose *Jude, the Obscure* had just been printed and expurgated in *Harper's*, as *Hearts Insurgent*) seemed to him "a gigantic writer." But Crane had never read "Balzac or Dostoywhat'shisname," [44] and to insinuate that he had leaned on Stendhal's *Charterhouse of Parma* (1839) in writing *The Red Badge of Courage* only made him angry.

THE WONDERFUL BOY Much less debatable is the part that he played in establishing naturalism as a branch of American literature. It is easier to chart in Norris, London, Dreiser, Anderson, Hemingway, or Faulkner the outlines of a scientific universe with its "struggle for exist-

[43] Quoted by Beer, Thomas, in his Introduction to Follett, Wilson (ed.), *op. cit.*, VII, xiii.

[44] Beer, Thomas, *Stephen Crane* (1923), p. 168.

ence." Yet Crane was plainly a preface to naturalism, with his gaunt "soldiers of fortune," Bowery toughs, cadavers, wars, morbid catastrophes, and mood of *laissez faire*. Action and atavism flavored his stories of lean, intrepid men, matching wits, muscle, and courage in pre-Adamic conflicts; and he ushered in a whole literature, devoted to cruelty, adventure, wayfaring, lechery, and "strong, silent men" who thirst for money, "life in the raw," or women, and run amok down the peaceful avenues of society. He lived in the "dime novel" days, when the public, feverish with prosperity and indifferent to the defects of this massive country, demanded fiction of a similar quality, in which "men were men," "shot at the drop of a hat," and "died in their boots." It was, significantly enough, the age of dawning pugilism, of Sullivan, Corbett, Fitzsimmons, Jefferies, and Johnson. The old frontier had gone, to be sure, but new ones were springing up in the Klondike, Mexico, the trenches of Cuba, the Bowery, the wheat pit in Chicago, and the open sea, where men still lived by craft and brute strength, where the strong devoured the puny, bravery counted for more than mercy, and reason chose Nature, amoral and impulsive, for its guide.

There, in that stormy region, "the wonderful boy" labored restlessly: a strange figure, "sallow, yellow-fingered, small and ugly," [45] whose life is prophetically cast up by one of his own stanzas:

> There was a man who lived a life of fire.
> Even upon the fabric of time,
> Where purple becomes orange
> And orange purple,
> This life glowed,
> A dire red stain, indelible;
> Yet when he was dead,
> He saw that he had not lived. [46]

[45] Garland, Hamlin, *op. cit.*, p. 196. By permission of The Macmillan Company, publishers.

[46] Follett, Wilson (ed.), *op. cit.*, VI, 97.

*

NORRIS AND THE BRUTE

*

THE BARBARIC INVASION   "Give us stories now," cried
Frank Norris, "give us men, strong, brutal men, with red-
hot blood in 'em, with unleashed passions rampant in 'em,
blood and bones and viscera in 'em, and women, too, that
move and have their being." [1]   Here is the tocsin of early
naturalism, the cult of the strong, embodying the ethics of
Hercules, seeking adventure on new frontiers, in war, on
the sea, in the Alaskan gold rush, and the marts of trade.
It represents the philosophy of men like Crane, Norris,
London, and Dreiser, the theories of Darwin, Haeckel's
view of man as a machine, and Spencer's concept of morals
based on pleasure and survival-value.   It is the doctrine of
indifference to literary style and tradition; obedience to
Nature's law of "struggle for existence"; and concentration upon dark violence, horror, and the animal that
sleeps under man's thin vest of civilization.   It is the
"red badge" of pride in blind strength, the colossal, the
dangerous, the crude, the vital, and the spectacular; the
literary home of prizefighters, financial titans, savages,
criminals, soldiers, revolutionists, and perverts.

The Gilded Age in America (1865–1890) coincided with
the growth of anarchy everywhere, and with the rise of
political tyrants like Nicholas I in Russia, Napoleon III in
France, Bismarck in Germany, Cavour in Italy, and Palm-
erston in England, men who stood as symbols of power and
war.   Since idealistic dreams were not safe after Darwin
and Spencer's refutation of moral progress, nations began

[1] Quoted in Walker, Franklin, *Frank Norris* (1932), p. 138.

45

to consider whether force and material gain might not be less disappointing. The romantics of society were held to have failed. Men turned to the sword and the dollar. Said Bismarck, "It is not by speeches and majority resolutions that the great questions of the day are to be decided — that was the mistake of 1848 and 1849 — but by blood and iron!" And on this side of the Atlantic, Roosevelt took up the refrain in his Chicago speech of April, 1899, when he roared:

I preach to you, my countrymen, that our country calls not for the life of ease, but for the life of strenuous endeavor. The twentieth century looms before us big with the fate of many nations. If we stand idly by, if we seek merely swollen, slothful ease and ignoble peace, if we shrink from the hard contests where men must win at the hazard of their lives and at the risk of all they hold dear, then the nobler and stronger peoples will pass us by, and will win for themselves the domination of the world.

The words here are Roosevelt's, but the melody is that of a naturalistic age imbued with Darwinism, "manifest destiny," the spirit of "the rough rider," imperialism, and David Harum's "Do to the other feller what he'd like to do to you, but do it first."

At the turn of the century, American magazines were becoming sensitive, in their columns of opinion, to Spencer, Zola, Ibsen, Tolstoy, and Nietzsche. There was a skeptical and pessimistic mood in the air; and for their new hopes men turned to science, with its "survival of the fittest," and sanctioning of hedonism. Science appeared to be something "real" and demonstrable. Its discoveries and inventions lent weight to its growing prestige; and after 1870 belief in science magnified surprisingly, carrying theology before it. Germany believed that it had won the War of 1870 because of its better scientific knowledge, and France decided that it had lost because of inferiority in the same department. The laws of Nature reigned supreme.

POLK STREET AND PARIS It was into this new world that Frank Norris was born, on the 5th of March, 1870, in Chicago. Far from being a product of the sordid environment that he wrote about in *McTeague*, Norris came of a prosperous family. His father was a rich wholesale jeweler, and his mother a person of sound New England ancestry. In 1884 his parents moved with their children to Oakland, California; returned to Chicago; and came back in 1895 to San Francisco, where they bought a large house, two blocks away from the Polk Street Norris was later to celebrate.

He was the oldest of three sons, the youngest of whom was Charles Norris, now a novelist in his own right. Like Crane he spent his childhood in reading the lurid romances of his day, and was especially fond of Scott and Stevenson, though his choice later swerved to Kipling, Richard Harding Davis, and Zola. In 1885 he was sent to a fashionable boys' school at Belmont, near San Francisco, where he promptly broke his arm at football and was dispatched home again. Along with Crane's love of athletics he shared the other's restless nature; and to beguile the hours of his convalescence, he began to take drawing lessons. But when it developed that he had artistic talent, his family (now reduced to four by the death of Frank's brother Lester) accompanied him to Paris. There they remained for a year, while Norris attended the Atelier Julian, played at elaborate games of toy soldiers with Charles, read Froissart's *Chronicles*, sketched medieval armor, and started a huge canvas on the Battle of Crécy. The others came home, and Norris was left behind to continue his studies. From Paris he sent Charles several installments of a cloak-and-dagger novel entitled *Gaston le Fox*, which was never completed. For one day his father discovered a chapter of it, and angry that his son should be wasting his time on literature instead of art, he called him back to San Francisco.

Norris returned, with sideburns and a walking stick, to enter the University of California in 1890. At college he became a "regular fellow," as Crane had, and declared that "an hour's experience is worth ten years of study." [2] He joined a fraternity, drew for the class book, played the banjo, and began to write in earnest; he fenced, went horseback riding, and enjoyed an occasional "spree." Though poor in mathematics, he was excellent in French; and he seems to have been deeply affected by a course that he took in evolution, if we may judge from his early stories, which are packed with references to scientific dogma and Darwin. He was enamored of the football hero, the "hardboiled" type, and the "primordial instincts" involved in fights between freshmen and sophomores at the university. "One good fight," he said, of these conflicts, "will do more for a boy than a year of schooling . . . it wakes in him that fine, reckless arrogance, that splendid, brutal, bullying instinct." [3]   From historical extravaganza he had turned by now to Kipling, who pictured the clash of fang and claw, and the beast in man that breaks out when he is faced by a crisis. Kipling's influence, for instance, is strong upon Norris in such early sketches as his tale of Lauth, a young medieval student who kills a man in a fray.

At the sight of blood shed by his own hands all the animal savagery latent in every human being awoke within him. *He could kill.* In the twinkling of an eye the pale, highly cultivated scholar, whose life had been passed in the study of science and abstruse questions of philosophy, sank back to the level of his savage Celtic ancestors. His eyes glittered, he moistened his lips with the tip of his tongue, and his whole frame quivered with the eagerness and craving of a panther in sight of his prey.[4]

It is a story that seems to foreshadow Norris's later *Vandover and the Brute*. Lauth, like Vandover, goes down and down, until he ends up as a pure organism, "a horrible

---

[2] Quoted in Walker, Franklin, *op. cit.*, p. 51.
[3] *Ibid.*, p. 66.   [4] *Ibid.*, p. 73.

shapeless mass lying upon the floor. It lived, but lived not as do the animals or the trees, but as the protozoa, the jellyfish, and those strange lowest forms of existence wherein the line between vegetable and animal cannot be drawn." [5]

While in school, Norris started *McTeague* and discovered Zola (whose novels he began carrying around with him in yellow-backed French editions). But after four years at the University of California, he decided that its academic atmosphere offered him small encouragement or liberty; and without graduating he went to Harvard for a year, where Professor Lewis E. Gates of the English department soon recognized his ability. Freshly inspired, he wrote *Vandover and the Brute*, which was lost during the San Francisco earthquake and not printed until 1914. Then, leaving Harvard, he traveled through South Africa on a commission for the San Francisco *Chronicle*, joined the British forces in the Boer War, was arrested by the Boer government, given thirty days to leave the country, and almost died of fever. When he was strong enough to move, he returned home to a job on *The Wave*, a small magazine in San Francisco. His work on this journal soon earned him a position in the East with S. S. McClure's syndicate, which sent him to Cuba in 1898, where his path as a war correspondent bisected that of Crane's. On his return to the United States, he married, read manuscripts for the new firm of Doubleday, McClure & Company, and published his novels *Moran of the Lady Letty* (1898), *Blix* (1899), *McTeague* (1899), *A Man's Woman* (1900), *The Octopus* (1901), and *The Pit* (1903). But in 1902 Norris's career was cut short by death, with his trilogy of *The Octopus*, *The Pit*, and *The Wolf* still incomplete.

ZOLA During the brief span of Norris's life, naturalism had been springing up like dragon's teeth in every country

[5] *Ibid.*, p. 74.

of Europe, especially in France, where this type of novel had begun with Balzac and Stendhal, passed to Flaubert, and been perfected by Zola.

Émile Zola, born in 1840, died in the same year as Norris. His father was a civil engineer, which perhaps influenced Zola himself to study science at Aix and Paris, though as a young man he was a furious romantic, devoted to the work of Rousseau, Hugo, Sand, and Musset. A turbulent youth, he was powerfully impressed by Rousseau's indictment of human civilization and "back to Nature" ideas. He was also struck by the theories of Darwin and Laplace, and once began a long poem on evolution, to be called "Genesis."

These influences gained upon him, until by 1870 he had thrown over (as Norris did) his earlier allegiance to the romantic dreams of Hugo. With burning zeal he began to collect, in a scientific way, the material for his great series of twenty novels. From streets and houses, conversations, books on heredity, and rabbit breeding, he compiled huge stacks of detail for this history of the Rougon-Macquart family. It was a study patterned on the titanic scheme of Balzac's *Comédie Humaine*, whose detached and documented method Zola so much admired.

"I believe that there is a great source of poetry," he said, "in the study of Nature, *as she is*," [6] not as she might be, had been, or should be. At the foundation of Zola's method lay a belief in scientific determinism, which conceives of man as an unimportant experiment in the vast laboratory of Nature, a being shaped and conditioned by circumstances beyond his control. The doctrine of *laissez faire* appealed to him; Nature he saw as an enlightened despot, whose harsh decrees could not be avoided, and whose example of careless fecundity could not be improved upon. "Ah! good earth," rhapsodized Zola:

[6] Quoted in Josephson, Matthew, *Zola and His Time* (1928), p. 78.

Take me, thou who art our common mother. O unique source of life, eternal and immortal, in which circulates the soul of the world, like a sap arising now in the stones and now in the trees, our great motionless brothers! . . . Yes, I desire to lose myself in thee; I feel thee down there, under my limbs pressing and arousing me; it is thou alone who shalt be as a pristine force in my works, the end and the means at once of all things." [7]

Naturalism he defined correctly when he termed it "a return to nature." [8]   Because in spite of its surface variety that is what it primarily means, with its basic tenet of *laissez faire* and filial respect for natural science.

Zola himself based his famous essay, *The Experimental Novel* (1880), on the investigations of Claude Bernard, an eminent French physiologist, as well as on the conclusions of Darwin. "Determinism," he remarked, "dominates everything." [9]

Man is not alone; he lives in society, in a social condition; and consequently, for us novelists, this social condition unceasingly modifies the phenomena. Indeed our great study is just there, in the reciprocal effect of society on the individual and the individual on society. For the physiologist, the exterior and interior conditions are purely chemical and physical, and this aids him in finding the laws which govern them easily. We are not yet able to prove that the social condition is also physical and chemical. It is that certainly, or rather it is the variable product of a group of living beings, who themselves are absolutely submissive to the physical and chemical laws which govern alike living beings and inanimate. From this we shall see that we can act upon the social conditions, in acting upon the phenomena of which we have made ourselves master in man. And this is what constitutes the experimental novel: to possess a knowledge of the mechanism of the phenomena inherent in man, to show the machinery of his intellectual and sensory manifestations, under the influence of heredity and environment, such as physiology shall give them to

[7] *Ibid.*, pp. 13–14.
[8] Zola, Émile, *The Experimental Novel* (1893), p. 114.   [9] *Ibid.*, p. 18.

us, and then finally to exhibit man living in social conditions produced by himself, which he modifies daily, and in the heart of
which he himself experiences a continual transformation.   Thus,
then, we lean on physiology; we take man from the hands of the
physiologist solely, in order to continue the solution of the problem, and to solve scientifically the question of how men behave
when they are in society.[10]

The naturalistic novel, continued Zola, "is a consequence of the scientific evolution of the century." [11] "It
no longer interests itself in the ingenuity of a well-invented
story, developed according to certain rules.   Imagination
has no longer place, plot matters little to the novelist, who
bothers himself with neither development, mystery, nor
dénouement; I mean that he does not intervene to take away
from or add to reality; he does not construct a framework
out of the whole cloth, according to the needs of a pre-
conceived idea.   You start from the point that nature is
sufficient, that you must accept it as it is, without modification or pruning; it is grand enough, beautiful enough
to supply its own beginning, its middle, and its end.   Instead of imagining an adventure, of complicating it, of
arranging stage effects, which scene by scene will lead to
a final conclusion, you simply take the life study of a person or a group of persons, whose actions you faithfully
depict.   The work becomes a report, nothing more; it
has but the merit of exact observation, of more or less
profound penetration and analysis, of the logical connec-
tion of facts.   Sometimes, even, it is not an entire life,
with a commencement and an ending, of which you tell;
it is only a scrap of an existence, a few years in the life of
a man or a woman, a single page in a human history,
which has attracted the novelist in the same way that the
special study of a mineral can attract a chemist." [12]

Modern criticism owes much to these theories of Zola,

[10] Zola, Émile, *op. cit.*, pp. 20–21.
[11] *Ibid.*, p. 23.   [12] *Ibid.*, pp. 123–124.

and to those of his contemporary, Hippolyte Adolphe Taine, who, in his *History of English Literature* (1863), laid the groundwork for a naturalistic system of esthetics. Taine felt that a book should be studied as Zola studied people, or as a geologist explains a fossil by reference to the rocks in which he has found it. Following the method of Sainte-Beuve, he tried to understand an author in the light of his race, surroundings, and epoch. With Zola he said, "It is not my intention to moralize . . . only to investigate, to *expose*, to lay all before you." The novelist or poet he saw as a mere result of his environment, without evaluating him in a moral or artistic sense; because according to science, vice and virtue are products "like vitriol and sugar," [13] not fixed or absolute, but relative to the cultures that originate them. "Genuine history," protested Taine, "is brought into existence only when the historian begins to unravel, across the lapses of time, the living man, toiling, impassioned, entrenched in his customs, with his voice and features, his gestures and his dress, distinct and complete as he from whom we have just parted in the street." [14] As Zola said:

The novelist and the critic start to-day from the same point, the exact surroundings, and the human data taken from nature, and they employ the same method to reach a knowledge and an explanation, on one side, of the work written by a man, and on the other, of the acts of a character, the written works and the acts being looked upon as the products of the human machine submitted to certain influences.[15]

WOLVES AND VALKYRIES Norris's earliest novel, *Vandover and the Brute*, is the story of a young man, caught in a duel between his spirit and flesh, who gives up more and more to the "brute" in him, spends his time in wine, women, and song, seduces a girl, is sued by her father when she

[13] Taine, H. A., *History of English Literature*, (1871), I, 6.
[14] *Ibid.*, I, 2.   [15] Zola, Émile, *op. cit.*, p. 228.

kills herself, gambles away his patrimony with college "pals," falls victim to a type of insanity known as lycanthropy, and gradually deteriorates into an animal, crawling around on all fours, mumbling "Wolf, wolf." In this tale Norris has echoed Darwin's remark "That man, with all his noble qualities, with sympathy which feels for the most debased, with benevolence which extends not only to other men but to the humblest living creature, with his God-like intellect which has penetrated into the movements and constitution of the solar system — with all these exalted powers — man still bears in his bodily frame the indelible stamp of his lowly origin." [16] To Vandover life meant a "great, mysterious force that spun the wheels of Nature and that sent it onward like some enormous engine, resistless, relentless; an engine that sped straight forward, driving before it the infinite herd of humanity, driving it on at breathless speed through all eternity, driving it no one knew whither, crushing out inexorably all those who lagged behind the herd and who fell from exhaustion, grinding them to dust beneath its myriad iron wheels, riding over them, still driving on the herd that yet remained, driving it recklessly, blindly on and on toward some far-distant goal, some vague unknown end, some mysterious, fearful bourne forever hidden in thick darkness." [17] There was no God, or else an impotent one. "Even that vast mysterious power to which he had cried could not help him now, *could* not help him, could not stay the inexorable law of nature, could not reverse that vast terrible engine with its myriad spinning wheels that was riding him down relentlessly, grinding him into the dust. And afterward? After the engine had done its work, when that strange other time should come, that other life, what then? No, not even then, nothing but outer darkness then and the gnashing of teeth, nothing but the deaf silence, nothing

[16] Darwin, Charles, *The Descent of Man* (1930), p. 634.
[17] Norris, Frank, *Vandover and the Brute* (1914), pp. 230–231.

but the blind darkness, nothing but the unbroken black-
ness of an eternal night." [18]   Projected against this background, Vandover saw "the course of his whole life, and
witnessed again the eternal struggle between good and
evil that had been going on within him since his very
earliest years.   He was sure that at the first the good had
been the stronger.   Little by little the brute had grown,
and he, pleasure-loving, adapting himself to every change
of environment, luxurious, self-indulgent, shrinking with
the shrinking of a sensuous artist-nature from all that was
irksome and disagreeable, had shut his ears to the voices
that shouted warnings of the danger, and had allowed the
brute to thrive and to grow, its abominable famine gorged
from the store of that in him which he felt to be the purest,
the cleanest, and the best, its bulk fattened upon the rot
and the decay of all that was good, growing larger day by
day, noisome, swollen, poddy, a filthy inordinate ghoul,
gorged and bloated by feeding on the good things that were
dead." [19]   In the end he is ruined by Geary, a comrade
with the naturalistic code of

Every man for himself. . . . It might be damned selfish, but
it was human nature; if he had to sacrifice Van so much the
worse . . . come whatever would, *he*, Geary, was going to be a
success.   Ah, you bet, he would make his way and he would make
his money.[20]

Moran of the Lady Letty, Norris's next volume, reminds
one of Jack London's *The Sea-Wolf*.   An idle young aristocrat named Wilbur is shanghaied aboard the *Bertha
Millner*, a shark-fishing vessel manned by coolies.   They
cross the path of the disabled *Lady Letty*, and rescue its
owner, a young Valkyrie, Moran Sternerson.   The *Bertha
Millner's* captain plans to keep the derelict for himself, as
salvage, but goes down with it in a storm, leaving his
own ship in the hands of Wilbur and Moran, who try to

[18] *Ibid.*, p. 245.   [19] *Ibid.*, p. 215.   [20] *Ibid.*, p. 251.

sail it back to port alone after the coolies desert, run into
a pack of beachcombers, almost sink, lose a lump of ambergris worth $150,000, recover their crew, and prepare to
retrieve the ambergris. Says Moran, a female Wolf Larsen:

There's no law and no policemen. The strongest of us are going
to live and the weakest are going to die. I'm going to live and
I'm going to have my loot too, and I'm not going to split fine hairs
with these robbers at this time of the day.[21]

The chief of the beachcombers is captured, and forced
to reveal the hiding place of the prize by the gentle Moran,
who files his teeth with a large rasp until he confesses. In
the fight that ensues, Wilbur the weakling proves himself
a real man and a fit mate for Moran.

The primitive man, the half-brute of the stone age, leaped to life
in Wilbur's breast — he felt his muscles thrilling with a strength
they had not known before. His nerves, stretched tense as harp-
strings, were vibrating to a new tune. His blood spun through
his veins till his ears roared with the rush of it. Never had he
conceived of such savage exultation as that which mastered him
at that instant. The knowledge that he could kill filled him with
a sense of power that was veritably royal. He felt physically
larger. It was the joy of battle, the horrid exhilaration of killing,
the animal of the race, the human brute suddenly aroused and
dominating every instinct and tradition of centuries of civilization.[22]

He even conquers Moran when she goes berserk during
the struggle and mistakes him for an enemy. "And, mate,"
she declares, "do you know, I love you for it." The last
chapter, however, sees Moran knifed by the same China-
man whose teeth she had filed, and Wilbur is forced to
watch her body drifting out to sea on the deck of the
derelict *Lady Letty.*

Blix (1899) is a pleasant love story, as innocent as *Moran
of the Lady Letty* was boisterous; but *A Man's Woman*

[21] Norris, Frank, *Moran of the Lady Letty* (1920), p. 191.
[22] *Ibid.*, pp. 214–215.

returns to the grand manner. It is a narrative of the Arctic, no doubt stimulated by public interest in the Alaskan gold rush, Nansen's trip to within four degrees of the Pole in 1895, and Andrée's attempt during 1897 to float over the crest of the world in a balloon. The story begins with a scientific expedition in the frozen North.

In the strange and gloomy half-light that filled the tent these survivors of the Freja looked less like men than beasts. Their hair and beards were long, and seemed one with the fur covering of their bodies. Their faces were absolutely black with dirt, and their limbs were monstrously distended and fat — fat as things bloated and swollen are fat. It was the abnormal fatness of starvation, the irony of misery, the huge joke that Arctic famine plays upon those whom it afterward destroys. The men moved about at times on their hands and knees; their tongues were distended, round, and slate-coloured, like the tongues of parrots, and when they spoke they bit them helplessly.

Near the flap of the tent lay the swollen dead body of Dennison. Two of the party dozed inert and stupefied in their sleeping-bags. Muck Tu was in the corner of the tent boiling his sealskin footnips over the sheet-iron cooker. Ferriss and Bennett [in love with the same girl "back home"] sat on opposite sides of the tent, Bennett using his knee as a desk, Ferriss trying to free himself from the sleeping-bag with the stumps of his arms. Upon one of these stumps, the right one, a tin spoon had been lashed.

The tent was full of foul smells. The smell of drugs and of mouldy gunpowder, the smell of dirty rags, of unwashed bodies, the smell of stale smoke, of scorching sealskin, of soaked and rotting canvas that exhaled from the tent cover — every smell but that of food.

Outside the unleashed wind yelled incessantly, like a sabbath of witches, and spun about the pitiful shelter and went rioting past, leaping and somersaulting from rock to rock, tossing handfuls of dry, dust-like snow into the air; folly-stricken, insensate, an enormous, mad monster gambolling there in some hideous dance of death, capricious, head-strong, pitiless as a famished wolf.[23]

[23] Norris, Frank, *A Man's Woman* (1900), pp. 37–38.

Yet Bennett, the leader, refuses to be defeated. "No, no, no; he was not beaten; he would live; he, the strongest, the fittest, would survive. Was it not right that the mightiest should live? Was it not the great law of nature?" [24] And soon he does manage to return to civilization, just in time to save Lloyd Seabright, the heroine, from a runaway, by beating the horse to death with a hammer.

The savagery of the whole affair stuck in Lloyd's imagination. There was a primitiveness, a certain hideous simplicity in the way Bennett had met the situation that filled her with wonder and with even a little terror and mistrust of him. The vast, brutal directness of the deed was out of place and incongruous at this end-of-the-century time. It ignored two thousand years of civilisation. It was a harsh, clanging, brazen note, powerful, uncomplicated, which came jangling in, discordant and inharmonious with the tune of the age. It savoured of the days when men fought the brutes with their hands or with their clubs. But also it was an indication of a force and a power of mind that stopped at nothing to attain its ends, that chose the shortest cut, the most direct means, disdainful of hesitation, holding delicacy and finessing in measureless contempt, rushing straight to its object, driving in, breaking down resistance, smashing through obstacles with a boundless, crude, blind Brobdignag power, to oppose which was to be trampled under foot upon the instant.[25]

Then Lloyd, a trained nurse, is called upon to tend the unlucky Ferriss, who has come back home only to fall sick of typhoid fever. Bennett refuses to let her risk her life on the case. There is a clash of wills over the bed of the patient. Bennett wins, and Ferriss dies for lack of attention. Later Bennett himself catches typhoid, is nursed back to health by Lloyd, marries her, and settles down to a quiet life. But in the end, prompted by Lloyd, he sails again for the Arctic, in order to prove himself "a man, and not a professor."

[24] *A Man's Woman*, pp. 44–45.
[25] *Ibid.*, pp. 105–106.

THE BLONDE BEAST *McTeague*, perhaps Norris's best novel, relates the tragedy of a huge, primitive dentist in San Francisco, "a blonde beast," clumsy, stupid, fond of steam beer, and given to relaxing in his stockinged feet. A friend, Marcus Schouler, introduces him to his cousin, Trina Sieppe, with whom he himself is a bit in love. McTeague, too, succumbs to her charms; and in a spirit of sacrifice, Marcus steps aside for him. But when Trina wins $5000 in a lottery, he sees that he has been too hasty with his altruistic gesture, and breaks off his friendship with the dentist. Trina and McTeague are married, and the former turns out to be a miser, hoarding her $5000 while McTeague sulks. At a picnic he and Schouler quarrel, and in a fierce wrestling match, McTeague breaks the other's arm.

The brute that in McTeague lay so close to the surface leaped instantly to life, monstrous, not to be resisted. He sprang to his feet with a shrill and meaningless clamor, totally unlike the ordinary bass of his speaking tones. It was the hideous yelling of a hurt beast, the squealing of a wounded elephant. He framed no words; in the rush of high-pitched sound that issued from his wide-open mouth there was nothing articulate. It was something no longer human; it was rather an echo from the jungle.[26]

Misfortunes come. Because he has no diploma, McTeague is forced to drop his practice, and together he and Trina sink back into the untidy, slothful habits of life from which she had begun to rescue him. They fight over her avarice and his growing taste for whisky. He becomes more and more intractable, and less ambitious, until finally he steals a few dollars from Trina and leaves. She is forced to take a job as a scrub-woman, broods over her lost gold, and continues to hoard the original $5000. But one day McTeague returns drunk, murders her for the lottery money, and escapes back to the mines where he had worked as a young man.

[26] Norris, Frank, *McTeague* (1899), p. 234.

The life pleased the dentist beyond words. The still, colossal mountains took him back again like a returning prodigal, and vaguely, without knowing why, he yielded to their influence — their immensity, their enormous power, crude and blind, reflecting themselves in his own nature, huge, strong, brutal in its simplicity.[27]

Learning that the sheriff is on his trail, he leaves the mines and heads into the alkali desert with a chance acquaintance; but despite their discovery of gold on the way, McTeague, pursued, is forced to continue across the blazing sand. Schouler, who has joined the posse, catches up with him, they grapple, and Schouler is killed. Yet even in death he is the victor; for as his body slumps to the ground, he manages to shackle it to McTeague, in a tremendous closing scene:

As McTeague rose to his feet, he felt a pull at his right wrist; something held it fast. Looking down, he saw that Marcus in that last struggle had found strength to handcuff their wrists together. Marcus was dead now; McTeague was locked to the body. All about him, vast, interminable, stretched the measureless leagues of Death Valley.[28]

Such an ending is indeed comparable to that of Crane's "Manacled," in which an actor, chained up during the course of a play, is left to burn to death when the theater catches fire and the other actors flee in panic.

Like Zola, Norris frequently wrote his novels around a symbol. In *The Octopus* and *The Pit* the symbol is wheat; and in *McTeague* it is gold. There is gold in the large burnished tooth that McTeague hangs out as an advertisement, the lottery prize Trina wins, Zerkow the junkman's thirst for the lost golden service plates of Maria Macapa, the gilt paint on the toys that Trina makes, the golden cage of McTeague's canary, and the vein of yellow metal that he strikes while crossing the desert. In

[27] *McTeague*, p. 387.   [28] *Ibid.*, p. 442.

fact Norris's first impulse was to name *McTeague* "The Golden Tooth." [29]

EPIC OF THE WHEAT   Toward the end of his life, Norris completed two volumes of a prospective trilogy, "the epic of the wheat." *The Octopus, The Pit,* and *The Wolf* (never begun) were to be "a serial about a cereal," involving the grain's production in *The Octopus,* its distribution in *The Pit,* and its consumption in *The Wolf,* where Norris intended to show it relieving famished humanity in some distant country.[30]   A torrential stream, a beneficent token of Nature's force and bounty, the wheat flows as inexorably as fate toward its goal; smashing all petty mortals who try to interfere with the working principle of *laissez faire;* entombing Behrman, the railroad agent in *The Octopus* who seeks to impede its progress; and ruining Jadwin, the speculator in *The Pit* who tries to "corner" it.

The Octopus, a powerful novel of bribery and bloodshed, chronicled an actual incident, the "Mussel Slough Affair" of 1878 in California.   It deals with the story of a war between ranchers in the San Joaquin Valley and "the octopus," a corrupt railway corporation with tentacles of steel.   Here again Norris has written of man's helplessness in the cold machinery of Nature: "Men were mere nothings, mere animalculae, mere ephemerides that fluttered and fell and were forgotten between dawn and dusk. Vanamee had said there was no death.   But for one second Presley could go one step further.   Men were nought, death was nought, life was nought.   Force only existed — Force that brought men into the world — Force that

[29] Howells, W. D., "Frank Norris," *The North American Review* (December, 1902), CLXXV, 773.

[30] "My idea," said Norris, "is to write three novels around the one subject of *Wheat.* First, a story of California (the producer), second, a story of Chicago (the distributor), third, a story of Europe (the consumer) and in each to keep to the idea of this huge Niagara of wheat rolling from West to East."   Howells, Mildred (ed.), *Life in Letters of William Dean Howells* (1928), II, 102–103.

crowded them out of it to make way for the succeeding generation — Force that made the wheat grow — Force that garnered it from the soil to give place to the succeeding crop." [31]

A saga of the soil, *The Octopus* resembles Zola's *La Terre* (1887) in its earth-worship and lusty metaphors.

Everywhere throughout the great San Joaquin, unseen and unheard, a thousand ploughs up-stirred the land, tens of thousands of shears clutched deep into the warm, moist soil.

It was the long stroking caress, vigorous, male, powerful, for which the Earth seemed panting. The heroic embrace of a multitude of iron hands, gripping deep into the brown, warm flesh of the land that quivered responsive and passionate under this rude advance, so robust as to be almost an assault, so violent as to be veritably brutal. There, under the sun and under the speckless sheen of the sky, the wooing of the Titan began, the vast primal passion, the two world-forces, the elemental Male and Female, locked in a colossal embrace, at grapples in the throes of an infinite desire, at once terrible and divine, knowing no law, untamed, savage, natural, sublime.[32]

Norris's second volume of this trilogy, *The Pit*, is a practice version of Dreiser's *The Titan*. Its characters are "bears" and "bulls"; its world is the Chicago "wheat pit" where these animals tear at each other's throats; and its hero, Jadwin, is Crane's soldier in *The Red Badge of Courage* transferred from the field of battle to the arena of business enterprise, a financial giant, asking no quarter and giving none, trampling down his enemies, and at last being thrust aside himself.

With his love of bulk and brawn, Norris stands in the main tradition of American naturalism. Just as *The Pit* seems to have been generated by Zola's *Money*, so Norris appears to have borrowed even his adjectives from the Frenchman. Everything in these novels is either "colossal," "prodigious," "vast," "monstrous," "gigantic,"

---

[31] Norris, Frank, *The Octopus* (1903), p. 634.   [32] *Ibid.*, pp. 130–131.

"brutal," "crude," "swollen," "inexorable," "mysterious," "horrible," "enormous," "huge," "infinite," "hideous," "savage," or "primitive." The naturalist is inclined to "write big," to italicize, to magnify, to plan works of epic scope, to depict the interplay of massive forces; in a word, to emulate the breadth of Nature, that "blind cyclops."

This same tendency is especially marked in Norris's choice of characters. Both his men and women are fit inhabitants of that rugged, primal world with which he dealt. There are, for instance:

Bennett, in *A Man's Woman*,

He was an enormous man, standing six feet two inches in his reindeer footnips and having the look more of a prize-fighter than a scientist. Even making allowance for its coating of dirt and its harsh, black stubble of half a week's growth, the face was not pleasant. Bennett was an ugly man. His lower jaw was huge almost to deformity, like that of the bull-dog, the chin salient, the mouth close-gripped, with great lips, indomitable, brutal.[33]

Moran, of the *Lady Letty*,

Her hands were red and hard, and even beneath the coarse sleeve of the oilskin coat one could infer that the biceps and deltoids were large and powerful. . . . She wore no hat, and her enormous mane of rye-colored hair was braided into long strands near to the thickness of a man's arm. The redness of her face gave a startling effect to her pale blue eyes and sandy, heavy eyebrows, that easily lowered to a frown. She ate with her knife, and after pushing away her plate Wilbur observed that she drank half a tumbler of whiskey and water.[34]

And McTeague,

a young giant, carrying his huge shock of blond hair six feet three inches from the ground; moving his immense limbs, heavy with ropes of muscle, slowly, ponderously. His hands were enormous, red, and covered with a fell of stiff yellow hair; they were hard

[33] *A Man's Woman*, p. 2.   [34] *Moran of the Lady Letty*, pp. 72–96.

as wooden mallets, strong as vises, the hands of the old-time car-boy. Often he dispensed with forceps and extracted a refractory tooth with his thumb and finger. His head was square-cut, angular; the jaw salient, like that of the carnivora.[35]

In Norris style itself degenerated into plethoric masses of words, bombast, and a perorative ringing of changes upon the terms "colossal" and "cruel." Like many naturalists (among them, London and Dreiser), he seems to have scorned the minor artistries of expression, as if he had decided that the vital and crude were of more importance than sensitive writing. With Crane he saw life in impressionistic fractions, a habit that appears to be characteristic of all naturalists, no matter whether they happen to be skilful craftsmen, as Crane was, or inept stylists, as Dreiser is. Reading Norris's description of South Water Street in *The Pit*, one is reminded of Zola's passages on Les Halles, in *The Belly of Paris* (1873), and of Dreiser's pachydermic paragraphs in *The Genius*, which do not "ring the bell" as Crane's images do, but gain in power what they lose in sharpness.

Provisions, market produce, "garden truck" and fruits, in an infinite welter of crates and baskets, boxes, and sacks, crowded the sidewalks. The gutter was choked with an overflow of refuse cabbage leaves, soft oranges, decaying beet tops. The air was thick with the heavy smell of vegetation. Food was trodden under foot, food crammed the stores and warehouses to bursting. Food mingled with the mud of the highway. The very dray horses were gorged with an unending nourishment of snatched mouthfuls picked from backboard, from barrel top, and from the end of the sidewalk. The entire locality reeked with the fatness of a hundred thousand furrows. A land of plenty, the inordinate abundance of the earth itself emptied itself upon the asphalt and cobbles of the quarter. It was the Mouth of the City, and drawn from all directions, over a territory of immense area, this glut of crude subsistence was sucked in, as if

[35] *McTeague*, p. 3.

into a rapacious gullet, to feed the sinews and to nourish the fibres of an immeasurable colossus.[36]

Norris's work, like Crane's, was often a mere sequence of pictures, but he possessed a larger ability to chink them with discussions and events; and for this reason he seems to have been more of a novelist than the author of *The Red Badge*, whose tinier and more concentrated narrative was better adapted to the short story. Yet Norris, too, had a fine sense of the isolated scene, as testified by his ending to *McTeague*, or his famous picture of the "Pit" which has been separately published. And his talent for dramatization, as well as his forceful use of symbols, prove him an artist of considerable proportions.

TOWARD SOCIALISM By the time Norris had reached *The Octopus* and *The Pit*, he was inclining away from naturalism toward a more humanitarian ideal. In these novels he continues to believe, as Spencer had insisted, that Nature, if left alone, will end up in its own kind of justice and goodness. "The larger view," he said in *The Octopus*, "always and through all shams, all wickednesses, discovers the Truth that will, in the end, prevail, and all things, surely, inevitably, resistlessly work together for good." [37] But he no longer glorifies, in these later books, the brawler and the strong man, as he did in his earlier stories. Now it is the race that counts.

The Responsibilities of the Novelist (1903) is also a product of his last years, when he had begun to discard pure naturalism that celebrates brute strength and the individual in favor of a naturalism adulterated with social protest. In fact it partakes less of Zola's *Experimental Novel* than of Tolstoy's *What Is Art?* with its central principle that "no art that is not in the end understood by the People can

---

[36] Norris, Frank, *The Pit* (1903), pp. 61–62.
[37] *The Octopus*, p. 652.

live or ever did live a single generation." [38]   The best kind of novel, it holds, is that which "preaches" and has a "purpose."   Yet "it preaches by telling things and showing things," [39] rather than by argumentation or moralizing.   To be a great force, it should work together "with the pulpit and the universities for the good of the people, fearlessly proving that power is abused, that the strong grind the faces of the weak, that an evil tree is still growing in the midst of the garden," [40] and that this evil tree is "man's inhumanity to man."   A far cry, surely, is this from Norris's youthful "men, strong, brutal men, with red-hot blood in 'em, with unleashed passions rampant in 'em, blood and bones and viscera in 'em, and women, too, that move and have their being."

[38] Norris, Frank, *The Responsibilities of the Novelist* (1903), p. 7.
[39] *Ibid.*, p. 27.   [40] *Ibid.*, p. 32.

*

MEN WITH THE BARK ON

*

RED BLOOD "What was 'elemental' in Frank Norris became 'abysmal' in Jack London. He carried the cult of 'red blood' in literature to an extreme at which it began to sink to the ridiculous, as in his lineal descendants of the moving picture. His heroes, whether wolves or dogs or prize-fighters or sailors or adventurers-at-large, have all of them approximately the same instincts and the same careers. They rise to eminence by battle, hold the eminence for a while by the same methods, and eventually go down under the rush of stronger enemies. London, with the strength of the strong, exulted in the struggle for survival. He saw human history in terms of the evolutionary dogma, which to him seemed a glorious, continuous epic of which his stories were episodes. He set them in localities where the struggle could be most obvious: in the wilds of Alaska, on remote Pacific Islands, on ships at sea out of hearing of the police, in industrial communities during strikes, in the underworlds of various cities, on the routes of vagabondage." [1]

WANDERLUST London derived from a restless breed of "frontier chasers," soldiers, backwoodsmen, and farmers. After his birth in San Francisco, January 12, 1876, his parents drifted around California until he was nine, when they returned to Oakland. There he went to the public schools, sold newspapers, and delivered "soap-box" lectures that earned him the local title of "Boy Socialist."

[1] Van Doren, Carl, *The American Novel* (1931), p. 268. **By permission of** The Macmillan Company, publishers.

His youth was a period of manual labor, and as he grew older his "passion for geography" sent him caroming from one job to another. He shipped before the mast at seventeen, on a schooner cleared for the Behring Sea, and worked in jute mills, canning factories, bowling alleys, and laundries. In 1894 he joined Kelly's Industrial Army (which marched upon Washington with Coxey's Army to demand employment); but after deserting, and being arrested in Buffalo for vagrancy, he began traveling over America, "riding the rods," and begging at kitchen doors with "the aristocracy of the Underworld . . . the lords and masters, the aggressive men, the primordial noble men, the *blond beasts* of Nietzsche, lustfully roving and conquering through sheer superiority and strength." [2]

THE PARLOR FLOOR   Back in Oakland, he set out to get himself an education. Thus far he had been living in what he termed "the cellar of society," and he meant to climb up to "the parlor floor." "Brains paid, not brawn." [3]   Therefore he would sell brains, not muscle; and with this intention he entered the University of California, where like Norris he found English unbearable and science intriguing. But gold was soon discovered up in the Klondike, or "backyard of the United States," and again he "hit the trail."

This trip, though unproductive of nuggets, proved a happy investment, in that it gave London the material for his earliest triumphs in fiction. He had already decided to become an author, tempted by rumors of the high prices paid for "best-sellers" (yet before placing his first story with *The Overland Monthly* in 1898, he received enough rejection slips to make a stack five feet high!). The year 1903 ushered in his biggest success, *The Call of the Wild.*

[2] London, Jack, "Rods and Gunnels," *The Bookman* (October, 1916), XLIV, 179.

[3] London, Jack, *John Barleycorn* (1913), p. 204.

He married, went about the country lecturing on the "Revolution," which many good citizens thought "just around the corner," marketed his tales for sizable checks, left to cover the Boer War as Norris was doing, found himself locked out by the same censorship that had expelled Norris, detoured to England, spent a few months among the "submerged tenth" of Whitechapel, wrote up his experiences there in *The People of the Abyss* (1903), was divorced, and married again. With his second wife, Charmian Kittredge, he bought a sailboat, and launched it upon a seven years' voyage in the South Seas. But by the time they had reached Australia he was brought low with a rare malady (which he called "Biblical leprosy"), and forced to return home. Then after a trip to Mexico in 1914 with General Funston's troops, and the purchase of a 1300 acre ranch near Glen Ellen, California, he settled down to wringing out a thousand words per day, until his death in 1916.

He died "burnt out" by the strenuous life he had led; yet during his brief literary career of eighteen years (sandwiched in between adventures), he found the opportunity to write over fifty books, or about three a year. His nonfiction consists, first, of socialistic essays in *People of the Abyss*, *War of the Classes* (1905), and *Revolution* (1910); and second, of autobiography in *Martin Eden* (1909), *The Cruise of the Snark* (1911), and *John Barleycorn* (1913), the story of London's fight against what used to be called "the liquor habit." His sketches deal with hobo life, and the struggle of man against man. Three volumes of these narratives, taken from his South Sea experiences, are entitled *A Son of the Sun* (1912), *South Sea Tales* (1911), and *The House of Pride* (1912); and others are to be found collected in *The Son of the Wolf* (1900), *Children of the Frost* (1902), *Tales of the Fish Patrol* (1905), *Moon-Face* (1906), *Love of Life* (1906), *When God Laughs* (1911), *The Strength of the Strong* (1914), and *The Turtles of Tasman* (1916).

A few of his novels are *A Daughter of the Snows* (1902), the story of Frona Welse, "a man's woman," and of Vance Corliss's regeneration from a "softy" into a fit "mate" for her (a favorite theme with both Norris and London); *The Call of the Wild* (1903), the novel of a dog who turned back into a wolf; *The Game* (1905), a brief and amateurish tale of a prizefighter, killed in his last bout; *White Fang* (1906), about a wolf who reverses the process of atavism depicted in *The Call of the Wild*, and becomes civilized; *Before Adam* (1907), a pre-historic romance, which was so similar to a previous novel, *The Story of Ab* (1897) by Stanley Waterloo, that London was charged with plagiarism; *Adventure* (1911), the story of a strong man and his "mate," surrounded by cannibals on a copra plantation in the Solomon Islands; *Smoke Bellew* (1912), presenting a lazy Bohemian spoiled by money, who finds love and "manhood" on the rough trails of the Yukon; *The Abysmal Brute* (1913), another story of the prize ring; *The Valley of the Moon* (1913), in which a huge teamster and his "mate" escape from poverty and industrial riots to a farm in the Sonoma Mountains, where London purchased his own ranch; *The Mutiny of the Elsinore* (1914), the narrative of a voyage around Cape Horn, with a tired wealthy youth coming to "manhood" under the inspiration of hardships and the captain's daughter, and with another Wolf Larsen in the second mate, who reads Zola, Anatole France, Heine, Flaubert, and Maxim Gorky; *The Scarlet Plague* (1915), the yarn of a great epidemic in the year 2013, which reduces the world to a primordial state; and *The Little Lady of the Big House* (1916), another novel of a man and his "mate," whose obvious locale is London's Glen Ellen estate. *Burning Daylight* (1910), London's contribution to that type of naturalistic literature represented by *The Pit* and Dreiser's *The Titan*, treats of the "struggle for existence" in commercial life and the rise of "giants" in American finance at the opening of the century. Elam

Harnish, a prospector in the Klondike makes a million, returns to San Francisco, and becomes a land speculator, a raging lion without morals, a savage gambler who treads into the earth all those who dare oppose him, a merciless profligate. But just as he seems to be losing his soul in the pursuit of gold, he grows enamored of his stenographer, and moves (like half of London's characters) to a ranch in the Sonoma Mountains.

London's most typical novel, however, is *The Sea-Wolf* (1904), which bears a strong resemblance to Norris's *Moran of the Lady Letty*, except that the despotic captain of London's story happens to be a man. Humphrey Van Weyden, another effete "scholar and dillettante," is standing on a ferry boat, musing over the fact that men are "mere motes of light and sparkle," when a collision occurs in the fog. He is thrown into the water, and rescued (as he is about to sink for the last time) by the schooner *Ghost*, "bound seal-hunting to Japan." The crew being short a hand, he is put to work as cabin boy by the diabolical skipper, Wolf Larsen, whom Van Weyden describes as follows:

His height was probably five feet ten inches, or ten and a half; but my first impression, or feel of the man, was not of this, but of his strength. And yet, while he was of massive build, with broad shoulders and deep chest, I could not characterize his strength as massive. It was what might be termed a sinewy, knotty strength, of the kind we ascribe to lean and wiry men, but which in him, because of his heavy build, partook more of the enlarged gorilla order. Not that in appearance he seemed in the least gorilla-like. What I am striving to express is this strength itself, more as a thing apart from his physical semblance. It was a strength we are wont to associate with things primitive, with wild animals, and creatures we imagine our tree-dwelling prototypes to have been — a strength savage, ferocious, alive in itself, the essence of life in that it is potency of motion, the elemental stuff itself out of which the many forms of life have been molded.[4]

[4] London, Jack, *The Sea-Wolf* (1904), pp. 18–19.

This Larsen, it transpires, is a vicious brute, fond of beating men into insensibility, a murderer who rules his ship with an iron hand, yet at the same time a man of some erudition, whose philosophy seems to be, as he expresses it to Van Weyden, that "life is a mess." "It is like yeast, a ferment, a thing that moves and may move for a minute, an hour, a year, or a hundred years, but that in the end will cease to move. The big eat the little that they may continue to move, the strong eat the weak that they may retain their strength." [5]   Life, he asserts, is the cheapest thing in the world.

There is only so much water, so much earth, so much air; but the life that is demanding to be born is limitless. Nature is a spendthrift. Look at the fish and their millions of eggs. For that matter, look at you and me. In our loins are the possibilities of millions of lives. Could we but find time and opportunity and utilize the last bit and every bit of the unborn life that is in us, we could become the fathers of nations and populate continents. Life? Bah! It has no value. Of cheap things it is the cheapest. Everywhere it goes begging. Nature spills it out with a lavish hand. Where there is room for one life, she sows a thousand lives, and it's life eats life till the strongest and most piggish life is left. [6]

He derides Van Weyden's belief in "such things as right and wrong." For him, "Might is right, and that is all there is to it. Weakness is wrong. Which is a very poor way of saying that it is good for oneself to be strong, and evil for oneself to be weak — or better yet, it is pleasurable to be strong, because of the profits; painful to be weak, because of the penalties." [7]

The voyage becomes "a carnival of brutality," with daily fights, knifings, storms, and mutiny, until one day they pick up a boatful of castaways: four men, and a woman named Maud Brewster, survivors of a mail steamer that has been wrecked in a typhoon. Wolf Larsen, of course,

[5] *The Sea-Wolf*, p. 50.   [6] *Ibid.*, p. 68.   [7] *Ibid.*, p. 79.

"desires" Maud; but at last Van Weyden finds his courage and makes off with her in a boat. After days on the open sea they land on a desert island, where they live on seal meat for a while. (London, who boasted that he had never written an obscene line, does not falter even in this situation; and the platonic purity of his two characters while on the island rings false to many readers of our present day.) Then one morning, to their dismay, the *Ghost* heaves in sight. On it they find only Wolf Larsen, deserted by his crew, half blinded by mysterious headaches, and no longer dangerous. Van Weyden, lacking the nerve to kill him, waits for him to die, which he soon does, of general paralysis, his last word *bosh*, "skeptical and invincible to the end." Whereupon Van Weyden and his "mate-woman" commandeer the *Ghost* and sail away, to be immediately rescued.

London's conclusion is flabby with sentiment, and worse than the lubricity he tried so hard to avoid. But let Van Weyden speak for himself.

Her lips met the press of mine, and, by what strange trick of the imagination I know not, the scene in the cabin of the *Ghost* flashed upon me, when she had pressed her fingers lightly on my lips and said, "Hush, hush."

"My woman, my one small woman," I said, my free hand petting her shoulder in the way all lovers know though never learn in school.

"My man," she said, looking at me for an instant with tremulous lids which fluttered down and veiled her eyes as she snuggled her head against my breast with a happy little sigh.

I looked toward the cutter. It was very close. A boat was being lowered.

"One kiss, dear love," I whispered. "One kiss more before they come."

"And rescue us from ourselves," she completed, with a most adorable smile, whimsical as I had never seen it, for it was whimsical with love.[8]

[8] *Ibid.*, p. 366.

In Norris and London naturalism reached the depths of mawkish melodrama.   Both attempted to suggest power and emulate the vast grandeur of Nature's sweep, only to overshoot the mark and lapse into the grandiose.   Their roots, perhaps, were not yet free of that romantic era of "rant and rococco" into which they had been born; and as a result, their naturalism seems to deserve the title, often given it, of "romanticism going on all fours."

Wolf Larsen, like London, was a self-educated man, who had reared himself on Spencer, Tyndall, Darwin, Huxley, Nietzsche, and Haeckel.   In his cabin were their books, and we may imagine him reading them, on a dark night, while outside great tongues of water curve over the bow. For instance, he might be reading Tyndall's *Address at Belfast* (1874), a cautious speech that had just shaken England and America profoundly, because of the tension to which Darwin's indirect attack upon theology had brought men of that day.   Or perhaps he abandons this short commentary on the advancement of materialism to pick up a volume by Thomas Henry Huxley, whose *Evolution and Ethics* (1894) did so much to clarify Darwinism for the lay student.   There he would find such utterances as these:

Man, physical, intellectual, and moral, is as much a part of nature, as purely a product of the cosmic process, as the humblest weed.[9]

For his successful progress, throughout the savage state, man has been largely indebted to those qualities which he shares with the ape and the tiger; his exceptional physical organization; his cunning, his sociability, his curiosity, and his imitativeness; his ruthless and ferocious destructiveness when his anger is roused by opposition.[10]

If he opened Spencer's *Data of Ethics* (1879), he might discover that "Sentient beings have progressed from low

[9] Huxley, Thomas H., *Evolution and Ethics, and Other Essays* (1902), p. 11.
[10] *Ibid.*, pp. 51–52.

to high types, under the law that the superior shall profit by their superiority and the inferior shall suffer from their inferiority. Conformity to this law has been, and is still, needful, not only for the continuance of life but for the increase of happiness." [11]

In large measure the adjustments of acts to ends which we have been considering, are components of that "struggle for existence" carried on both between members of the same species and between members of different species; and, very generally, a successful adjustment made by one creature involves an unsuccessful adjustment made by another creature, either of the same kind or of a different kind. That the carnivore may live herbivores must die; and that its young may be reared the young of weaker creatures must be orphaned. Maintenance of the hawk and its brood involves the deaths of many small birds; and that small birds may multiply, their progeny must be fed with innumerable sacrificed worms and larvae. Competition among members of the same species has allied, though less conspicuous, results. The stronger often carries off by force the prey which the weaker has caught. Monopolizing certain hunting grounds, the more ferocious drive others of their kind into less favourable places. With plant-eating animals, too, the like holds: the better food is secured by the more vigorous individuals, while the less vigorous and worse fed, succumb either directly from innutrition or indirectly from resulting inability to escape enemies. That is to say, among creatures whose lives are carried on antagonistically, each of the two kinds of conduct delineated above, must remain imperfectly evolved. Even in such few kinds of them as have little to fear from enemies or competitors, as lions or tigers, there is still inevitable failure in the adjustment of acts to ends towards the close of life. Death from starvation from inability to catch prey, shows a falling short of conduct from its ideal. [12]

Conduct is right or wrong according as its special acts, well or ill adjusted to special ends, do or do not further the general end of self-preservation. [13]

[11] Spencer, Herbert, *The Data of Ethics* (1886), p. 198.
[12] *Ibid.*, pp. 17–18.   [13] *Ibid.*, p. 23.

No school can avoid taking for the ultimate moral aim a desirable state of feeling called by whatever name — gratification, enjoyment, happiness.[14]

If he turned from this hedonism to Haeckel's *Riddle of the Universe*, he might read that "The supreme mistake of Christian ethics, and one which runs directly counter to the Golden Rule, is its exaggeration of love of one's neighbor at the expense of self-love. Christianity attacks and despises egoism on principle. Yet that natural impulse is absolutely indispensable in view of self-preservation; indeed, one may say that even altruism, its apparent opposite, is only an enlightened egoism." [15]

(1) The universe, or the cosmos, is eternal, infinite, and illimitable. (2) Its substance, with its two attributes (matter and energy), fills infinite space and is in eternal motion. (3) This motion runs on through infinite time as an unbroken development, with a periodic change from life to death, from evolution to devolution. (4) The innumerable bodies which are scattered about the space-filling ether all obey the same law of substance; while the rotating masses slowly move towards their destruction and dissolution in one part of space others are springing into new life and development in other quarters of the universe. (5) Our sun is one of these unnumbered perishable bodies, and our earth is one of the countless transitory planets that encircle them. (6) Our earth had gone through a long process of cooling before water in liquid form (the first condition of organic life) could settle thereon. (7) The ensuing biogenetic process, the slow development and transformation of countless organic forms, must have taken many millions of years — considerably over a hundred. (8) Among the different kinds of animals which arose in the later stages of the biogenetic process on earth the vertebrates have far outstripped all other competitors in the evolutionary race. (9) The most important branch of the vertebrates, the mammals, was developed later (during the Triassic period) from the lower amphibia and reptiles. (10) The most perfect and

14 Spencer, Herbert, *op. cit.*, p. 46.
15 Haeckel, Ernst, *The Riddle of the Universe* (1900), p. 353.

most highly developed branch of the class mammalia is the order of primates, which first put in an appearance, by development from the lowest prochariata, at the beginning of the Tertiary period. (11) Consequently, the so-called history of the world — that is, the brief period of a few thousand years which measures the duration of civilization — is an evanescently short episode in the long course of organic evolution, just as this, in turn, is merely a small portion of the history of our planetary system; and as our mother-earth is a mere speck in the sunbeam in the illimitable universe, so man himself is but a tiny grain of protoplasm in the perishable framework of organic nature.[16]

Transvaluation of Values   In a letter to a friend, London once said, "I have always inclined toward Haeckel's position. In fact, 'incline' is too weak a word. I am a hopeless materialist. I see the soul as nothing else than the sum of activities of the organism plus personal habits — plus inherited habits, memories, experiences, of the organism. I believe that when I am dead, I am dead." [17] Yet his right hand went out to another prophet of the age, and a greater: Friedrich Wilhelm Nietzsche, of whom it might be said that wherever you scratch modern life, there you will find him. Nietzsche recognized only two classes of men, the masters and the slaves. The first were noble because they had no hampering morals, and because they had strength, craftiness, and were swift to avenge an insult or injury. The second were ignoble slaves because they respected Christian tradition and human morals, and because they were humble, generous, and forgiving. To be merciful led to impotence, to be hard and selfish led to power. In one bold move Nietzsche reversed the values of Christianity. He saw all standards as based on habits, customs, and the desires of various nations and races, always changing. From this he argued that no fixed idea

[16] *Ibid.*, pp. 13–14.
[17] Quoted in Houck, Calvin B., "Jack London's Philosophy of Life," *The Overland Monthly* (May, 1926), LXXXIV, 141.

of good or evil could exist.   Man would have to call good
that which satisfied and suited him at the moment.   Life
was an exploitation; and an individual should judge everything by its effect on his own welfare.   Free will, charity,
peace, democracy, theology, morals, humanitarianism,
compromise, and governmental regulations were deceits
practiced upon the strong by the weak, in order to make
them weak, too.   And for this reason, Nietzsche, a natural
aristocrat, decried the leveling influences of both Christianity and socialism.   He wanted the distinctions between
master and slave left there.

We may easily picture Wolf Larsen, in his lonely cabin,
tasting and enjoying such remarks as these from the works
of Nietzsche:

This new table, O my brethren, put I over you: *Become hard!* [18]

What is good?   All that enhances the feeling of power, the Will
to Power, and power itself in man.   What is bad? — All that
proceeds from weakness.   What is happiness? — The feeling
that power is *increasing*, — that resistance has been overcome.
Not contentment, but more power; not peace at any price, but
war; not virtue, but efficiency. [19]

Pangs of conscience are indecent. [20]

Here are almost the very words of Wolf Larsen himself,
or of London's earlier character, Jacob Welse, a "captain
of industry" in the Arctic fur trade, who says to his indomitable daughter, "Conventions are worthless for such
as we.   They are for the swine who without them would
wallow deeper.   The weak must obey or be crushed; not
so with the strong.   The mass is nothing; the individual
everything; and it is the individual, always, that rules the
mass and gives the law." [21]

[18] Nietzsche, Friedrich, *The Complete Works of Friedrich Nietzsche* (1924),
XI, 262.   By permission of The Macmillan Company, publishers.

[19] *Ibid.*, XVI, 128.   By permission of The Macmillan Company, publishers.

[20] *Ibid.*, XVI, 2.   By permission of The Macmillan Company, publishers.

[21] London, Jack, *A Daughter of the Snows* (1902), p. 184.

One of Nietzsche's forerunners was Max Stirner, who promulgated in *The Ego and His Own* (1845) a doctrine of the most rampant individualism. Another was Schopenhauer, whose *The World as Will and Idea* (1819) held the instinct of self-preservation to be at the root of everything. Both were read widely in the United States by the end of the nineteenth century, though Nietzsche's own fame in this country was not large before 1908, when H. L. Mencken published his *Philosophy of Friedrich Nietzsche*. But by 1913 this book had gone into its third large edition, and Dr. Oscar Levy had completed the last of his eighteen-volume English translation of Nietzsche's works. In 1905 Bernard Shaw's *Man and Superman* came from England to our shores; a few years later James Huneker published *Egoists: A Book of Supermen;* and by 1912 "the word superman was firmly on its feet in America." [22] So that when Dr. William Osler, the famous physician, advocated (in a joking way) that men were useless after forty and should be chloroformed at sixty, many people were ready to take him seriously and interpret his remark in the light of Nietzsche's contention that the "weak and botched" ought to be helped to perish.

In every country, writers like Jack London were choosing supermen for their heroes. But most of them, in converting the theories of science and philosophy to their own uses, did not always tell "the whole truth and nothing but the truth." Instead they selected only the more striking ingredients of such doctrines as "evolution," and ignored the important qualifications that belong to them. True, they often said no more than Spencer or Huxley; the fault is that they did not say as much. In their treatment of Darwinism too many modifying clauses were left out. Spencer, as a matter of fact, did insist that behavior should be founded on its utility to the individual; but in

[22] Casseres, Benjamin de, *The Superman in America*, The University of Washington Chapbooks (1929), No. 30, 15.

transferring his hypothesis to their pages, some authors have forgotten to include his codicil, to the effect that the highest good is the welfare of society as a whole. Nor do they seem to remember that Huxley, for all his comments on the "struggle for existence," went on to say that

Society differs from nature in having a definite moral object; whence it comes about that the course shaped by the ethical man — the member of society or citizen — necessarily runs counter to that which the non-ethical man — the primitive savage, or man as a mere member of the animal kingdom — tends to adopt. The latter fights out the struggle for existence to the bitter end, like any other animal; the former devotes his best energies to the object of setting limits to the struggle.[23]

Even Nietzsche, in the last analysis, saw a higher destiny for his superman, a stage of noble development to which the "Blonde Beast" would some day climb in the course of his evolution, and thus become a figure of humanitarian significance rather than a mere roving beast of prey.

NEW FRONTIERS   London's success as a writer depended to a great extent upon his generation's taste for popularized scientific ideas, and also upon its appetite for novels about "new frontiers," localities on the globe never before exploited in fiction. Kipling, for example, found India; Bret Harte discovered California; Stevenson unearthed the South Seas; Richard Harding Davis annexed the rising profession of "newspaper life"; Crane wrote about that new genus "the war correspondent"; O. Henry struck gold in Bagdad-on-the-Subway; Zane Grey warmed over the "West" in such novels as *Riders of the Purple Sage* (1912); Stewart Edward White in *The Blazed Trail* (1902) and James Oliver Curwood appropriated the northern wilds; and Rex Beach, in a series of novels beginning with *The Spoilers* (1906), staked out a claim with London on the

[23] Huxley, Thomas H., *op. cit.*, p. 203.

Alaskan scene. London also did some spade work in "Trampland," a field since taken over by Harry Kemp in his autobiographical *Tramping on Life* (1922), and by Jim Tully in *Beggars of Life* (1924).

There was another province, too, in which London did some pioneering, that of socialism. In 1905 he was given the Socialistic nomination for Mayor of Oakland, and beaten. During his later years he became an ardent crusader for the abolition of child labor, "dirty" literature, the whisky traffic, and trained animal acts (on the grounds that they are inhumane). And his books on reform topics, such as *People of the Abyss*, *Revolution*, and *The Iron Heel* (1907), continue to enjoy, with the works of Upton Sinclair, a spectacular renown in foreign countries, especially Soviet Russia, where London was read and admired by Lenin himself.

But London's socialism is his own brand, and nearer to anarchy than anything else. Impatient and inclined toward violence, he resigned in 1916 from the Socialist party, because (as he said) "of its lack of fire and fight and its loss of emphasis on the class struggle," [24] though he continued to sign his letters "Yours for the Revolution." The point is that he never was a true socialist; he was too much of an individualist. Much as he reviled the great industrial barons in his later work, he never ceased believing that only the strong should survive. In *Martin Eden* London pictures himself addressing a Socialist meeting in this way:

The old law of development still holds. In the struggle for existence, as I have shown, the strong and the progeny of the strong tend to survive, while the weak and the progeny of the weak are crushed and tend to perish. The result is that the strong and the progeny of the strong survive, and, so long as the struggle obtains, the strength of each generation increases. That is development. But you slaves — it is too bad to be slaves, I grant —

[24] Bamford, Georgia Loring, *The Mystery of Jack London* (1931), p. 224.

but you slaves dream of a society where the law of development will be annulled, where no weaklings and inefficients will perish, where every inefficient will have as much as he wants to eat as many times a day as he desires, and where all will marry and have progeny — the weak as well as the strong. What will be the result? No longer will the strength and life-value of each generation increase. On the contrary, it will diminish. There is the Nemesis of your slave philosophy. Your society of slaves — of, by, and for, slaves — must inevitably weaken and go to pieces as the life which composes it weakens and goes to pieces.[25]

Nor did he ever lose his reverence for Nietzsche. Though he soon began to call his Nietzsche period the "long sickness," he was at the same time enthusiastically recommending the German's works to his wife.

The fallacy in this stance is well noted by C. Hartley Grattan, a recent critic, when he says, "London had a passion to dominate — men, women, things. He had many of the characteristics which Dreiser attributes to his financiers. The drive of his personality was in the direction of domineering individualism, which is hostile to collectivism. Thus, while his head argued socialism his nature argued individualism." [26] Poisoned by this spiritual conflict he came in the end to look upon life with a jaundiced eye. For what appeared to be scant reason, he began to alienate people who had befriended him. That he thought of suicide as a way out of his melancholia is testified by *Martin Eden;* and notwithstanding the fact that he died of intestinal uremia, Upton Sinclair hints that he took his own life. At any rate it would appear that he did little to save himself from dying.

More bad literature has been written about London (especially in praise of his "masculinity") than he wrote himself. He seems to have been the object of feminine encomia

[25] London, Jack, *The Works of Jack London* (1917), VII, 329.
[26] Grattan, C. Hartley, "Jack London," *The Bookman* (February, 1929), LXVIII, 670.

almost to the extent that D. H. Lawrence was; and both of them have had their biographies compiled, for the most part, by women. A great deal has also been published on the subject of London's early hardships (and certainly they were formidable), but what his enraptured critics have neglected to observe is that Jack London's worst enemy was Jack London. He desired only two things: to be thought a rough, virile MAN, and to have power, as represented by money.

It was by way of obtaining this first end that he began drinking at an early age, on the waterfronts of Oakland, "in order to demonstrate to myself," he confesses, "how much I was a man." [27] For the same reason he had barbers cut his hair "shaggy," and asked people to call him "Wolf." As one writer puts it, "London is always getting the reader to feel his biceps" (a request that he carried over into his personal life). In the phraseology of William James, he wanted people to believe that he was "tough-minded" [28] and not "tender-minded," that he could endure the "sting" of bitter experiences. He "could steer any kind of boat through any kind of sea; he could 'mush' over Chilkoot Pass, drink a straight quart of whisky, contend with prize-fighters and carry off the Sabine women. Therefore, he admired and portrayed types that could steer, mush, drink, box, and overcome. And his types were nearly always Jack London himself transposed to a heroic key." [29] Like Crane's hero in *The Red Badge of Courage*, he wanted to prove his bravery and stamina in the face of a brutal, lawless world. Yet there is something adolescent in his cult of barbarism, a kind of playing at "cowboys and Indians," or confession of basic weakness;

[27] *John Barleycorn*, p. 65.

[28] James described the "tough-minded" person as empirical, sensationalistic, materialistic, pessimistic, irreligious, fatalistic, pluralistic, and skeptical. James, William, *Pragmatism* (1908), p. 12.

[29] Dargan, E. Preston, "Jack London in Chancery," *The New Republic* (April 21, 1917), X, 7.

because "to be so preoccupied with vitality is a symptom of anaemia." [30]

London's other ambition, to possess power, springs from his desire to be one of Nietzsche's "masters," and not one of his "slaves." He wanted to dominate others, to assert his mastery, to overcome people, to "spread himself" (as the slang phrase has it); and for this he needed money. His life, therefore, was spent "in pursuit of dollars, dollars, dollars." It can scarcely be said that he loved literature for itself, since he turned to writing as a young man because "A 'best-seller' will earn anywhere between fifty and a hundred thousand dollars — sometimes more and sometimes less; but, as a rule, pretty close to those figures." [31] When his first story brought him only five dollars, instead of the expected forty or more, he abused *The Overland Monthly* in *Martin Eden*, to compensate for his disappointment. The rôle of conqueror appealed to him more than literary fame. As he said:

I'd rather win a water fight in the swimming pool, or remain astride a horse that is trying to get out from under me, than write the great American novel.[32]

From his point of view dollars meant "power," a huge estate in the mountains of California, blooded horses, and yachts. Did it matter if he had to grind out a thousand words per day in order to pay for these insignia of power? Editors gave him twenty cents a word, and "quality" was only a word like the rest. "The prophet of freedom," complains Mencken, "he yet sold himself into slavery to the publishers, and paid off with his soul for his ranch, his horses, his trappings of a wealthy cheese-monger." [33]

[30] Santayana, George, *Little Essays* (1921), p. 163.
[31] *The Works of Jack London*, VII, 190.
[32] Quoted in Colbron, Grace Isabel, "Jack London," *The Bookman* (January, 1917), XLIV, 441.
[33] Mencken, H. L., *Prejudices*, First Series (1929), p. 239.

*

THE HINDENBURG OF THE NOVEL

*

BEFORE THE LOOKING GLASS When his literary remains have been embalmed in a uniform edition, they should bear as a title, "The Confessions of Theodore Dreiser." In their pages we find again the solipsism that actuates Sherwood Anderson, Marcel Proust's *Remembrance of Things Past*, Bernarr Macfadden's popular magazine, *True Story*, and psychoanalytic patients. But Dreiser, in turning autobiography into fiction, has done so with a bristling honesty that is rare. He disrobes in public, "kisses and tells," and refuses to apologize for his candor. He is part of a recent tendency in literature for writers to use their books as mirrors in which to dramatize themselves, whether out of conceit or to achieve, in defiance of our machine age, an individuality by proxy. To borrow a phrase from Agnes Repplier, he has accomplished a "repeal of reticence."

THE BANKS OF THE WABASH This life of which he has spoken so plainly has not been, despite the jeremiads of his generation, "An American Tragedy." From *A Hoosier Holiday*, *Twelve Men*, *A Book About Myself*, *A Gallery of Women*, *Dawn*, and his novels, it emerges as forty years of mountainous labor, garnished with mistakes and erotic apocrypha. He has been forced to create his own audience. But today, after a brave season of effort, his name is often in the mouths of critics, and his novels are in the movies. Doors that were once closed to him have been opened. The "pariah" has outlived his epithet. He has conquered, as Sherwood Anderson once phrased it, "the wilderness of Puritan denial."

Dreiser was born in Terre Haute, Indiana, on August 27, 1871, of German parents. There were thirteen children in the family, writes Dreiser, "more or less under the domination of my dogmatic father, who was a Catholic and a bigot." [1] It was not a good start; and when his father's woolen mill burned down, they were left penniless. The boys picked up coal along railway tracks; the girls married, scattered, died. As their fortunes sank, his mother took three of the children, including Dreiser, and set out to live with friends, ending up in Warsaw (Indiana) under the wing of her son Paul, who had come into money and renown as a composer of popular songs, notably "On the Banks of the Wabash." Later his mother packed up again and moved to Evansville, where Dreiser went to parochial school; and one summer they journeyed to Chicago, decided it was too vulgar, and returned to Warsaw.

There Dreiser spent the rest of his youth, tortured, as he informs us in *Dawn*, by dreams of girls and a lust for self-aggrandizement. "My body," he says, "was blazing with sex, as well as with a desire for material and social supremacy — to have wealth, to be in society." [2] He read zealously among innocent volumes, *Water Babies*, *The Scarlet Letter*, Irving, Goldsmith, Shakspere, *Ben Hur*, Macaulay, Taine, Dickens, and Scott; yet he did not think of becoming an author himself. Nor did he ever imagine that he might some day arrive at a reputation almost as universal as that of Nietzsche, whose fame, he had heard, girdled the earth.

Without finishing high school he left for Chicago alone, at the age of sixteen, where he slaved as a dishwasher, scene painter, and shipping clerk in a hardware firm, until realizing his unfitness for a mercantile career, he accepted

[1] Dreiser, Theodore, *A Hoosier Holiday* (1916), p. 284.
[2] Dreiser, Theodore, *A Book About Myself* (1922), p. 106.

his employer's advice and went to college at the University of Indiana. After a year he turned up in Chicago again.

Back in The Windy City he worked for a while at driving a laundry wagon and collecting bills for an installment house; but the fever was strong in him to become a newspaper man, and ignoring disappointments, he kept his eye on this objective until he had landed a berth with the Chicago *Daily Globe*. He soon advanced to jobs on the St. Louis *Globe-Democrat* and Cleveland *Leader*, and while in Cleveland started *Sister Carrie*, his first novel, which was published in 1900 by Doubleday, Page and Company upon the recommendation of Frank Norris, only to be apprehensively withdrawn when reviewers objected to its abrupt treatment of human frailty and excommunicated Dreiser from polite society as a "moral leper."

BALZAC From Cleveland he went to Pittsburgh, where he worked on the *Dispatch* and discovered the novels of Balzac. "It was for me," he remembers, "a literary revolution." [3] Contrary to a wide misconception, Dreiser does not derive from Zola. Instead he pays tribute to the author of *Comédie Humaine*, and to Henry B. Fuller, whose two stories of Chicago, *The Cliff-Dwellers* (1893) and *With the Procession* (1895), were the birth cries, according to Dreiser, of naturalism in this country. Studying Balzac he began to see the possibilities of the American scene in fiction. He wanted to do for such cities as Pittsburgh what Balzac had done for Paris, to chart their teeming life and block out their ponderous silhouettes. In the organization of modern business enterprise, with its "captains of industry," its magnates, and its brutality, lay the material ready to his hand; and resolved to conjure an epic from it, he cast about for a hero, finally deciding upon Charles T. Yerkes, the traction king of Philadelphia and Chicago. He departed for Philadelphia, where Yerkes' early cabals

[3] *Ibid.*, p. 411.

had been projected, read everything in the newspaper files that applied to him, and thoroughly studied the history of the city, without (it is said) taking a single note. Then he did the same for Yerkes' later "deals" in Chicago, and documented *The Financier* and *Titan* (volumes I and II in his unfinished "Trilogy of Desire") entirely from memory.

WHO? WHAT? WHERE? WHEN? HOW? By 1894 Dreiser was in New York; but here he failed, and gave up newspaper work at the very moment Stephen Crane was riding to prominence on his *Red Badge of Courage*. Of journalism as a profession he did not think very highly, and he has signified his agreement with Mencken's remark that "The average American newspaper, especially the so-called better sort, has the intelligence of a Baptist evangelist, the courage of a rat, the fairness of a prohibitionist boob-bumper, the information of a high-school janitor, the taste of a designer of celluloid valentines, and the honor of a police-station lawyer." [4]   Too fond of words, and emotionally implicated in his assignments, he was not a good reporter. More and more he realized that he was not suited to this life, which required one's expression to be drained of personality. He could not tie himself down to simple accuracy, to "Who? What? Where? When? How?" The "Why?" intrigued him more, though it entirely baffled him and still does.

He turned to the magazines. In 1904 he became editor for Street, Smith and Company, publishers of sensational "wood pulp" fiction; in 1905 he was made literary editor of *Broadway Magazine;* and in 1907 he assumed the editorship of Butterick Publications, while grinding out "potboilers" for other periodicals: special articles entitled, for example, "Why the Indian Paints His Face," "The Making of Stained-Glass Windows," "Fruit Growing in

[4] Quoted in *A Book About Myself*, p. 465.

America," and "Scenes in a Cartridge Factory." [5] Undismayed by his troubles with *Sister Carrie*, he wrote *Jennie Gerhardt* in 1911; and since that year we have had from his pen *The Financier* (1912); *A Traveller at Forty* (1913), a European travelogue; *The Titan* (1914); *The Genius* (1915); *Plays of the Natural and Supernatural* (1916); *A Hoosier Holiday* (1916), Dreiser's pilgrimage back to his home state of Indiana; *Free and Other Stories* (1918); *The Hand of the Potter* (1918), a four-act play dealing with the rape of a child by an imbecile; *Twelve Men* (1919), a dozen biographies; *Hey Rub-a-Dub-Dub* (1920), philosophical essays; *A Book About Myself* (1922), Dreiser's story of his newspaper days; *The Color of a Great City* (1923), sketches of New York during the years 1900 to 1914; *An American Tragedy* (1925); *Moods, Cadenced and Declaimed* (1926), poetry; *Chains, Lesser Novels and Stories* (1927); *A Gallery of Women* (1929), a companion volume to *Twelve Men; Dreiser Looks at Russia* (1928); *Tragic America* (1931); and *Dawn* (1931), an intimate record of Dreiser's youth.

Sister Carrie is the story of a young girl who comes to Chicago from a small western town, and tempted by the luxury that confronts her, just out of reach, surrenders first to the blandishments of Drouet, a salesman, and then to Hurstwood, manager of a bar. But in attaining her own success as an actress, she proves to be the agent of Hurstwood's final deterioration, which Dreiser traces in the most sensitive chapters he ever wrote. Jennie Gerhardt, Carrie's literary "double," is a "daughter of poverty," whose family seems to have been modeled after Dreiser's own. Befriended by a Senator, she allows him, out of gratitude, to seduce her. When he dies, leaving her with a child, she drifts, with the usual abulia of Dreiser's heroines, into the rôle of mistress to a "strong, intellectual bear of a man, son of a wealthy manufacturer." Members of

[5] See McDonald, Edward D., "Dreiser Before 'Sister Carrie'," *The Bookman* (June, 1928), LXVII, 369–374.

his family try to disrupt the *ménage;* and finally he too dies, after deserting Jennie for a woman of his own social level. *The Genius,* called by William Marion Reedy a "multiplication of amours," details the adventures of a painter, Eugene Witla, who makes the favorite hegira of Dreiserian characters from a midwestern village to Chicago, and later goes on to New York. There he becomes an artist, with a taste for the same raw, volcanic qualities admired by his author. He marries an older woman, tires of her, falls in love with a young girl, gives up his art after a long sickness, becomes a laborer, makes a fortune in publishing, ruins his career with another intrigue, and after his wife's death, returns to painting.

His life, in fact, seems to be based on the supposition that a man must experience every desire before he can be free of them, or upon William Blake's avowal that "You never know what is enough unless you know what is more than enough." "The genius," said Nietzsche, "is necessarily a squanderer: the fact that he spends himself constitutes his greatness. . . . He flows out, he flows over, he consumes himself, he does not spare himself, — and does all this with fateful necessity, irrevocably, involuntarily, just as a river involuntarily bursts its dams." [6] It would be hard to find a better description of Dreiser's Witla.

An American Tragedy relates the story of Clyde Griffiths, son of evangelistic parents, who takes a job as a bellhop, is involved in an accident, escapes to another city, finds work in a rich uncle's manufacturing plant, splits his affection between an heiress and a factory girl, learns that the latter is pregnant, entices her to a distant lake, drowns her, and pays for his crime in the electric chair. It is a huge work of two volumes, replete with Dreiser's usual turgidity, "chemic compulsions," and melodrama; yet its

[6] Nietzsche, Friedrich, *The Complete Works of Friedrich Nietzsche* (1917), XVI, 103. By permission of The Macmillan Company, publishers.

style is an improvement upon his earlier products. Though it lacks the vibrancy of *Sister Carrie*, and though it might be shortened to advantage, *An American Tragedy* is one of the most important books of this day. The loneliness of young men and women in American cities and the economic extremes of wealth and poverty that tempt them to disaster have found here a poignant expression. Over the whole length of this novel hangs an atmosphere of social protest, a mood of despair, and a sense of irrational fate. And there is in it a profundity of tone and variety of life that few other modern writers have been able to achieve.

SOPHOCLES VERSUS SHAKSPERE Dreiser's idea of tragedy is Shaksperian, not Greek. His Clyde Griffiths is a moral coward and weakling, instead of a hero in the Athenian sense; he is a victim of his environment. The criminal, as Dreiser emphasizes here and in *The Hand of the Potter*, cannot be held responsible for his misdeeds. He is the product of forces beyond his control, an Othello, not an Oedipus punished for the deliberate transgression of an ethical law; he is broken on the wheel not because he deserves it, but due to cosmic accidentia. Shakspere's tragedies are "fortuitous calamities," whose characters are often the innocent frauds of chance; whereas in the Greek, tragedy was a just dispensation of the gods for an infraction of their code.[7] "As flies to wanton boys," said the Bard, "are we to the gods; They kill us for their sport." But Dreiser's true complaint is not against "the gods"; it is aimed at a human society that tries to polarize the natural currents of life. In common with Nietzsche he believes that man is contaminated by regulations, that he is "beyond good and evil," and that

The criminal type is the type of the strong man amid unfavorable conditions, a strong man made sick. He lacks the wild and

[7] See Frye, Prosser Hall, "The Idea of Greek Tragedy," in Foerster, Norman (ed.), *American Critical Essays* (1930), pp. 364–425.

savage state, a form of nature and existence which is freer and more dangerous, in which everything that constitutes the shield and the sword in the instinct of the strong man, takes a place by right.   Society puts a ban upon his virtues.[8]

MACHIAVELLI (NEW STYLE)   Though not his best, the key novels of Dreiser are *The Financier* and *The Titan*, in which Charles Yerkes has been given the character of Frank Cowperwood, a "corporation-breaking, vote-corrupting, jury-bribing, non-ethical, non-moral buccaneer of American finance." [9]

"Synchronously with the growth of the evolutionary theory," writes one historian, "arose the economic doctrine of *laissez faire*, culminating in the Manchester school which held that a world of economic order would develop mechanically from the free play of individuals upon one another without the intervention of any governmental and, so to speak, external regulation of competition.   It was the perfect counterpart to the Darwinian notion of the survival of the fittest amidst the accidental and competitive variation of individuals." [10]   Yet in this case, theory had merely overtaken an established fact;   the practice of *laissez faire* in economics goes back much farther than the nineteenth century.   "Every man for himself" is a naturalistic concept as old as the earth.

American industry, with its huge resources of wood, oil, coal, waterways, and metal to be exploited, began to mass and differentiate early.   Though at first awkward, it boomed steadily after 1790, with the ratification of a Constitution favorable to the property classes, the War of 1812, western land speculation, canal and turnpike enthusiasm, and the Tariff of 1816.[11]   During 1819 infant capitalism

[8] Nietzsche, Friedrich, *op. cit.*, XVI, 103–104.   By permission of The Macmillan Company, publishers.

[9] Rascoe, Burton, *Theodore Dreiser* (1925), pp. 13–14.

[10] More, Paul Elmer, *Shelburne Essays*, Seventh Series (1910), pp. 254–255.

[11] Simons, A. M., *Social Forces in American History* (1914), p. 160.

suffered growing pains, but persevered over rudimentary banking methods with its definite emergence from a domestic to factory stage. Manufacturing assumed strength as iron and textiles began to direct tariff policies. A century of invention soon revolutionized the steel industry and loom wares. Recovery was swift from the Panic of 1837; and commercial forces sprang into adult supremacy with the development of western markets, the railroad, the telegraph, the postal system, and express companies. The Civil War saw a further growth in the "machine" system, due to a shortage of labor caused by military demands for men. America was coming into a new destiny, says Garet Garrett, and in the years from 1850 to 1860, "destiny surrendered."

There was that rare coincidence of seed, weather, deep ploughing, and mysterious sanction which the miracle requires. The essential power of the American was suddenly liberated. There was the discovery of gold in California. There was the Crimean War, which created a high demand abroad for our commodities. The telegraph put its indignities upon time and space. The idea of a railroad as a tool of empire seized the imagination. Railroads were deliriously constructed. The map of 1860 shows a glistening steel web from the seaboard to the Mississippi.

The gigantesque was enthroned as the national fetich. Votive offerings were mass, velocity, quantity. True cities began. The spirit of Chicago was born. Bigness and be-damnedness. In this decade the outlines of our economic development were cast for good.[12]

"The manipulation of war finances poured such a golden flood into the vaults of a clique of New York bankers as to give them domination within the capitalist ranks,"[13] and from then on, industry, in spite of two panics, grew with logarithmic speed.   "In the next fifty years down to 1910,

[12] Stearns, Harold E. (ed.), *Civilization in the United States* (1922), p. 403.
[13] Simons, A. M., *op. cit.*, p. 280. By permission of The Macmillan Company, publishers.

we built half as much railroad mileage as all the rest of the world. Population trebled. This fact stands alone in the data of vital statistics. Yet even more remarkable were the alterations of human activity. The number of city dwellers increased 3½ times faster than the population; the number of wage-earners, 2 times faster; clerks, salesmen, and typists, 6½ times faster; banks, 7 times faster; corporations, 6½ times faster; miners, 3 times faster; transportation-workers, 20 times faster; and the number of independent farmers decreased. Wealth in this time increased from about $500 to more than $1,500 *per capita*." [14]
"With capital at hand, with natural resources to be had for the asking or the taking, with stalwart labor ready for the fray, with a vast domestic market assured, with politicians impatient to co-operate and share the fruits, and unhampered by a powerful aristocracy, lay or clerical, attached to other manners and other ideals, American business men leaped forward as strong runners to the race." [15]

Great financial barons issued from this tempest of profit, "titans" like Andrew Carnegie, John D. Rockefeller, James J. Hill, Edward H. Harriman, J. Pierpont Morgan, and scores of lesser men. The subsidization of railroads, displacement of iron by steel, adaptation of electricity, exhaustion of free lands in the West, strangling of the farmer, political and judicial control of the dollar, rise of corporations, and piratical gulping of small firms by larger ones, all contributed to a pronounced and perilous concentration of wealth. And when these "titans" were called to order, Roosevelt shouted down their critics with the epithet "muckrakers," the implication being (as it still is) that America was a giant, and that giants are bound to have a few negligible errata in their construction.

[14] Stearns, Harold E. (ed.), *op. cit.*, pp. 403–404.
[15] Beard, Charles A., and Mary R. Beard, *The Rise of American Civilization* (1930), II, 172. By permission of The Macmillan Company, publishers.

From this struggle there emerged so many financial wolves, infected with moral ataxia, that it is not surprising to find the superman type well represented in our recent literature. His footprints are to be found weaving through such novels as Henry Kitchell Webster's *The Banker and the Bear* (1900), Charles K. Lush's *The Autocrats* (1901), David Graham Phillips' *The Master-Rogue* (1903), Frank Norris's *The Pit* (1903), Robert Herrick's *The Memoirs of an American Citizen* (1905), Francis Lynde's *The Empire Builders* (1907), Will Payne's *The Automatic Capitalists* (1909), Robert Grant's *The Chippendales* (1909), Garet Garrett's *The Driver* (1922), based on the life of E. H. Harriman, and Lester Cohen's *The Great Bear* (1927). But among these harpies of the marketplace, Frank Cowperwood is surely the best known.

The Financier shows him first as a young boy in Philadelphia, the son of a banker. One day he sees a lobster devour a squid in a window aquarium, and decides "That's the way it has to be, I guess."

The incident made a great impression on him. It answered in a rough way that riddle which had been annoying him so much in the past: "How is life organized?" Things lived on each other — that was it. Lobsters lived on squids and other things. What lived on lobsters? Men, of course! Sure, that was it! And what lived on men? he asked himself. Was it other men? Wild animals lived on men. And there were Indians and cannibals. And some men were killed by storms and accidents. He wasn't so sure about men living on men; but men did kill each other. How about wars and street fights and mobs? He had seen a mob once. It attacked the *Public Ledger* building as he was coming home from school. His father had explained why. It was about the slaves. That was it! Sure, men lived on men. Look at the slaves.[16]

From the start he shows a natural aptitude for business, and following a preliminary success on the grain exchange,

[16] Dreiser, Theodore, *The Financier* (1927), p. 5.

he goes into a note-brokerage company of his own. After marrying the statuesque widow of a shoe merchant, he edges over craftily into politics, aims at a "corner" in the new field of street-railway securities, scores one coup after another, manipulates city officials, dips into graft, and achieves prestige, dominance, and wealth. "It was an illegitimate gain, unethical; but his conscience was not very much troubled by that. He had none, truly." [17]

The thing for him to do was to get rich and hold his own — to build up a seeming of virtue and dignity which would pass muster for the genuine thing. Force would do that. Quickness of wit. And he had these. "I satisfy myself," was his motto; and it might well have been emblazoned upon any coat of arms which he could have contrived to set forth his claim to intellectual and social nobility. [18]

Growing tired of his sickly and much older wife, he forms an "illicit relationship" with the young daughter of a henchman. But the girl's father discovers their liaison, organizes Cowperwood's enemies against him, and has him sent to prison for embezzling municipal funds, though he is pardoned after a year or so, and enters business again in Philadelphia on a modest scale. Then, just as a chance catastrophe (the Chicago fire in 1871) had helped ruin him, so the failure of Jay Cooke in 1873 enables Cowperwood to exploit the market in excess of a million dollars. With this sum he leaves for Chicago, accompanied by his mistress, his wife having divorced him soon after his release from the penitentiary.

A RAKE'S PROGRESS   *The Titan* is a virtual duplication of this first volume, in the words of Stuart Pratt Sherman, a "huge club-sandwich composed of slices of business alternating with erotic episodes." [19]   It deals with the commer-

[17] *The Financier*, p. 109.   [18] *Ibid.*, p. 135.
[19] Sherman, Stuart P., *On Contemporary Literature* (1917), p. 98.

cial and polygamous activities of Cowperwood in Chicago, where he devotes himself even more assiduously to a bold stalking of women and money. Cowperwood, in his greed for power, is a new Machiavelli, and in his erotic peccadillos, a modern Don Juan. "There was a great talk concerning morality, much praise of virtue and decency, and much lifting of hands in righteous horror at people who broke or were even rumored to have broken the Seventh Commandment. He did not take this talk seriously." [20] Nor does Dreiser. "A raging, destroying bull," he avers,

which insists on gormandizing all the females of a herd, is the product of nature, not of man. Man did not make the bull or the stallion, nor did they make themselves. Is nature to be controlled, made over, by man, according to some theory which man, a product of nature, has discovered? [21]

THE FINANCIAL TYPE   As for those who insist that Dreiser did not condone the behavior of Cowperwood, let them turn to his essays in *Hey Rub-a-Dub-Dub*, where he has set down, without equivocation, his opinion of the "merchant prince" and "sexual freelance." He saw the superman as "one who has dreamed out something." The mass, he said, "only moves forward because of the services of the exceptional individual." [22]   Hence "it is folly not to wish that the significant individual will always appear and will always do what his instincts tell him to do." [23]

Dreiser found "an epic quality in the rise of individuals to merciless and remorseless power through the adaptation of their combative instincts to the peculiar conditions of the American struggle for existence." [24]   But he is aware that this conflict has today been modified. As Nietzsche pointed out, "where there is a struggle" now, "it is a

[20] *The Financier*, p. 38.
[21] *A Hoosier Holiday*, p. 378.
[22] Dreiser, Theodore, *Hey Rub-a-Dub-Dub* (1920), p. 89.
[23] *Ibid.*, p. 89.
[24] Rascoe, Burton, *Theodore Dreiser* (1925), p. 78.

struggle for power," and not for simple existence.[25]   Even London, exponent of "the strong," realized that our modern competition for "survival" differs from the old. "Primitive strength," he explains,

was in the arm; the modern strength in the brain.   Though it had shifted ground the struggle was the same old struggle.   As of old time, men still fought for the mastery of the earth and the delights thereof.   But the sword had given away to the ledger; the mail-clad baron to the soft-clothed industrial lord, and the center of imperial political power to the seat of commercial exchanges.[26]

To Dreiser's mind this was as it should be; these polypous lords of trade and money had the complete sanction of Nature. "An interviewer once questioning me," he says, "in regard to the significance of the American financial type (it was just after I had published 'The Financier'), raised the question as to whether the American financial type, then so abundant and powerful, had ethically the right to be as it was or to do as it was doing, seeing that it was being and doing about as it pleased.   My answer was, and I still see no reason for changing it, that, in spite of all the so-called laws and prophets, there is apparently in Nature no such thing as the right to do or the right not to do." [27]

The financial type is the coldest, the most selfish, and the most useful of all living phenomena.   Plainly it is a highly specialized machine for the accomplishment of some end which Nature has in view.   Often humorless, shark-like, avid, yet among the greatest constructive forces imaginable.[28]

LOQUENTIA PRAECOX   Crane, Norris, and even London were not entirely bereft of proportion in their style.   De-

---

[25] Nietzsche, Friedrich, *op. cit.*, XVI, 71.   By permission of The Macmillan Company, publishers.

[26] London, Jack, *A Daughter of the Snows* (1902), p. 58.

[27] *Hey Rub-a-Dub-Dub*, p. 87.   [28] *Ibid.*, p. 74.

spite their new material and philosophy, they seemed to restrain their novels within the older patterns, from which
Dreiser, with his scorn for tradition, has seceded. He appears to have taken to heart the advice given by Hamlet's
mother to Polonius, "More matter, with less art." The
subject matter of his books is not assimilated by artistic
handling. He leaves it strewn around in chunks, like blocks
of unused granite. To him the thought of adjusting anything is petty. Style is a minor affair; "He writes to a theme
rather than to a plot." [29] His novels are a return to the
picaresque, an imitation of Nature in their inconsecutive-
ness, partaking of impressionism in their "snowstorms of
detail" (as one critic has termed them). It is the modern
habit of viewing life as a series of isolated events, without
meaning, ethical pigmentation, or authority. The Dreiserian novel is usually, in its plot, a mere skeleton of two
or three bones, upholstered with sagging details, and moving forward "like a large but immature lumber-wagon
loaded to the ricks with laboriously collected and most
conscientiously specified and authenticated downright in-
dubitable matters of fact." [30] His heavy doses of exposition
take on the aspect, for some, of rhetorical filibustering,
though his aim is only to express, with the strictest veracity, his own view of life. But such precision is out of
place in imaginative literature. Art is artificial, and must
be kept so; an entirely literal transcription of experience into
words always looks distorted, while a shaded transcription
seems to be true. Literature deals with imaginative truth,
not scientific.

HANGOVER Darwin's theory, it should be remembered,
was born into an era soaked with demure theatricalism,
vestiges of which lingered on in Crane, Norris, London,
and Dreiser. As we have already noted, their romanticized

[29] Boynton, Percy H., *Some Contemporary Americans* (1924), p. 134.
[30] Eastman, Max, *The Literary Mind* (1931), p. 326.

concept of evolution is not truly accurate in terms of the laboratory.   Early American naturalism, in brief, suffered a kind of "hangover" from the historical and local color novels that flourished during Dreiser's youth.   His habit of inserting "editorial" passages addressed to the reader is an anachronism that betrays this influence; and the same might be remarked of such candied excerpts as:

You have heard the wood-dove calling in the lone stillness of the summertime; you have found the unheeded brooklet singing and babbling where no ear comes to hear.   Under the dead leaves and snow-banks the delicate arbutus unfolds its simple blossom, answering some heavenly call for color.[31]

JUST SO MUCH STRAW   Dreiser's style has been called "a great grey sea of flat phrases, clichés, grammatical errors, and broken backed sentences," a description that would also fit Norris and London.   Their main concern was for breadth and power, "a return to Nature," which often sacrifices grace to grandeur.   "Let the chips fall where they may," we can hear Dreiser saying; and for the most part circumstances conspired to fix him in this attitude. He was told by his English teachers and his mentors in journalism that technique meant nothing.   Facts alone counted, especially in newspaper work, where Dreiser and most naturalists have gained their literary training.   The average "sheet" cannot require sleek compositions, based on "unity, coherence, and emphasis."   There is no time, when writing against a "dead-line," to draft polished articles.   Writing becomes a catch-as-catch-can affair.

"All this talk about style," says Dreiser, "what does it amount to?   Just so much straw!"[32]   Yet does it argue complete indifference that he has on several occasions turned his cyclopic manuscripts over to friends to be edited?   Both in material and style he seems to be ani-

---

[31] Dreiser, Theodore, *Jennie Gerhardt* (1926), p. 99.
[32] Quoted in Dudley, Dorothy, *Forgotten Frontiers* (1932), p. 468.

mated by a tough veracity and hatred of literary vanity. Few authors of his eminence would so unhesitatingly expose their lives to public criticism, or confess an inability to edit their own work.   No matter what he does, he is governed by a distaste for sticky hypocrisy, or the "naive American" who with one hand "takes and executes with all the brutal insistence of Nature itself," and with the other "writes glowing platitudes concerning brotherly love, virtue, purity, truth, etc., etc." [33]   There are no pretensions in his prolixity;   it is merely a part of his desire to be candid and consistent at any expense.

AN ORPHAN IN SPACE   The substance of Dreiser's philosophy can be melted down into one word, skepticism. Such an attitude maintains that nothing is positive, everything doubtful;   there are no conclusive facts in life.   Nothing can be proved;   we do not know anything for certain. The usual retort to this view has, of course, always been, "How, then, can you be sure that even your theory is right and true?"   But Dreiser is prepared;   his simple answer is, "I can't."   He is the perfect skeptic.

In all their ramifications, his hypotheses never wander far from this terminal concept.   For Dreiser life is "a mere idle rocking of force in one direction or another," [34] and man, only "an orphan in space," an "evoluted arrangement of attractions and repulsions, arranged by chemicals and forces which desire or cannot escape whorls or epitomes of complicated motions and emotions." [35]   Every process of man is brought about, he claims,

by the inescapable chemical and physical reactions and compulsions of seemingly blind forces, as Crile and Loeb have shown. . . . Even as to his so-called thought how close are the Behaviorists to the material mechanics which produce it.[36]

[33] *Hey Rub-a-Dub-Dub*, p. 272.
[34] *Ibid.*, p. 209.
[35] *Ibid.*, p. 242.
[36] *Ibid.*, p. 247.

BEHAVIORISM   The materialism of London traces back to
Haeckel, but Dreiser's found its inspiration in the work of
more recent investigators. Jacques Loeb, who saw life as
a series of "tropisms," wrote *The Mechanistic Conception of
Life* (1912), one of the most startling and disputed books
of our generation; and the Behavioristic theory owes most
of its fame to the researches of John B. Watson, published
in his volume *Behaviorism* (1925).   Together with C. Lloyd
Morgan, E. L. Thorndike, and others, Watson conceives of
man as a pure animal, a reaction-mass, operating like a
clock and capable of being measured by scientific instruments.   Thought, he says, is a muscular phenomenon.
Substituting Pavlov's "conditioned reflexes" for the older
psychological term "instincts," he looks upon the human
being as an organism with a body but no soul, and with
no mind, or at best a mind snared in an unbroken circuit
of "stimulus and response," and helpless to interfere.

Another book that has influenced Dreiser is Carl Snyder's
The World Machine (1907); but the most important sources
of his faith were opened to him while he was still twenty-
three years old.   "At this time," he states, "I had the fortune to discover Huxley and Tyndall and Herbert Spencer,
whose introductory volume to his *Synthetic Philosophy* (*First
Principles*) quite blew me, intellectually, to bits.   Hitherto,
until I had read Huxley, I had some lingering filaments of
Catholicism trailing about me, faith in the existence of
Christ, the soundness of his moral and sociologic deduc-
tions, the brotherhood of man.   But on reading *Science and
Hebrew Tradition* and *Science and Christian Tradition*, and
finding both the Old and New Testaments to be not com-
pendiums of revealed truth but mere records of religious
experiences, and very erroneous ones at that, and then
taking up *First Principles* and discovering that all I deemed
substantial — man's place in nature, his importance in the
universe, this too, too solid earth, man's very identity save
as an infinitesimal speck of energy or a 'suspended equa-

tion' drawn or blown here and there by larger forces in which he moved quite unconsciously as an atom — all questioned and dissolved into other and less understandable things, I was completely thrown down in my conceptions or non-conceptions of life." [37]   He began to feel that "spiritually one got nowhere, that there was no hereafter, that one lived and had his being because he had to, and that it was of no importance.   Of one's ideals, struggles, deprivations, sorrows and joys, it could only be said that they were chemic compulsions, something which for some inexplicable but unimportant reason responded to and resulted from the hope of pleasure and the fear of pain. Man was a mechanism, undevised and uncreated, and a badly and carelessly driven one at that." [38]

The race was to the swift and the battle to the strong.   All great successes, as I was beginning to discover for myself, were relatively gifts, the teachings of the self helpers and virtue mongers to the contrary notwithstanding.   Artists, singers, actors, policemen, statesmen, generals, were born and not made.   Sunday-school maxims, outside of the narrowest precincts, did not apply. People might preach one thing on Sunday or in the bosom of their families or in the meeting-places of conventional social groups, but they did not practice them except under compulsion, particularly in the marts of trade and exchange.   Mark the phrase "under compulsion."   I admit a vast compulsion which has nothing to do with the individual desires or tastes or impulses of individuals.   That compulsion springs from the settling processes of forces which we do not in the least understand, over which we have no control and in whose grip we are as grains of dust or sand, blown hither and thither, for what purpose we cannot even suspect.   Politics, as I found in working as a newspaper man, was a low mess; religion, both as to its principles and its practitioners, a ghastly fiction based on sound and fury, signifying nothing; trade was a seething war in which the less subtle and the less swift or strong went under, while the more cunning succeeded; the professions were largely gathering-places of weak-

[37] *A Book About Myself*, pp. 457–458.   [38] *Ibid.*, p. 458.

lings, mediocrities or mercenaries, to be bought by, or sold to, the highest bidder.[39]

DREISER IN WONDERLAND   There is about him Nature's own mistrust of stagnation.   He sees a universe of shifting atoms, where good and bad have been replaced by strong and weak, tries to discern in its blankness a trapdoor to truth, and failing, sinks back into long Saharas of pessimism.   Down every walk of life he goes, and comes out with an impression of the world as an insane, nebulous thing, striated with mystery, wherein men cause all the mischief by their vain attempts to tag and restrict the flow of Nature.   The naturalistic code of *laissez faire* infuses almost everything he has ever written.   "We are inherent in some greater thing than man," he says, "Nature Herself. Only She knows." [40]   "Nature's way is correct." [41]   "Leave it to Nature." [42]

Motivating Dreiser's thought is the belief that men and women are not responsible for their behavior.   He does not say that God is the Devil; he does not know.   What he does say, however, is that man is only a chemical compound, ignorant and futile amid a web of natural forces which are both good and evil.   And because his conduct is a thing for which man cannot be held to blame, and since Nature itself frowns upon every human effort to confine it in moral harness, conventions are folly.   Life cannot be forced to "mark time" for the sake of an ethical standard. "Old prejudices must always fall, and life must always change." [43]   It will not be

boxed in boxes.   It will not be wrapped and tied up in strings and set aside on a shelf to await a particular religious or moral use.   As yet we do not understand life, we do not know what it is, what the laws are that govern it.   At best we see ourselves

[39] *Hey Rub-a-Dub-Dub*, pp. 255–256.   [41] *A Book About Myself*, p. 427.
[40] *Ibid.*, p. 141.   [42] *Hey Rub-a-Dub-Dub*, p. 264.
[43] *A Book About Myself*, p. 428.

hobbling along, responding to this dream and that lust and unable to compel ourselves to gainsay the fires and appetites and desires of our bodies and minds.   Some of these, in some of us, strangely enough (and purely accidentally, of that I am convinced) conform to the current needs or beliefs of a given society; and if we should be so fortunate as to find ourselves in that society, we are by reason of these ideals, favorites, statesmen, children of fortune, poets of the race.   On the other hand, others of us who do not and cannot conform (who are left-over phases of ancient streams, perhaps, or portentous striae of new forces coming into play) are looked upon as horrific, and to be stabilized, or standardized, and brought into the normal systole-diastole of things.   Those of us endowed with these things in mind and blood are truly terrible to the mass — pariahs, failures, shams, disgraces.   Yet life is no better than its worst elements, no worse than its best.   Its perfections are changing temporalities, illusions of perfection that will be something very different tomorrow.   Again I say we do not know what life is — not nearly enough to set forward a fixed code of any kind, religious or otherwise.   But we do know that it sings and stings, that it has perfections, entrancements, shames — each according to his blood flux and its chemical character.   Life is rich, gorgeous, an opium eater's dream of something paradisiacal — but it is never the thin thing that thin blood and a weak, ill nourished, poorly responding brain would make it, and that is where the majority of our religions, morals, rules and safeguards come from.   From thin petered out blood, and poor, nervous, non-commanding weak brains.

Life is greater than anything we know.

It is stronger.

It is wilder.

It is more horrible.

It is more beautiful.

We need not stop and think we have found a solution.   We have not even found a beginning.   We do not know.[44]

Life is a dizzy, glittering game of trapping and fishing and evading, and slaying and pursuing, despite all the religious and so-called moral details by which we surround it.   Nature itself

[44] *A Hoosier Holiday*, pp. 285–286.

has an intense love of the chase. It loves snares, pitfalls, gins, traps, masks and mummeries, and even murder and death — yes, very much murder and death. It loves nothing so much as to build up a papier-mâché wall of convention, and then slip around or crash through it. . . . Justice, truth, mercy, right are all abstractions and not to be come at by any series of weights or measures. We pocket our unfair losses or unearned gains and smile at our luck.[45]

Religions come and go. Laws are written and fade away. Moral laws change with groups and climates.[46]

Convention has not made, and cannot make, any headway against a chemical scheme of life which puts sex desires first.[47]

Life cannot be put into any mold, and the attempt might as well be abandoned at once.[48]

He does not believe in ethical geometry; his only conclusion is that no conclusions exist. It is a philosophy to end philosophies. "All we can know is that we cannot know."[49] But life for Dreiser is magnetic, even in its dirt, poverty, and evanescence; it is vibrant, with its orgies, ruthlessness, conflicts, and defeats. He is like a boy watching a parade. He does not care where it is going; the important thing is its music and magnificence, its stridor and bulk.

What he has seen has dazed him, because he refuses to use the labels that make life endurable for other men. To apply a moral classification to life is a thing he will not do. And that seems to be the root of his confusion. He has tried to swallow life whole, without cutting it up, or proportioning it to his capacity. His books, in consequence, have become pipe organs with only two stops, Awe and Despair. Humor he lacks, taste he holds finical, and sophistication he disdains. Though not a "peasant," as so many critics seem fond of terming him, he does stagger

[45] *A Hoosier Holiday*, p. 377.   [47] *Ibid.*, p. 139.
[46] *Hey Rub-a-Dub-Dub*, pp. 159–160.   [48] *The Financier*, p. 146.
[49] *Hey Rub-a-Dub-Dub*, p. 21.

as he writes, as if under the weight he has forced himself to carry alone.

Like Lewis Carroll's Alice, he sees a world of infinite magic, without being able to understand it. Perhaps he even prefers his sprawling amazement and "the chemic thrill of life" to a condition of knowledge. "Why pray in beggarly fashion," he asks, "for that which will be, whether we pray or not — which, as the mechanists believe and show, cannot escape its own destiny? Rather sing and be joyful, I should say, for one's unescapable share in so great a spectacle. The game is open, free, a thrashing, glorious scene." [50]

Life is as it is — active, dancing, changeful, beautiful, at once brutal and tender — regardless of how our theories would seek to make it seem, and though it does as it chooses at times, or appears to, and invents or assumes various guises of perfection, it is as it has always been, both good and bad, yet held in a kind of equational vise or harmony — neither too good nor too bad — or we would not now be here at all, any of us, to tell the tale.[51]

FOOD FOR DREAMS Critics have often placed Dreiser among the sociological writers of our day, just as they have mistaken Floyd Dell for a naturalist. But naturalism and socialism are antipodal philosophies. The first stands for the individual as opposed to the interests of society, and does not believe in progress; the second feels a solicitude for the masses, demands that the individual be subordinated to the larger welfare of humanity, and has a mastering faith in "the ultimate perfectability" of mankind. It is not diffi-cult, remembering this distinction, to mark a slight change in Dreiser's point of view. A few years ago, he was a rampant individualist, praising the "financial superman." Today he holds that "the one hope of the world lies in teaching people the folly of this crazy chasing after wealth and power." His recent volumes, *Dreiser Looks At*

[50] *Ibid.*, p. 180.   [51] *Ibid.*, p. 178.

Russia (1928) and *Tragic America* (1931), both deal with the economic injustice of modern life, and he is an active member of such organizations as the National Committee for the Defense of Political Prisoners. In a word, he seems to be taking the path followed by most naturalists since Zola, from individualism into socialism. However, there is evidence that he has not entirely deserted his faith in the "genius," the alienated dreamer. Even as early as 1891, he had come to feel "a great contempt for the average mind. So many people were so low, so shifty, so dirty, so nondescript. They were food for dreams; little more." [52] "I don't care," he says, "a damn about the masses. It is the individual that concerns me." [53] Reform he has called "suave inanity," adding that "What we really need is a better stomach for life as it is." [54]

THE FOURTH DIMENSION   Authors with the sansculottic ideas of Dreiser do not often escape public notice, and yet for many years division of opinion upon his novels ran a submerged course. They were damned, to an extent, by silence. It was not until after his *Genius* was banned by the New York Society for the Suppression of Vice that Stuart Pratt Sherman and Mencken (who termed him "The Hindenburg of the Novel") chose up sides and brought the fight out into the open. A few critics praised him; others like Don Marquis tomahawked him by calling his work "a representation of the junk life left behind when it departed." [55] But after 1916 everybody read him.

Carl Van Doren was one of the first to lower a drawbridge for Dreiser and let him pass over into the textbooks. And it is to Van Doren that we are indebted for a criterion

[52] *A Book About Myself*, p. 32.
[53] Quoted in Dudley, Dorothy, *op. cit.*, p. 442.
[54] *Hey Rub-a-Dub-Dub*, p. 211.
[55] Marquis, Don, in *The Saturday Review of Literature* (October 15, 1932), IX, 174.

by which to judge naturalistic literature as a whole. To the traditional questions, "Is it good?" "Is it true?" "Is it beautiful?" he has tacked a "fourth dimension," "Is it alive?" "The critic," he declares,

who is aware of this fourth dimension of the art he studies saves himself the effort which critics less aware contrive to squander in trying to explain their art in terms merely of the three dimensions. He knows that life began before there were such things as good or evil; that it surges through both of them; that it will probably outlast any particular conception of either one or the other: he knows that it is not the moral of so naive a tale as *Uncle Tom's Cabin* which makes it moving but the life which was breathed into it by fiery passion. He knows that the amount of truth in poetry need not always be great and often indeed is much exaggerated; that a ruthless hand can find heaps of theological slag in Milton and corners full of metaphysical cobwebs in Plato and glittering excrescences of platitude in Shakespeare: he knows that these poets now live most in those parts of their work in the creating of which they were most alive. He knows that a powerful imagination may beget life even upon ugliness: he knows it because he has felt the vibrations of reality in Browning's cranky grotesques and in Whitman's long-drawn categories and in Rabelais' great dung-cart piled high with every variety of insolence and wisdom. Not goodness alone nor truth alone nor beauty alone nor all of them in one of their rare fusions can be said to make great literature, though these are the tools of that hard trade. Great literature may be known by the sign that it communicates the sense of the vividness of life.[56]

Meanwhile, above these voices saying "yea" and "nay" to him, we hear the grave tones of Dreiser, protesting against being added up, refusing to be placed, and concluding with this brief negation: "I can make no comment on my work or my life that holds either interest or import for me. Nor can I imagine any explanation or interpretation of any life, my own included, that would be either

[56] Van Doren, Carl, *The Roving Critic* (1923), pp. 19–20.

true — or important, if true. Life is to me too much a welter and play of inscrutable forces to permit, in my case at least, any significant comment. One may paint for one's own entertainment, and that of others — perhaps. As I see him the utterly infinitesimal individual weaves among the mysteries a floss-like and wholly meaningless course — if course it be. In short I catch no meaning from all I have seen, and pass quite as I came, confused and dismayed." [57]

[57] Dreiser, Theodore, "Statements of Belief," *The Bookman* (September, 1928), LXVIII, 25.

BROKEN FACE GARGOYLES

Both Dreiser and Sherwood Anderson despise cerebration and morals, pine for a "return to Nature," see the cosmos as an incoherent mixture, tilt against standardization in ethics and industry, place their faith in instinct, and confess themselves absolutely bewildered by life. Yet Anderson is even more confused (if possible) than Dreiser. His sentences are less articulate, and his philosophy a thing of "sex and sqush." [1] Crane, Norris, London, and Dreiser were for the most part objective. Despite romantic alloys they dealt in environment, or the tug and mass of outward phenomena. But Anderson works inwardly. His books are an incestuous mingling of psychical gleams; the "subconscious" and Freud have appropriated his pen. He has deserted the world that he could not understand.

The late war played havoc with earlier theories of naturalism. What good was the strong man's muscle or money if they could be destroyed by bullets and blockades? Here was something bigger than McTeague, Wolf Larsen, or Cowperwood; it was Hercules committing suicide, using his mighty strength to pull down the temple of Darwin upon himself. If men were equal when it came to inhaling poison gas, and if capitalists could not ward off such financial panics as those initiated by post-war deflation, where did that leave "survival of the fittest"? Weak and strong alike were seen to be puppets in the hands of a merciless Nature, which seemed to have taken this occa-

[1] Gerould, Katharine F., "Stream of Consciousness," *The Saturday Review of Literature* (October 22, 1927), IV, 234.

sion to put its "Cowperwoods" in their place, and demonstrate to "Jack Londons" that it was still their master. "You go along in life," groans Anderson, "not thinking very much, not feeling very much, not knowing very much — about yourself or anyone else — thinking life is so and so, and then — bang! Something happens. You aren't at all what you had thought you were. A lot of people found that out during the war." [2]   And so did naturalism. Dreiser, of course, had already come to realize that biceps were not enough in this modern world; money, he thought, was. But the war and its sequel "depressions" soon convinced many naturalists that this too was folly. Nothing was left except to do as Anderson did: throw Spencer out of the window, and sink into oneself.

He did; he sank so far that he touched the floor of Freud's "subconscious," and there he found his materials for fiction, in what Lewis Mumford has termed "the Cloaca Maxima of the personality."

Anderson is Dreiser with the backbone removed. With his advent naturalism changed from muscles to nerves; but in a sense he has been the victim of his times. Naturalism has been driven in upon itself by the war and by civilization's transition from an agricultural to an industrial stage. From a rural nation America has changed into an urban (if not urbane) one. People have crowded themselves together in cities, desperately pursuing employment. Surrounded by walls, factories, pavement, delicatessens, motor cars, subway tunnels, and hedges of noise, the average citizen has begun to suffer a bit from what psychologists have termed "claustrophobia," or a terror of small places. Prevented from early marriage by high standards of living and low wages, he has been cut off from normal sex expression, and left the prey of ulcerous maladies, drugs, pessimism, homosexuality, intoxicants, suicide, and the movies. To use another word from psychoanalysis, he is "repressed."

[2] Anderson, Sherwood, Dark Laughter (1925), p. 139.

The older naturalist, like Crane, Norris, London, and Dreiser, tried to confine himself to the external facts of life, "which, however, he could not avoid perceiving subjectively. But the modern advanced novelist tries to deal more and more exclusively with the internal facts of human existence: he transfers his gaze from the external to the internal environment, the 'inner life' of man." [3] After Dreiser naturalism began to turn morbid, though he himself was not. True, he was obsessed with certain ideas, but apart from occasional lapses into sentimentality, not sickly. His work was not highly introspective; instead it dealt with things in an outright fashion. Anderson, on the contrary, fled inward to a shadowy world of conflicts and voices. In his work naturalism's first bold advocacy of man's animal instincts shifted to a fumbling with symbols, demons, epicycles, and mixed personalities. The simple, lusty characters of Dreiser turned in Anderson to complex ones, aching and impotent.

Perhaps the reason for this change lies in the fact that our emotions are never able to catch up with our intellect. Man sees that Nature has no sense of morals, but his own heart continues to nurse an ethical view of life; he knows that science has destroyed old illusions, and yet he is homesick for them. His spirit cannot swallow what his mind has thought up, until long after his mind has moved on to newer positions ; and the confused temper of modern fiction springs, to a degree, from this dilemma: man's difficulty in playing "the animal's part without the animal's unconscious acquiescence." [4]

Anderson resembles a Whitman gone to seed, or a bacchic St. Francis of Assisi, with his lush nonsense about a "sweeter brotherhood," "virgins," the "soft lips" of men and women on his hands, and his spiritual orgasms. He sees himself as a "sacred vessel," as the womb of unborn

[3] Munson, Gorham B., *Style and Form in American Prose* (1929), p. 173.
[4] Sockman, Ralph W., *Morals of Tomorrow* (1931), p. 168.

dreams; he eats excrement, throws himself face downward on the ground, laughs drunkenly at the stars, runs naked in the rain, and caresses the earth in a pantheistic sweat. If he is "pregnant" (as he is so fond of insisting), it is partly with maudlinism. "Creeping, I come out of the corn," he sings,

> Wet with the juice of bruised corn leaves —
>   out of the corn I come
>
> Eager to kiss the fingers of queens,
> Eager to stand with kings,
> To breed my kind and stand with kings.
>
> Out of the corn at daybreak,
> Brother to dogs,
> Big brother to creeping, crawling things
> Stretched full length on the long wet grass
>   at the edge of the cornfields,
> Waiting,
> Here I lie through the day, waiting and waiting.
>
> Come, tired little sister, run with me.
> See — I kiss your lips — soft — to entice you.
> In the still young night we begin our running,
> Stripping our clothes away. . . .
>
> Come, tired little sister, run with me.
> Let's lie down on this hill-side here.
> Let our soft mid-western nights creep into you.
> See the little things, creeping, creeping,
> Here, in the night, the little things creeping,
> Let's be creeping.
> Let's be creeping.
>
> I've got a strong man's love for you.
> See the muscles of my legs — how tense.
> Now I leap and cry like a strong young stallion.

Let's away.
West of Chicago the endless cornfields.
Let's be running.
Come away.[5]

It is of those who have been shell shocked and frustrated by modernity that Anderson writes, "the misfits, the mutterers, the crazy rebels, the hall-bedroom brooders, the mad doctors . . . sex-starved, life-starved Americans . . . gregarious but unsocial, drowned in stark solitude of soul,"[6] whose warped processes of thought seem to have infected his own. "I have not achieved clearness often," he admits. "In my work I have seldom come quite clear."[7] At one moment we find him campaigning against present conditions, and in the next deciding with other naturalists that, "I like people just as they are. I do not want to change any one."[8] He is symbolic of a contemporary attitude that " promenades its incertitudes," that

prides itself upon its seriousness and upon its confusions, upon the seriousness of its confusions, with the pain of living balanced by the fear of dying, the need of believing by the habit of doubt . . . and a taste for not believing by the desire to dare to believe in one's unbelief.[9]

As suggested by one of his story titles, he has traveled in his philosophy "Out of Nowhere Into Nothing." "To me," he once wrote in a letter to Upton Sinclair, "there is no answer for the terrible confusion of life."[10] And yet, whether we admire his work or not, we can hardly escape the conclusion that he has influenced the literature of contemporary America more than any other writer, not excepting Dreiser.

[5] Anderson, Sherwood, *Mid-American Chants* (1918), pp. 58–59.
[6] Fadiman, Clifton, "Sherwood Anderson: the Search for Salvation," *The Nation* (November 9, 1932), CXXXV, 456.
[7] Anderson, Sherwood, *Sherwood Anderson's Notebook* (1926), p. 168.
[8] Dickinson, L. R., "Smyth County Items," *The Outlook* (April 11, 1928), p. 581. Now *New Outlook*.
[9] Putman, Samuel (ed.), *The European Caravan* (1931), p. 10.
[10] Quoted in Sinclair, Upton, *Money Writes* (1927), p. 119.

Anderson was born in Camden, Ohio, September 13, 1876, the third child of a strange, nomadic family. His father, whose portrait he has engagingly drawn in *A Story Teller's Story*, appears to have been the village Munchausen, "a ruined dandy from the South," by trade a house painter; but his mother, a dark silent woman, died before Anderson was fifteen. During his youth he read "Jules Verne, Balzac, the Bible, Stephen Crane, dime novels, Cooper, Stevenson, our own Mark Twain and Howells and later Whitman," sold papers, went infrequently to school, lounged around saloons and livery stables, and after his mother's death, wandered through the Middle West as a laborer, tramp, and race-track follower. When the Spanish-American War broke out, he enlisted, to escape factory work and receive the crowd's applause; demobilized, he attended Wittenburg College for six months, married, entered business, and became president of a paint company in Elyria, Ohio.

He began life hungry for power, as did London and Dreiser. "I would like so well," he said,

the things money buys — cigarettes, horses, warm clothes, a fine house to live in. I would so like to have a great deal of money. Why does not someone who has ten or fifteen million dollars give me a million, or a half million, anyway? If you meet a man bothered by his money tell him about me. I would like to wear clothes made of delicate fabrics, gay, brightly-colored neckties, flashing vests, plaid socks. I would like a string of race horses, a farm, a yacht. There is in me something that likes to strut before men, make a splash of color in the street where I walk.[11]

And so he reasoned, "I will become a man of action, in the mood of the American of my day. I will build railroads, conquer empires, become rich and powerful."[12] But as he approached forty the conviction rapidly grew upon him that in surrendering to the lure of material ease

[11] *Sherwood Anderson's Notebook*, p. 171.
[12] Anderson, Sherwood, *A Story Teller's Story* (1924), p. 218.

he had "prostituted" himself, that in aiming for "success" he had become, somehow, "unclean." Gradually the idea occurred to him that it would be "nice to be unknown, to slip quietly through streets, seeing life while remaining unseen and unknown." [13] Then, in Anderson's parlance, "something happened," and suddenly he ran away to Chicago, and found a job in an advertising agency.[14]

RENAISSANCE, 1912–1930 For months, as a prosperous manufacturer, he had been tentatively scrawling down his thoughts; and now, freer to do as he pleased, he turned to writing. His first tales were published in *The Little Review* and *Seven Arts*, two periodicals that had just been established for the purpose of sponsoring experimental literature. Since 1912 dozens of "magazinelets" had been bubbling up all over Europe and America, furnishing asylum for daring and original prose or verse that could not gain entrance to the larger and more conservative journals; introducing to the world such writers as Hemingway, Carl Sandburg, Joyce, and Elizabeth Madox Roberts; fighting "vice" societies; being denied the mails by postal authorities; and usually dying (with the second issue) of financial sclerosis. During and after the War many others appeared, among them *The Glebe, Palms, Transatlantic, Contemporary Verse, The Double Dealer, Rhythmus, The Dial, Muse and Mirror, The Masses, Star-Dust, The Midland, 1924, Laughing Horse, Pagany, The Gyroscope, Broom, transition, Contact, Parnassus, Forge, Palo Verde, The Fugitive, All's*

---

[13] *Sherwood Anderson's Notebook*, p. 177.

[14] "When he had accomplished half the span of life allotted by the psalmist to man," writes one critic, "he heard a voice saying: 'It is hard for you to kick, but you are the chosen vessel to bear the message: Life is sex, death is sex-repression; living is sex-awareness; pleasure is sex-indulgence; beauty is sex-realisation; salvation is dependent upon the development of sex sensibilities.' The scales fell from his eyes and he went to the typewriter and struck off his 'Apology for Crudity' — his credo concerning the true inwardness and inherent mission of American literature." Collins, Joseph, *Taking the Literary Pulse* (1924), p. 33.

Well, The Measure, S4N (standing for "the principle of growth through disagreement"), *Lariat, Poetry: A Magazine of Verse, This Quarter,* and *Voices.*[15]   It was a period of literary ferment everywhere, marked by radical secessions from tradition; rendered comic at its edges by a lunatic fringe; influenced by such events as the founding of The Modern Library in 1918, Haldeman-Julius's Little Blue Books in 1919, and *The American Mercury* in 1924; encumbered by its own brand of esthetic snobbery; justified on the whole by its renovation of fictional art; and hospitable to modern thought in all of its idiosyncrasies.

CATHARSIS   Even more than Dreiser, Anderson has used his own life as a motif for his novels.   *Windy McPherson's Son* (1916) is the story of a boy, Sam McPherson, in the small Iowa town of Caxton.   His father, Windy, is a "cracked" veteran of the Civil War, laughed at by the other citizens for his senile braggadocio; and Sam, feeling that he must in some way make up for this shame, decides to "Make money!   Cheat!   Lie!   Be one of the men of the big world!"[16]   In time he moves from Caxton, becomes the vulpine executive of a firearms plant, and marries the daughter of his employer.   His bank account grows, and before long he has pushed his father-in-law out of control in the company.   But soon discovering, as Anderson did, that such victories were really Dead Sea fruit, beautiful without and dust within, he takes to drinking, decides to leave "money hunger" behind him, packs a bag, and deserts his wife and job.

In his mind he had no definite idea of where he was going or what he was going to do. He knew only that he would follow the message his hand had written. He would spend his life seeking truth.[17]

[15] Troy, William, "The Story of the Little Magazines," *The Bookman* (January and February, 1930), LXX, 476–481 and 657–663.

[16] Anderson, Sherwood, *Windy McPherson's Son* (1922), p. 75.

[17] *Ibid.,* p. 255.

Beginning over again as a carpenter and socialist, he tries to protect a community from Chicago grafters, but is misunderstood and driven away. For months he leads a gypsy existence, abandons it after two years to go big game hunting in Africa, sinks into a prolonged coma of inebriacy, adopts three children, and returns home with them to his wife, convinced that "I cannot run away from life. I must face it."[18]

Marching Men (1917), dedicated "To American Working Men," is another expression of Anderson's resentment against a mechanized America. Like Sam McPherson his Beaut McGregor of this novel begins in a small maggoty town, Coal Creek, Pennsylvania. He is disgusted to see, among the miners, how "Losing step with one another, men lose also a sense of their own individuality,"[19] and hating the town's larval inhabitants he goes, as McPherson did, to Chicago. With his "two fists" he brawls his way up to the position of foreman in an apple warehouse, reading law at nights, and now and then feeling "the call of sex." When his mother dies in Coal Creek, he goes back for her funeral; and as he watches the miners fall into step behind her coffin, something comes over him in a flash (the usual Andersonian "catharsis"). "Some day," thinks Beaut,

A man will come who will swing all of the workers of the world into step like that. . . . He will make them conquer, not one another but the terrifying disorder of life. . . . Suppose they could just learn to march, nothing else. Suppose they should begin to do with their bodies what their minds are not strong enough to do — to just learn the one simple thing, to march, whenever two or four or a thousand of them get together, to march.[20]

He decides to teach them this lesson himself, studies to be an attorney while working in a restaurant, achieves celeb-

[18] *Ibid.*, p. 349.   [19] Anderson, Sherwood, *Marching Men* (1917), p. 12.
[20] *Ibid.*, pp. 148–149.

rity by his successful defense of a "framed" prisoner, and devotes the rest of his life to organizing the Marching Men Movement (an even worse type of regimentation than Anderson's prime nemesis, "The Machine Age").

All over the country men were getting the idea — the Marching Men — old Labour in one mass marching before the eyes of men — old Labour that was going to make the world see — see and feel its bigness at last.   Men were to come to the end of strife — men united — Marching!   Marching!   Marching! [21]

In *Mid-American Chants* (1918), a book of verse that appeared during the next year (smelling powerfully of Sandburg and Whitman), Anderson has told in poetry this same story of a business man's "middle-aged" revolt.

> In the rain in the streets of my city I stood.
>   My clothes were foul.   In the woven cloth that
> covered my body the dust of my city had lodged.
> The dust of my civilization was in my soul.   I
> was a murderer — a weeping prostitute standing
> by a wall.   In a jail they had lodged me.   I was
> one condemned to be hanged.   There was filth on
> my shoes — my shoes were filthy.

> It was night and I had come into my room.   I was
> cold and my body trembled.   I was afraid.   The
> pencil was gripped in my cunning fingers.   Words
> came.   Over the paper my pencil ran — making the
> words — saying the words.

> There is a song in the pencil that is held in my
> cunning fingers.   Out — out — out — dear words.
> The words have saved me.   There is rhythm in the
> pencil.   It sings and swings.   It sings a great
> song.   It is singing the song of my life.   It
> is bringing life in to me, into my close place.

[21] *Marching Men*, p. 286.

Out — out — out — out of the room I go. I am become
pure. To the homes of the people I go. Here in
these words I am become a man. The passions and
lusts of men have taken hold of me.

I have gone into the woman's chamber, into the secret
places of all women and all men I have gone. I have
made love to them. Before me in the chamber lies
the naked body of a woman. She is strong and
young.

Do you not see, O my beloved, that I am become strong
to caress the woman! I caress all men and all women.
I make myself naked. I am unafraid. I am a pure
thing. I bind and heal. By the running of the pencil over the white paper I have made myself pure. I
have made myself whole. I am unafraid. The song of
the pencil has done it.[22]

Winesburg, Ohio (1919), *The Triumph of the Egg* (1921),
Horses and Men (1923), and *Death in the Woods* (1933) are
collections of brief narratives, dealing with melancholic
scarecrows who stride along talking to themselves, ponder
imponderables, and suddenly break into tears: Peeping
Toms, and hot-eyed gymnosophists with "tics" of personality. Yet it is in these volumes (especially *Winesburg*) that
Anderson lives at his durable best. Such tales as "The
Sad Horn Blowers," "I Want to Know Why," and "The
Egg" have a poignance and originality that must place
them among the highlights of our literature. They "are
written out of the depths of a prolonged brooding over
the fascinating spectacle of existence, but they combine
that quality with a marvelous faculty of precise observation.
Thus, the impression of surface realism is reinforced by that
deeper realism which sees beyond and beneath the exterior
world to the hidden reality which is the essence of things." [23]

[22] *Mid-American Chants*, pp. 26–28.
[23] Boyd, Ernest, in his Introduction to Sherwood Anderson's *Winesburg,
Ohio*, The Modern Library.

Poor White (1920) chronicles the vicissitudes of another midwestern youth, Hugh McVey. Born in Mudcat Landing, Missouri, he soon finds himself sickened by the ugliness and stupor of his environment, and moves East, plagued by dreams and erotic visions. Settling down in Bidwell, Ohio, he catches a glimpse of the "machine age" just ahead; invents a plant-setting device, an apparatus for unloading coal, and a corn cutter; becomes wealthy; and marries the daughter of a rich farmer. Bidwell grows into a robust industrial center, fed by McVey's contrivances. But it is not long before a reaction sets in against the invasion of "large scale" industry. Strikes break out; a harness maker, ruined by the competition of machine products, slays two men; and in the end McVey himself is left fettered to a gnawing sense of blighted hope, as he realizes what terrible genii have been released upon America by his hands and brain.

In *Many Marriages* (1923) Anderson has repeated his favorite text of the Rotarian who, stricken by a sudden dislike for his mercenary life, undergoes a spiritual eruption, and walks dramatically out of his family's bosom into the "dawn of a new day," henceforth to be a seeker of the "truth." John Webster is a washing machine manufacturer in a Wisconsin town, with a wife and daughter, when the "light" hits him. The idea invades his mind that he has been missing LIFE, and that it is very wrong of people to wear clothes. Each night he walks naked up and down before a picture of the Virgin Mary in his room, hoping in this way to bring "grace and meaning" into his existence. One night, while in the midst of this ceremony, he calls his startled wife and daughter and tries to explain to them what he is doing. Then he dresses, and goes off with his stenographer, a certain Natalie Swartz. His wife takes poison.

Sherwood Anderson's Notebook, published in 1926, contains articles and memoranda on such topics as standardization, realism, dreams, Negroes, prose style, and Gertrude Stein. "I make notes only of fragmentary things," he writes, indicating his "impressionism." "In one moment a dozen moods may pass through me." [24] *Tar*, in the same year, relates the story of Anderson's "midwest childhood." *A New Testament* (1927) offers scraps of mystical poetry, written in a kind of pseudo-biblical rhythm. And *Hello Towns* (1929) is made up of clippings from the two country newspapers that Anderson bought and began to edit in Marion, Virginia, during 1928.

His most popular novel, *Dark Laughter*, which came out two years after *Many Marriages*, is an even worse misfire, another "wistful idealization of the male menopause." [25] It narrates the fortunes of Bruce Dudley, a factory hand in the town of Old Harbor, Indiana. His real name is John Stockton and he had once been a journalist in Chicago; but an increasing contempt for his wife and the shoddy wordmongering of newspaper life (plus too much reading of Mark Twain) had sent him floating down the Mississippi to New Orleans.

It was a little trick he had always wanted to do. Since he was a kid and had read Huckleberry Finn, he had kept some such notion in mind. Nearly every man who lived long in the Mississippi Valley had that notion tucked away in him somewhere. The great river, lonely and empty now, was, in some queer way, like a lost river. It had come to represent the lost youth of Middle America perhaps. Song, laughter, profanity, the smell of goods, dancing niggers — life everywhere.[26]

Later he returns north, under an alias, to his birthplace, Old Harbor, and begins work in a carriage plant. "He had a vague notion that he, in common with almost all American men, had got out of touch with things — stones

[24] *Sherwood Anderson's Notebook*, p. 125.
[25] Quoted in Smith, Rachel, "Sherwood Anderson," *The Sewanee Review* (October, 1929), XXVII, 159.
[26] *Dark Laughter*, p. 17.

lying in fields, the fields themselves, houses, trees, rivers, factory walls, tools, women's bodies, sidewalks, people on sidewalks, men in overalls, men and women in automobiles." [27]   That was what he wanted to get back to, what had driven him to flight from the artificial routine of Chicago.   He becomes the paramour of his employer's wife, Aline, and to facilitate their adultery takes a job as her gardener.   A pair of Negro servants in the house watch, and mock the wary progress of the intrigue.   "When a negro woman wants to go live with another man she does," explains Anderson.   "White women furnish negro women with endless hours of amusement." [28]   High bleating laughter flows up from "below stairs" at intervals during the last half of the volume.   Aline's husband eventually discovers her with Bruce, only to be told to his face that they are leaving together; and after their departure, he hears again, from somewhere in the house, one of the Negro women laughing, "I knowed it, I knowed it, all the time I knowed it." [29]

CLAUSTROPHOBIA   From this review of his books we can see that what was "confession" in Dreiser approaches "exhibitionism" in Anderson.   The plots of his stories, in fact, are almost carbon copies of the plot he himself followed in first coveting "the almighty dollar," experiencing a pang of revulsion, and at last running away.   In an earlier day Anderson might have "gone West" to escape the rising factory system of the East; but the frontier had disappeared.   The result, in Anderson's case, has been to *invert* him, to breed in his work a modern species of Hamletism, forcing him to seek new outlets for his stifled ego in

[27] *Dark Laughter*, pp. 62–63.

[28] *Ibid.*, p. 291.

[29] *Ibid.*, p. 319.   Since *Dark Laughter*, Anderson has written only one novel, *Beyond Desire* (1932), the story of youthful Red Oliver who returns from college to work in a cotton mill, goes through the usual sexual glozings, and dies a martyr in a labor strike.

vagabondage and in skylarking with words. While his brother "prisoners" have been "facing the music," Anderson and his heroes have been playing hide and seek with stern reality, trying to drown their troubles in sensory magnifications, "alcoholidays," dreams, the subconscious, and a "return to Nature."

STANDARDIZATION Ever since he began writing, Anderson has been trying to tell "the story of the American man crushed and puzzled by the machine," [30] and in *Perhaps Women* (1931) he attempts it again. He preaches against

Speed, hurried workmanship, cheap automobiles for cheap men, cheap chairs in cheap houses, city apartment houses with shining bathroom floors, the Ford, the Twentieth Century Limited, the World War, jazz, the movies.[31]

But principally he condemns standardization in industry, just as Dreiser concentrated his attack upon standardization in morals. Both are protesting against a loss of that individualism so essential to the naturalistic theory.

As a boy Anderson had seen "the machine triumph in America, like an unleashed giant striding everywhere, surveying the land, raising a new class of men to positions of power. Railroads had already been pushed out across the plains; great coal fields from which was to be taken food to warm the blood in the body of the giant were being opened up; iron fields were being discovered; the roar and clatter of the breathing of the terrible new thing, half hideous, half beautiful in its possibilities, that was for so long to drown the voices and confuse the thinking of men, was heard not only in the towns but even in lonely farm houses, where its willing servants, the newspapers and magazines, had begun to circulate in ever increasing numbers." [32] Modern unrest he calls "a disease of life

---

[30] Anderson, Sherwood, *Perhaps Women* (1931), p. 112.
[31] *A Story Teller's Story*, p. 81.
[32] Anderson, Sherwood, *Poor White* (1920), p. 63.

due to men getting away from their own hands," [33] and
as a remedy he has offered the old love of craft, the arti-
san's previous respect for the materials of his handiwork,
in other words, a return to the artistic sensitivity that
builds its products less with an eye to haste than with a
regard for their permanence and quality.[34] "Standardization," he proclaims, "is a phase. It will pass. The tools
and material of the workmen cannot always remain cheap
and foul. Some day the workmen will come back to their
materials, out of the sterile land of standardization." [35]
In *Perhaps Women*, however, he has come to the conclusion
that "modern man cannot escape the machine, that he
has already lost the power to escape," [36] that he has sacrificed his manhood to the spinning loom, and come at last to
impotence. And yet all may not be lost, continues Anderson; "perhaps women" can lead men out of this stalemate.

Because, as I have already tried to point out, the woman, at her
best, is and will remain a being untouched by the machine. It
may, if she becomes a machine operator, tire her physically but it
cannot paralyze or make impotent her spirit. She remains, as
she will remain, a being with a hidden inner life. The machine
can never bring children into the world. . . . If these machines
ever are controlled, so that their power to hurt men, by making
them impotent, is checked, women will have to do it.

They will have to do it perhaps to get men back, so that they
may continue to be fertilized, to produce men.[37]

It should appear evident from this that as a thinker Anderson is miserably ragged. To use a phrase of Robert Littell's,
a belief seems to be something "he thinks, rather than what
he has thought out." [38] His concern with ideas is a poetic
one, a mere concern with such phobias as "impotence."

[33] *Dark Laughter*, p. 98.
[34] See Veblen, Thorstein, *The Instinct of Workmanship* (1914).
[35] *A Story Teller's Story*, p. 295.
[36] *Perhaps Women*, p. 138.
[37] *Ibid.*, p. 140.
[38] Littell, Robert, *Read America First* (1926), p. 205.

What does he mean by it? Does he refer to sexual impotence, which obviously cannot be termed an imminent result of the machine while the birth rate remains higher among factory laborers than among professors? Or does he mean "spiritual" impotence, which is more reasonable, but has little to do with the kind of "fertilizing" he mentions? [39] Today Anderson seems mired deeper in the swamp of mental confusion than ever before.

THE BABEL OF THE PSYCHE About 1881 an Austrian physician named Sigmund Freud entirely upset our current ideas of human behavior. The first psychological laboratory was founded by Wundt at Leipzig in 1879; and following 1890 psychology began to be established in universities as a separate branch of science, operating upon the "pleasure principle" of hedonism, or the theory that men tend to act toward pleasant stimuli and away from unpleasant ones. [40] But Freud wanted to find something beyond this notion; what happened, for instance, when people refused to obey their instincts and sidetracked normal reactions in favor of duty or shame?

Briefly, his concept holds that every person is like an iceberg, with his largest area submerged beneath the threshold of consciousness. That portion remaining below he calls the "subconscious." (Anderson terms it "the well.") Into this nether compartment each man forces the thoughts and impulses that he is ashamed of, or unable to acknowledge and use. Standing guard at the stairway leading up to the "conscious" from the "subconscious" is an invisible agent known as "the censor," who "turns the damper down" on undesirable thoughts, and prevents them from escaping their prison except during sleep, when they often emerge as dreams to furnish the individual with a kind of vicarious gratification.

[39] See *A Story Teller's Story* (1924), p. 195.
[40] *Cf.* McDougall, William, *Outline of Psychology* (1929), p. 218.

But when any one "represses" a desire or a memory long enough, because it is not one toward which public opinion is friendly, trouble usually develops. If his *libido* (or life force) happens to be strongly enough organized behind this thwarted element, it may upset his balance, and lead him into minor forms of insanity, hysteria neuroses, complexes, and fixations. The task of the psychoanalyst is to elicit from the patient an introspective account of his past life, in order to make him aware of whatever he has suppressed. Once this is identified and fished up into "consciousness," the situation will be automatically relieved and a healthy equilibrium restored.

Such a theory of human conduct had already been implied by earlier psychologists, and in Nietzsche's statement that

When a man has to do that which he is best suited to do, which he is most fond of doing, not only clandestinely, but also with long suspense, caution and ruse, he becomes anaemic; and inasmuch as he is always having to pay for his instincts in the form of danger, persecution and fatalities, even his feelings begin to turn against these instincts.[41]

Yet it was not until Freud's daring enunciation of the problem that men and women could display an intelligent interest in it. Freudianism crossed to America in 1906, when it was first mentioned in an article by Boris Sidis, "The Psychopathology of Everyday Life." "By 1909, medical periodicals had much of it. In September of that year, Freud came in person to deliver a series of lectures 'Concerning Psychoanalysis,' at Clark University." [42] After 1910 the newspapers were packed with references to this new doctrine; and men in the street began quoting a jargon of strange phrases like "censorship," "ambivalence," "introjection," "psychosis," and "abreaction."

---

[41] Nietzsche, Friedrich, *The Complete Works of Friedrich Nietzsche* (1927), XVI, 104. By permission of The Macmillan Company, publishers.

[42] Sullivan, Mark, *Our Times* (1932), IV, 168.

The whole idea met with a landslide of protest and denial. "To the average American of about 1910, it would be difficult to imagine anything more repellent. A not too imaginative reader would have interpreted Freud's theory to mean that a devotee kneeling before the Cross is unconsciously satisfying a sublimated form of desire of the flesh, and does not differ from a pagan bowing before a phallic symbol; that every baby in his cradle is a leering philanderer; that a boy-child throwing his arms about his mother is an incestuous libertine; that every girl-child has an incestuous love for her father accompanied by a murderously jealous hate of her mother; that protective tenderness shown by an adult toward a child of the opposite sex is a scandal." [43] Nevertheless, there were more than two hundred books on Freudianism by 1920, and by 1927 the word had forced its way into Webster's Dictionary. Everywhere people were talking about

"Psychoanalysis," meaning the study of a man's sub-conscious motives and desires, or the act of a practitioner in analyzing the sub-conscious mentality of an individual; "sublimation," meaning the diverting of sexual energy into intellectual or creative work; "fixation," meaning the unconscious arrest and crystallization at any early age of a sub-conscious tendency, for example, the affection, alleged by Freud to be wholly or mainly sexual, of a child for a parent; "repression," meaning the keeping from consciousness of primitive desires or mental processes that would be painful for the conscious to admit; "complexes," meaning obscure mechanisms arising in the sub-conscious as a result of the tyranny of the conscious or of the outside world — a series of associated ideas, the touching of any one of which stirs the whole series into action; "libido," meaning originally sexual hunger but broadened to include what the philosopher Bergson termed the "vital impetus." [44]

Repercussions of this doctrine were soon heard in art, fiction, poetry, and the drama. One author, Floyd Dell,

[43] *Ibid.*, IV, 169–170.   [44] *Ibid.*, IV, 171.

had himself "psyked" and declared the operation a success. Eugene O'Neill adopted Freudianism almost entirely in such plays as "Desire Under the Elms." And in Harvey O'Higgins' *The American Mind in Action* (1924), the lives of Mark Twain, Lincoln, Andrew Carnegie, Anthony Comstock, Franklin, Longfellow, Julia Ward Howe, Whitman, and Margaret Fuller were interpreted as reactions against Puritanism, "gestures of the ego," or "fixations."

From the presses, since then, have issued such novels as Evelyn Scott's *The Narrow House* (1921), which deals with a narcistic wife and humid perversions; O'Higgins' *Clara Barron* (1926), the story of an "inhibited woman" ("an animal," complains the author, "who refuses to live like an animal"); *Madonna Without Child* (1929), Myron Brinig's record of a maternal complex; *Shadows Waiting* (1927), Eleanor Carroll Chilton's study of an artist's attempt to reconcile his inner and outer worlds; *Victim and Victor* (1928), John Rathbone Oliver's case history of a psychoneurotic priest; Thomas Wolfe's *Look Homeward, Angel* (1929), "A Story of The Buried Life," turbulent with hermetic conflicts; Julian Green's *The Dark Journey* (1929), a nightmare of cancerous desires in a French town; Wilbur Daniel Steele's *Meat* (1928), in which youth finds itself curdled by the New England conscience; and Floyd Dell's autobiographic *Moon-Calf* (1920), which deals, he has said, with an inner conflict "between the narcistic and sexual-social impulses." [45] "If the twentieth century," notes one critic,

has contributed anything whatsoever to the advance of the novel, or to its decline, we must look for it in the influence of Havelock Ellis, Freud, Jung, and other investigators of the sex mind of man. They have not created a new set of emotions, of characters, or of plots for the author. They have given him a new approach and a new jargon. They have succeeded somehow, in making the

[45] Dell, Floyd, "A Literary Self-Analysis," *The Modern Quarterly* (June–September, 1927), IV, 149.

abnormal, if not palatable, at least popular. They have turned the author even further inward. He was often introverted, but he now finds himself conscious of his introversion, calling it by name, using it for his purposes much as he would a pet dog. Instead of using his sensitivity to reflect the character of the world at large, he tends to characterize only himself. Instead of creating new characters, he either willingly capitalizes his ego or betrays it.[46]

Dreiser's men are more or less the pawns of their environment and instinct; but Anderson's are the prey of forces in the "unconscious." They "lead their lives behind a wall of misunderstanding they themselves have built"[47] by repressing their instincts. In a "pluralistic universe" they have acquired split-personalities by not letting "their right hand know what their left hand doeth." Below the surface of their daily lives they are gnarled, irrational, withered, sallow: "broken face gargoyles," to use one of Sandburg's phrases.

Where Mr. Dreiser like a giant mole with strong flat hands tore up the soil and prepared the ground for a more liberal treatment of sex in American literature, Mr. Anderson, nervous and mystical, follows along like the anxious white rabbit in Alice in Wonderland, clasping instead of a watch the latest edition of Sigmund Freud.[48]

"If there is anything you do not understand in life," says Anderson, "consult the works of Dr. Freud."[49] He asks that man's "inner self" be pardoned and released from the bondage in which it is kept by discretion. "Why," he queries, "must one commit rape, rape of the conscious, rape of the unconscious?"[50] He appeals for a surrender to the instincts, and begs for the liberation of those cold

[46] Farrar, John, "Sex Psychology in Modern Fiction," *The Independent* (December 11, 1926), CXVII, 669.

[47] *Poor White*, p. 227.

[48] Gregory, Alyse, "Sherwood Anderson," *The Dial* (September, 1923), LXXV, 246.

[49] *Dark Laughter*, p. 230.

[50] Anderson, Sherwood, *Many Marriages* (1923), p. 185.

Freudian monsters that society holds in check by means of opinion and law. "Obsessed with the experience of sudden self-discovery, the single moment in which the subconscious rises up to enforce its demands upon the total personality," [51] he dares to predict that "If one kept the lid off the well of thinking within oneself, let the well empty itself, let the mind consciously think any thoughts that came to it, accepted all thinking, all imaginings, as one accepted the flesh of people, animals, birds, trees, plants, one might live a hundred or a thousand lives in one life." [52] And "Dark hidden things, festering in the well" would come out, to express themselves in beautiful deeds and images.

SEX O'CLOCK "How did the vogue of the sex novel arise? Perhaps from the great attention which was in the last century given to the sciences of biology and physiology; and perhaps, more especially from the popularization of these sciences. Love was, under the spell of science, translated by the novelists into sex." [53] After Freud sex became a topic of conversation in "mixed company" as never before. Magazines and movies began catering to a public taste for frankness (and aphrodisiacs), now that the long drouth and "impure hush" of Puritanism had elapsed in America. "It's sex o'clock," remarked William Marion Reedy in 1915; but by 1930 Freudianism had waned in popular interest, and readers were laughing at James Thurber and E. B. White's *Is Sex Necessary?* (1929), a humorous satire on psychoanalysis.

In the novel Freud's influence evidenced itself both as a valuable solvent, conducive to a better understanding of life, and as an argument for moral anarchy. Of this second tendency Maxwell Bodenheim (himself the author of

[51] Fadiman, Clifton, "Sherwood Anderson: The Search for Salvation," *The Nation* (November 9, 1932), CXXXV, 454.

[52] *Many Marriages*, pp. 190–191.

[53] Muir, Edwin, *We Moderns* (1918), pp. 25–26.

Naked On Roller Skates, 1931, and *Replenishing Jessica*, 1925) has taken the opportunity to remark that "In this country psychoanalysis has been widely accepted by critics and creators who were longing for a diagrammed excuse for their sensual admirations, and these people, of course, have plastered it with phallic exaggerations. It began with the modest claim, advanced by Freud, that dreams were directly or indirectly symbolic of physical desires and repressions and that men, by studying the trend and imagery of their dreams, could become aware of these hidden longings and thus cast a light upon the personal problems of their lives. But the disciples of psychoanalysis, being very substantial creatures, were not content to cling to the realm of dreams, since the dream after all is merely flimsy and tantalizing food for the depths of sensual desires. . . . Thus the disciples of Freud have changed his modest premise into the contention that sex underlies and dominates all human motives and is the basis of all creations." [54] "American novels have rapidly formed themselves into the following classes: the sensual melodrama, written in an awkwardly forced style and unsuccessfully wavering between Whitman and Baudelaire, such as Waldo Frank's 'Rahab'; the novel in which sensuality adopts a heavy, clumsy, and naively serious mien, such as the stories and novels of Sherwood Anderson, in which young men lie upon their backs in cornfields and feel oppressed by their bodies, etc.; the novel in which sensuality becomes half flippant and half sentimental and plays the youthful ape to sophistication, such as the creations of F. Scott Fitzgerald; the novel in which sensuality, sordid and undressed, fights with longings for business success, a proceeding that occurs in the ponderous fiction of Theodore Dreiser; the novel in which sensuality sneers at itself and wonders whether the gain is worth the effort involved, a quality

[54] Bodenheim, Maxwell, "Psychoanalysis and American Fiction," *The Nation* (June 7, 1922), CXIV, 683.

recently exhibited in Ben Hecht's 'Eric Dorn'; and the endless novels in which sensuality runs after romance, nobility, and domestic bliss. . . . Back of this farce stands the psychoanalyst, with his enticing implication that nothing exists in human beings except sex, and its open or indirect manifestations. He has, indeed, become the godfather of most contemporary American prose and poetry, and he is, indeed, very much in need of a metaphysical spanking." [55]

The naturalist's glorification of the primordial has been extended to love. From a sublimated and ritualized phenomenon, it has become in recent novels (such as those of Donald Henderson Clarke and the Ben Hechtics) a matter of swift, careless ecstasy, followed by a period of mental torment and disappointment. In the words of Aldous Huxley, it has turned into a mere "sweating of palm to palm." "*What is home without another?* might be the motto," says one critic, "for numbers of novels published every season." [56] But the "literotic" novel, for so long a direct revolt against social conventions, has gradually begun to deal with the individual's problems of adjustment, now that a kind of triumph over Comstockery has been won. As Joseph Wood Krutch has pointed out:

Most sex novels of the past have been concerned chiefly with what might be called the right to love. They have combated an extremely old idea which Christianity found congenial and embodied in the conception of love as a part of the curse pronounced upon man at the Fall, and hence at best a necessary evil . . . and they have had to fly in the face of all laws and social customs which are seen, if examined closely, to rest upon the assumption that desire is merely a dangerous nuisance, fatal to efficiency and order, and hence to be regimented at any cost. It is now pretty gener-

[55] Bodenheim, Maxwell, " Psychoanalysis and American Fiction," *The Nation* (June 7), CXIV, 684.
[56] Drew, Elizabeth A., *The Modern Novel* (1926), p. 57.

ally admitted among the educated class that love is legitimate, even that it has an aesthetic as well as a utilitarian function.   We have got back to the point which Ovid had reached some two thousand years ago of realizing that there is an art of love. During the next quarter of a century fiction will be concerned, I think, more with the failure or success of individuals to attain this art than with the exposition of theses which most accept.[57]

THE NOBLE SAVAGE Just as Stephen Crane saw "the noble savage" in children, as Defoe saw him in Robinson Crusoe, as Edgar Rice Burroughs saw him in Tarzan, as D. H. Lawrence saw him in the Mexican Indian, as Kipling saw him in Kim, and as others have seen him in the American cowboy, so Anderson sees him in the Negro. The white man, he says in *Dark Laughter*, has been corrupted by civilization; and today only the Negro has escaped, to laugh at the "paleface" with his moral scruples and synchronized life.   What Anderson petitions for is a return to that age when

> Man, entirely free, alone and wild
> Was blest as free — for he was Nature's child. . . .
> Confessed no law but what his reason taught,
> Did all he wished, and wished but what he ought.[58]

He is a descendant of Jean Jacques Rousseau (who said that "man is naturally good and that our social institutions alone have rendered him evil"),[59] and a brother of such modern Rousseauists as John Cowper Powys, English novelist and advocate of "the ichthyosaurus-ego," or "animal-vegetable rapture."[60]   His is a philosophy opposed to logic, tradition, conscience, standardization, thrift,

[57] Krutch, Joseph Wood, "New Morals for Old: Modern Love and Modern Fiction," *The Nation* (June 25, 1924), CXVIII, 735–736.

[58] Wordsworth, in a poem dated 1791.

[59] In his "Discourse on the Arts and Sciences" (1750).

[60] See his *In Defence of Sensuality* (1930).   This whole philosophy of savage-worship and the return to primitivism is interestingly treated in Wyndam Lewis's *Paleface* (1929).

self-restraint, the "hot, fussy, feverish set of human ideals," and policemen; it favors "a life of sensations rather than of thoughts," and counsels resignation to the naked incentives of Nature.

Anderson believes that the Negro is happier than other men, because he is more aboriginal, never concerned with Freudian "repressions," and in love with "bright gaudy colors, food, the earth, the sky, the river . . . song and laughter, night, drink, and lust." [61] "Could it be," he asks,

that force, all power, was a disease, that man on his way up from savagery and having discovered the mind and its uses had gone a little off his head in using his new toy?   I had always been drawn toward horses and dogs and other animals and among people had cared most for simple folk who had no pretense of having an intellect, workmen who in spite of the handicaps put in their way by modern life still loved the materials in which they worked, who loved the play of hands over materials, who followed instinctively a force outside themselves they felt to be greater and more worthy than themselves — women who gave themselves to physical experiences with grave and fine abandon. [62]

Negroes "like good things.   Good big sweet words, flesh, corn, cane.   Niggers like a free throat for song." [63]   They scorn inhibitions, and possess an "Unconscious love of inanimate things lost to the whites — skies, the river, a moving boat — black mysticism — never expressed except in song or the movement of bodies." [64]   Therefore, reasons Anderson, we should envy and imitate them.

His attitude is that of many contemporary Negrophiles, who, afraid that romance and liberty are dying, try to recognize lingering vibrations of them in unassimilated racial groups.   This same spirit, which explains the modern influence of African art upon sculpture, helped lure Paul Gauguin, a French painter, to the South Seas, after

---

[61] *Sherwood Anderson's Notebook*, p. 65.
[62] *A Story Teller's Story*, p. 269.
[63] *Dark Laughter*, p. 80.
[64] *Ibid.*, p. 106.

a "catharsis" that would have done credit to an Andersonian character. It has also contributed to an esthetic revival of interest in Amerindian culture (led by Mary Austin), and to the anthropological novels of Thames Williamson, *The Earth Told Me* (1930) and *Sad Indian* (1932).

STREAM OF CONSCIOUSNESS   One "bible" of this age has been Henri Bergson's *Creative Evolution* (1907), in which he pictures life as a cosmic river or

current passing from germ to germ through the medium of a developed organism. It is as if the organism itself were only an excrescence, a bud caused to sprout by the former germ endeavoring to continue itself in a new germ. The essential thing is the *continuous progress* indefinitely pursued, an invisible progress, on which each visible organism rides during the short interval of time given it to live.[65]

And from this "impressionistic" theory, which reduces existence to a flux, many authors have drawn their inspiration. We find it shadowed in Marcel Proust and Elizabeth Madox Roberts' *The Time of Man* (1926), a novel of itinerant poor farmers in the South which pictures a fluent blend of events as the seasons wing over. But its chief function in literature has been to serve as the basis of what has come to be known as the introspective, or "stream-of-consciousness" novel, a term derived from William James's "the stream of thought."

This type of novelist has been defined as "the one who attempts to portray life and character by setting down everything that goes on in his hero's mind; notably all those unimportant and chaotic thought-sequences which occupy our idle or somnolent moments, and to which, in real life, we pay, ourselves, little attention." [66]   It is a kind of mental solitaire, played by such authors as Herbert Gorman in his *Gold by Gold* (1925); Conrad Aiken in *Blue*

[65] Bergson, Henri, *Creative Evolution* (1911), p. 27.
[66] Gerould, Katharine F., "Stream of Consciousness," *The Saturday Review of Literature* (October 22, 1927), IV, 233.

Voyage (1927); William Faulkner in *The Sound and the Fury* (1929); Rex Stout in *How Like a God* (1929), a story told in a man's mind as he walks up several flights of stairs; Aaron Mark Stein in *Spirals* (1930); and Hilda Doolittle in *Palimpsest* (1926), a confused novel that deals with terraces of time and their merger. As an example of their technique, we may take this passage from Evelyn Scott's *The Narrow House:*

She cried a long time. The work would have to go. At last she crept off the bed and undressed herself and put out the light, but she lay awake and the darkness remained electric and horrible.

Mama and Papa Farley. What was wrong between them? Sex. Horror. She tried to keep her thoughts from integrating. Child. She bit her wrist again and turned over in bed. Too proud to hate Winnie. Other girls. Their faces opened against hers. They were white and flowering in the dark. Eyes open, waiting to receive men. She shivered. One must think about these things. Winnie's maternity. Bobby seemed slimed all over with Winnie. To wash Bobby clean — clean of Winnie.

Alice was still awhile. She was dark inside, but the dark grew calm. She began to go over things very clearly. What was passion? Fourteen years old. Pain. Words written on back fences.

I am glad to be out of it. Poor little Winnie. Outside, cool. Cool ache of being outside life.[67]

The best known of those using this narrative device is James Joyce, "the literary Bolshevist," for whose work Bruce Dudley (in *Dark Laughter*) admits a passion.[68] Joyce's famous novel, *Ulysses*, was first published in *The Little Review* from 1918 to 1921, and brought out as a volume in the next year. Covering about nineteen hours in the life of Stephen Dedalus, an Irish Hamlet, it is said to be founded, in its symbolism, upon Homer's *Odyssey*,

[67] Scott, Evelyn, *The Narrow House* (1921), p. 36.
[68] Joyce, however, was not the father of the "interior monologue." It is said to have first come into literature in Edouard Dujardin's *Les Lauriers Sont Coupés* (1886), a book to which Joyce has confessed his debt.

Dedalus taking the part of Telemachus and Leopold Bloom, his friend, standing for Ulysses. In this book the "stream-of-consciousness" receives its most consistent expression. For forty-five pages, without punctuation of any kind, we are given the thoughts of Bloom's wife, as she lies in bed musing upon the lovers she has had:

as for them saying theres no God I wouldnt give a snap of my two fingers for all their learning why dont they go and create something I often asked him atheists or whatever they call themselves go and wash the cobbles off themselves first then go howling for the priest and they dying and why why because theyre afraid of hell on account of their bad conscience ah yes I know them well who was the first person in the universe before there was anybody that made it all who ah that they dont know neither do I so there you are they might as well try to stop the sun from rising tomorrow the sun shines for you he said the day we were lying among the rhododendrons on Howth head in the grey tweed suit and his straw hat the day I got him to propose to me yes first I gave him the bit of seedcake out of my mouth and it was leapyear like now yes 16 years ago my God after that long kiss I nearly lost my breath yes he said I was a flower of the mountain yes so we are all flowers of a womans body.[69]

Though other novelists, like Henry James, Dorothy Richardson, and Virginia Woolf, have used this method of telling a story, no one has ever employed the "stream-of-consciousness" with greater force or versatility than Joyce. Among those who have tried to bend this bow, it has often become no more than a trick of style, or an excuse for novelists who are afraid to join life's fragments together for fear the addition might come out wrong.

A PROSE PICASSO But Anderson's style was influenced less by Joyce than by another stormy petrel of modern fiction, Gertrude Stein. Her first book to attract notice was *Tender Buttons* in 1914. Then followed such curious

[69] Joyce, James, *Ulysses* (1934), p. 767.

literary fauna as *Have They Attacked Mary He Giggled — A Political Satire* (1917); *Geography and Plays* (1922); *Useful Knowledge* (1928), a play consisting of long lists of phrases divided into acts; *Lucy Church Amiably* (1930); and *How to Write* (1931). Before 1914 she had already written her most intelligible books in *Three Lives* (1909), "the stories of three servant girls in terms of their hidden minds," and *The Making of Americans* (not published until 1925). Since then she has grown rapidly more obscure. Gertrude Stein, insists a recent critic, "has outdistanced any of the Symbolists in using words for pure purposes of suggestion — she has gone so far that she no longer even suggests. We see the ripples expanding in her consciousness, but we are no longer supplied with any clew as to what kind of object has sunk there." [70] Here, for instance, are three specimens taken from *Geography and Plays:*

A clatter registered has a calming center. That is the outlasting of a sight of all. If it is possible that there is the result then certainly no one would think so. Every one does. There is no sense in such a history. There is no sense at all. Not a bit of broom has the windows open, not a bit.[71]

To begin on again.
It was said and well said it was well said and avoiding, it was avoided by instantaneous crowning it was mounted by sullen points it was suddenly anticipated and nearly by a trinket. What is a trinket.

I was disappointed in eggs.
Sweet oh sweet oh sweet sweet sweet

Acting
An amazing cow. Simply an amazing cow. Not in sobbing. Not in clenching. An amazing cow. So shot. When.[72]

I saw a spoken leave leaf and flowers made vegetables and foliage in soil. I saw representative mistakes and glass cups, I saw a

---

[70] Wilson, Edmund, *Axel's Castle* (1931), pp. 243–244.
[71] Stein, Gertrude, *Geography and Plays* (1922), p. 177.
[72] *Ibid.*, p. 299

whole appearance of respectable refugees, I did not ask actors I asked pearls, I did not choose to ask trains, I was satisfied with celebrated ransoms. I cannot deny Bertie Henschel is coming tomorrow. Saturdays are even. There is a regular principle, if you mention it you mention what happened.

What do you make of it.

You exceed all hope and all praise.[73]

Soon after 1914 *Tender Buttons* came to Anderson's attention. "How it had excited me!" he says. "Here was something purely experimental and dealing with words separated from sense — in the ordinary meaning of the word sense." [74] "After Miss Stein's book had come into my hands I spent days going about with a tablet of paper in my pocket and making new and strange combinations of words. The result was I thought a new familiarity with the words of my own vocabulary. I became a little conscious where before I had been unconscious." [75]

He seems to have learned from Gertrude Stein "his recurrent repetitions with their effect of ballad refrains and his method of telling a story in a series of simple declarative sentences of almost primer-like baldness." [76]

I am sick of my old self that protested against the machine. I am sick of the self in me, that self in me, that self in me, that would not live in my own age.

> That self in me.
> That self in me.
> That self in me.
>
> In my own age.
> In my own age.
> In my own age.
> Individuality gone.
> Let it go.[77]

---

[73] *Ibid.*, p. 156.   [74] *A Story Teller's Story*, p. 359.
[75] *Ibid.*, p. 362.   [76] Wilson, Edmund, *op. cit.*, p. 239.
[77] *Perhaps Women*, p. 14.

The trouble is that he has become *too* "conscious." Words are for him ends in themselves, not means to an end. As he has remarked:

One works with words and one would like words that have a taste on the lips, that have a perfume to the nostrils, rattling words one can throw into a box and shake, making a sharp, jingling sound, words that, when seen on the printed page, have a distinct arresting effect upon the eye, words that when they jump out from under the pen one may feel with the fingers as one might caress the cheeks of his beloved.[78]

Yet for all his discussions about the "perfume" of words his vocabulary remains among the most limited in American literature, and his style one of the driest. Never more than a species of echolalia, it has descended in recent volumes to even less; with his phobic absorption in words it has become a welter of mannerisms. Those words that lie in him, as he often says, like "seeds," have sprouted at last; and he is lost in their branches.

SPONTANEOUS ME Joyce, Stein, and Anderson, in their variations from the normal, are emblematic of a literary theory known as "expressionism," based on the principle that every man's style should be as unique as his fingerprints, that "all eminence and distinction lies out of the beaten road," and that art should flout all laws, to become merely a "vehicle of the artist's personal reaction." [79] It is a child, at least in large part, of science, which considers the world as a multiverse of entirely unlike things: a notion which literature has interpreted to mean that since things are different, the more we stress their difference, the better the art. The more ingenuity, the more genius.

[78] Anderson, Sherwood, in his Introduction to Gertrude Stein's *Geography and Plays* (1922).

[79] Beach, Joseph Warren, *The Twentieth-Century Novel* (1932), p. 9. The descent of this theory is traced in Babbitt, Irving, *Rousseau and Romanticism* (1919).

There are certain landmarks in the growth of this idea. In 1759 Edward Young, the English poet, wrote his *Conjectures on Original Composition*, defending in it the local, the specific, and the unusual; repudiating tradition; and denying the existence of any fixed or universal standards in literature. The same implications were contained in Buffon's remark that "the style is the man," in Swinburne's observation that "the manner of doing a thing is the essence of the thing done, the purpose or result of it the accident," in de Maupassant's Introduction to *Pierre and Jean* in which he says to the author, "Give me something fine in any form which may suit you best, according to your own temperament," [80] and in Zola's statement that "You can write badly, incorrectly, like the devil, and yet, with it all, retain a true originality of expression." [81] With the artist's growing skepticism and uncertainty about the "subject matter" of life, he has begun to seek refuge in naked style, which he no longer subordinates to the meaning of his work. "Why use art to conceal art?" he inquires.

Young's doctrine later found sanction in Taine's theory of criticism, which viewed each writer as a highly individualized product of a special milieu, and also in Hamlin Garland, who was influenced by Taine. Garland's *Crumbling Idols* (1894) was "intended to weaken the hold of conventionalism upon the youthful artist." It wanted to smash the old gods, asked for "freedom from past models," and confessed a "passion for truth and for individual expression."

The most recent prophet of Young's "original genius" theory has been Elias Spingarn, whose own concepts are founded upon the work of Benedetto Croce, an Italian historian and philosopher. It was Croce's idea that "since every work of art expresses a state of the soul, and the

[80] In his Introduction to *Pierre and Jean* (1906), p. 9.
[81] Zola, Émile, *The Experimental Novel* (1893), p. 221.

state of the soul is individual and always new," the reader should love "each work for itself, for what it is, as a living creature, individual and incomparable," knowing "that each work has its individual law."

On March 9, 1910, Spingarn delivered his lecture "Creative Criticism" at Columbia University, in which he said that he believed in "no rule except the whim of genius and no standard of judgment beyond individual taste." [82] He declared himself against arbitrary formulae and haloed generalizations on the topic of art. "We have done with all moral judgment of literature," he announced.[83] "To say that poetry is moral or immoral is as meaningless as to say that an equilateral triangle is moral and an isosceles triangle immoral." [84] "Beauty's world is remote from both these standards; she aims neither at morals nor at truth." [85] Art is "its own excuse for being." "Every poet re-expresses the universe in his own way, and every poem is a new and independent expression." [86] "When Criticism first propounded as its real concern the oft-repeated question: 'What has the poet tried to express and how has he expressed it?' Criticism prescribed for itself the only possible method." [87]

AMERICA FIRST   Applied to the literature of various countries, this theory of "original genius" takes the name and form of *nationalism*, or the principle that every country, like every individual, has its own peculiar message for the world. Changing Spingarn's phrase a bit, we learn that "Every locality re-expresses the universe in its own way." It is "the whim of genius" translated into patriotic terms.

Nationalism in America first sprang from a conception of this new continent as "the Promised Land" (offering the hope of a natural paradise), and from resentment against England during the Revolution. The work of Irving and

---

[82] Spingarn, J. E., *Creative Criticism* (1917), p. 10.   [83] *Ibid.*, p. 31.
[84] *Ibid.*, p. 32.   [85] *Ibid.*, p. 33.   [86] *Ibid.*, p. 29.   [87] *Ibid.*, p. 42.

William Cullen Bryant's *American Life and Fiction* supplied further arguments for an indigenous literature. Then with Longfellow, Whittier, Lowell, and Emerson the trend was halted for a time; "each experimented in youth with the doctrine of a local and unique literary nationalism, but each in his maturity came to stand for the universal rather than the national . . . for those aspects of life which men of all times and lands have in common rather than those aspects in which men and nations differ." [88] In Whitman's prose and poetry, however, the idea of a national literature was revived, as it was in William Dean Howells and Garland. *Crumbling Idols* affirmed that here in this country "Themes are crying out to be written," [89] and that "each locality must produce its own literary record, each special phase of life utter its own voice. There is no other way for a true local expression to embody itself. The sun of truth strikes each part of the earth at a little different angle; it is this angle which gives life and infinite variety to literature." [90]

THE REDISCOVERY OF AMERICA   Nationalism was spurred, to an extent, by the International Copyright Act of 1891, which prevented American publishers from reprinting European books for nothing, and led them to buy more manuscripts from authors on this side of the Atlantic. It was also fostered by the Columbian Exposition of 1892, marking the 400th anniversary of America's discovery. Garland's book lent it further impetus in 1894; and in 1913 the cause was supported by John Macy's *The Spirit of American Literature*. Van Wyck Brooks, in his *America's Coming of Age* (1915) and *Letters and Leadership* (1918), brought the question into the critical arena, and "called for debate about America, her ideals and traditions, and

[88] Clark, Harry Hayden, "Nationalism in American Literature," *The University of Toronto Quarterly* (July, 1933), II, No. 4, 509.
[89] Garland, Hamlin, *Crumbling Idols* (1894), p. 14.   [90] *Ibid.*, p. 22.

her hope for the future. He got his response in the challenge to tradition led by Mr. Mencken, who gained the most listeners because he shouted the loudest; in the defence of tradition, led by Mr. Sherman, who spoke for the conservatives; in the attempts to reconsider America as an heir to Europe in the books of Lewis Mumford, Waldo Frank, and Frederic Paxson; and in the attempts to revaluate America as it stands, by groups of younger critics," [91] such as Randolph Bourne, and Matthew Josephson in his *Portrait of the Artist as American* (1930).

Mencken in *The American Language* (1919) and George Philip Krapp in *The English Language in America* (1925) supplemented this "battle of the books" with a new philological "declaration of independence" from England and Europe. Meanwhile slang had come to be looked upon as a distinct gift of America to civilization. George Ade in his *Fables in Slang* (1899), Ring Lardner, and sports writers everywhere were putting it into astringent prose; and it was even being introduced into poetry by John V. A. Weaver, at the instigation of Mencken.

After 1870 Bret Harte and many others carried nationalism one step farther and applied it to various regions of America, as well as to the country as a whole. Schools of "local color" lifted their heads in every part of the nation, gradually faded as communication improved, and were replaced by novels dealing with class instead of sectional differences. But today this regionalism in literature is experiencing a revival in such books as Janet Lewis's *The Invasion* (Great Lakes country), Nard Jones's *Oregon Detour* (the Northwest), Edwin Granberry's *The Erl King* (Florida), Thames Williamson's *The Woods Colt* (the Ozarks), Richard Warren Hatch's *Into the Wind* (New England), Gladys Hasty Carroll's *As the Earth Turns* (Maine), Glenway Wescott's *The Apple of the Eye* (Wisconsin), John Towner Frederick's *Green Bush* (Michigan), Marjorie Kinnan Raw-

[91] Boynton, Percy Holmes, *The Challenge of Modern Criticism* (1931), p. 104.

lings' *South Moon Under* (Florida), Charles Morrow Wilson's *Acres of Sky* (Arkansas), Charles Malam's *Slow Smoke* (Vermont), Leroy McLeod's *Years of Peace* (Indiana), James Gould Cozzens' *The Last Adam* (Connecticut), Ellen Glasgow's *Barren Ground* (Virginia), Julia Peterkin's *Scarlet Sister Mary* (Carolina), T. S. Stribling's *Teeftallow* (the South), Harvey Fergusson's *The Blood of the Conquerors* (Southwest), Dorothy Scarborough's *The Wind* (Texas), Maristan Chapman's *The Happy Mountain* (Tennessee), and Walter D. Edmonds' *Rome Haul* (upstate New York).[92]

DADAISM Expressionism, as it operates in the individual author, has been responsible for many changes in the novel's form. Having departed from the old carefully built story, with its complex scaffolding of plot, many characters, definite climax, and unobtrusive style, the modern novel is marked by a static Freudian plot, dealing with inner crucialities instead of overt circumstances; few characters, selected for their striking rather than universal traits; and various novelties of style. Since Bergson there has been a tendency to discard the climax in favor of a level flowing plot, indicating the new character of life as a stream of time, with no beginning and no end. Fiction today does not always have Aristotle's "beginning, middle, and end." Plot has become a flux, an impressionistic blur, which rarely comes to a boil. In *Manhattan Transfer* (1925), *42nd Parallel* (1930), and *1919* (1932), John Dos Passos has converted this technique into a method for fiction, which gives his stories the disconnected variety of a news reel, or a tabloid paper. Such a style is obviously related to science's view of a "pluralistic universe," filled with unique events and people, and is well adapted to mirror the confusing and divergent nature of our present world.

[92] See McWilliams, C., *The New Regionalism in American Literature*, University of Washington Chapbooks; and Hibbard, C. A., *The South in Contemporary Literature*, The University of North Carolina Press.

Structural innovations of real interest may be found in such books as Hemingway's *The Sun Also Rises* (1926), Joyce's *Ulysses*, Aldous Huxley's *Point Counter Point* (1928), Glenway Wescott's *The Grandmothers* (1927), Thornton Wilder's *The Bridge of San Luis Rey* (1927), Evelyn Scott's *The Wave* (1929), Tess Slesinger's *The Unpossessed* (1934), Jonathan Leonard's *The Meddlers* (1929), Frances Newman's *The Hard-Boiled Virgin* (1926), Felix Riesenberg's *Endless River* (1931), Babette Deutsch's *In Such a Night* (1927), Myron Brinig's *The Flutter of an Eyelid* (1933), Kay Boyle's *Plagued by the Nightingale* (1931), George Anthony Weller's *Not to Eat, Not for Love* (1933), Edwin Seaver's *The Company* (1930), and Leonard Ehrlich's *God's Angry Man* (1932). But among other writers the spirit of "expressionism" has produced only freakishness. The older concept was that literature was designed for communication. In certain quarters today, however, the view holds that literature is an instrument of self-indulgence, designed to exhibit the author's random and often fragmentary impulses, which the reader may or may not understand. The author becomes an isolated figure, "talking to himself in public," [93] and art "a tendency toward privacy." [94]

After 1916 this "tendency" was represented in France by the cult of Dada, aggravated by the modern belief that life is a kind of venereal vaudeville, and by a post-war feeling of despair. Dada, says one writer, "denies all values save the immediate intuition, inspiration, of the individual, who is therefore sole judge of his product — and, one may sometimes feel, alone in his enjoyment." [95] The 1918 manifesto of this group contained the following explanations:

[93] Eastman, Max, *The Literary Mind* (1931), p. 96.
[94] *Ibid.*, p. 79.
[95] Shipley, Joseph T., *The Literary Isms*, University of Washington Chapbooks, No. 49 (1931), p. 31.

DADA MEANS NOTHING [96]

there is no beginning and we do not tremble, we are not sentimental. We rend, furious wind, the linen of clouds and of prayers,
and prepare the great spectacle of disaster, the conflagration,
decomposition. Prepare the suppression of sorrow and replace
tears with sirens stretched from one continent to the other. Pa-
vilions of joy intense and widowed of the sadness of poison. . . .
DADA is the banner of abstraction; advertising and business are
likewise poetic elements. I do away with the drawers of the
brain and those of the body social: to bring demoralization everywhere and to cast the hand of heaven on hell, the eyes of hell on
heaven, to re-establish the prolific wheel of a universal circus in
the real potentialities and the fantasy of each individual.[97]

America has produced only one Dadaist novel, Robert
M. Coates' *The Eater of Darkness* (1929). But its obscur-
ity has been exceeded by several other books, like E. E.
Cummings' Joycean travelogue, *Eimi* (1933), from which
this description of a train ride has been taken.

SHUT seems to be The Verb:gent of lower ("ça ne vous fait rien
si je me déshabille?")whose baggage strangles a sickly neatness of
deuxième coffin Shut the window(don't you think we'll have too
much smoke?)and tactfully funeral director,upon glimpsing
milord today drowsing after cakes & ale by mister mome,Shut
our door(this morning I was thoroughly amazed:met, en route
to breakfast,Fresh Air!—in a troisième common grave)

and lunch was more Shut than a cemetery:4 separate corpses
collectively illatease:no ghost of conversation. Ponderous grub;
because(last night, Shut in a breathless box with a grunting doll)
I rushed sidewise into Germany(but that swirling tomb of horizon-
tality was less Shut than the emptiest rightangledness which called
itself "essen")

lowering weather through SHUTnesses — dank dark fields,
smutted towns. Enlivened by

[96] In Putnam, Samuel (ed.), *op. cit.*, p. 93.
[97] *Ibid.*, p. 95.

(1)a trainmaster(or whatever)in colours remembering how those children who are our ancestors would emblazon images of hourglass-ladies-fair(displayed, with other touching nonsense, on quais)

(2)Das Magazine — at least 2 really delicious allbutetc. girlies

(3)astonishly armears of windmill poking over a brief world-edge

(4),,00"

(5)hugest(andtoadreamstreamlined)locomotive-nakedly-floating-most-lazily-who(throughhanoverstation)slid-whispering-extinction

and framed with

> nie wychylać sie
> omwierać drzwi
> podczas biegu pociągu [98]

[98] Cummings, E. E., *Eimi* (1933), p. 3.

*

GRACE UNDER PRESSURE

*

AN AMERICAN BYRON   While Anderson played Virgil to
his *libido* among the purgatorial depths of Freud, other
novelists eschewed his sentimentality and looked with
more favor upon Nietzsche's injunction to "Be hard!"   It
was this spirit of cynicism that marked "The Jazz Age,"
and found its voice in the books of Cyril Hume and F. Scott
Fitzgerald.   *This Side of Paradise* (1920) is a marginal
comment upon our sin-copated period of "flaming youth,"
cocktail parties, joy rides, and the saxophone; and teamed
with Norris's *Vandover and the Brute*, it achieves further importance as the precursor of such "undergraduate" novels
as Katherine Brush's *Glitter* (1926), Betty White's *I Lived
This Story* (1930), William McNally's *The Barb* (1923),
Percy Marks' *The Plastic Age* (1924), Alexander Laing's
End of Roaming (1930), Aaron Mark Stein's *Spirals* (1930),
John Earl Uhler's *Cane Juice* (1931), David Burnham's *This
Our Exile* (1931), John Hermann's *What Happens* (1926),
and the finest volume of its kind, George Anthony Wel-
ler's *Not to Eat, Not for Love* (1933).

But for the starkest expression of that "blue Monday"
after the war we must go to Ernest Hemingway, whose
vogue in 1932 eclipsed even Fitzgerald's during the 20's.
Hemingway, though he won his first renown with Anderson's help, represents a distinct revolt from the cloying
emotionalism of *Dark Laughter*, which he humorously par-
odied in *The Torrents of Spring*.   He is a reversal, in fact,
of everything Anderson holds dear.   To naturalism he
has lent a bald objectivity of theme and style, rescuing

151

it from the potpourri of raptures into which Anderson escorted it, purifying it of false romanticism, introducing a cosmopolitan point of view, correcting its tendency to lapse into mysticism, and erasing with the aid of antiseptic wit Anderson's "Peter Pantheism." "An American Byron" is the phrase applied to Hemingway by a recent critic, who completes the analogy by pointing out that both Hemingway and Byron defy conventional morality, worship the violent, cruel and ghastly, exploit athleticism, are fascinated by the more *outré* aspects of sex, exalt sport, irony, and sophistication, prefer wild romantic localities, and spring from a post-war *Weltschmerz*, or pessimistic belief that the ethics and ideals of civilization have defaulted in their promises. "He cultivates to the point of fetichism," notes this same critic (in giving us what is so far our best diagnosis of Hemingway),

those primal emotions which cannot betray him, as his hands and feet cannot betray him. Among these emotions may well be the fear of death and the delight in it, the stoic joy of battle and the pleasurable acceptance of the flesh and the muscles. In the last analysis he worships his reflexes, tending to exalt any activity which the act of introspection cannot corrode. He reverts, however subtly, to the primitive and even the brutal, because on these levels he finds no echo of the culture which has cheated him. He attempts to cling to the hands of the clock, to become a non-political animal, an individualist contemning all creeds, individualism included.

Having forsworn both his national and his class roots, he is at home in all countries. He puts his faith in simple things rather than in complicated words and shakes off all phrases that smack of the metaphysical or the moral. He seeks the companionship and tries to share the experience of booze-fighters, killers, athletes, and sportsmen, men who lead careers of physical sensation, superficially insulated from the main current of the life of their time. He may even cultivate a special interest in the reactions of animals, creatures unspoiled by the general infection of the world. . . . He is the frontiersman of the loins, heart, and biceps, the stoic

Red Indian minus traditions, scornful of the past, bare of sentimentality, catching the muscular life in a plain and muscular prose.[1]

Ernest Hemingway was born in Oak Park, Illinois, July 21, 1898, and educated in the public schools there. During the war he served on the Italian front, and afterwards became a newspaper correspondent in Europe. *In Our Time* (1925), his first important volume, revolves chiefly around a youth named Nick, and contains sketches of a Michigan lumber camp, fishing, adolescent love, war, Italy, and matadors. In 1926 he published *The Torrents of Spring*, and in the same year, *The Sun Also Rises*, which brought him instant fame. *The Sun Also Rises*, a study in truncated emotion, is concerned with what Gertrude Stein once called "the lost generation," those young men and women who came out of the war minus their previous faith in humanity, duty, and religion. Like Maurice Samuel's *The Outsider* (1921) it deals with a group of "expatriate" writers, artists, and nymphomaniacs in Paris, who, to cover their boredom and loss of direction, march through one set of drinks after another, and take innumerable baths to sober up. They have reduced life to a sequence of physical sensations, feeling that the war complicated existence, and that in order to simplify it they must try not to think about anything, except drinking, loving, dancing, fishing, and watching bull fights in Spain. From this they gain no pleasure; it is a mere anodyne, to help them endure what they cannot improve. Under a blanket of nimble conversation they seek to disguise from themselves their uprooted condition.

"Here," I said. "Utilize a little of this."
We uncorked the other bottle.
"What's the matter?" I said. "Didn't you like Bryan?"
"I loved Bryan," said Bill. "We were like brothers."

[1] Fadiman, Clifton, "Ernest Hemingway: An American Byron," *The Nation* (January 18, 1933), CXXXVI, 63–64.

"Where did you know him?"

"He and Mencken and I all went to Holy Cross together."

"And Frankie Fritsch."

"It's a lie.   Frankie Fritsch went to Fordham."

"Well," I said, "I went to Loyola with Bishop Manning."

"It's a lie," Bill said.   "I went to Loyola with Bishop Manning myself."

"You're cock-eyed," I said.

"On wine?"

"Why not?"

"It's the humidity," Bill said.   "They ought to take this damn humidity away."

"Have another shot."

"Is this all we've got?"

"Only the two bottles."

"Do you know what you are?" Bill looked at the bottle affectionately.

"No," I said.

"You're in the pay of the Anti-Saloon League."

"I went to Notre Dame with Wayne B. Wheeler."

"It's a lie," said Bill.   "I went to Austin Business College with Wayne B. Wheeler.   He was class president."

"Well," I said, "the saloon must go."

"You're right there, old classmate," Bill said.   "The saloon must go, and I will take it with me."

"You're cock-eyed."

"On wine?"

"On wine."

"Well, maybe I am."

"Want to take a nap."

"All right."

We lay with our heads in the shade and looked up into the trees.

"You asleep?"

"No," Bill said.   "I was thinking."

I shut my eyes.   It felt good lying on the ground.

"Say," Bill said, "what about this Brett business?"

"What about it?"

"Were you ever in love with her?"

"Sure."

"For how long?"

"Off and on for a hell of a long time."

"Oh, hell!" Bill said. "I'm sorry, fella."

"It's all right," I said. "I don't give a damn any more."

"Really?"

"Really. Only I'd a hell of a lot rather not talk about it."

"You aren't sore I asked you?"

"Why the hell should I be?"

"I'm going to sleep," Bill said. He put a newspaper over his face.

"Listen, Jake," he said, "are you really a Catholic?"

"Technically."

"What does that mean?"

"I don't know."

"All right, I'll go to sleep now," he said. "Don't keep me awake by talking so much." [2]

Men Without Women (1927) is a second volume of stories about matadors, scenes of agony in field hospitals, a young man persuading his sweetheart to have an abortion, gangsters, pederasts, a frozen corpse in the Alps, prize fighters, and dope fiends. In *A Farewell to Arms* (1929), hymned by its publishers as "the powerful story of a love conceived in the muck of war which evolves into beauty," Hemingway returned to the novel form. Catherine Barkley, an English nurse in Italy during the war, and Frederic Henry, an American volunteer in the ambulance service, meet behind the lines. He is injured, placed in a Milan hospital, and visited by Miss Barkley, who spends the night with him. In a few months he is ordered back to the front, gets lost in a confused retreat, escapes arrest for desertion, rejoins Catherine, and together they go to Switzerland, where she dies in childbirth. *Death in the Afternoon* (1932), which has been termed "a Baedeker of bulls," is a large handbook on the matador's art, interspersed with remarks on life in general. And *Winner Take*

---

[2] Hemingway, Ernest, *The Sun Also Rises* (1929), pp. 126–128.

Nothing (1933), his latest volume, is another collection of sketches.

PLAYING THE GAME In private life Hemingway is an active sportsman; and in each of his books there appear frequent references to baseball, skiing, fishing, horse racing, and boxing. This interest in sport may perhaps be founded on our modern assumption that when the mind and social ideals abdicate (as they did in the war), the body must take charge; at any rate, existence has become for Hemingway a mere contest, bitter and trenchant.

You did not know what it was about. You never had time to learn. They threw you in and told you the rules and the first time they caught you off base they killed you.[3]

Yet he does not complain of this brutality. He is the athlete, the "tough-minded" hero, embracing a fatalistic philosophy. The important thing is to "play the game," accepting both victories and defeats with laconic calm, and retaining your "grace under pressure." His principal desire is to keep things from becoming complicated, to keep them simple, by reducing everything to its lowest terms, as he has morals. "I know," he explains, "only that what is moral is what you feel good after and what is immoral is what you feel bad after."[4] His "design for living" involves only rudimentary and physical acts. "I was not made for thinking," Frederic Henry declares, in *A Farewell to Arms*, "I was made to eat. My God, yes. Eat and drink and sleep with Catherine."[5] Understatement he prefers to overstatement. "The Hemingway character, who only *does* and *is*, says nothing but the barely and bleakly necessary, and despises all subtleties of thought and emotion."[6] "He instinctively mistrusts explicitness, anal-

[3] Hemingway, Ernest, *A Farewell to Arms* (1929), p. 350.
[4] *Death in the Afternoon* (1932), p. 4.
[5] *A Farewell to Arms*, p. 249.
[6] Hazlitt, Henry, "Salvation for the Modern Soul," *The Nation* (June 10, 1931), CXXXII, 637.

ysis, imputation of motives, investigation of the souls of others, qualifying adjectives and a heart worn on the sleeve." [7] "I was always embarrassed," says Frederic Henry,

> by the words sacred, glorious and sacrifice and the expression in vain. We had heard them sometimes standing in the rain almost out of earshot so that only the shouted words came through, and read them, on proclamations that were slapped up by bill posters over other proclamations now for a long time, and I had seen nothing sacred, and the things that were glorious had no glory and the sacrifices were like the stockyards at Chicago if nothing was done with the meat except to bury it. There were many words that you could not stand to hear and finally only the names of places had dignity. Certain numbers were the same way and certain dates and these with the names of the places were all you could say and have them mean anything. Abstract words such as glory, honor, courage, or hallow were obscene beside the concrete names of villages, the numbers of roads, the names of rivers, the numbers of regiments and the dates.[8]

Faced with the confusion and cruelty of life, Hemingway has resigned himself to stoicism; he is determined "to grin and bear it." Anderson's introspection is of no avail; indeed "you are better when you don't think so deeply." Courage is man's last refuge, now that he can no longer believe in God or reason. "Nothing," he has decided, "ever happens to the brave," [9] a sentiment that we find echoed, with variations, in other novels similar or tributary to Hemingway's, such as Morley Callaghan's *A Broken Journey* (1932), John Hermann's *Summer Is Ended* (1932), John V. Craven's *The Leaf Is Green* (1931), W. R. Burnett's *Little Caesar* (1929), and John M. Cain's *The Postman Always Rings Twice* (1934).

[7] Littell, Robert, "Notes on Hemingway," *The New Republic* (August 10, 1927), LI, 305.

[8] *A Farewell to Arms*, p. 196.

[9] *Ibid.*, p. 149.

WESTERN UNION Even in his style Hemingway evinces this same concern for the non-committal and deliberately barren. As someone has remarked, everything he writes "sounds like a crisis in a cable." Having decided that life is vain, he seems to be conserving his strength, by restricting himself to ordinary American "lingo." It is an application to literature of "Occam's razor" theory, which held that all unnecessary abstractions should be discarded. Yet there is nothing "unconscious" about his technique, as Anderson has sometimes pretended in regard to the studied disorder of his own work. Like Anderson he is an artificer; and like Anderson he has drawn much of his inspiration from the fugal experiments of Gertrude Stein. It is easy, for example, to catch his abrupt rhythms in *Geography and Plays*.

Helen Furr had quite a pleasant home. Mrs. Furr was quite a pleasant woman. Mr. Furr was quite a pleasant man. Helen Furr had quite a pleasant voice a voice quite worth cultivating. She did not mind working. She worked to cultivate her voice. She did not find it gay living in the same place where she had always been living. She went to a place where some were cultivating something, voices and other things needing cultivating. She met Georgine Skeene there who was cultivating her voice which some thought was quite a pleasant one. Helen Furr and Georgine Skeene lived together then. Georgine Skeene liked travelling. Helen Furr did not care about travelling, she liked to stay in one place and be gay there. They were together then and travelled to another place and stayed there and were gay there.[10]

They did not live together then Helen Furr and Georgine Skeene. Helen Furr lived there the longer where they had been living regularly together. Then neither of them were living there any longer. Helen Furr was living somewhere else then and telling some about being gay and she was gay then and she was living quite regularly then.[11]

[10] Stein, Gertrude, *Geography and Plays* (1922), p. 17.   [11] *Ibid.*, p. 22.

But at his best, Hemingway has a style that is his very own, a style frequently aped though never equaled. In spite of his unvarying "I said's" and "he said's," which now and then tend to congeal upon him and become monotonous, there runs throughout most of his work a tingling insight and live limpidity of language that should assure his volumes of future respect.

*

THE CULT OF CRUELTY

*

REDUCTIO AD ABSURDUM After Hemingway there remains little to say of William Faulkner. By positing a more ghastly and anarchic cosmos than previous novelists, and then cynically resigning himself to it, he has managed to simulate an even greater fortitude, or "stoicism." This appears to be his major purpose in writing. He is the *reductio ad absurdum* of American naturalism.

"The world of William Faulkner echoes with the hideous trampling march of lust and disease, brutality and death," [1] as if he had decided that in a universe bereft of authentic proprieties and the accents of logic, violence is the only source of emphasis and intensity left in fiction. Like Hemingway he views every species of human behavior with anesthetized tolerance, and reclines upon a glacial note of pessimism. "No battle is ever won," he says in *The Sound and the Fury*, "They are not even fought. The field only reveals to man his own folly and despair, and history is an illusion of philosophers and fools." [2] In *Soldiers' Pay* he insists that "we learn scarcely anything as we go through this world, and that we learn nothing whatever which can ever help us or be of any particular benefit to us, even." [3] "Breath is to a man but to want and fret a span," [4] he continues. "We are here to work.

---

[1] Hicks, Granville, "The Past and Future of William Faulkner," *The Bookman* (September, 1931), LXXIV, 17.

[2] Faulkner, William, *The Sound and the Fury* (1929), p. 93.

[3] Faulkner, William, *Soldiers' Pay* (1926), p. 69.

[4] Faulkner, William, *A Green Bough* (1933), p. 26.

It is either sweat or die. Where is there a law requiring we should be happy?" [5]

He has been compared, in his zest for the cruel and morbid, to Robinson Jeffers, the California poet. But Jeffers' deeds of crime, perversion, and sadism are symbols that lift us above the deed, while Faulkner's never transcend the level of bare perception. There is nothing, we feel, behind his atrocities, no cosmic echo; each gamy detail exists for itself alone, and seems to be designed more to "thrill" the reader than to awaken his conceptual faculties. Jeffers has a genuine vision of evil, as a principle of existence; Faulkner uses it merely as a false face, which he dons to frighten people. He refuses to believe that "The only legitimate 'shock' in the field of prose is the shock of unexpected truth." [6]

SAVAGERY AMONG THE HONEYSUCKLES Faulkner was born September 25, 1897, in New Albany, Mississippi. His ancestral background included governors, statesmen, and generals; and one of his grandfathers had been a popular author of Southern romances. In Oxford, Mississippi, he went to high school, and 1918 found him in France with the British Royal Air Forces. After the Armistice he spent two years at the state university, and then returned to Oxford, where he lives today on his own farm. In 1925 he worked his passage to Europe on a freighter; stayed there for about eight months, chiefly in Italy; and met Sherwood Anderson, upon whose suggestion he began to write fiction (an interesting fact when we remember that Hemingway, too, was encouraged by Anderson). Faulkner had already published a volume of pastoral verse called *The Marble Faun* (1924), but *Soldiers' Pay* (1926), his first novel, strikes out more fiercely, betrays the influence

[5] Quoted in Smith, Marshall L., "Faulkner of Mississippi," *The Bookman* (December, 1931), LXXIV, 417.

[6] Gerould, Katharine F., "Stream of Consciousness," *The Saturday Review of Literature* (October 22, 1927), IV, 234.

of the war upon him, and concerns a tragically mangled aviator, Donald Mahon, who comes back home to Charleston (Georgia), his unfaithful sweetheart, and a world quivering with baffled lust, death, and moral disintegration. *Mosquitoes*, a sophisticated book that came out in the next year, deals with a coterie of artists and social climbers on a yacht party lasting several days, and satirizes, in the manner of Aldous Huxley, the buzzing banality of these cognoscenti. With *Sartoris* (1929), however, Faulkner repeated his theme of the discharged soldier, who in this volume returns to Jefferson, Mississippi, with his mind unbalanced by the war, tries to kill himself two or three times, and finally does end his life in an airplane crash, thus bringing to a close the wild adventures of a desiccated Southern family.

The Sound and the Fury (1929) also treats of a diseased, imbecilic group; one of this household is an idiot, another is a prostitute, and a third commits suicide. In *As I Lay Dying* (1930), which its author considers his best work, he has chronicled the macabre journey of a shiftless insane family, as they cart a putrefying corpse halfway across the state to bury it. *Sanctuary* (1931), intentionally penned as a "hair-raiser," records a vicious rape by an impotent moron, as well as a lynching; and *Light In August* (1932) features the castration of its hero, a mulatto named Joe Christmas, who, by way of concluding an ugly affair with a middle-aged white woman, murders her. Between these last two novels there appeared a collection of stories, entitled *These Thirteen* (1931); and in 1933 Faulkner published his second book of verse, *A Green Bough*, which rustles with A. E. Housman, "e. e. cummings," and poetical clichés, and elegizes Philomel, dead kings, Lilith, and nymphs with a pagan, Elizabethan touch. His latest book, *Doctor Martino* (1934), is a group of fourteen short stories.

Faulkner's volumes, both in prose and verse, are singularly void of philosophy, apart from the implication that

one must devour life in order to be safe from it. He is
more occupied with experiments in the narrative structure
of his novels. *The Sound and the Fury*, for example, borrows
part of its method from the "stream-of-consciousness"
school, and bases some of its episodic quality upon a modern tendency (best exemplified in John Dos Passos) to construct a blended picture out of successive fragments and
non sequiturs.

Nobody else there but her and me. If we could just have done
something so dreadful that they would have fled hell except us.
I have committed incest I said Father it was I it was not Dalton Ames
And when he put Dalton Ames. Dalton Ames. Dalton Ames.
When he put the pistol in my hand I didn't. That's why I didn't.
He would be there and she would and I would. Dalton Ames.
Dalton Ames. Dalton Ames. If we could have just done something so dreadful and Father said That's sad too, people cannot do
anything that dreadful they cannot do anything very dreadful at
all they cannot even remember tomorrow what seemed dreadful
today and I said, You can shirk all things and he said, Ah can
you. And I will look down and see my murmuring bones and
the deep water like wind, like a roof of wind, and after a long
time they cannot distinguish even bones upon the lonely and
inviolate sand. Until on the Day when He says Rise only the
flat-iron would come floating up. It's not when you realise that
nothing can help you — religion, pride, anything — it's when
you realise that you dont need any aid. Dalton Ames. Dalton
Ames. Dalton Ames. If I could have been his mother lying
with open body lifted laughing, holding his father with my hand
refraining, seeing, watching him die before he lived. *One minute
she was standing in the door* [7]

With Anderson and Hemingway, he is the highly conscious architect of plot and style, working like Poe to freeze
the reader's blood. But when his floating point of view
and "stream-of-consciousness" are employed to describe the
mental associations of an idiot, as they are in *The Sound*

[7] *The Sound and the Fury*, pp. 97–98.

and the Fury, he becomes more incoherent than Joyce, whose presence is often felt in his pages.

To Faulkner the novel is a problem in art and fictional strategy, rather than a transfiguration of wisdom. He cultivates, not so much the inherent values of action or character, as their expression. For his skilful manipulation of words he has been highly praised. And it cannot be denied that his style is both vivid and original, the two qualities that impressionism always seeks to embrace. He is Crane brought up to date, with sex added; and his language is clever and dappled, writhing, luscious, and coagulated with sensory appeals.

The violet dusk held in soft suspension lights slow as bell-strokes. Jackson square was now a green and quiet lake in which abode lights round as jellyfish, feathering with silver mimosa and pomegranate and hibiscus beneath which lantana and cannas bled and bled. Pontalba and cathedral were cut from black paper and pasted flat on a green sky; above them taller palms were fixed in black and soundless explosions. The street was empty, but from Royal street there came the hum of a trolley that rose to a staggering clatter, passed on and away leaving an interval filled with the gracious sound of inflated rubber on asphalt, like the tearing of endless silk.[8]

There is something Swinburnian in his flow of prose, and his first novel, *Soldiers' Pay*, is one long "purple passage," composed of such units as "The sky, so remote, so sad, spurned by the unicorns of gold, that, neighing soundlessly from dusk to dawn, had seen them, had seen her — her taut body prone and naked as a narrow pool sweetly dividing: two silver streams from a single source."[9] His style is a vehicle for transporting sound, motion, and color, but not meaning. Like Anderson, Faulkner's reply to existence is a drifting, emotional one. Even when he utters such words as Death, Sex, Time, and Beauty, he seems to

[8] Faulkner, William, *Mosquitoes* (1927), pp. 14–15.
[9] Faulkner, William, *Soldiers' Pay* (1926), p. 196.

do so with an esthetic and sophisticated rather than moral purpose, using them more to lend a dark beat to his lines than to create an ethical frame of reference. In his employ they become ornamental, not elemental words. What he has to say is that there is nothing to say. A windy melancholy tosses in his pages, lighted here and there with firefly phrases. Nihilism, the only philosophy apparent in Faulkner, is as much an implication of his style as his treatment of character. He belongs to the perennial school of Poe, Crane, and Ambrose Bierce. All of them deal with terror, pain, violence, and degeneration; and all of them are expert technicians. Yet their roots do not go far down into life, do not draw their strength from the wells of being as Dostoievsky's do when he treats of sickness, death, and horror. In the truly great novel, whether gentle or tragic, goodness and evil use each other as sounding boards, reflect significance upon each other, and produce a third element, that sense of life's wonder, which marks all authentic literature and evokes a variety of religious awe in the reader. But in Faulkner's circumscribed world of sensation, evil goes round and round with its tail in its mouth; and as a result, his books lack what might be termed "spiritual resonance."

DEAD END   The popularity of such volumes as Faulkner's *The Sound and the Fury*, Vardis Fisher's *In Tragic Life* (1933), and Kay Boyle's *Plagued by the Nightingale* (1931) is founded, in part, upon the tendency of our neurotic age to read sweetness into cruelty, freaks, and self-inflicted wounds. Few readers peruse Faulkner to learn what disposition he has made of communal questions, or what synthesis he has devised of emotion and reason. His stories treat of death only as death, not as a phenomenon with universal overtones; and the incidents of his novels have no moral momentum for carrying them over from the concrete into the abstract, from fact into symbol. Under the pressure of economic unrest and spiritual confusion, we seem to be passing from an extrovert period into an introvert one. And Faulkner's morbidity is a symptom of this change.

Crane, Norris, London, Dreiser, Anderson, Hemingway, and Faulkner have all missed the best spirit of naturalism. The first three mistook it for a love of power, and ended in Dreiser's skepticism (which, in his case, is not a preparation for knowledge but a denial of it); Anderson drove it just as far inward as Dreiser had pushed it outward; while Faulkner and Hemingway have tried to elude both extremes by courting nihilism. Faulkner, therefore, does not stand for a perfected naturalism, but for a kind of blind alley into which it has wandered.

As a matter of fact, it is doubtful whether any one can hope to develop naturalism any farther along the lines marked out by Faulkner. "Those who play the game of *frisson nouveau* find that its stakes are continually rising; each must raise his predecessor's ante." [10] But who can outbid *Sanctuary*, without defeating his own purposes? If naturalism goes much farther in the direction of diablerie and the gruesome, it will become a parody of itself, and like parts of Erskine Caldwell's *Tobacco Road* (1932) step over into the ridiculous. For just beyond horror lies humor.

The vital tradition of naturalism, which is at heart broad in its sympathies and warm in its "passionate recognition" [11] of life, cannot rest upon such a specialized, reptilian art as that of Faulkner's; it requires thought to justify its style and meaning to adorn its emotion. It should be a "mansion of philosophy," invigorating as well as vigorous, and a source of inspiration for all those who draw their values from Nature rather than Man, not a haunted house, dark and cold, inhabited only by spiders and morons.

[10] Thompson, Alan Reynolds, "Sanctuary: A Review," *The Bookman* (April, 1931), LXXIII, 188.

[11] Soule, George, "Realism as Confession," *The New Republic* (August 19, 1916), VIII, 64.

* BEYOND LIFE

To look fate into the eyes makes one sicker;
One gladly would shake off broodings on sorrow, —
Find makeshift escape from thought of the morrow.
Hence some use lies and some use liquor;
And we — well, we used the fairy tales told
Of princes and trolls and beasts manifold.
Of bride-reaving, too!

HENRIK IBSEN

SINGERS OF AN EMPTY DAY

∗

FAREWELL TO FREEDOM   America woke up to the fact, about 1890, that it was being strangled to death by two forces, (1) the "tightening grasp" of Nature, and (2) the tentacles of "big business."   Haeckel and Darwin had razed the old universe, and presented us with a new one, from which religion, morals, immortality, and pity had been stringently ejected.   Nature, a blind vortex of atoms, protoplasm, and raw energy, had taken over the scepter of God.   Man, no longer the "captain of his soul," had been wedged into a parasitic circle of plants and animals, victims and victors.   Deprived of an independent mind, he found himself embroiled in a "struggle for existence," governed by a web of causes and effects.

The naturalist, laced into this straitjacket of natural law, decided to accept the modern world of science and take things as he found them.   Nature, he insisted, could develop its secret plans without human or divine interference.   Man's duty was to recognize in his instincts the signals of Nature, and obey them, wherever they led.   He should also forfeit the idea of ethical perfection, and abandon such chimeras as sympathy, chivalry, patriotism, charity, purity, generosity, altruism, honor, justice, courtesy, loyalty, truth, and conscience.   They were only "crutches," invented by weaklings to help them bear life and hamstring their masters, the strong.   It was just as reasonable to suppose that anarchic Nature might be heading toward a system based on the virtues of the praying mantis as toward one which embraced these feeble devices or the prescriptions of Christ. But whether man wished to believe this or not, he had no choice; sans free will, he would have to espouse the theory of *laissez faire*, and play "follow the leader" with Nature.

BLUE MONDAY   It is to this concept that the novels of Crane, Norris, London, Dreiser, Anderson, Hemingway, and Faulkner are radial; and yet long before *laissez faire* had entered our fiction, it had made itself at home in economics. American business men saw in Darwin and Spencer only a philosophical confirmation of practices they had already set in motion. During The Gilded Age (1865–1890) trade had been placed entirely in the hands of Nature, to be worked out by the natural process of supply and demand. No efforts were made to restrain commercial enterprise; and for a time, misled by increasing prosperity and the fact that those who felt dissatisfied with this arrangement could always go West, America made no complaint. But after the depression of 1873 a wave of disappointment swept the country. In 1890 it was discovered that cheap land out West was almost exhausted, and discontent gave way to panic.

The closing of the frontier was a tragic factor in our history, an incident that has determined, to a large extent, the vanishing morale of America. So long as we could "run away," the hardships of a plutocratic civilization might be endured, and even smiled at. However, when it became necessary to stand and "face the music," to suffer the burden of growing poverty among the urban working classes, to watch the *nouveau riche* lighting their cigars with hundred dollar bills, to see our pristine land tainted with smoke and grime, to realize that the whole tempo of modern life was being adjusted to the pace of swift machines, and to smell the fumes of political graft everywhere, men began to feel quite definitely that in the zone of happiness a period of diminishing returns had ensued, and to agree with E. L. Godkin (founder of *The Nation*) that ours had surely become a cheap, ugly "chromo civilization."

In 1893 the Columbian Exposition at Chicago, with its theatrical splendors, opened on the eve of a great railway strike and the march of Coxey's Army. A change began to drift over the spirit of our dream. No false display of wealth could hide the true situation. Legislation had become a rank exchange of favors; and if the sentiment of "In God We Trust" still existed, it was only on the dollar. God had been shouldered aside by Mammon, just as He had been crowded out of philosophy by Science. Workingmen scowled at the perfumed tribe known in metropolitan society as "The Four Hundred." Curses were let fly at the "gold bugs" of the East, Wall Street, and the "trusts." That optimism long associated with America was being rapidly dispersed. Now it served only as a deodorant. The eagle of liberty had begun to moult; and many sacred precepts of American belief were suddenly found to be counterfeit. A few of them have recently been listed by Ernest Sutherland Bates:

1. Freedom of speech (illustrated by laws restricting it in thirty-one states).
2. Government by the people (illustrated by Tammany, the Republican machine in Pennsylvania, etc., etc., etc.).
3. Free education for the masses (illustrated by the instance of Southern Negroes).
4. Equal opportunity to rise (illustrated by the instance of six million unemployed).
5. Honesty is the best policy (illustrated by the history of the railroads, Standard Oil, Public Utilities, etc., etc., etc.).
6. The sanctity of the home is the basis of our civilization (illustrated by our divorce rate).
7. We are a God-fearing people (illustrated by the decline of our churches).
8. The rights of children must not be put in jeopardy (illustrated by child labor).

9. We are a peaceful people (illustrated by our spending more on armament than any other nation).
10. No entangling alliances (illustrated by our policy of foreign loans).
11. Competition is the life of trade (illustrated by corporations, trusts, and mergers).
12. Respect for law and order (illustrated by gang warfare in every large city).[1]

Nervousness was heightened by the plight of the farmer. Freight rates, grain speculators, and rent had almost reduced him to a state of peonage. And despair was accentuated by the fact that thirty per cent of the people in this country had shifted to the city. From 1850 to 1900 our population had increased over fifty million; immigration had risen alarmingly; our natural resources were approaching an end; corporations had seized a monopoly of business; high tariffs were being levied for the benefit of a few key industries, to the detriment of the consumer; financiers were invading politics through a back door; and our currency system had fallen out of joint. Civil liberties were being violated; "third degree" methods were put to use by the police, free speech was curtailed, professors were discharged for propagating "unpopular" ideas, and radicals were deported. School textbooks were being filled with propaganda, chiefly patriotic. The birth rate was sinking, the divorce rate was soaring; women were going from the home into offices and factories, parental control over youth was relaxing, and the automobile and restaurant were weakening family ties. In morals the old criteria had been eaten away by a hedonistic philosophy based on science. The "yellow peril" was lifting its head in California. The South had taken a tip from its conqueror and begun to change from an agricultural to an industrial section; our last citadel of aristocracy, the plantation, was giving way to a new aristocracy of wealth.

[1] Schmalhausen, Samuel D. (ed.), *Our Neurotic Age* (1932), p. 444.

There was a biological assimilation of the immigrant that alarmed many, who feared that the future American might turn out to be a dark, stunted individual if this racial dilution continued.   In 1900 there were still six million illiterates in this country.   Fights were raging over temperance, feminism, and the Negro; and upon some of our most talented spirits there had fastened a dawning misanthropy that may be found reflected in the last stories of Mark Twain and *The Education of Henry Adams* (1907).

RUNAWAYS FROM REALITY   But not every American writer in 1890 became a naturalist, participated in the tumult aroused by "rugged individualism," resigned himself to *laissez faire*, and consented to the amputation from life of its illusions.   Though harried from the earth by science, chivalry and beauty and honor continued to thrive in history and fantasy; and nothing could prevent men from returning to imagination and the past, in order to be with these outlawed sentiments again.

To many for whom science thus seemed to establish the essential meaninglessness of all existence and all striving, the ivory tower of art furnished the only solace and refuge.   Only in discerning beauty in the passing show, since all action is beyond our power, and we must do as the eternal laws of nature bid us, can man find that which will make his existence worth while and lift him above the brute.   For many a despairing soul during the last few generations, it has seemed that man's hopes can rest only in the ideal world of beauty; and aestheticism has proved the natural way of life in the Alien World.[2]

A few novelists, disgusted by the sordid materialism and ugliness of this country, left it to pursue in foreign environments a fairer climate of intellect and propriety.   Bret Harte fled to Scotland, F. Marion Crawford to Italy, Stuart Merrill (the poet) to Paris, and Henry Harland to London, where he became an associate editor of the notori-

[2] Randall, John Herman, *The Making of the Modern Mind* (1926), p. 568.

ous *Yellow Book*. Lafcadio Hearn, another of these expatriates, went to Japan in 1891, taught English at the University of Tokyo, married a Japanese wife, became converted to Buddhism, and wrote a number of volumes on Nipponese folk lore. And James Huneker, with others, escaped into Murgerism.[3]

Some of those in whom romance died hard turned to art and decadence for solace. Carl Van Vechten, for example, tried to surprise in "art for art's sake" a substitute for reality. Many esthetes, hypnotized by the *Yellow Book* and Petronius's *Satyricon* (then being introduced to America), wavered along with Edgar Saltus in the wake of those European diabolists, Oscar Wilde and Baudelaire, flirted with pagan religions, tasted of vicarious vice, fashioned a protective coloration from "the rouge of life," and alienated themselves by sophistication from their vulgar habitat. But other writers, less interested in the purely orchidaceous, turned to such types of "escape" fiction as: the "folksy" story (by Booth Tarkington out of Edgar Guest); the "hammock" book, a sparkling cocktail of young love, exchanged wedding rings, or the *haut monde;* tales of "adventure"; the "detective" or "mystery" story, a ghoulish type of "subway reading" (now creating what might be termed a literary crime wave); the "historical" novel, which deserts the present for customs and costumes of a time long dead; and "romance," a variety with a strong tincture of the "unreal."

THE SEARCH FOR ELSEWHERE   It is not an easy task to diagnose the philosophy of naturalism. Dreiser and Hemingway even deny that they believe anything; and Anderson, instead of reasoning, just broods. The naturalist abhors consistency, and seems bent on purifying his own

[3] Another name for Bohemianism, derived from Henri Murger, who was one of the first to interpret the *vie de Bohême* in his *The Latin Quarter* (1901). For a study of this phenomenon in America, see Parry, Albert, *Garrets and Pretenders*, Covici, Friede, 1933.

remarks of it. He is fond of delusive gestures and emotional detours. Very often he does not know where he is going or what he is talking about, in spite of the fact that he always winds up by saluting *laissez faire*, the noble savage, and "return to Nature." Escapism, however, is a different matter entirely. There are few barriers in the way of sounding out its purpose, which is merely to play truant from this world of "fact and fatality," by dreams or other methods. The escapist, whose stomach is not tough enough to digest naturalism, refuses to abide in a milieu empty of *fables convenues*. Poetry and life, he feels, beauty and reality, "are irreconcilably opposed to each other, and he for his part is on the side of poetry and the 'ideal.' " [4] He bolts the workaday scene, pretends that he is living in a more congenial age or clime, and "makes believe" that the older glories of man and America have not been eclipsed by newer and less enchanting ones. In the words of Montaigne, he has decided that "To abandon life for a dream is to appraise it at its true value." "Buttering his bread with dreams," he spins out

> A shroud of talk to hide us from the sun
> Of this familiar life which seems to be
> But is not — or is but quaint mockery
> Of all we would believe.[5]

His days are trances, a mélange of comfortable pretenses, masking his environment in the cosmetics of fancy. He is one who has "hitched his wagon to a star," who in every adversity runs (not walks) to the nearest exit. "Dreamer of dreams," he argues,

> born out of my due time,
> Why should I strive to set the crooked straight?
> Let it suffice me that my murmuring rhyme
> Beats with light wing against the ivory gate,

[4] Babbitt, Irving, *Rousseau and Romanticism* (1919), pp. 84–85.
[5] Shelley, Percy Bysshe, *The Complete Poetical Works of Percy Bysshe Shelley* (1901), p. 393.

> Telling a tale not too importunate
> To those who in the sleepy region stay,
> Lulled by the singer of an empty day.[6]

Like Hans Vaihinger, author of *The Philosophy of "As If"* (English translation, 1924), the escapist believes that man must construct for himself a fictional copy of the world. This "fictional copy" will not be an accurate transcription of reality; but since he has made it himself, he will be able to move familiarly about in it, to feel at home and at peace in it, something he is not able to experience in real life. He must seek what Élie Faure has termed an "organizing illusion," and act "as if" he had a free will, "as if" we possessed a soul, "as if" there were a God, "as if" the cult of "business efficiency" and "time is money" had not plowed under many of our loveliest traditions. For the sake of beauty and expediency he must operate upon delusional concepts, upon hypotheses and deliberate errors; because to his mind the sentiments that make life sweet, "or at any rate tolerable, spring from a falsehood and are fed on illusions." [7]

[6] Morris, William, *The Earthly Paradise* (1872), p. 2.
[7] France, Anatole, *The Garden of Epicurus* (1923), p. 22.

*

THE JOURNEYS OF JURGEN

*

SANCTUARY   Of this whole tendency, James Branch Cabell is perhaps the best and most comprehensive instance.   He itches to escape from this pedestrian world, this crass Suburbia.   "It is because he is terrified at the meanness of what practical men call reality, that Mr. Cabell turns away from it to find the true life in dreams." [1]   As he says in *The Cream of the Jest:*

I find my country an inadequate place in which to live. . . . Oh, many persons live there happily enough! or, at worst, they seem to find the prizes and the applause of my country worth striving for whole-heartedly.   But there is that in some of us which gets no exercise there; and we struggle blindly, with impotent yearning, to gain outlet for great powers which we know that we possess, even though we do not know their names.   And so, we dreamers wander at adventure to Storisende — oh, and into more perilous realms sometimes! — in search of a life that will find employment for every faculty we have.   For life in my country does not engross us utterly.   We dreamers waste there at loose ends, waste futilely.   All that we can ever see and hear and touch there, we dreamers dimly know, is at best but a portion of the truth, and is possibly not true at all.   Oh, yes! it may be that we are not sane; could we be sure of that, it would be a comfort. But, as it is, we dreamers only know that life in my country does not content us, and never can content us.   So we struggle, for a tiny dear-bought while, into other and fairer-seeming lands in search of — we know not what! [2]

[1] Parrington, Vernon Louis, "The Incomparable Mr. Cabell," *The Pacific Review* (December, 1921), II, 359.
[2] Cabell, James Branch, *The Cream of the Jest* (1920), pp. 31–32.   By permission of Robert M. McBride & Company.

It is the business of the author, Cabell has declared, "to tell untruths that will be diverting," to charm away the cares of man and render him insensible to tedious circumstances. "He temporarily endows his followers with the illusion of possessing what all alchemists have sought, — unfading youth, wealth, and eternal life. He engineers the escape for which men have always longed." [3] The artist writes to evade boredom, and to season vexatious things more to his palate. "Man lived, for the major part of his conceded time," as one might put it, "a meagre and monotonous and unsatisfying existence: this he alleviated by endlessly concocting fictions which be-drugged and diverted him." [4]

Since his birth in Richmond, Virginia, on April 14, 1879, Cabell has taught French and Greek at William and Mary College (1896–1897), worked on newspapers in Richmond and New York, contributed stories to magazines, done original research in genealogy, and written almost thirty books of fiction, essays, and verse, among them *The Eagle's Shadow* (1904), *The Line of Love* (1905), *Gallantry* (1907), *The Cords of Vanity* (1909), *Chivalry* (1909), *The Soul of Melicent* (1913), *The Rivet in Grandfather's Neck* (1915), *The Certain Hour* (1916), *From the Hidden Way* (1916), *The Cream of the Jest* (1917), *Beyond Life* (1919), *Jurgen* (1919), *Figures of Earth* (1921), *The Lineage of Lichfield* (1922), *The High Place* (1923), *Straws and Prayer-Books* (1924), *The Silver Stallion* (1926), *The Music from Behind the Moon* (1926), *Something About Eve* (1927), *The Way of Ecben* (1929), *These Restless Heads* (1932), and *Special Delivery* (1933). *Branchiana* (1907) and *Branch of Abingdon* (1911) are studies of his own ancestry. *From the Hidden Way* is an adaptation of poetry from doubtful Old French sources. *These Restless Heads* and *Special Delivery*, together with *Straws and Prayer-*

---

[3] Cabell, James Branch, *Straws and Prayer-Books* (1924), p. 69. By permission of Robert M. McBride & Company.
[4] *Ibid.*, pp. 280–281. By permission of Robert M. McBride & Company.

Books and *Beyond Life*, are saucy critiques of present-day standards and "realism." And his latest book, *Smirt* (1934), which he has subtitled "An Urbane Nightmare," is an excursion into the land of dreams. The rest of these volumes make up units in Cabell's lengthy saga of rogues, which he has given the inclusive title of "Biography."

His Biography is constructed on the outlines of a fugue, with recurring situations and personalities, to indicate the "interchangeable symbols of the changeless desires of men." In this opus he tilled again that field of synthetic romance already worked by Maurice Hewlett in his *Forest Lovers* (1898) and *Richard Yea-and-Nay* (1900). The scene of its earliest action is laid mainly in Poictesme, a mythical and medieval country along the Mediterranean, bounded on the west by Nimes, on the east by the town of Castres, on the south by Asia Minor, and on the north by Arthurian England. But some of its later installments take place in the eighteenth century, and a few in the modern and fictitious city of Lichfield, Virginia.

Poictesme is a land inhabited by fiends, beautiful damsels, magicians, dragons, gnomes, dryads, the rakhna, and centaurs. The ruler of this province is Dom Manuel, a swineherd who rises to be Count of Poictesme, and turns into a kind of Redeemer after his death. His children, the heroes and heroines of subsequent parables, are reincarnations of Manuel and of Jurgen, the progenitor of a secondary cycle in the Biography. Manuel is supposed to be the man of action, Jurgen the man of intelligence; and Dorothy la Desiree, Melicent, Hovendile, Gerald Musgrave, Felix Kennaston, Robert Etheridge Townsend, and others are their spiritual progeny. The complete story, as a matter of fact, embodies an intricate tissue of relationships not easy to understand, and Cabell, realizing this, has supplied the reader with a family tree of Manuel and his descendants in *The Lineage of Lichfield*.

In this land of Poictesme he has built himself a sanctuary, hatched a microcosmic world of magic, knavery, and imagination, and become a citizen of it. "There are those," notes a recent critic, "and Cabell is one of them, who simply cannot face life as it is. Their means and methods of escape are many and varied and, sometimes, strange. Occasionally they have, like Cabell, creative ability. There is, for example, the actual instance of the man who felt compelled to do nothing but construct small models of cities. The models were of no practical value but, having made them, their creator was able to escape into them. The laying out of the streets, squares, parks, and public buildings satisfied in some measure their maker's sense of beauty and of pattern. In time these fancied cities grew so real to him that he lived only in them, and gradually lost touch altogether with the world about him. He succeeded in escaping. Cabell is not unlike him." [5]

The motif of his novels is a simple and constant one. "Cabellian heroes, in pursuit of a vision, journey into the unknown and after a series of erotic and esoteric adventures, find that the vision is unattainable; then, as grim reality comes back to take possession, they resign themselves to settle down to enjoy the irony of a fate which makes the elusive Unreal the only and abiding Real." [6] "There is but one fable," pronounces Cabell, "which holds true everywhere. The man goes upon a journey: that is all." [7]

You are all bound on one journey, which you begin in diapers and finish in a shroud. You journey from the cradle to the schoolroom and so to the puzzled ardors and the blundering desires of your prime. You journey thence toward the more sedative workaday life of offices and counting houses and courts of law and quiet libraries; you journey toward the farther side of official

[5] Farrar, John (ed.), *The Literary Spotlight* (1924), pp. 178–179.
[6] Hooker, Edward Niles, "Something About Cabell," *The Sewanee Review* (April, 1929), XXXVII, 194.
[7] Cabell, Branch, *These Restless Heads* (1932), p. 219. By permission of Robert M. McBride & Company.

desks and of typewriters and of shop counters: so do you journey
perforce from out of your youthfulness toward one or another
means of earning that daily food which will sustain you to continue journeying. You journey toward marriage and parent-
hood, goaded after the manner of beasts by the blind and irresist-
ible instincts of a beast. You journey toward fattening wits and
more sluggish senses and the stigma of public approval, now
that you journey as a well-thought-of citizen. Though the
vigor and desire die out of you like guttering candles, do you old-
sters yet pluck up heart, and know that you still journey quite as
speedily as may the alert young, in the while that you all journey
together toward a black door with silver-plated handles. And at
no moment of your journey is there any pausing as you travel
upon that part of a highway which you have never trodden before
and are not ever again to revisit.[8]

But he is not content to accept the ordinary ending of fairy
tales in which the hero, returned from his quest, lives "happily ever after." Instead, he prefers to remember that
"aged Jason was killed by the falling of a tree, and that the
last exploit of gray Theseus was to tumble over a cliff."   I
recall, he says, "that both Heracles and Odysseus were accidentally poisoned in late middle life — the one with a
second-hand shirt and the other with the scratch of a fish-
bone." [9] His hero always ends up as a responsible house-
holder; his husbands are all foiled poets, lured back to the
hearth and finally domesticated. Bent on escaping "the
asphalt ways of conformity," they are jerked back from
dreams to wear out their years as respectable mediocrities.
For in Cabell's work there is a good deal of irony, of that
variety common to poets who "kill the thing they love,"
and gnaw at their own hearts. Early in his career he
struck upon

a formula expressed perfectly in the figure used by Jean Paul
Richter to describe his own novels, and first applied to Cabell by
Carl Van Doren: hot baths of sentiment alternating with cold

[8] *Ibid.*, pp. 214–216. By permission of Robert M. McBride & Company.
[9] *Ibid.*, pp. 207–208. By permission of Robert M. McBride & Company.

douches of irony.   Mr. Cabell ridicules sentiment, but only after
having revelled in it.   This device of emotional somersaults is
appropriately called romantic irony, because it is the revulsion
of the author's intelligence against his own romantic sentiments,
and because it thus differs essentially from the classic irony which
is based on the objective observation by a normal individual of
extravagances in others.[10]

In *The Cream of the Jest* the questing hero is Felix Kennaston, an author who dreams himself into one of his
stories as the thwarted lover of Etarre, the Ageless Woman.
Coming back to "real" life from this fictional world, he
happens upon a small half disk of burnished metal, similar to the "broken sigil of Scoteia" given to him as a
token by Etarre during his revery.   He returns to Lichfield, Virginia, with its mean bromidic routine, and to his
faded materialistic wife, but continues to dream of Etarre
and fondle the sigil.   Each night he goes on strange metem-
psychosic tours.   But with the dawn he is once again just
an impotent misfit, declining toward old age; and in the
end, he finds that his talisman is only the top of a cold cream
jar.   His dream, therefore, has played him false, and this
is the "cream of the jest."

The Music from Behind the Moon tells of Madoc, young
court poet to Netan, the High King of Marr and Kett, and
of how he tries to flee from a confusing music that haunts
his songs, a melody sent by Etarre from a prison behind the
moon in which she is being held.   He rescues the witch,
and escorts her down to earth, but in time discovers that
she has turned into a chronic scold; and both forget their
love of music under the burden of children, rheumatism,
and increasing years.   The same thing occurs in *Jurgen*,
where a henpecked pawnbroker, after a mental holiday
spent in visions of black magic, demons, and "sexquisite"
women, comes back to his shrewish wife, the bubble pricked

[10] Thompson, Alan Reynolds, "Farewell to Achilles," *The Bookman*
(January, 1930), LXX, 468.

and his spirit resigned to compromise with the common-place.

MASQUERADE In his style Cabell has tried to capture an atmosphere of medievalism and Latinity. Yet in spite of its effective correspondence to his themes, it has been the object of too much simpering praise. His Biography is written in a tricky anachronistic prose, which gives off "light rather than heat," [11] and suffers from an addiction to lingual and orthographic japes or symbolisms. Even in his use of language, Cabell is a cabalist; many of the proper names in his work are said to be anagrams, like these in *Something About Eve:*

> Caer Omn — Romance
> Doonham — Manhood
> Lytreia — Reality
> Turoine — Routine
> Land of Dersam — Land of Dreams

His narratives are decked out with romantic moonshine, scholiastic hocus-pocus, and such pedantic words as sic-cative, ventripotent, and mundivagant. It is a kind of "left handed" style, that smells of the lamp and outworn masquerades. So much time does Cabell waste in intro-ductory gambits and fake quotations that many readers are apt to desert him without troubling to sieve out the gist of his literary *hors d'œuvres.* He is continually "winding up" to deliver a pitch that (if it does appear) never seems worth its gusty preliminaries. There is also his monotonous habit of beginning every fifth or sixth sentence with "for," and his practice of ending every other paragraph with ellipsis marks. But it is only fair to add that his last three volumes (in which he has pruned his name to Branch Cabell) display signs of an improved style and healthier dexterity of wit.

Cabell has pickled the fruits of his philosophy between the covers of *Beyond Life.* Nature, he believes, guides man, not

[11] Beach, Joseph Warren, *The Twentieth-Century Novel* (1932), p. 85.

by his instincts (as the naturalist holds), but by his dreams, and by putting his wits to sleep with such "dynamic illusions" as womanly beauty, etc.   Temporarily blinded by the mistaken notion that the lady of his choice represents a deathless love, man finds himself trapped into marriage and used by Nature to produce a new generation.   It is not a happy trick, but Cabell seems to feel that it is a wholesome one.   "The philtres of romance," he says,

are brewed to free us from this unsatisfying life that is calendared by fiscal years, and to contrive a less disastrous elusion of our own personalities than many seek dispersedly in drink and drugs and lust and fanaticism, and sometimes in death.   For, beset by his own rationality, the normal man is goaded to evade the strictures of his normal life, upon the incontestable ground that it is a stupid and unlovely routine; and to escape likewise from his own personality, which bores him quite as much as it does his associates. So he hurtles into these various roads from reality, precisely as a goaded sheep flees without notice of what lies ahead. . . .

And romance tricks him, but not to his harm.   For, be it remembered that man alone of animals plays the ape to his dreams.   Romance it is undoubtedly who whispers to every man that life is not a blind and aimless business, not all a hopeless waste and confusion; and that his existence is a pageant (appreciatively observed by divine spectators), and that he is strong and excellent and wise: and to romance he listens, willing and thrice willing to be cheated by the honeyed fiction.   The things of which romance assures him are very far from true: yet it is solely by believing himself a creature but little lower than the cherubim that man has by interminable small degrees become, upon the whole, distinctly superior to the chimpanzee.[12]

Most of Cabell's "stag and stallion" stories can be reckoned as a thumbing of the nose at those authorities who in 1920 haled *Jurgen* into court for its alleged indecency. His patience is highly offended by prudes.   In the words of Henry Seidel Canby, he is "a talented gentleman who has

[12] Cabell, James Branch, *Beyond Life* (1919), pp. 355–357.   By permission of Robert M. McBride & Company.

lost his temper " [13] and decided to bait his prosecutors by writing about "the ultimate cause of population" in elegant phrases that cannot be proved to have an inelegant meaning. Because of this aim, he inclines toward a refined phallicism, *double entendres*, and "fescennine" expressions. He has, or thinks he has, been driven "to make a pose of his indecencies, to sophisticate them, elaborate them, conceal them, play with them, until it is not the human quality but the craftsmanship, not the humor but the challenging fact, not the truth but the exhibitionism, which asks for attention." [14]

In this purpose he has been abetted by most critics. Whereas it was once unfashionable to tolerate sexual innuendoes in fiction, it has now become popular to accept everything. The benefit of the doubt once lay with the reader in the case of books suspected of pornography; now it lies with the author. Dreiser, Anderson, Bodenheim, and Cabell have all been made martyrs as a result of charges levied against them by ubiquitous vice societies; and the publicity accruing from such attacks has solidified many of these novelists in their contempt for the ordinary reader, tripled their royalties, and left reviewers afraid to object to anything. The average critic has turned into The Great Appreciator, intent only on playing safe, on finding significance in our age (whether it is there or not), and on justifying modern fiction to himself. But what we really need is a small boy to exclaim, "Why, these kings are naked!"

UNDER TWO FLAGS Cabell's fame has no doubt been injured by the preference of readers today for books dealing with contemporary problems. In an age when volumes of non-fiction are selling with a new vigor, and treating of such topics as science, marriage, Russia, sex, and technoc-

[13] Canby, Henry Seidel, "Something About Fig Leaves," *The Saturday Review of Literature* (October 29, 1927), IV, 250.
[14] *Ibid.*

racy, his dreams of an enchanted and watery fairyland must lose some of their earlier appeal. Yet perhaps another reason for his waning vogue is that he has lately given up his revolt against social tabus, virginity, monogamy, Mrs. Grundy, and "the practical man," and joined the ranks of those "philistines" he formerly despised. Once he insisted that "should monogamy ever become prevalent among us, we should be deliberately abating one of the more considerable pleasures of an existence wherein pleasures are not over-frequent." [15] Today he has drawn the teeth of all his previous arguments, and destroyed the entire foundation of his work, by going over to the enemy, and saying:

It is better to be content. It is better to be content with the dear, common happenings of human life, shared loyally with the one woman whose love for me is limitless and does not change, for all that it is blind to none of my failings. It is the part of wisdom to know that these things are enough and very far beyond my deserts. It is the part of an honest husband not ever to be insanely hankering after any more high-hearted manner of living, which is out of my reach, or, at any rate, is attained through more trouble than it is probably worth. And in the cordial glow of his own hearth-fire each one of us discovers by-and-by that the middle way of life is best. [16]

Jurgen has come home.

[15] *Straws and Prayer-Books*, p. 88. By permission of Robert M. McBride & Company.
[16] *These Restless Heads*, pp. 139–140. By permission of Robert M. McBride & Company.

*

COSTUMES BY HERGESHEIMER

*

SUCCESS STORY   A few other romances that, like *Jurgen*, try to escape "the ache of the actual" are Christopher Morley's *Where the Blue Begins* (1922), the puckish fable of a dog who leads, instead of "a dog's life," the career of an idealistic gentleman in search of far horizons; Robert Nathan's dulcet fantasies, *The Puppet Master* (1924) and *The Fiddler in Barly* (1926); Donn Byrne's *Messer Marco Polo* (1921), which Cabell has said is "the only contemporary book that ever I actually sought the privilege of reviewing"; [1] and Elinor Wylie's *Jennifer Lorn* (1923).

Yet the only escapist whose reputation seems to be equal to that of Cabell's is Joseph Hergesheimer, author of *The Lay Anthony* (1914), *Mountain Blood* (1915), *The Three Black Pennys* (1917), *Java Head* (1919), *Linda Condon* (1919), *Cytherea* (1922), *The Bright Shawl* (1922), *Balisand* (1924), *Tampico* (1926), *The Party Dress* (1930), *The Limestone Tree* (1931); four volumes of short stories, *Gold and Iron* (1918), *The Happy End* (1919), *Quiet Cities* (1928), and *Tropical Winter* (1933); *Swords and Roses* (1929), a book of *belles-lettres; San Cristóbal de la Habana* (1920), a description of Cuban social life; *A Presbyterian Child* (1923) and *From an Old House* (1925), autobiographical notes; *Sheridan* (1931), a biography; and *Berlin* (1932), the record of a trip through Germany and Austria.

Hergesheimer, the son of Pennsylvania Dutch parents, was born in Philadelphia, February 15, 1880.   Due to poor health, his youth was necessarily an idle one.   He read

[1] Cabell, James Branch, *Straws and Prayer-Books* (1924), p. 57.

paper-bound love stories and Ouida, attended a Quaker school in Germantown (where he did not shine), and later entered the Philadelphia Academy of Fine Arts to study painting.   At twenty-one he inherited a bit of money, went to Italy, stayed there until his funds were depleted, and came back.   On his return he began keeping "low company," until one day, after helping a popular authoress "read proof" (and noting the wretchedness of her work), he decided to take a flyer in literature himself.   Retiring with a broken typewriter to the hill country of Virginia, he produced a tale, rewrote some parts of it a hundred times, and gave it up as a bad job.   It was fourteen years later, after an interval of steady endeavor, that he sold his first manuscript. But since then his stories have brought him at least $500,000 from the *Saturday Evening Post* alone; and in 1922 he won a *Literary Digest* poll as "the leading American novelist."   Today he resides with his wife at West Chester, Pennsylvania, in a stone mansion furnished with antiques, travels widely, wears silk, and smokes only the most expensive Havana cigars.

EARLY AMERICAN   *The Lay Anthony*, his earliest volume, has been summarized by Hergesheimer as the story of "a boy's purity — in a world where that quality is a cause for excruciating jest."   It records the "temptations" of Anthony Ball, a young man tortured by problems of sex and disgusted by the moral poverty of his home town.   He meets a girl named Eliza, conceives for her a Petrarchean kind of love, nurses it with scrupulous care during two years that he is forced to spend away from her, keeps his armor bright, returns to find Eliza dead, and loses his life in a bawdy house. "He had a vision of purity," says the author, "as something concrete, something which, like a priceless and fragile vase, he guarded in his hands.   It had been a charge from her, a trust that he must keep unspotted, inviolable, that she would require — but she was gone, she was dead." [2]

[2] Hergesheimer, Joseph, *The Lay Anthony* (1919), p. 304.

Hergesheimer's second novel, *Mountain Blood*, has for its locale the mountains of Virginia, and for its hero a stage driver, Gordon Makimmon, who, in avenging an insult to a girl, has drawn upon himself the reprisal of a creditor. Forced to pay up his debt in order to save the house where he lives with his invalid sister Clare, he raises the amount by gambling, but has to use it to send Clare to the hospital for an operation. His job is taken from him, the house is sold at public auction, and Clare dies. Then by a trick he marries the daughter of the richest man in that section. Their marriage, however, is not successful, and lured by the torso of Meta Beggs, a mercenary school mistress, he plans to run away from his pinched wife, Lettice. The latter's death upon learning of his perfidy arouses him to his mistake, and feeling that he must make amends, he decides to use his wealth in helping his townsmen; but his motives are misinterpreted, he loses everything, goes back to his old job of driving the stage, and dies in an accident. The theme of this novel, explains Hergesheimer, is "the failure of an aged man to repair a spiritual wrong with gold."

In *The Three Black Pennys* Hergesheimer has traced the history of a strange, passionate family. He shows us first Howat Penny, son of a Pennsylvania ironmaster in the eighteenth century, a tempestuous spirit afraid of being caged by conventions, who instinctively

resisted every effort to make him a part of any social organization, however admirable; he never formed any personal bonds with humanity in particular. He had grown into a solitary being within whom were immovably locked all the confidences, the spontaneous expressions of self, that bind men into a solidarity of common failings and hopes.[3]

Howat's mad Welsh blood, the "black" blood of the Pennys, drives him into an affair with another man's wife, which his "rugged individualism" defends against every moral con-

[3] Hergesheimer, Joseph, *The Three Black Pennys* (1917), p. 7.

sideration, until at last he is rewarded by the husband's death. Jasper, the second of this dark breed, acts out his part in the nineteenth century. But his ancestor's strength of purpose burns with less ardor in him, and in trying to break off with a mistress whom he no longer loves, he makes a mess of his life. The third Penny, also named Howat, is a twentieth-century lawyer wooed from his profession by a bemused taste for beauty. Dead is the wild streak. The metal of the generations of Pennys has been "refined to the point of producing an immaculate dilettante, accustomed to a gentle leisure," [4] and the "black" blood has run thin.

Java Head is a drama of Salem during Polk's administration. The Ammidon family, around which the story revolves, consists of Grandfather Jeremy, an old salt and hardy Federalist, wrapped in dreams of past adventure; his son William, a junior partner in the Ammidon shipping business, and an advocate of certain progressive methods (like clipper ships and opium trading) to which his father, doubting their honor, is opposed; William's wife Rhoda; their four girls; and Gerrit, the younger son of Jeremy, who has, like his father, a lingering veneration for the older ways, and who has chosen, instead of a land job, to follow the sea. At the opening of the book Gerrit is on his way home from China; but when he arrives, it is found that he has brought with him a Chinese wife, Taou Yuen. Salem, unable to appreciate her Manchu birth, regards her as a heathen, a situation which she faces with a wise and inscrutable patience that bears her above every indignity, and serves Gerrit, too, as an antidote against his native town. Then her new world begins to break in pieces. Edward Dunsack, a sardonic wastrel and opium addict, is mastered by a passion for her; Jeremy dies, crushed by the flow of time that he cannot impede; and Gerrit himself is caught between his admiration for Taou Yuen and his love for Nettie Vollar,

---

[4] Kelley, Leon, "America and Mr. Hergesheimer," *The Sewanee Review* (April-June, 1932), XL, 178.

a pitiful outcast. But everything is solved by Taou Yuen, who, learning of her husband's affection for Nettie, stoically commits suicide, in order to escape Dunsack's lust and release Gerrit.

The principal character of *Java Head* is always this quiet daughter of the East. By pure simplicity of spirit, she finds "her way to beauty and to the preservation of her own exquisite serenity — first through all the deviousness of social Salem, against the background of the Ammidon's commercial greatness and general prestige; then through the complications of an astounding intrigue of which she becomes, innocently, the center. Clinging faithfully in her bewilderment to the few simple ideals of conduct which scores of generations have bred into her blood as well as her mind, maintaining to the end the poise of her own fatalistic philosophy, she gives a sense of living exclusively with fundamentals and essentials, in the midst of a society preoccupied with trivial externals. It is she, the alien, who lives at the center of the life she has entered, working her way with a patient simplicity to the core of its realities, while the others, the indigenes — even Gerrit the individualist and rebel — live, by comparison, unreally and at the fringe of things, making motions they hardly know the sense of. They exist, as it were, from hand to mouth, letting the effect achieved in one moment supply the conduct of the next, exactly like a realistic novel; whereas Taou Yuen is living, at every moment, as for eternity." [5]

Linda Condon is the story of a girl reared in a cheap, kaleidoscopic world of resorts, hotels, velvet, jewels, and scented luxury, a child with a passion for beauty and perfection. Her early years are spent in a materialistic atmosphere, which numbs her spirit and obstructs the realization of her ideals. But later on she meets a sculptor, who, thwarted of her love, models her secret charm into

[5] Follett, Wilson, "Factualist Versus Impressionist," *The Dial* (May 3, 1919), LXVI, 450.

a product of his genius, and discovers in her his inspiration. So that at last each is enabled to find in this bronze masterpiece some compensation for his or her losses in real life.

The hero of *Cytherea* is Lee Randon, a forty-seven-year-old broker, soured by the passing of his youth. On a trip to New York he sees a doll in a window, endows it with the name Cytherea, and keeps it in his thoughts as an emblem of Venus, the goddess of love. Weary of his aging wife, and yearning "to escape from life, from the accumulating limiting circumstances" and conventional proprieties in which he feels he has been snared, he runs away to Cuba with Savina Grove, a married woman, whom he has got mixed up in his mind with the doll, Cytherea. But Savina dies, and Randon is left conscious that he has been tricked by his dreams, just as the heroes of Cabell are duped by Etarre, the illusion of deathless romance. From the slavery of a hypocritical existence he has been dragged down into spiritual impotence, a new slavery worse than the old.

The Bright Shawl concerns a young American, Charles Abbott, who goes to Cuba for his health (just before the War of 1898); gets entangled in the Cuban fight for independence; worships a dancer, La Clavel; barely escapes after her death, minus even the bright red shawl that he had meant to keep as a token of their passion; and ends up as a middle-aged bachelor, alone with his memories, and puzzled by the emotional inertia and cynicism of our "lost generation."

In *Balisand* Hergesheimer wrote a novel that partakes of his best talents. It is the story of Richard Bale, a Virginia colonial, jealously devoted to George Washington during those days of hot dispute after the Revolution, when Federalist and Jeffersonian engaged in fierce debates over the question of democracy. Bale was an aristocrat, a member of the Continental Congress, a sensitive gentleman, disturbed by the growth of sedition in America and living in the past as Abbott did in *The Bright Shawl*. He falls in love with Lavinia, the fiancée of Gawin Todd, a member of Jefferson's rising party and an enemy to the Tory ideals of the old Virginia planters. Gawin challenges him to "pistols for two," but before the event Lavinia is killed and the duel is called off. The second half of the book pictures Richard nine years later, still dreaming of Lavinia. He marries Lucia Mathews, a young gentlewoman, instead of trying to re-enter Congress and compete with Gawin, whose political star is now in the ascendant. After Jefferson is elected in 1800, the story closes with the defeat of the Federalists and Bale's death in a duel at the hands of his old enemy Gawin.

Tampico describes the decline and fall of Govett Bradier, a rather shady *entrepreneur* in the oil game, who returns to the scene of his earlier triumphs in Mexico for further operations. There he becomes involved in a liaison with Vida Corew, wife of another official in his company. Her husband is killed, and Bradier discovers that he does not love her after all. In the end he is shown on his way back to the United States, a relic (like so many of Hergesheimer's characters) of a more heroic age that has been overwhelmed by time and newer devices.

The Party Dress, which deals with Mina Henry, her husband Wilson, and their swanky Eastlake Country Club set, is an invertebrate body of references to "dresses by Ishtarre," bath soaps, roses, Lalique atomizers with gilt tops, diaphonous handkerchiefs, China crêpe drawers, feathered garters, champagne, jeweled wrist watches, cracked ice, rum swizzle, kisses in a corner, naked bathing parties, the tango, golf, frothy conversation, marital defections, and people who are "sick of being decent."

Hergesheimer's latest novel is *The Limestone Tree*. Another chronicle of "mountain blood," it traces the fortunes of an old Kentucky family from about 1769 to 1890. But its flow is choked by tufts of historical data, local color, and genealogical lore; and it is not probable that many readers will agree with its author when he says, "I like *The Limestone Tree* better than anything else I have ever done."

CABELL AND HERGESHEIMER   From this synopsis of Hergesheimer's work, certain points of resemblance between his novels and those of Cabell stand out.   Both are glad that they have been spared, as Hergesheimer puts it, "the dreary and impertinent duty of improving the world."   What they are most interested in is flight from an America that does not satisfy them; and in this discontentment they are joined by Louis Bromfield (another "expatriate"), now living in France, whose four novels *The Green Bay Tree* (1924), *Possession* (1925), *Early Autumn* (1926), and *A Good Woman* (1927) bear the collective title of *Escape*, exhibit a deep respect for sensuous beauty, and unfavorably contrast the accoutrements of life in America with the culture of Europe.[6] Hergesheimer's volumes recall with affection the decayed gentility of colonial America and the Old South.   They are never quite without that jasmine fragrance so noticeable in Stark Young's *Heaven Trees* (1926), or Glenway Wescott's nostalgia, in *The Grandmothers* (1927), for our pioneer virtues of bravery, dignity, and "love of life," which have always seemed to Hergesheimer to be heroic facts.   "To recall them," he has said, "stirred me with a fine revivifying emotion, and what I had hopes of was by them to stir others."[7]

Cabell, in his private life, has surrounded himself with tomes of medieval romance, Hergesheimer with early American furniture, in an effort to perpetuate bygone glories and build an asylum for their spirits.   Both select, for their characters, men and women who are aristocrats, if not always in breeding, at least in bearing.   Neither is very

[6] See Field, Louise Maunsell, "Louis Bromfield: Novelist," *The Bookman* (April, 1932), LXXV, 43–48.   Of *The Farm* (1933), his latest book, Mr. Bromfield has said, "It was an escape for me all the time I wrote it."   The New York *Herald Tribune* (Sunday, October 22, 1933), I, 17.

[7] Hergesheimer, Joseph, *From an Old House* (1925), p. 92.

much pleased with our modern, three-ring circus age of soda fountains, Al Capones, "Service-with-a-Smile," chain stores, speakeasies, Florida booms, Amos 'n Andy, ballyhoo, flagpole sitters, marathon dancers, bathing beauty contests, murder trials, ticker tape, cross-word-puzzles, bunion derbies, Ford cars, beauty parlors, "The Bringing Up of Father," Hollywood, sheet music, Tammany, the Ku Klux Klan, "the hero racket," bureaucracy, skyscrapers, noise, miniature golf, Scopes trials, transatlantic flights, wine bricks, installment plans, censorship, and patent medicines, an age that Hergesheimer calls "a different, an inferior, a threatening period." [8] "If I write a great deal about our earlier America," he says, "I do that because I prefer the relief of its hushed, its quiet, life to the loudness around me." [9] "I don't care a whoop about the world in general. My interest is all for and in relation to my own chosen little world in particular." [10]

Both Hergesheimer and Cabell lament the hostility of our realistic generation to sentiment, and regret the passing of such values as serenity, gallantry, self-sacrifice, loyalty, individualism, beauty, and tradition. They write their stories with a threnodic pen, and seek in fiction a means of refuge. They believe, not so much in "art for art's sake" as in art for the sake of diversion. Says Hergesheimer, "An imaginative book, as Mr. Cabell has so often made clear, is a way of escape for its author." [11] Both are fond of ceremony. Cabell delights in the secret rituals of magic, Hergesheimer in the social formalities of aristocracy; for etiquette of any kind has the effect of setting man

[8] Quoted in Kelley, Leon, "America and Mr. Hergesheimer," *The Sewanee Review* (April-June, 1932), XL, 176.

[9] Hergesheimer, Joseph, "James Branch Cabell," *The American Mercury* (January, 1928), XIII, 41.

[10] Quoted in Phillips, Henry Albert, "A Novelist's Uphill Road," *The World Today* (July, 1928), LII, 152-153.

[11] Hergesheimer, Joseph, "James Branch Cabell," *The American Mercury* (January, 1928), XIII, 39.

at one remove from the material reality of things, and protecting him from the chafed surface of events.

All the stories of Hergesheimer are constructed upon the lines of a quest; his formula is the same as that of Cabell's, the search for something "beyond life." Both are after the remote ideal; each makes "the old gesture toward the stars." Hergesheimer's characters are "ultra romantics, content to hang their world upon a single hair. Their lives are governed not by a complication of interests, a balance of values, but by one interest, one value, alone. They are lonely dreamers, haunted by a vision of strange beauty, for whose sake they would consider the world well lost. Even where they are shown immersed in all manner of affairs, we know that they are nursing some secret desire or some burning remembrance that alone keeps the blood stirring in their veins." [12] "Nearly all the men in Mr. Hergesheimer's books are hag-ridden by one or another sole desire which spurs them toward a definite goal at every instant of their mimic lives." [13] They are Jurgens, family men, and poets at heart, men like the three Pennys, Lee Randon, and Gordon Makimmon, who reach "the dangerous age" of middle years, decide to escape from a life that they feel is ugly and unworthy of them, worship " the slow arrow of Beauty," and end up in the frustration of Cabell's Felix Kennaston.

AN OPTIC WORLD   What they appear to be striving for is the beauty that still enhances certain ideals now obsolescent in our modern age of science. "Where beauty is concerned," notes Hergesheimer, "the standards of the past must remain valid." [14] Yet despite this apparent interest of his in *le beau ideal*, his real interest is in physical, rather

[12] Squire, J. C. (ed.), *Contemporary American Authors* (1928), p. 192.

[13] Cabell, James Branch, "In Respect to Joseph Hergesheimer," *The Bookman* (November-December, 1919), L, 267–268. This article, in a more mature form, was later reprinted as part of *Straws and Prayer-Books*.

[14] Quoted in Kelley, Leon, *op. cit.*, XL, 174–175.

than psychical, beauty.   Notwithstanding the "lip service" paid by his characters to various forms of lost *spiritual* beauty, he seems to be more intent upon the beauty of *things*, more devoted to material loveliness than character, more concerned with intensity of experience than wisdom, goodness, or peace.   "The continuous minor tragi-comedy of workaday existence has no real place in his fiction.   His narratives do not depend upon the clash of character, the stealthy encounter of opposing motives, the comedy that waits upon the interplay of personalities," [15] or the solution of economic and social problems.   He slights the meaning of his drama for its background or scenery; and many of his heroes, instead of symbolizing an abstract beauty, serve him as mere "clothes horses."   Their beauty is only skin deep. His women, for instance, are just "troublingly ornamental odalisques . . . fine costly toys, tricked out in curious tissues: and, waiting for the strong man's leisure, they smile cryptically. . . . Sometimes they are embodied ideals, to be sure, remotely prized as symbols or else grasped as trophies to commemorate the nearing of the goal: but for the most part they rank candidly as avocational interests." [16]

Thus it is that they remain in our memories not as living people but as bright pictures, the brightest in a world of bright pictures. The most impressive of them all is the most fantastic, Taou Yuen, that Manchu lady who brought her little painted face, her gorgeous robes, her elaborate ceremonials, among the startled crinolines of old Salem; and what is she but a figure created out of silk and lacquer and porcelain?   La Clavel, in "The Bright Shawl," is simply that shawl touched, in a dream, with a fleeting kind of feminine life.   Savina Grove is only the doll Cytherea made life size, wound up and set going until it collapses, with a whir of wheels, under the brazen sky of Cuba.[17]

[15] Squire, J. C. (ed.), *op. cit.*, pp. 182–185.
[16] Cabell, James Branch, "In Respect to Joseph Hergesheimer," *The Bookman* (November-December, 1919), L, 268.
[17] Squire, J. C. (ed.), *op. cit.*, pp. 197–198.

The novels of Hergesheimer are Whistleresque studies in color.   One critic has even termed *Java Head* "An Arrangement in Gold, Black, Drab, Scarlet, Blue Laws, Blue Water, Opium, Happy Childhood, and Chinese Poetry."   And the rest of Hergesheimer's volumes, which "flash and glitter like so many fricasseed rainbows," [18] might be classified in the same way.   He has brought to literature a painter's eye; he is absorbed, not so much in his heroes or the concepts they represent, as in their "optic world."   "The years in which I had failed to be a painter," he has said, "naturally left me with an enormous interest in surfaces; I used words precisely in the way I had used colours, striving for the same effects." [19]   In consequence his pages wear the devitalized aspect of "a painted ship upon a painted ocean." He is "delighted with colors and shapes and textures, the more luxurious the better. . . . Opening his 'Linda Condon' almost at random, we are asked to remark, in two pages, 'morocco beauty-cases and powder-boxes,' 'slipper and garter buckles extravagant in exquisite metals and workings,' 'limousines with dove-coloured upholstery and crystal vases of maidenhair fern and moss-roses,' 'black chocolates from painted boxes ruffled in rose silk,' 'a restaurant of Circassian walnut and velvet carpets,' 'eggs elaborate with truffles and French pastry.'   We begin to feel slightly dizzy and sick.   In such passages the still-life painter and the lover of mere luxury and magnificence join hands, with a somewhat unfortunate result." [20]

His people are rendered from complexion to coat-tail buttons, and the reader is given precisely the creasing of the forehead and the pleating of all underlinen.   Mr. Hergesheimer's books contain whole warehousefuls of the most carefully finished furniture in literature; and at quaint bric-à-brac he has no English equal.   It is all visioned, moreover, very minutely.   Joseph Hergesheimer

[18] Nathan, George Jean, "Hergey," *The Borzoi, 1925* (1925), p. 142.
[19] *From an Old House*, p. 38.
[20] Squire, J. C., (ed.), *op. cit.*, p. 185.

makes you observe his chairs and panelings and wall-papers and window-curtains with an abnormal scrutiny.[21]

Beauty is always the key to Hergesheimer, but it is a superficial beauty, the beauty of objects rather than values.[22] An easy emotionalism, a tendency of his heroes to be stifled by their feelings, and a tropicality of style have taken possession of him. His protagonists simply burn with that "hard gemlike flame" which Pater said was "success" in life; and words have turned upon him (as they did on Anderson) and gulped him up. Prose in his books has degenerated into a species of adjectivitis, a pure "torrent of mobile chimeras," with a purpose that seems to be largely decorative. His desire to escape from an empty world has led him into an even emptier one, marked not by degrees of good and evil but by gradations of sensory poignance. In evading the real he has arrived at the theatrical, not the unreal or ideal. The cardboard stage he has set for his drama has absorbed the actors. Though charming, it lacks the vivifying presence of a moral symbolism. His beauty does not penetrate beyond the eye, and has nothing to say to the heart or mind, no carrying power. Paint does not turn into spirit on his canvas; it remains a thin film of gorgeous but inanimate color, uninhabited by that vital mingling of sense and sensation so necessary to important and significant art.

[21] Cabell, James Branch, "In Respect to Joseph Hergesheimer," *The Bookman* (November-December, 1919), L, 271.

[22] A fact particularly evident in his stories on China, Pewter, Glass, Maple, Oak, Silver, and Walnut that he wrote for *The Saturday Evening Post* in 1923 and 1924.

✳ NEW WORLDS FOR OLD

God is merely Humanity with a crown on.
FREDERIC HARRISON

*

LITERATURE INSURGENT

*

THE AGE OF GUILT   After 1890 social conditions in America
reached a new low.   The Gilded Age had defaulted on its
promises to pay, and we seemed to be entering an "Age of
Guilt."   A confederation of domestic evils had opened fire
upon the average man; and democracy found itself en-
circled (like Childe Roland) by many dangers.

The "state of the nation" was enough to freeze the bravest
heart.   A treaty had been signed between capitalism and
the government.   State and municipal politics crawled
with graft; and "vested interests" darkened party councils.
Bribery was rampant, and in New York City, the "tiger"
of Tammany walked arm in arm with the underworld.
Many national scandals had been exposed, as for instance,
the Crédit Mobilier, the Tweed Ring, the "Star-Route"
frauds, the Whisky Ring, and the Belknap case, which
involved Congressmen, a Secretary of War, and even the
honor of a President.

"Frenzied Finance" had triumphed, by an insolent
decimation of our natural resources, by intrigues, and by
combinations in restraint of trade.   Honest men had been
seduced, newspapers "bought," and lawyers "retained" to
help concentrate wealth in the hands of a favored few.   A
passion for lucre ruled business, a kind of gold fever.   Obese
companies fed upon their weaker kin.   Great industrial
dinosaurs, such as Jay Gould, William H. Vanderbilt,
Collis P. Huntington, James J. Hill, John D. Rockefeller,
Andrew Carnegie, William A. Clark, and Philip D. Armour,
savagely clawed one another, imported cheap labor from

abroad to drive down wages, manipulated the money market to wring a profit from their debtors, evaded taxes, participated in "land grabs," stamped out the lives of farmers and factory workers in their giant duels, and dictated prices by means of protective tariffs. As for the State, it had come to act only as a "passive policeman," for the purpose of safeguarding private property. "Let business work itself out by the natural laws of competition," said the Goulds and Rockefellers. "*Laissez faire.* Hands off." Yet at the same time, they were seeking land grants and subsidies from Congress, and forming monopolies that actually had the effect of voiding competition. On Mondays, Wednesdays, and Fridays, they warned the government not to interfere with trade; and on Tuesdays, Thursdays, and Saturdays, they asked for State aid. In familiar parlance, they were "playing both ends against the middle."

As one astute humorist observed in 1897, the crowning work of our age was "th' cash register." America, to quote Bryan, was being "crucified on a cross of gold." Dividends were going up, and wages were going down. The "full dinner pail" had not materialized; men were starving in the midst of plenty. And to evidence of revolt on the part of an aroused working class, employers replied with "black lists," armed thugs to break up strikes, European labor, "scabs," blanket injunctions against picketing, and spies. Labor was fast becoming a chattel; and by 1921 men would be sold like slaves on an auction block in New York. Quantity production had begun in 1901, together with large-scale advertising. Strikes paralyzed the country, and were accompanied by rioting and bloodshed. In several industrial centers, street fighting occurred, and brought with it tragedy and property loss. The moral and cultural poverty of America that drove Cabell and Hergesheimer to "escape" from it was matched by an economic poverty. Two-thirds of all male workers over sixteen received less than $12.50 a week; one-tenth of the people owned nine-tenths of the wealth; and queues of hungry men stood in lengthening bread lines. It was growing apparent that Lincoln had not freed the slaves, or at least not all of them.

The Populist Party, in 1892, described the situation as follows: "Corruption dominates the ballot box, the Legislatures, the Congress, and touches even the ermine of the bench. The people are demoralized. Many of the States have been compelled to isolate the voters at the polling-places in order to prevent universal intimidation or bribery. The newspapers are subsidized or muzzled, public opinion silenced, business prostrated, our homes covered with mortgages, labor impoverished, and the land concentrated in the hands of capitalists. The urban workmen are denied the right of organization for self-protection; imported pauperized labor beats down their wages; a hireling standing army, unrecognized by our laws, is established to shoot them down, and they are rapidly degenerating into European conditions. The fruits of the toil of millions are boldly stolen to build up colossal fortunes unprecedented in the history of mankind, and the possessors of these in turn despise the Republic and endanger liberty. From the same prolific womb of governmental injustice we breed the two great classes — paupers and millionaires." [1]

The tools man had invented to subdue the wilderness, his railroads and corporations, were now mastering him; the machine, as a weapon in the service of capital, had begun to degrade taste, ruin craftsmanship, focus riches, rob men of work, encourage waste, and delete man's self-reliance. Big business had become "an organized appetite," instead of a power for the good; and "To many thoughtful men in the opening years of the twentieth century it seemed that America in making her fortune was in peril of losing her soul." [2]

[1] Watson, Thomas E., *The People's Party Campaign Book, 1892*, pp. 123–124.
[2] Faulkner, Harold Underwood, *The Quest for Social Justice* (1931), p. 81. By permission of The Macmillan Company, publishers.

THE MAN WITH THE HOE   Agriculture, too, was having its troubles; the farmer, like the laborer, was about to go down for the third time.   After the Civil War, migration had begun again into the West and Northwest.   The "middle border" was rapidly settled by unemployed factory hands from the East, demobilized soldiers, and hordes of immigrants.   Lured by the "ballyhoo" of railway promoters and land speculators, and panting for a home of their own, they staked out claims, reared their large families, and planted their corn or wheat.   Hope embroidered their dream, optimism colored the air they breathed, and they envisioned in the frontier a rich country of peace and plenty, a "new Eden."

But this mirage soon melted away when they found, to their sorrow, that the railways had not tempted them westward for nothing.   Freight rates were pushed sky high on them, almost at once; it became cheaper, with corn selling at ten cents a bushel, to use it for fuel than to ship it anywhere; and down in Kansas they were saying that it was about time to "stop raising corn and start raising hell." Nor had the "land sharks" invited them to the frontier out of pure altruism.   Many of the homesteads had to be rented from absentee landlords in Europe and New York, who had "sneaked in on the ground floor" and secured huge chunks of western America from the government (by fraud or favor) which they in turn leased out to tenants.   By 1900 over a third of all farms in the United States were being tilled in this way, and mortgages on rural property amounted to more than a billion dollars.   As the economic value of the frontier rose under cultivation, an "unearned increment" flowed into the bulging pockets of a few men in silk hats, either in the form of rent or interest on loans.   In most cases a non-resident owner was waiting back East,

to reap profits from the increase in the value of the lands through the development of society and the growth of population.   He was making no improvements, buying no goods in the stores, shouldering none of the burdens of the new society — except the payment of taxes. He was actually excluding people from settlement except at his own terms by holding his lands out of use.[3]

The farmer was being "milked," and yet to an extent, he had brought this misfortune upon himself; for his intense pioneer individualism prevented him from organizing, his greed for land often drove him to borrow more than he could repay, and he continued to vote shyster lawyers into office, instead of men from his own group. Droughts, cyclones, and insect plagues swept across the open plains, laid waste to crops, and brought ruin to "the middle border." The hounds of dismay were on hope's traces; the "new Eden" had been visited by the snake; the "promised land" had turned out to be a desert.

To solve this problem of agriculture, Henry George wrote his celebrated *Progress and Poverty* (1879), in which he developed the idea of a "single tax" that would take from the bloated landlord the privilege of profiting from the sweat of others. And Hamlin Garland, called "the first actual farmer in literature," soon began to introduce George's theory into a series of novels and sketches. Joseph Kirkland had already described, in his *Zury* (1887), the way one man's character had been destroyed by "the struggle for existence" in Illinois; and Edward Eggleston had penned, in *The Hoosier Schoolmaster* (1871), a story of backwoods Indiana. But Garland's fiction, though influenced by these two books, was a more severe indictment of the situation than either. He believed, as Henry George did, that agrarian despair proceeded from an unjust land system, and felt with Rousseau that "Nature is not to blame. Man's laws are to blame."

"The lives of these farmers are hard," he wrote. "They wear filthy clothing the year round. I hear no words of affection in their homes. All is loud, coarse, but rudely

[3] Quick, Herbert, *The Hawkeye* (1923), p. 21. Used by special permission of the publishers, The Bobbs-Merrill Company.

wholesome. They fear to be polite. They consider it a weakness. They are all packhorses and they never lay down their burdens. No wonder the boys are discontented and that the girls marry early. No beauty, no music, no art, no joy — just a dull and hopeless round of toil." [4] His *A Spoil of Office* (1892) was a story of Iowa during the Granger movement of the nineties; *Jason Edwards* (1891) told of a mechanic who went West to seek in Boomtown, Dakota, an escape from the industrial rigors of Boston, only to find death and bitterness; "Up the Coolly," in *Main-Travelled Roads* (1891), voiced an inflamed protest against those circumstances that forced some men to drudge like animals in dark barnyards, and gave to others the decent comforts of existence; "Under the Lion's Paw," in the same volume, pictured the average tenant farmer, knee deep in mud and mortgages; and *A Son of the Middle Border* (1917), which is autobiographical, traced the pioneer spirit in its dying fall "from hope to hopelessness."

More recently, other novelists have taken up the tragic theme of Garland's work. The destitution (moral and financial) of the frontier has been reported in Mr. and Mrs. Haldeman-Julius's *Dust* (1921), the drab landscape of a Kansas farm. Herbert Quick's *Vandemark's Folly* (1922), *The Hawkeye* (1923), and *The Invisible Woman* (1924), form a trilogy of early Iowa from about 1857 to the end of the century, when the farmer's sun was setting in clouds of "single tax" controversy. Martha Ostenso's *Wild Geese* (1925) provides an instance of how frontier frustrations corroded the human qualities of a few Scandinavian home-steaders in the Northwest. Dell H. Munger's *The Wind before the Dawn* (1912) is a study of hard times on the Kansas prairie, of man's conflict with drought, grasshoppers, and mortgages, and of barren lives. G. D. Eaton's *Backfurrow* (1925) pictures rural melancholy in Michigan, with force

---

[4] Garland, Hamlin, *Roadside Meetings* (1930), pp. 114–115. By permission of The Macmillan Company, publishers.

and finesse. Vardis Fisher's *Toilers of the Hills* (1928) depicts the struggle of a man and his wife amid the dry wastelands of Idaho. Walter Muilenburg's *Prairie* (1925) is another novel of hardships in the West. Cornelia James Cannon's *Red Rust* (1928) relates the fight made by a young man against poverty and wheat rust in Minnesota. And O. E. Rölvaag's *Giants in the Earth* (1927) dramatizes, with epic "surge and thunder," the heartsick aspirations of a band of Norwegian settlers in Dakota Territory, who have severed their spiritual and physical ties with the homeland to grow up in loneliness and tragedy on the frontier. All these, and others, treat of the moral stagnation and material privation that brutalized life on "the middle border" after 1870, and ask again, in regard to Markham's "The Man with the Hoe" (1899):

> Who made him dead to rapture and despair,
> A thing that grieves not and that never hopes,
> Stolid and stunned, a brother to the ox?
> Who loosened and let down this brutal jaw?
> Whose was the hand that slanted back this brow?
> Whose breath blew out the light within this brain? [5]

THUNDER ON THE LEFT   Even literature had become a "trust" by 1890. With money everywhere in power, it was hardly safe for magazines and newspapers to print material that might damage the *status quo*, however much they might want to. Advertisers would boycott magazines that included incendiary articles or fiction among their pages; and editors were forced to use "the soft pedal." Manuscripts were picked that would not scare away "Business," or offend "home and fireside" readers. Radicalism and sex were outlawed. "The facts of life," either in morals or economics, were not allowed to reach "the masses." Though many great captains of industry had discarded ethics, it was considered best to let the proletariat linger on

[5] Markham, Edwin, *The Man with the Hoe* (1931) p. 16.

in the belief that ethics still existed. "Polite" fiction was left
to consist mainly of "moral pap for the young," as Louisa
May Alcott described her own stories; and the effete
romance of Crane's youth held sway. The public was
carefully "spoon fed" on the work of such foreign novelists
as Dickens, James Barrie, Conan Doyle, Charles Reade,
Wilkie Collins, George Eliot, Kipling, and Stevenson,
because they did not deal with American questions of social
justice, and because books already published in Europe could
be copied and sold here without the payment of royalties.

But in 1891 an International Copyright Act put a stop to
this trick of "pirating," and opened up the market for native
authors. The novel of protest could at last become articulate; and before the century's end, the holy league of "slick
paper" periodicals in the East, like *Harper's*, the *Atlantic*,
Scribner's, and the *Century*, had been broken. Patrician and
mildewed magazines ("safe as a graveyard, decorous as a
church, as devoid of immorality as an epitaph")[6] were being
challenged by other journals more hospitable to problems
of the day, to the "advance guard" of socialism, to sexual
candor, and to experimentation. There arose a number of
brochures, the *Chap-Book*, founded in Chicago; *The Lark*,
edited in San Francisco by Gelett Burgess; and *The Philistine*, Elbert Hubbard's venture in East Aurora, New York,
whose combined purpose, as Burgess expressed it, was to

overthrow the staid respectability of the larger magazines and
to open to younger writers opportunities to be heard before they
obtained recognition from the autocratic editors. Their outbreak was a symptom of the discontent of the times, a wide-felt
protest of emancipation from the dictates of old literary tribunals.[7]

New publishing houses sprang up, Stone and Kimball in
Chicago, Bobbs-Merrill in Indianapolis, and The Arena

[6] Walker, Franklin, *Frank Norris* (1932), p. 146.
[7] Quoted in Walker, Franklin, *Frank Norris* (1932), p. 136. See also
Bragdon, Claude, "The Purple Cow Period," *The Bookman* (July, 1929),
LXIX, 475–478.

Publishing Company in Boston, to which rebels like Hamlin Garland could turn. The literary center of America had shifted from Boston to New York; and a liberal press, given almost entirely to social opinion, soon began to growl out "thunder on the left." *The Nation*, since 1865, had been urging "The maintenance and diffusion of true democratic principles in society and government," and in 1911 it was joined by *The Masses*, "a monthly magazine devoted to the interests of the working people" and "the co-operative side of Socialist activity." *The New Republic* appeared in 1914, under the editorship of Herbert Croly, to advocate "sound and disinterested thinking"; in 1920 *The Freeman* came out, in order "to meet the new spirit of inquiry which recent events have liberated, especially in the field of economics and politics"; *The Modern Quarterly* made its bow in 1923, edited by V. F. Calverton, and dedicated "to scientific synthesis — the co-ordination of the discoveries and conclusions of the life and physical sciences into an accurate and comprehensive sociology"; and in 1926, *The New Masses*, a more revolutionary journal than any of the others, issued its first volume.

NEARER TO THE HEART'S DESIRE   The years from 1890 to 1934 were more than a period of sick disappointment. America became, during that time, more sternly aware of the need for reform, more conscious of itself, and more definitely criticial of those factors in its social body that hinder progress. The first realization that *laissez faire*, as a way of life, was not going to redeem its promises of universal prosperity froze America in its own despair. Many deserted to the enemy, a few (who could) ran away, and the rest were almost convinced, for a while, that our plutocratic system had got itself too firmly entrenched to be ousted. But by 1890 the forces of hope and insurgency were in the saddle, and reconstruction had finally begun.

The end of the last century saw an awakening interest in

social reform throughout the whole of western civilization. Men of all countries seemed to feel as Matthew Arnold did, when he said, "Our present social organization has been an appointed stage in our growth; it has been of good use, and has enabled us to do great things. But the use is at an end, and the stage is over." What Arnold, a conservative, had declared in restrained tones, other men, suffering heavier abuses of fear and hunger, were echoing in louder and angrier voices. Agitation for reform was on the up grade. In England there were such leaders as William Morris, Arnold Toynbee (whose name was given to the first great settlement in London), and William Booth, founder of the Salvation Army; in Germany, Karl Marx and Friedrich Engels had fostered their International Workingmen's Association; in Norway, Henrik Ibsen was attacking bourgeois hypocrisies in a series of problem plays; in Russia, Tolstoy was declaiming the brotherhood of man and Peter Kropotkin was being exiled for spreading revolutionary propaganda; and in America, Jane Addams was starting Hull House. Churches were establishing rescue missions; Pope Leo XIII was issuing his encyclical *On the Condition of Labor* (1891); George Bernard Shaw was betraying social wrongs in his dramas; and H. G. Wells was composing his first Utopian romances, which were being duplicated on this side of the Atlantic by Edward Bellamy's "fairy tale of social felicity," *Looking Backward, 2000–1887* (1888); Henry Olerich's *A Cityless and Countryless World* (1893); S. Byron Welcome's *From Earth's Center* (1894); and David Lubin's *Let There Be Light* (1900).[8]

A philosophy of reform had been slowly achieved, and one important contributor to it was Auguste Comte, the Frenchman, who in his *Positive Philosophy* (1842) had demonstrated the possibility of grouping social phenomena under

[8] For other Utopian romances and a discussion of their social importance, see Forbes, Allyn B., "The Literary Quest for Utopia, 1880–1900," *Social Forces* (December, 1927), VI, 179–189.

laws, laid the groundwork for our present science of sociology, and outlined a "religion of humanity." Yet an even more potent mind to whom the world, in its crisis, had turned was Karl Marx, a German journalist, political exile, and at one time European correspondent for Greeley's New York *Tribune*. "Workingmen of all lands, unite!" trumpeted Marx. "You have nothing to lose but your chains!" In his *Communist Manifesto*, which came out in 1848 ("the year of revolutions"), he said, "The history of all human society, past and present, has been the history of class struggles." And in his later *Capital* he enunciated another of his primary theories, the idea of "surplus value," which holds that capitalists, by forcing labor to produce more than it needs or receives for its own subsistence, are enabled to skim off this profit, or "surplus value," and use it to create more capital, just as Henry George's landlords drained off an "unearned increment" from their real estate.

Fired by Marx's vision of class warfare, both labor and the farmer set about to organize for what Eugene V. Debs was heralding as a "battle between the producing classes and the money power of the country." The National Labor Union, formed in 1866, gained a membership of 168,000 in the next three years; the Knights of Labor, which appeared in 1869, won 700,000 new recruits in 1886 alone; and the powerful American Federation of Labor, begun in 1886, numbered about a half million members by 1898. The proletariat, having no representation left in either of the major parties, began initiating political movements and parties of its own, like the Greenbackers, the Farmers' Alliance, the Grangers, the Populists, and in 1897, the Socialist Party, which by 1912 had office holders in more than three hundred cities and towns. Then, stealing a page from the technique of capital, these organizations opened a subtler campaign of "blocs," "lobbies," and newspaper editorials; and during the last fifty years, they have aided "progressives" of both parties in the achievement of such reforms as the Civil Service Act of 1883, the Australian Ballot, the Interstate Commerce Act of 1887, the Sherman Anti-Trust Law (1890), a Department of Labor (1913), an act requiring publicity for campaign contributions (1911), a constitutional amendment for the popular election of senators (1913), the income tax law of 1913, the enfranchisement of women (1920), and the Immigration Acts of 1924 and 1929. These victories, however, have been chiefly peripheral. The Anti-Trust Law has not prevented the merger of great industrial units, the Civil Service Act has not eliminated "the spoils system," and the votes cast by women have not endangered many parasitic politicians. The real source of economic infection in America has not been dried up; for business continues to operate, in spite of every opposition, on the naturalistic principle of *laissez faire*, which holds that plagues, panics, wars, and low wages are necessary to keep down (in a "natural" way) our surpluses of population and labor, and prevent them from assuming disastrous proportions. From this point of view poverty is a definite good, since by killing off many of the working-class, it enables the remainder to enjoy higher wages. Therefore, charity is a positive evil, because it perpetuates the weak, and so reduces the standard of living for the rest. As Spencer said:

The poverty of the incapable, the distresses that come upon the imprudent, the starvation of the idle, and those shoulderings aside of the weak by the strong, which leave so many "in shallows and in miseries," are the decrees of a large, far-seeing benevolence.[9]

Laissez faire, as a theory of economics, dates from Adam Smith's *Wealth of Nations* (1776), which contended that the State's only duty was, not to keep an eye on business, but to guard property rights; and it was for this very purpose, in fact, that our own eighteenth-century Constitution was devised, rather than for guaranteeing "natural rights" to the

---

[9] Spencer, Herbert, *Social Statics* (1865), pp. 353–354.

proletariat. Hamilton, Madison, and Adams believed that property owners must in some way be insured against the depredations of those who own no property. Democracy was not being safeguarded; we were being safeguarded against too much democracy. Gerry, Franklin, Randolph, and other Federalists subscribed to a "natural aristocracy of the wise, the rich, and the good." Hamilton saw in every democracy a "mediocracy." His plan was to check "the mob," and rear defenses for our wealthy middle class. To him the people represented "a great Beast," which could be tamed only by placing all authority in the grasp of citizens whose ownership of lands or bonds rendered them conservative and responsible, by centralizing the government, and by uniting business and politics. America, he felt, should be ruled by benevolent despotism, by a plutocracy, by the dictatorship of a "civilized minority."

Jefferson, on the other hand, felt more inclined to agree with Rousseau, the Frenchman, who protested that all men are born good, and turn impure only when subjected to the hampering and perversive influence of human laws. Remove the restrictions that men like Hamilton would put upon them, and they will return to their original state of goodness, and prove quite capable of living in "natural" harmony, without being watched over by policemen and paymasters. The majority, said Jefferson, should decide its own issues; we must have a "popular" government, not one dominated by "the well-born and wealthy." But by 1900 there remained little to choose between the two parties, despite the fact that Democrats are supposed to have inherited the policies of Jefferson, and Republicans the policies of Hamilton. Politicians of both groups had discovered that the proper formula for securing votes in America was to "talk" Jeffersonian and "act" Hamiltonian.

Hamilton and Jefferson each wanted a "dictatorship" instead of a "co-operative" commonwealth, Hamilton the dictatorship of a rich minority, and Jefferson the dictatorship of a poor majority. Both, as individualists, believed in "the less government the better," except that Hamilton did want the State to rein in the poor, and Jefferson wanted it to rein in the wealthy. Each of them approved of *laissez faire* for his faction, but not for the other; and today neither theory seems to fit the situation. The dangers of Hamilton's *laissez faire* are already evident; and Jefferson's "masses," when given complete freedom from law, have matched "the idle rich" in faults. If a business "aristocracy" is an unsafe form of State, a "democracy" (it has been proved) is no less so; for in addition to being just as greedy and even more intolerant, it has been found to be the easy dupe of war-time hysteria, patent medicines, demagogues, economic panaceas, "experts," catchwords, flags, parades, the spectacular and picturesque, incense, "human interest" stories, advertising, "happy endings," "get-rich-quick" schemes, and all types of propaganda, though it should not be forgotten that those moguls of the profit system who feed, and feed upon, proletarian stupidity are largely responsible for its ignorance. Both types of *laissez faire* are perilous; Marx's "dictatorship of the proletariat" and Hamilton's "dictatorship" of the moneyed class are alike bad. The true kind of a democracy should exclude the concept of dictatorship, and base itself upon some arrangement that would protect the majority from minorities, and minorities from the majority. There needs to be a realization by all parties concerned that, just as in a man's personal government of his mind and body, the keyword must be co-operation. Difficult as it may be, the motive of reform should be to bring about a condition of "all for one and one for all."

BALLOTS OR BULLETS? A number of methods have already been proposed for achieving this new condition, but they all boil down to the Communistic and the Socialistic, the revolutionary and the revisionary. Communism, which is based in a rough way on Marx's "dictatorship of the proletariat," holds that a struggle to the death exists beween capital and labor, and that the former should be "overthrown," without waiting for it to "suffocate in its own fat." Socialism, on the contrary, is willing to collaborate with capital in remedial legislation for the proletariat.   It is opposed to sudden revolution, and wants to get whatever reforms it can, even if this means going slow and compromising with those forces now in authority.   The programs involved, then, are of two kinds (1) the apocalyptic, which demands class war to the bitter end, refuses to arbitrate with capital, and aims at the overthrow of capital by "revolution," and (2) the pragmatic, which tends to minimize the class battle, delay reform until it has the sanction of public opinion, educate rather than coerce, and remedy present conditions by means of directed "evolution."   But in other respects, these two philosophies are similar.   For, briefly stated, both desire

(a) To utilize the collective resources for the promotion of the good of the associated members in the sense of securing to each individual the minimum facilities for the fulfilment of his capacities for good.

(b) To control such differences in power and possessions as arise in a society with the object of preventing those who have acquired excess of power from abusing it and forcing others into conditions incompatible with the requirements of the good life.[10]

THE DEBUNKERS   It is true that most of the constructive thinking along the lines of social improvement has been done by philosophers, economists, and statesmen. The social novelist has chiefly been occupied with the "exposure" of governmental, educational, cultural, and economic maladies.   Yet "they also serve" who only help destroy unsatisfactory and shameful conditions, in order that just and

[10] Ginsberg, M., "Social Philosophy," *The Encyclopaedia Britannica*, 14th edition (1929), XX, 900.

satisfactory ones may be created in their place. The task of the reformer in literature has been to "debunk" old shams and established usages that stand in the way of public welfare.

The word "debunk" has lost some of its popularity since it was first introduced into American fiction by W. E. Woodward, in his novel *Bunk* (1923). However, it is a word that may still be used to indicate that growing party of authors who have dedicated their art to a criticism of "the way things are being run," and who are trying, like gadflies, to sting injustice to death. Since 1890, or thereabouts, American writers have produced a vast body of novels that examine various problems of modern life, purge our thought of self-deceit, and "answer the social ? with a literary !" [11] The plight of the "under-privileged" has been described in Isaac K. Friedman's *By Bread Alone* (1901), Ernest Poole's *The Harbor* (1915), Frank Harris's *The Bomb* (1908), Edward Dahlberg's *Bottom Dogs* (1930), Rollo Walter Brown's *The Firemakers* (1931), Charles Rumford Walker's *Bread and Fire* (1927), James Oppenheim's *The Nine-Tenths* (1911), Catherine Brody's *Nobody Starves* (1932), Robert Cantwell's *Land of Plenty* (1934), William Rollins' *The Shadow Before* (1934), Jack Conroy's *The Disinherited* (1933), James T. Farrell's *The Young Manhood of Studs Lonigan* (1934), Louis Colman's *Lumber* (1932), Agnes Smedley's *Daughter of Earth* (1929), Myra Page's *Gathering Storm* (1932), and Idwal Jones' *Steel Chips* (1929). Socialism has been expounded in Ernest Poole's *Blind* (1920), Max Eastman's *Venture* (1927), Hutchins Hapgood's *The Spirit of Labor* (1907), Elias Tobenkin's *The Road* (1922), Alexander Black's *The Seventh Angel* (1921), Arthur Bullard's *Comrade Yetta* (1913), and George Cram Cook's *The Chasm* (1910). Miscreant politicians have been attacked in Isaac K. Friedman's *The Radical* (1907), Gertrude

[11] Littell, Robert, "Notes on Hemingway," *The New Republic* (August 10, 1927), LI, 306.

Atherton's *Senator North* (1900), Samuel Hopkins Adams' *Revelry* (1926), Winston Churchill's *Coniston* (1906), David Graham Phillips' *Plum Tree* (1905), Henry Adams' *Democracy* (1880), Paul Leicester Ford's *The Honorable Peter Stirling* (1894), Alfred Henry Lewis's *The Boss* (1903), Frederick Hazlitt Brennan's *God Got One Vote* (1927), Harvey Fergusson's *Capitol Hill* (1923), Mark Lee Luther's *The Henchman* (1902), Frederick Trevor Hill's *The Minority* (1902), Brand Whitlock's *The Thirteenth District* (1902), and Elliott Flower's *The Spoilsman* (1903). The problems of the immigrant in America's "melting pot" have been emphasized in Anzia Yezierska's *Bread Givers* (1925), Ernest Poole's *The Voice of the Street* (1906), Myron Brinig's *Singermann* (1929), Elias Tobenkin's *Witte Arrives* (1916), O. E. Rölvaag's *The Boat of Longing* (1933), Sholom Asch's *Uncle Moses* (1920), David Cornel De Jong's *Belly Fulla Straw* (1934), Michael Gold's *Jews Without Money* (1930), and Abraham Cahan's *The Rise of David Levinsky* (1917). Social conditions in "the new South" have been dealt with in Edith Summers Kelley's *Weeds* (1923), Fielding Burke's *Call Home the Heart* (1932), Grace Lumpkin's *To Make My Bread* (1932), Clement Wood's *Mountain* (1920), and Mary Heaton Vorse's *Strike!* (1930). Feminism and the "emancipation" of women have been debated in Samuel Hopkins Adams' *Siege* (1924), Floyd Dell's *Janet March* (1923), Gertrude Atherton's *Julia France and Her Times* (1912), Robert Herrick's *The Gospel of Freedom* (1898), Charles G. Norris's *Bread* (1923), Robert Grant's *Unleavened Bread* (1900), Susan Glaspell's *Fidelity* (1915), Mary Austin's *A Woman of Genius* (1912), Sarah Grand's *The Heavenly Twins* (1893), Alfred Kreymborg's *Erna Vitek* (1914), Mary Johnston's *Hagar* (1913), and David Graham Phillips' *A Woman Ventures* (1902). The horrors and injustices of war have been impugned in George Blake's *The Path to Glory* (1929), William March's *Company K* (1933), Charles Yale Harrison's *Generals Die in Bed* (1930), Thomas Boyd's

Through the Wheat (1923), William T. Scanlon's *God Have Mercy on Us!* (1929), and James Stevens' *Mattock* (1927). Marriage and divorce have been treated of in Floyd Dell's *The Briary Bush* (1921), Gertrude Atherton's *Perch of the Devil* (1914), Robert Herrick's *Together* (1908) and *One Woman's Life* (1913), Charles G. Norris's *Brass* (1921), David Graham Phillips' *Old Wives for New* (1908), Edgar Lee Masters' *The Nuptial Flight* (1923), James Oppenheim's *Idle Wives* (1914), George F. Hummel's *After All* (1923), and Harold H. Armstrong's *For Richer, For Poorer* (1922). The "souls of black folk" and the Negro's changing status in American life today have been reflected in Rudolph Fisher's *Walls of Jericho* (1928), John L. Spivak's *Georgia Nigger* (1932), George S. Schuyler's *Black No More* (1931), Roark Bradford's *This Side of Jordan* (1929), Clement Wood's *Nigger* (1922), Langston Hughes' *Not Without Laughter* (1930), Nella Larsen's *Passing* (1929), Claude McKay's *Banjo* (1929), Walter White's *The Fire in the Flint* (1924), Wallace Thurman's *The Blacker the Berry* (1929), Jessie Fauset's *There Is Confusion* (1924), Waldo Frank's *Holiday* (1923), and Howard Odum's *Rainbow Round My Shoulder* (1928). Capitalism and "the leisure class" have been arraigned in Charles G. Norris's *Pig Iron* (1926), James Oppenheim's *The Olympian* (1912), and Robert Herrick's *Waste* (1924). The "bitch-goddess, Success" has been ridiculed in Harold H. Armstrong's *The Groper* (1919), Maurice Samuel's *Whatever Gods* (1923), Robert Herrick's *The Web of Life* (1900), W. E. Woodward's *Lottery* (1924), and William Allen White's *A Certain Rich Man* (1909). And society's present attitude toward the criminal has been flayed in Brand Whitlock's *The Turn of the Balance* (1907), Nathan Kussy's *The Abyss* (1916), Mr. and Mrs. Haldeman-Julius's *Violence* (1929), and Charles Yale Harrison's *A Child Is Born* (1931).

MAGNA CHARTA   What these novels are protesting against, for the most part, are things like the American passion for "bigness" and success, high-pressure salesmanship, shoddy commercial products, poor housing conditions in urban areas, the narrow, lethargic, platitudinous and often hysterical mob mind, corruption in government, labor injunctions, racketeering, standardization in education, industry, and art, the deportation of radicals, the abridgment of our constitutional liberties, the "contract" system of prison labor, militarism, the subsidizing of large corporations, political patronage, "blue laws," nationalism, the legalized extortion of "big business," sweat shops in the needle trades, racial prejudice, the "stretch" system in factories, inelastic marriage statutes, capital punishment, the entrance of religion into politics, imperialism, profiteering, a nation "half boom and half broke," jingoism, rate inflation by public utilities, law evasions, our present jury system, election frauds, bigotry, child labor, the Ku Klux Klan, and wage slavery of every kind. What they favor (at least by implication) are such improvements as equal rights for women, profit sharing in industry, penal and judicial reform, a dynamic religion, a minimum wage law, the public ownership of natural resources, a stabilized prosperity that will not be subject to the fluctuations of supply and demand or the victim of stock speculation, unemployment and old age insurance, increased leisure, birth control, higher wages, lower tariffs, protection for the Negro, increased taxation on the higher income levels, civil liberty, co-operative marketing, direct election of the President, organization of the worker and consumer, disarmament, the outlawing of war, proportional representation, and the perfection of political and economic democracy: in short, all those ideas which are slowly, but too slowly making headway against a world that would rather exorcise poverty with soup kitchens than socialism.

NATURALIST, ESCAPIST, REFORMIST. But if these novels are less creative than accusative, they are at least motivated by definite theories of reform, which are widely at variance with those of naturalism and escapism. For instance, the naturalist does not believe in progress. He is willing to concede that humanity may be holding its own, yet he refuses to admit that it is improving. In the first place, if we have no free will, we cannot take advantage of our past mistakes; we are no more able to better our own condition by an effort of volition than an amoeba. And in the second place, there would be no way of deciding what we were to call progress, even if we had free will. Moral values are always changing, and what might seem a virtue to one generation might seem a vice to the next. Ethical ideas are, like men, just products of their environment. Science's "evolution" does evolve, but it points neither up nor down in any moral sense.

The escapist, for his part, does not even feel inclined to grant that society is holding its own in the matter of progress; to him it appears that we are going backwards, that yesterday was a more desirable age to live in than the present. But the reformist (to endow the author of social fiction with a generic name) retains his faith in "the ultimate perfectability" of mankind. He believes, to be sure, that man is "a product of his environment"; yet he also believes that his environment is conditioned by man, and that since this action is reciprocal, man can improve himself by improving his environment. He is also aware that values change, and should change, to fit the different requirements of different generations; but by stepping outside the stream of history for a moment (a thing the naturalist never does), he thinks he can discern a few permanent indices of progress, such as increased wisdom, the production of men of genius, decrease in crime, rise in the average duration of life, the diffusion of culture, an increased understanding of man and his world, education of the social conscience, freedom of thought, and equality before the law.

He does not believe in God's ability to raise these barometers of progress, but he does not believe, either, in the power of Nature to guide mankind aright. The naturalist places his destiny in the hands of Nature; the reformist does not. He is not convinced, as Dreiser is, that "Mother Nature" knows best. He turns away from the principle of *laissez faire*, because Nature's idea of justice (if it has one) is obviously not that of man. The natural laws of science and free trade may, if left alone, shape our behavior and commerce. Yet such laws as those of "the struggle for existence" or supply and demand seem to favor only the strongest and richest among us. The reformist feels that Nature may represent order, but not equity. Every act of Nature may conform to rigid laws (in a physical way), but these same acts (from a philosophical point of view) appear to be just mere products of chance, because they have no apparent purpose.

Misery flourishes in the world; yet the naturalist does not trouble himself about repairing it. He walks through life with his hands in his pockets, saying with Zola, "We are not willing to correct what is by what should be." [12] But the reformist finds this ruthless code too dreadful and ugly. Naturalism and *laissez faire*, he notes, are splendid for those fortunate beings who have been blessed by Nature with the power and health to withstand Nature. "Rugged individualism" is quite satisfactory for the "rugged individual," yet in order that all may possess equal opportunities to be happy, some human discipline must be enforced upon the raw processes of evolution. The individual's instincts must be warped, says the reformist, into conformance with the best aims of society. Nature, it is plain, will not lead us to a paradise on earth. It is more apt to lead us to a jungle. Unless chastened by foresight and legislative checks and balances, Darwin's "struggle for existence" will divide us into Nietzsche's "masters and slaves," and business, left to

[12] Zola, Émile, *The Experimental Novel* (1893), p. 127.

itself, will always bear a crop of Frank Cowperwoods, with the creed of "dog eat dog."

Many naturalists are "intellectual vagabonds," who try to blame their own confusion upon the universe, and who do not want life to seem capable of being interpreted and understood, because that would be a reproach to them for their failure "to undertake the task of reconstructing our social, political, and economic theories, and in consonance with these, our ideals of a good life." [13] The reformist, however, cherishes a feeling that

society can no longer be left to develop and function without guidance, but that intelligent social control of its forces is fundamental, and that such control must be devoted to the welfare of the entire community. Men must work out what the good life should be, and they must consciously plan, in the light of scientific knowledge and practice, how best to bring it nearer to man. [14]

The naturalist would have it that whatever is, is true and beautiful and good; but while the escapist and reformist both might agree that whatever is, is true, the escapist does not feel that it is beautiful, and the reformist will not admit that it is good. Nor does the reformist believe in any biologic or esthetic aristocracy. The naturalist is an individualist; he believes in "every man for himself," and sees the world as a series of discontinuous objects and events (of which he is one), each beautiful, true, and good only in itself, each with no duty or meaning beyond its own existence and welfare. He is an egoist and an aristocrat; he feels sure that Nature intended for some men to emerge as masters, and his attitude toward "the herd" is that of Nietzsche, who said:

The masses seem to be worth notice in three aspects only: first as the copies of great men, printed on bad paper from worn-out plates, next as a contrast to the great men, and lastly as

[13] Dell, Floyd, *Intellectual Vagabondage* (1926), p. 249.
[14] Randall, John Herman, *The Making of the Modern Mind* (1926), p. 628.

their tools: for the rest, let the devil and statistics fly away with them![15]

The escapist, too, is an aristocrat, because he feels that the masses cannot appreciate beauty, serenity, or culture, that they care more for Irving Berlin than Bach, more for the comic strips than El Greco, more for "bread and circuses" than for "the old gesture toward the stars," more for the present than the past. But the reformist is not an individualist; he is a democrat, an altruist, and a friend of "the great majority." He rejects the notion that Nature should not be tampered with by man, protests against abandoning the weak to the not very tender mercies of the strong, and denies the idea that beauty is worth more than bread. He realizes that men are not born equal in physical and mental strength, or in the ability to appreciate life's subtler values; but he does contend that they are born equal in their right to be happy. The naturalistic novel wins his displeasure, because it fails to pity those lowly creatures it so often deals with. Yet the escapist novel, which takes to its heels at the approach of any problem, is even more a victim of his criticism. Instead of running away from the painful realities of the present, he believes with Glenn Frank that "Only by frankness concerning the truth that hurts can we secure a sustained respect for the truth that helps." Instead of trying to "escape," it is better to remain behind and edit unpleasant situations into pleasant ones. "Life," he feels, "is not changed by the few who stand outside the mêlée . . . and shout 'In the name of God!' It is changed from within — such change as there is."[16] The naturalist lives in the present and the escapist in the past, but the reformist lives for the future. To build a new world, he has decided, would be less difficult than to understand the old. Nor does he believe in "art for art's sake," as the naturalist does,

[15] Nietzsche, Friedrich, *The Complete Works of Friedrich Nietzsche* (1911), V, 84. By permission of The Macmillan Company, publishers.
[16] Samuel, Maurice, *Whatever Gods* (1923), p. 321.

or in art for the sake of beauty and escape, as Cabell and Hergesheimer do; he believes in "art for Marx's sake," in art for the sake of humanity. Pegasus, he feels, should be harnessed to the plow.

The reformist and naturalist, however, are both pragmatists. They agree that nothing is a virtue unless it is "useful." "Pretty is as pretty does," the pragmatist declares. "I am not interested in abstract qualities of truth, beauty, and goodness; what I am interested in is the utility of objects and events. For if a thing is serviceable, it will also be good, true, and beautiful in my eyes." A belief has no pertinence, to him, except as it applies to action or behavior. The world exists as a logical problem, which he tries to solve by experimental methods and the adjustment of means to ends. He attempts to objectify knowledge and reconstruct society by "creative intelligence." He avoids thought that has no relation to facts, and approves of philosophy only when it ceases to be a device for "philosophizing" and becomes a method for dealing with the problems of man. "*Theories thus become instruments*," [17] wrote James, and ideas not just "good," but "good for something."

The moral value of a deed or thought is of less importance than its effect. The reformist is not concerned with any paradise but an earthly one; he wants to enjoy this world, not the next. He does not care for the promise implied in

> Hope and pray,
> Work all day,
> Live on hay.
> You'll eat pie
> In the sky,
> Bye and bye.

In a way he feels as Marx did, that "religion is the opium of the people," because it preaches resignation instead of action. The reformist ranks humanity before God. Or as an English disciple of Comte once said, "God is merely

[17] James, William, *Pragmatism* (1931), p. 53.

Humanity with a crown on." Even if a man does not say his prayers or go to church, he need have no fear of the inferno. A good citizen will make a good angel.

Science has told the reformist that miracles do not exist, and that divinity is a bogus fact. Therefore he has decided to improve his own lot, rather than wait for some heavenly ukase to put an end to social misery, which he feels is caused, not by sin, but by stupidity. "I think," he says,

> that Galahad and his Holy Grail
> Had best make way for some less gilded plan.[18]

The reformist does not believe in a blind loyalty to existing standards of conduct, or in perpetuating traditions when once they have ceased to bear fruit. If companionate marriage serves mankind better today than a strict form of monogamy, it cannot be bad; and if trusts are harmful to humanity, they cannot be good. He asks himself, not, "Is this God's wish?" but "Will this action injure me or other human beings?" "A deed," he says, "is good if it is the sort of deed that has good results; whether any one recognizes it as good is quite secondary. Any act that is of the sort to have harmful results is a bad act, whether or not any one condemns it." [19] The reformist is in revolt against our present system of abstract vice and virtue; he wants to discard a religious morality in favor of a social one, inasmuch as our theological scheme of right and wrong has hardened into a creed and lost its elasticity.

Not being founded upon a study of the consequences of conduct . . . it is not open to correction by the sight of disastrous results. It may be exploited by fanatics and schemers, as when it was made to sanction the Crusades, and later the Inquisition. In our day it is interfering with education (as in the anti-evolution bills) and preventing multitudes from learning important facts about human life.

[18] Ficke, Arthur Davison, *Selected Poems* (1926), p. 16.
[19] Drake, Durant, *The New Morality* (1929), p. 18. By permission of The Macmillan Company, publishers.

Nothing can save men from such irrationalities and cruelties but a clear recognition of the fact that morality is made for man, not man for morality.   Men have suffered innumerable deprivations and been the victims of untold suffering because they have not seen that it lay within their power to shake off their loyalty to irrational commandments and adapt their conduct to their actual interests and needs.[20]

THE LAST CRUSADE   Since 1890 our social system has undergone many changes.   There has been a growth in the freedom of women; the liberal arts have moved over to make room for science in education; birth rates have sagged and divorce rates have gone up; the American family no longer seeks those pleasures lauded by Burns in his "Cotter's Saturday Night"; machines have revolutionized industry; and the urbanite, with his relaxed social consciousness, has replaced the more communal farmer.   But our moral system has not kept pace.   It is out of date, protests the reformist, and should be modernized.   Reason has not been applied to the solution of our economic problems as it has to the solution of our scientific problems. We have not made the same progress in understanding business cycles and crime that we have in understanding the principles behind electricity and celestial mechanics. "Those in positions of authority still hold to the political and moral and economic principles worked out in the eighteenth century, under the reign of strictly Newtonian conceptions and methods, and in response to the strictly eighteenth-century social needs of an overwhelmingly agricultural and commercial society.   But today we no longer live in the Newtonian world nor in an agricultural and commercial society; we have discovered biology and psychology, and we have felt the full effects of the Industrial Revolution.   Our fundamental scientific conceptions and our social needs have both been profoundly altered, and

[20] Drake, Durant, *op. cit.*, pp. 9–10.   By permission of The Macmillan Company, publishers.

there is good reason for believing that principles developed in the eighteenth century and highly efficacious under those conditions are no longer adequate to meet our modern problems." [21]

We are still attempting to order our political life through beliefs and institutions conceived in terms of the problems of the rural and frontier colonial civilization; we are still trying to direct an economic society in which the giant corporation and centralized finance are the chief features, by ideas developed to meet the needs of eighteenth-century commercial and agricultural England and France; we are still seeking to regulate our international relations upon principles perhaps necessary to the world just emerging in the fifteenth and sixteenth centuries from the universal dominion of the Church; we are still endeavoring to adjust our conduct and our human relationships by an ethical code that originated in ancient Palestine over two thousand years ago.[22]

The great need of the present day, contends the author of social fiction, "is to bring our social, economic, and political institutions up to something like the same level of efficiency and objectivity which has been reached in science and technology." [23]   And he views it as part of his duty to remove whatever prejudices of the past cannot be translated into present values, to bring a new mind to our new industrial order, to catch up with the facts of life and place them again under moral jurisdiction, and to control by reason what science has created by reason.   His point of view is that of John Stuart Mill, the English philosopher, who said that the problem of society was "how to unite the greatest liberty of action, with a common ownership in the raw material of the globe, and an equal participation of all in the benefits of combined labor." [24]   He believes in "the greatest good for the greatest number,"

[21] Randall, John Herman, op. cit., p. 309.
[22] Ibid., p. 595.
[23] Barnes, Harry Elmer, Social Science: The Hope of Democracy (1931), p. 14.
[24] Mill, John Stuart, Autobiography (1874), p. 232.

that the motive of service must be substituted for the motive of profit, and that we should "take from every man according to his ability, and give to every man according to his need." The desires of the individual, he says, must be subjugated to the welfare of the whole, and the whole dedicated to the welfare of the individual. We require a "planned society," tailored to the peculiar conditions of modern life; and so the reformist has set out on another crusade, this time not to recapture the Holy Land, but to find a Happy Land.

"The world is so full of a number of things," sang Stevenson, "I'm sure we should all be as happy as kings." And he might have added, "If only we would let ourselves enjoy them." Man, according to the reformist, stands in his own light, stumbles over his own feet. Nature has placed at our elbow food, shelter, and a bountiful supply of the elements necessary to happiness, which touched by the wand of human knowledge could be transmuted into usefulness and pleasure. But we are prevented from accepting this miraculous gift by our own superstition, intolerance, inertia, selfish habits of mind, and imperfect systems of government and economics. Viewed in this way, Hamlin Garland's words take on a real meaning. "Nature is not to blame. Man's laws are to blame."

*

PLAIN TALK

*

THE MAN WITH THE MUCKRAKE   By 1900 storms were brewing against the "trust," and always sensitive to meteorological changes in popular opinion, S. S. McClure (editor of *McClure's* magazine) stumbled upon the idea of providing the forces of revolt with documented evidence, which they could use in support of their attacks on political misrule and business avarice in America. In 1902 he launched his experiment with a series of articles on the Standard Oil Company by Ida M. Tarbell; and the result, measured in public interest, surprised even McClure.   The circulation of *McClure's* leaped; and almost at once, less original editors, climbing on the bandwagon, began to investigate other suspicious phases of our national life. *McClure's* went on to publish Ray Stannard Baker's study of the railroads and Lincoln Steffens' articles on municipal graft; *Everybody's* aired Thomas W. Lawson's "Frenzied Finance" and Charles Edward Russell's exposure of "the beef trust"; *Collier's* chimed in with Samuel Hopkins Adams' betrayal of the patent medicine "racket"; *Cosmopolitan* brought out David Graham Phillips' "Treason of the Senate"; *The Arena* printed Rudolph Blankenburg's story of Pennsylvania politics; and other "buzzard geniuses" threw a curative light upon such infamies as commercialized vice and the life insurance business.

Most of these writers spent a great deal of time on their work; for instance, it took Miss Tarbell five years to prepare and draft her eighteen installments anent the Standard Oil Company, and Lincoln Steffens, in over two years, produced only ten articles.   But not every author devoted as much time and integrity to his research.   There was the usual "lunatic fringe" of those who rushed to extremes or spoke without any basis in fact; and it is these that Theodore Roosevelt is supposed to have meant when he turned down the damper on this "literature of exposure" by comparing its writers to that character in Bunyan's *Pilgrim's Progress* who, offered a celestial crown for his muckrake, continued to rake to himself "the filth of the floor."

"Muckraking," by 1908, had largely died out of the magazines; its climax had come, in fact, only a few weeks before Roosevelt's outburst, with the publication of a very sensational novel, entitled *The Jungle* (1906), by a young man named Upton Sinclair.

The Jungle is a savage indictment of labor and sanitary conditions in the stockyards of Chicago, for which Sinclair had spent seven weeks gathering material, on $500 given him by *The Appeal to Reason*, a Socialist weekly.   Its plot deals with Jurgis Rudkus, a Lithuanian immigrant, and his fellow workers in the abattoirs of "Packingtown," with

their struggle to get ahead, to own a home, to bring up their children decently, while all the time they are brutally exploited, preyed upon, robbed, outraged, by the unscrupulous forces which find in their poverty and ignorance and helplessness mere opportunities for enrichment.   One group is crushed, one by one, in the struggle; the old men are thrown on the scrap-heap to starve, the women are drawn into prostitution to keep body and soul together, the children die; Jurgis himself goes to prison for smashing the face of a brutal boss, and when he comes out his little world has been destroyed as if by an earthquake — and he is left to wander, getting wisdom as he wanders, and coming at last to believe in a Socialist reconstruction of this hideous world.[1]

But *The Jungle's* "story" was far overshadowed by its ghastly revelation of malpractices in the packing industry.

[1] Dell, Floyd, *Upton Sinclair* (1927), pp. 104–105.

So vivid were Sinclair's anecdotes of men falling into rendering vats and coming out as Durham's Pure Leaf Lard that his readers were scandalized, and began to demand a governmental probe. For a while the country lost its appetite for meat products; and Roosevelt, though more inclined to ballast than blast the "profit system," felt compelled to act. The upshot of his inquiry was the Pure Foods Law of 1906 (an act that was all "bark" and no "bite"). Yet a fright had been thrown into "big business" by *The Jungle*, which had been quickly translated into seventeen languages, and termed by Jack London (in an introduction that he wrote for it) "the 'Uncle Tom's Cabin' of wage-slavery." Almost overnight, Sinclair found himself regarded as "the plumed knight" of Socialism.

THE SOCIAL DETECTIVE   Upton Sinclair was born in Baltimore, September 20, 1878, of a family long prominent in Southern history. His father, a liquor and straw-hat salesman, drank himself to death, the fate of many "drummers" in those days when it was customary to seal every business contract or sale with a glass of whisky. His mother's relatives were wealthy, but owing to his father's inability to keep the money that he made, Sinclair's childhood was spent in frequent transformations from comparative ease to poverty and back again. When his father would bring home some banknotes, they would live in comfort for a time; then, after a few weeks, they would be back in some verminous boarding house, sleeping three in a bed. But once in a while Sinclair would be invited to the home of his maternal uncle, who was president of a large insurance company. So he came to know, as "a poor relation," both faces of our social medal, the dark and the bright; and it is with contrasting these two different sides of American life that his novels are concerned.

He was ten years old before he entered grade school in New York, where his parents had moved a year or two earlier. But at thirteen he was ready to continue his studies in the City College of New York (which, properly speaking, was at that time only a high school); and four years later he enrolled at Columbia University, where he specialized in philosophy and literature, though his mother had wanted him to become a lawyer. Meanwhile he had begun to look upon the educative process as "a dreary routine" that did not take note of a student's aptitudes, but fed him into a machine which turned out, each semester, a fresh batch of standardized minds, like so many sausages. His faith in the tenets of Christianity had also started to droop, and it was not long before he had shaken off his allegiance to formal worship and adopted that religion favored today by most reformists, who hold that "to labor is to pray."

By the age of seventeen he was selling jokes and stories to magazines, to help support his family, and reading a great deal of Shelley and Shakspere. To pay his way through Columbia, he wrote "pulp fiction" for Street and Smith (the same firm that Dreiser had worked for as a young man), and did other literary hackwork from which his style has never recovered. By his twentieth birthday he was turning out more than two million words a year in the form of "half dime novels" and very bad romances with such titles as *In the Days of Decatur* and *In the Net of the Visconti*. Then, weary of grinding out these cheap narratives, he decided to write "the great American novel," and renting a cabin near a small Canadian lake, he produced *King Midas*, which he describes as "the story of a woman's soul redeemed by high and noble love."

While at this hermitage, he met again a girl he had known in his youth; and finding that they were both fond of music and German poetry, they promptly fell in love. Despite the protests of their parents, they married "on a shoestring"; the "great American novel" was rejected by a half dozen publishers; and Sinclair had to return to the manufacture of "potboilers." But like Crane he determined to print his first book himself, and like Crane he soon found the expense justified. Even as Crane's *Maggie* had caught the attention of Garland and Howells, so Sinclair's *King Midas* won an unexpected friend in the editor of the *Literary Digest*. Funk and Wagnalls issued the volume under its own imprint, and Sinclair, with his wife, went to the Thousand Islands, where they lived in a tent, and he worked on his next novel, *Prince Hagen*.

But *King Midas* (1901), a prattling romance of much soulful yearning and raving raptures, did not overwhelm its audience; and Sinclair, now a father, was forced back into writing jokes and book reviews, while he labored on a new story. *Prince Hagen* (1903), the "story of a Nibelung, grandson of the dwarf Alberich, who brings his golden treasures up to Wall Street and Fifth Avenue, and proves the identity between our Christian civilization and his own dark realm," [2] did not satisfy the public either; and the fate of Sinclair's next book was not much better. This last, *The Journal of Arthur Stirling* (1903), is supposed to be the diary of a twenty-two-year-old "genius," a poet who, outraged by the world's indifference to geniuses, had taken his own life. It is the story of a youthful Chatterton; a fine sample of what extremes of sentiment can be bred in a young poet by the suspicion that he embodies a "divine afflatus"; and probably one of the world's worst novels.

Though it received favorable notice from the critics, *The Journal of Arthur Stirling* was not a success in the bookshops; and Sinclair was driven to seek aid from George D. Herron, a Socialist lecturer, in order to build a shack in the woods near Princeton, New Jersey, and begin work on a trilogy dealing with the Civil War. Such a trilogy, it may be remembered, had previously entered the mind

[2] Sinclair, Upton, *American Outpost* (1932), p. 116.

of Frank Norris; but whereas Norris's plan did not mature, Sinclair was able at least to finish his first volume, which he labeled *Manassas*. *Manassas* (1904) is the story of a boy, Allan Montague, son of a Mississippi planter, who grows up to manhood during the Civil War, becomes a defiant Abolitionist, and joins a Massachusetts regiment when the fighting begins. From a literary point of view this novel is one of Sinclair's best; here, for example, is his report of the first shot fired upon Fort Sumter:

And then suddenly the crowd whirled about, startled into silence, transfixed. Across the harbor there had shone out a sudden far-off gleam of fire — instantaneous, like a flash of heat-lightning close to the horizon. At the same moment a pale spark of light was seen to shoot up into the sky. It went up in a curving track, trembling, scintillating; slowly and more slowly it moved — then seemed to stand still — hovering, hesitating, shaking like a star. And then it fell, faster and faster — and suddenly, like a meteor, disappeared. A moment later there came across the waters a dull and heavy boom, — and from the throats of the startled crowd burst a roar.[3]

Thus far, Sinclair had felt that all the world's great problems had been left on his doorstep; but now he began to come into contact with Socialists like Herron, to read Shaw and *The Appeal to Reason*, to discover that Socialists were not "cranks" or madmen (as he had always imagined), and to realize that he was not alone in his objections to social injustice. Says Sinclair, "It was like the falling down of prison walls about my mind; the most amazing discovery, after all these years — that I did not have to carry the whole burden of humanity's future upon my two frail shoulders!" [4] He had been constantly aware of a need to identify himself with something, and Socialism appeared to fill this need. He began writing "radical" manifestoes for *The Appeal to Reason* and other magazines,

[3] Sinclair, Upton, *Manassas* (1923), pp. 302–303.
[4] *American Outpost*, p. 143.

and in 1906 ran for Congress on the Socialist ticket.[5]
Manassas came out, in this interval, and like all the rest of
his novels failed.   But *The Jungle* brought Sinclair instant
renown, and what was even more welcome, thirty thousand
dollars in royalties.

He founded the Intercollegiate Socialist Society, which
later ripened into the present League for Industrial Democracy; and inspired by Charlotte Perkins Gilman's *The
Home* (1903), he decided to establish a kind of "co-operative
boarding house," where a few people of liberal sympathies
might live together on a communal basis.[6]   A building
was located near Englewood, New Jersey, on two or three
acres of land, and after Sinclair had managed to round
up a group of members, the colonists began to apply "the
machine process to domestic affairs" and try out their
new solution of the servant problem.   The site of this
experiment was called Helicon Hall by its inhabitants, and
a "free-love nest" by reporters.   But whether it would have
proved with time to be feasible was never determined, for
after a few months it was burned to the ground by a fire
of mysterious origin.   One boarder was killed; and all
that remained of Sinclair's "beautiful Utopia" was a pile
of smoking ashes.   His thirty thousand dollars were gone,
but undaunted, he pitched his tent in the Adirondacks,
and started on another book.   Having portrayed the
plight of labor in *The Jungle*, he meant this time to draw a
picture of the rich.[7]

The Metropolis (1907) relates the experiences of a second
Allan Montague, son of the hero in Sinclair's *Manassas*.
A young lawyer, thirty years old, he arrives in New York
from the South to join his brother Oliver, who has already

[5] Sinclair has announced his intention of running for Governor of California in 1934, on the Democratic ticket.   His platform is contained in
I, The Governor (1933).

[6] See his article on this "home colony" in *The Independent* for June 14, 1906.

[7] The same thing has been done more recently in James Noble Gifford's
Caviar for Breakfast (1931).

come to "the metropolis" to seek his career. On his first
night there he hears a Socialist orator addressing a crowd,
as follows:

They force you to build palaces, and then they put you into tenements! They force you to spin fine raiment, and then they dress
you in rags! They force you to build jails, and then they lock
you up in them! They force you to make guns, and then they
shoot you with them. They own the political parties, and they
name the candidates, and trick you into voting for them — and
they call it the law! They herd you into armies and send you out
to shoot your brothers — and they call it order! They take a
piece of coloured rag and call it the flag and teach you to let yourself be shot — and they call it patriotism! First, last, and all the
time, you do the work and they get the benefit — they, the masters
and owners, and you — fools — fools —*fools!* [8]

But he scarcely has time to consider what these words
may mean, before he is swept off by his brother into a
tempest of rich living. He becomes a student of life in
the Metropolis. He moves here and there among "The
Four Hundred," awed and disturbed by the luxury and
extravagance of everything he sees. At Mrs. Robbie
Wallings' "hunting lodge" (which turns out to be a granite castle!) he is almost stifled by the display of wealth,
and meets a bevy of gluttons, dilettantes, and oafs; at
Mrs. Winnie's house on Fifth Avenue (which is all of white
marble and cost two million to build) he learns about the
casual way that marriage and divorces are treated among
the sybaritic elect, and is shocked by the fact that Mrs. Winnie has spent millions upon pictures and furniture that she
cannot appreciate. He meets arbiters of fashion, cotillion
leaders, a young man named Reggie (of indeterminate
sex), débutantes, and polo players; and on every side,
there flows around him a liquid nightmare of perfume,
orchids, sexual delinquencies, limousines, glittering man-

[8] Sinclair, Upton, *The Metropolis* (1923), pp. 17–18.

sions, deep carpets, magnificent gowns, wine, blazing jewels, lace, solid gold candlesticks, and lavish viands. He goes to the Horse Show, to the Opera, to church, and to the "Millionaires'" Club; everywhere he finds the same story of wealth easily or fraudulently won, and sickeningly displayed, the same story of depraved men and women, drunken with money. And then there comes to him a memory of that Socialist orator he had heard on his first night in the city. He thinks, with weak terror, of all the human lives and toil upon which this blind and sensual riot is founded, and finally breaks away from "Society," to find out "if there isn't some way in New York for a man to earn an honest living."

The Moneychangers (1908), which trails Allan Montague into the mazes of Wall Street, gives us an "inside story" of the 1907 panic; and with the money earned by these two books, Sinclair was able to take a trip to California, do a few plays, and try to regain his health, which poverty and hard work had brought dangerously low. Returning East, he wrote *Samuel the Seeker* (1910), the story of a boy's search for an answer to the naturalistic hypothesis that since there is "not enough to go around" some of us must die and leave the comforts of existence to those who are fit to "grab" them and hang on.

After a period of wandering with his family from Michigan to Alabama, and of further attempts to improve his health by fasting and other methods,[9] Sinclair joined a group of "single tax" enthusiasts at Arden, Delaware, and composed *Love's Pilgrimage* (1911). In this book the author has chronicled his own boyhood and first marriage, a boyhood embittered by his father's taste for bitters and a marriage ruined by sexual ignorance. As a novel *Love's Pilgrimage* is as pathetic as its title; but like *The Journal of Arthur Stirling*, it does give us an interesting (if romanticized) "portrait of the author as a young man," a young man a

[9] See his *The Fasting Cure* (1911).

bit too eager, it seems, "to defy the world for the sake of his ideal."

In 1911 Sinclair went to New York to obtain a divorce; but unable to secure it under the peculiar laws of that state, he left for Holland the next year, where the separation was granted. Vexed by America's moral inertia, he decided that he never wanted to see this country again; and for a time he lingered in Europe and worked at *Sylvia* (1913), a tale of "the deep south." But with the outbreak of the war, he came back home, married again, resigned from the Socialist Party because it had voted for American neutrality, and in 1918 began his own magazine, *Upton Sinclair's*, to sponsor the policies of President Wilson.

From 1914 to 1934 Sinclair has continued to besiege the world with novels and pamphlets. *Sylvia's Marriage* (1914) is a sequel to *Sylvia*, and *King Coal* (1917) is a study of labor conditions in the coal mines of America. In the latter book, Hal Warner, a young man of "the upper crust," tries to obtain a job in a Colorado mining camp, in order to see for himself "how the other half lives." He is suspected of being a union sympathizer, beaten, and thrown out. But after he has turned hobo, lost some of his outward luster, and grown a beard, he manages to find work in the mines as "Joe Smith."

He soon discovers that many of the miners are starving, that accidents are never reported, and that an espionage system has been erected by the owners to spy upon employees; and when he starts to organize a union as a means of protest, he is "framed" and jailed. A mine explosion occurs, dozens of workers are trapped below, and the company seals them up to prevent the coal from burning. Hal, released by this tragedy, goes for outside help; but the police refuse to intercede, the miners are left to their fate, and the story ends on a mingled note of hope and despair.

The Profits of Religion (1918) berates supernaturalism "as a Source of Income and a Shield to Privilege," and in *The Brass Check* (1919), Sinclair makes the charge that American newspapers and magazines have sold themselves out to high finance, that the press is a prostitute, and that most "free thinkers" are victims of a journalistic conspiracy. *Jimmie Higgins* (1919) deprecates the part played by the United States in 1918, when Japanese, British, French, and American troops were sent to Vladivostok to protect Siberian railroads from the Bolsheviks. *100%* (1920) renders the Mooney case into fiction, and censures that period after the Armistice known as "The Great Red Scare." *They Call Me Carpenter* (1922) is a short fantasy in which the figure of Christ steps out of a stained-glass window, walks about on this troubled earth until he is mistaken for a Bolshevik and tossed in a blanket, and then hurries back to the shelter of his window, quavering, "I meant to die for this people. But now — let them die for themselves!" [10]   *The Goose-Step* (1923) raises the point that American universities are dominated by "big business," religion, and pedantry. And in *The Goslings* (1924), Sinclair applies this same indictment to our preparatory schools.

Mammonart (1925) states that artists, down through the ages, have always been ready to trade their souls for thirty pieces of silver; and *Money Writes* (1927) brings to a close Sinclair's "Dead Hand" series, in which he has tried to show how the dead hand of reactionism holds religion, journalism, education, and art in its grasp. *Money Writes*, itself, is "a study of American literature from the economic point of view. It takes our living writers, and turns their pockets inside out, asking, 'Where did you get it?' and 'What did you do for it?'"

Oil! (1927), perhaps Sinclair's best novel, is "a picture of civilization in Southern California," an exciting drama of the petroleum industry, stock frauds, land deals, drilling

[10] Sinclair, Upton, *They Call Me Carpenter* (1922), p. 218.

operations, bribery, labor troubles, Red-baiting, war fever, and racial prejudice, whose hero, "Bunny" Ross (the radical son of a great oil magnate) finds like many of Sinclair's heroes that he cannot accept his father's code of business ethics. After the latter's death, he uses his inheritance to found a labor college and fight that "evil Power which roams the earth, crippling the bodies of men and women, and luring the nations to destruction by visions of unearned wealth, and the opportunity to enslave and exploit labor." [11]

Mountain City (1930) is the story of Jed Rusher, who, reared amidst poverty and hardship in the beet fields of Colorado, determines to break into the upper circle of wealth, obtains a job as companion to an invalid capitalist, marries his employer's granddaughter (in order to get into the family, though she is pregnant by another man), swindles two ignorant ranchers out of rich oil property, organizes the Tar-Bucket Operating Corporation, becomes a great petroleum king, controls the stock market, bribes editors, directs banks, gets indicted for fraud, uses more fraud to obtain his liberty, loses his wife to her first lover, puts her out of his mind in his greed for more wealth, and in the end is shown giving a college president $50,000 for the purpose of endowing a chair to combat the "single tax" theory. "The ranch-boy who had tended cattle and crawled about in the muck of the beet fields had solved the modern Aladdin problem; he had found out where money comes from and how it is 'made' — and he had 'made' it. Unaided, he had forced his way into the sacred Garden of Privilege, and staked out a generous section of it for his private reserve. He had, and would forever after, have unlimited money to buy all the things he wanted: oil derricks and office buildings, to say nothing of politicians and newspapers and banks, and all the thousand other things needed for the developing of the Tar-Bucket

[11] Sinclair, Upton, *Oil!* (1927), p. 527.

enterprise. Jed would take this money and expend it wisely; he would buy what was needed, at the lowest possible prices; he would be a careful custodian and steward of wealth. The only point upon which he would insist was that all the oil derricks and storage tanks and pipe-lines and trucks and office buildings should belong to him, and not to anybody else in the world!" [12]

Boston (1928) dramatizes the Sacco-Vanzetti case. *The Millennium* (1929), "A Comedy of the Year 2000," which was taken from Sinclair's four-act drama of the same name, closes with the starvation of the last capitalist. "He had been too lazy to work," notes the author, "so he had perished; and with him perished his system — and the Co-operative Commonwealth reigned for ever after." [13] *The Way Out* (1933), a series of letters addressed to "the white collar class" of America (just as *Letters to Judd*, 1926, were addressed to "the average American workingman"), explains what Sinclair believes the future holds for us. *The Wet Parade* (1931), Sinclair's blast against "demon rum," is a novel partly inspired by the tragic rôle that liquor played in his own father's life. *Roman Holiday* (1931) describes how Luke Faber, the idealistic son of a millionaire, after being knocked out in an automobile race, dreams that he is back in Rome during the years of its twilight, and wakes up to draw a parallel between the fall of Rome and the threatened decline of modern America, based on a resemblance between the social injustice to be found in each. And *Upton Sinclair Presents William Fox* (1933) deals with the alleged corruption of certain money interests, under the subtitle: "A Feature Picture of Wall Street and High Finance."

A Radical Harold Bell Wright Sinclair has been branded as a "Prophet for Profit," and to this charge his

---

[12] Sinclair, Upton, *Mountain City* (1930), pp. 271–272.
[13] Sinclair, Upton, *The Millenium* (1929), p. 246.

genius for advertising himself and his ability for making literature pay him dividends both leave him open. But they do not constitute enough evidence to prove that his motives have been mercenary. If he has made money from his crusading volumes, he has also spent a small fortune on social projects of every description and has on several occasions mortgaged his future to do so. Were profit his only object, he could serve himself better by renouncing reform and going into business. *American Outpost* (1932), his autobiography, does not reveal him as a "whited sepulchre," but as a sincere humanitarian, loyal to his friends, tactless, generous to a fault, perennially young, disputatious, energetic, dedicated, and idealistic.

His credo is, in brief, "Communism in material production, Anarchism in intellectual production." Yet he does not entertain "revolution" as a means of achieving this. He expresses a confidence that "the hope of humanity is not in any new machinery or process to be discovered or invented, but in the opportunities already existing, and now owned and operated for purposes of exploitation." [14] He does not believe in confiscating the factories of America and turning them over to the worker, but thinks they should be purchased and run by the government, with all "unearned increment" going into the public treasury. He stands for a minimum wage law, with special salary scales for those in intellectual and agricultural work, and with a method of adjusting wages to tempt men into the more unpleasant trades and professions. No one need be drafted for anything; for performing the disagreeable tasks of society men should be paid slightly more. In his "ideal state" if a man wanted to starve, he could; or he might live in the woods on berries. The only demand that Sinclair would make is this: if a man buys any products, he should be made to pay for those products "with his

[14] Sinclair, Upton, "A Home Colony," *The Independent* (June 14, 1906), LX, 1404.

own labor, and not with some other man's labor." [15] "To take command of life," he says, "to replace instincts by reasoned and deliberate acts, to make the world a conscious and ordered product — that is the task of man." [16]

But a "reasoned and deliberate" point of view is something he has never been able to master in his own novels. He is an inveterate idealist; and this idealism has, in fact, led him into many mistakes. It betrayed him, for instance, into espousing militarism during the War, and it lured him to predict in *The Industrial Republic* (1907) that a great "house cleaning" would take place in America about the year 1913. Sinclair has been termed "a radical Harold Bell Wright." He is a born romanticist, whose "three friends" are Jesus, Hamlet, and Shelley, all visionaries like himself. His *Prince Hagen, The Millennium, They Call Me Carpenter*, and *Roman Holiday* are frankly fantastic; his *Journal of Arthur Stirling* and *King Midas* almost lead one to conclude that "to make the world safe for poets" it is only necessary to wipe out selfishness with sonnets; and even his strongest novels take on the aspect of romances, because, prompted by a romantic zeal, he constantly overtaxes the reader's belief. No matter how irrefutable they may be, the uncompromising energy with which he advances his facts keeps them from *sounding* convincing. As Lincoln Steffens once said to him, "The things you tell are unbelievable. I have a rule in my own work — I don't tell things that are unbelievable, even when they are true." [17] And Sinclair might put this advice to good use.

His stories are partisan, and his deep sympathy for "the under dog" forever prevents him from treating of economic and social questions in an impartial way; his fury against capitalism leaks through every line he has ever written.

[15] Sinclair, Upton, *The Book of Life* (1926), II, 204.
[16] Sinclair, Upton, *The Profits of Religion* (1918), p. 306.
[17] Quoted in Sinclair, Upton, *The Brass Check* (1919), p. 32.

The French statesman, Talleyrand, once observed that "Society is divided into two classes, the shearers and the shorn," and added that he preferred being on the side of the former. But Sinclair, for his part, feels more inclined to echo Eugene V. Debs, who said:

> While there is a lower class, I am in it.
> While there is a criminal element, I am of it.
> While there is a soul in jail, I am not free.

Sinclair is an evangelist, not a calm historian. He states "facts," but not for both sides; his crusading ardor does not tolerate a philosophic margin of hesitation, or admit of qualifications. He is a public prosecutor of "the idle rich," who comes to the case determined to gain a verdict of guilty against "the leisure class," and convict it of malfeasance and injustice. In the reformist novel, social groups have replaced individuals as the heroes and villains. As Sinclair sees it, the hero is the proletariat; the villain, capital. The fiscal and material facts of each one's case are a part of his knowledge. He has been in jail, and in palatial hotels; he knows I.W.W.'s and he knows bank presidents. The conditions of their lives are well understood by him. But whereas he may know the outward features of their different states, and realize what the laborer is thinking of, he does not, it seems, entirely comprehend the thought processes and rationale of the plutocrat. The ordinary human being, whether rich or poor, is a complex soul, a fact that Sinclair does not recognize. Or perhaps he does not want to recognize it, since his novels would be much less successful if they pictured the "captain of industry" as a many-sided personality with moments of kindness as well as moments of cruelty. If he rendered an absolutely true report of the financial baron, he would be forced to equivocate now and then; and equivocation would weaken his point. It is much more effective to describe his man of wealth as dominated by one greedy purpose and blind to every other impulse,[18] than it would be to describe him as "a colony of souls," some of them good and some of them bad.

This, in short, is the chief flaw in his work; it lacks artistry and imaginative truth, just as Hergesheimer's does. Both authors, though of radically opposed faith, fail in that they use their characters as lay figures, upon which Hergesheimer drapes his silks, and Sinclair hangs his socialistic arguments.

PUPPETS ON PARADE   To Sinclair the alignments of American life are simple; in fact, too simple. The rich, to his way of thinking, are bad and the poor are good, without much variation. He does not bother with nuances of personality, but loads his villains with vices and his heroes with virtues. His members of the capitalist group are mere symbols, highly conventionalized. They bear the obvious names of Robert van Rensselaer, Mrs. Smythe, Freddie Vandam, or Mrs. Lumley-Gotham; their homes are all frescoed with gold; and their own persons are eloquent with jewels. Sinclair's "captain of industry" is not a man; he is a dummy, plastered with dollar signs (the way cartoonists used to draw Mark Hanna). There is nothing subtle about Sinclair's satire. His weapon is not the rifle, but the shotgun; he "lays it on thick" and uses no half tones in his pictures. The rich are presented as insane cannibals and coupon clippers, and left at that; his working girls are all madonnas or flaming Valkyries, and his men of labor are "ragged philosophers." "Here all the workers wear haloes of pure golden sunlight and the capitalists have horns and tails."[19] For what Sinclair has always done has been

to flay an evil with mannikins instead of men; he has visualized a situation, conceived of its totality in terms of its theme, and then

[18] The father in *Oil!* is an exception.
[19] Brooks, Van Wyck, *Emerson and Others*, (1927), p. 212.

made his characters fit into that situation in order to illustrate its logic. As a result his characters have become the appendages of action instead of the creators of action, and have been no more real than puppets on parade.[20]

Sinclair has remarked that his concept of a novel is that of William Lyon Phelps: "a good story well told." But in his own work he violates this criterion. His stories are neither "good" nor "well told." They are, it is to be feared, hardly stories at all, in the usual sense; they are lectures in novelistic clothing. As someone has said of Sinclair's fiction, you can almost "hear the author whisper between each line 'I rather think that will bite you.'" He is not interested in character portrayal; he is interested in social renewal, and in plans for "the millennium." His books do, now and then, manage to convince us of their factual verisimilitude, but not of their imaginative truth. They do not strike us in the heart, but in the head, or, as Sinclair himself confessed of *The Jungle*, in the stomach.

"All art is propaganda," avows Sinclair.[21] Yet he seems to forget that in fiction, at least, the author must interest us in individual men before he can interest us in the problems of mankind as a whole. Characters and the theses they are designed to propagate must be integrated in art. The average reader will not swallow theories raw; they must be dipped in "human interest." Sinclair has ideas aplenty, but he does not know how to write "a good story well told." The gods gave him sincerity, a generous soul, and a capacity for hard work; but they left out the fictional touch. There is too much "finger-pointing" in his work.

Many authors, whose only aim is to cater to popular taste, and escapists like Cabell and Hergesheimer, geld unsavory truths by gilding them with sentimentalities. These novelists are concerned only with not leaving a bad

[20] Calverton, V. F., *The Liberation of American Literature* (1932), p. 464.
[21] Sinclair, Upton, *Mammonart* (1925), p. 9.

taste in the mouth; the literary meals they serve up consist always of *hors d'œuvres*, never of strong meat. And against their doctrine of authorship Sinclair does right to object. Yet he should recognize that in the novel the way to a reader's mind is through his emotions. In non-fiction the reverse is true. The man who picks up a book of essays is prepared to *think* first and feel afterwards; the man who picks up a novel expects to *feel* first and think later. "Literature, like all the arts, is primarily emotive in essence, and it is most successful in dealing with ideas, and 'gets across' its propaganda most effectively, when it is *emotionalized* instead of cerebralized." [22] Here and there, of course, are a few hardy readers who can digest both kinds of writing without benefit of emotion, but they are at present few in number, and most of them are already on Sinclair's side. To reach that far greater and as yet unconverted public, he must learn to convey his message through the clash of personalities and the psychological or moral development of individuals. As V. F. Calverton has said:

Revolutionary art has to be good art first before it can have deep meaning, just as apples in a revolutionary country as well as in a reactionary country have to be good apples before they can be eaten with enjoyment.[23]

[22] Calverton, V. F., "The Upton Sinclair Enigma," *The Nation* (February 4, 1931), CXXXII, 133.

[23] Calverton, V. F., *The Liberation of American Literature* (1932), p. 460.

*

THE VILLAGE VIRUS

*

BAD BOY Helicon Hall had been operating only a few months, when a knock was heard at the outer gate, and "Enter two students from Yale, asking for work." One was Allen Updegraff, who later married Sinclair's secretary, Edith Summers Kelley (author of *Weeds*); and the other was a young man with very red hair. His name, he told the colonists, was Sinclair Lewis. They made him janitor.

Lewis, son of a village doctor, was born February 7, 1885, in Sauk Center, Minnesota. As a youth, he was considered by the neighbors to be a trifle "queer," and in *Main Street* he has taken ample revenge upon his birthplace for its ugly, insular habits of mind. Surcease he found in introspective reveries, *Ivanhoe* (his favorite book), Dickens, walks about the countryside, and poetry. At fourteen he peddled a few of his own poems to the magazines, but without any luck; and to vent his *furor scribendi*, he tried to interest his classmates in a student paper, and took a job on the Sauk Center *Herald*.

High school over, he decided to go to Harvard, which he had read about in Charles Flandrau's *Harvard Episodes* (1897). Sauk Center, of course, warned him that "If you go off to one of these Eastern colleges, you'll get a lot of expensive tastes and not be able to earn one cent more money." But his father, though a bit skeptical of this Harvard idea, had been born near New Haven, and in the end they were able to compromise on Yale. So Lewis studied for six months at Oberlin Academy, to pass his entrance examinations at the university, and in 1903 went East.

During his college days, he twice worked his way to Europe on a cattle boat, contributed prose and Swinburnean poetry to the Yale *Courant*, helped edit the *Yale Literary Magazine*, and did reporting for a New Haven newspaper. At the beginning of his senior year, he left school (with his friend Updegraff) and came down to Sinclair's "co-operative boarding house," in New Jersey. But the other residents of Helicon Hall soon got on his nerves; he sickened of jaundice, and when he recovered, gave up his janitorship for an editorial berth on *Transatlantic Tales*. A bit later he went steerage to Panama, hoping to find work there; but discovering none, he came back and finished his last year at Yale. In 1908 he graduated, obtained a job as proof reader and dramatic critic on a Waterloo (Iowa) paper, lost it, and returned to New York to work for the Charity Organization Society.

Writing took up most of his spare time. He managed to place two or three stories, and a great many verses for children. And then with a few dollars in his pocket, he threw everything aside and went out to California, to earn his living as an author. Once there, however, he realized that he had nothing to write about; and the next three months found him busy on the San Francisco *Bulletin*. He worked three months more for The Associated Press (and was "fired" from both jobs for incompetence), went back to free lancing, and sold "plots" for stories to Jack London at ten dollars each. But when his own tales did not find a market, he retreated to Washington, D. C., became editor of the *Volta Review for the Deaf*, "read manuscripts" for Stokes Publishing Company (at $12.50 per week), worked for *Adventure Magazine*, and ended up as advertising manager with the book firm of George H. Doran, in New York. In 1914 he wed Grace Livingstone Hegger (who, after their divorce, is said to have drawn a portrait of him in her novel *Half a Loaf*, 1931). His second wife, whom he married in 1928, is Dorothy Thompson, author of *The New Russia* (1928) and other political works.

Meanwhile he had been perfecting his art, reading and learning from the volumes of H. G. Wells and Hamlin Garland;[1] and after a seven-year plague of rejection slips, he "broke into print" in *The Saturday Evening Post*. His first novel, *Our Mr. Wrenn*, was typed out after working hours, and printed in 1914. *The Trail of the Hawk* (1915) took shape on the train that carried him to and from his desk in New York. *The Job* appeared in 1917, and in the same year, *The Innocents*. *Free Air* tagged along in 1919; and then, "the bad boy of American letters" gathered himself together, borrowed $500 from his father, and sat down to write a novel that would blow America out of the water.

Main Street, "that pioneering work which with a swing of the pen hacked away the sentimental vegetation from the American small town,"[2] first occurred to Lewis while he was a sophomore at Yale. He sketched it out; entitled it "The Village Virus"; centered it about the pivotal figure of a village lawyer; and put it aside three times before finishing it, though at one time it did reach the length of thirty thousand words. In 1920 it came out in its final draft, with Carol Kennicott as its heroine, and by 1922 its readers numbered over 390,000. *Main Street* became, in fact, the smash hit of contemporary literature, and Lewis the curse of thousands and the toast of hundreds.

Babbitt (1922), written abroad (to enable him to escape from the literary lion hunters), solidified his fame. He

---

[1] "In Mr. Garland's 'Main-Travelled Roads,' " he says, "I discovered that there was one man who believed that Midwestern peasants were sometimes bewildered and hungry and vile — and heroic. And, given this vision, I was released; I could write of life as living life." Lewis, Sinclair, *Addresses by Erik Axel Karlfeldt and Sinclair Lewis, on the Occasion of the Award of the Nobel Prize* (1931), p. 22.

[2] Wharton, Edith, "The Great American Novel," *The Yale Review* (July, 1927), XVI, 648.

settled down in Hartford, Connecticut, for a deserved rest; but almost at once he met Paul H. de Kruif, a bacteriologist who had been with the Rockefeller Institute; and their discussions of medical education in the United States aroused in Lewis the desire to write a novel on this subject. With de Kruif he wandered for three months in Barbados, Panama, and Europe, visiting leper asylums, dispensaries, and laboratories; and when together they had worked out a long outline for the projected book, Lewis stayed on in France for a year to write it. His father, grandfather, brother, and uncle had been, or were, practicing physicians; and from the earliest days of his career, he had entertained the idea of a volume with "a doctor hero." *Arrowsmith* (1925) is that ambition satisfied.

Mantrap,[3] an inferior book, came out in 1926; and 1927 found Lewis in Kansas City, gathering material for his "preacher novel," and shocking the country by standing up in a pulpit, jerking out his watch, and giving God ten minutes to strike him dead for stating that he did not believe in the existence of a Divine Being. Luther Burbank's recent death, clergymen were saying, had been a judgment from heaven, because he was a skeptic. But Lewis thought otherwise. Wasn't it just possible, he insisted, that Burbank had died of hardening arteries?

In 1927 a loud Bang! resounded over the nation. That was Lewis blasting the ministry, as he had previously lighted giant crackers under the Babbitts, Main Streets, and medicos of America. In the twinkling of an eye, critics had chosen up sides on *Elmer Gantry*, Mencken had decorated Lewis for bravery in whacking the philistines, and even more voices had proclaimed him a "rascal" of the blackest dye. With this book, it was said, Lewis had "sent the preachers a comic valentine."

[3] The story of a New York lawyer's vacation in the Canadian woods, which Lewis quite frankly wrote to make a few dollars. Later it served as a vehicle for Clara Bow.

The Man Who Knew Coolidge followed in 1928; in 1929 *Dodsworth* came out; *Ann Vickers* issued from the press in 1933; and *Work of Art* (1934) brings him up to date.   In 1926 he refused the Pulitzer Prize for *Arrowsmith* because he felt that its donor's preference for books that echoed "the wholesome atmosphere of American life and the highest standard of manners and manhood" smacked of provincialism.   But in 1930 he did accept the Nobel Prize for Literature, and became the first American to receive that honor.

APPRENTICE PIECES   The hero of *Our Mr. Wrenn* is a clerk in the Souvenir and Art Novelty Company of New York, "a cornered mouse," an exact duplicate of Webster's "Timid Soul," "a meek little bachelor — a person of inconspicuous blue ready-made suits, and a small unsuccessful mustache." [4]   Yet there beats within his thin chest a heart that is hungry for a more poetic existence.   And so one day off he goes on a cattle boat to England, where he finds romance sitting in the eyes of Istra Nash, a red-haired art student.   Then love fades, he comes back, marries Nellie Croubel, a department store buyer, sinks into his background again, and is shown in the last line coming home to his wife with a paper in one hand and seven cents worth of potato salad from a delicatessen in the other.   A somewhat puerile book, and less real than raffish, *Our Mr. Wrenn* nevertheless has Lewis's signature on it, with its occasional swipes at "the live wire," business slogans, the Y.M.C.A., correspondence schools, "highbrows," Salvation Army types of religion, and men whose only idea of conversation is, "Some car you got.   What's your magneto?"

Hawk Ericson, in *The Trail of the Hawk*, is another "restless seeker of romance."   As a boy in Joralemon,

[4] Lewis, Sinclair, *Our Mr. Wrenn* (1914), p. 1.

Minnesota, he learns from Bone Stillman, the town atheist, that

Life is just a little old checker game played by the alfalfa contingent at the country store unless you've got an ambition that's too big to ever quite lasso it. You want to know that there's something ahead that's bigger and more beautiful than anything you've ever seen, and never stop till — well, till you can't follow the road any more. And anything or anybody that doesn't pack any surprises — get that? — *surprises* for you, is dead, and you want to slough it like a snake does its skin. You want to keep on remembering that Chicago's beyond Joralemon, and Paris beyond Chicago, and beyond Paris — well, maybe there's some big peak of the Himalayas.[5]

He goes to the jerkwater college of Plato, a place (says Lewis) "as earnest and undistinguished, as provincially dull and pathetically human, as a spinster missionary." [6] There he tries to help a professor who is being ostracized for radical views, is forced out of school as a heretic, wanders about the country, labors as a mechanic, travels with a road show, tends bar in the Bowery, ships for Panama to get a job (as Lewis did), moves on to Mexico, then California, enrolls as an aviation student in the early days of airplane building, joins a "flying circus," becomes a famous pilot, and invents a new type of automobile, the "Touricar." The Joralemon "state of mind" pursues him, however, in the person of one Gertie Cowles, until he falls in love with Ruth Winslow, a social worker. They marry, almost settle down into a "Normal Married Life," but are "saved" from that by a quarrel. The War comes, motor cars sell madly, and Hawk finally sails to become manager of an automobile corporation in South America, his "freedom" still unimpaired either by money or matrimony.

The Job is the story of Una Golden, a young girl brought up as a lawyer's daughter in the village of Panama, Penn-

---

[5] Lewis, Sinclair, *The Trail of the Hawk* (1915), p. 50.   [6] *Ibid.*, p. 58.

sylvania, and in the faith that a woman's duty is simply to maintain a "virginal vacuousness," keep respectable, and secure a husband. When her father dies, she revolts against the stale rectitude of her home town, bustles off with her mother to New York, attends a commercial college, gets a job on *The Motor and Gas Gazette*, begins to ask herself "what women in business can do to make human their existence of loveless routine," [7] tries to win Walter Babson, a hectic migratory co-worker, loses him when he breezes on to another job, meets a flashy paint salesman on her vacation, weds him to escape the daily grind of "the job," watches him cheat on her, thinks of suicide when he turns into a drunken beggar, returns to "the job" again to escape from her husband, works her way up in the realty game, goes into hotel publicity, and at last runs into her old lover, Babson. The "fade out" is a rather too obviously happy ending; but *The Job*, with all its faults, is one of the best novels ever done on the life of a wage slave in Manhattan, and seems to anticipate Lewis's later book about a "woman who did," *Ann Vickers*.

Lewis himself has termed *The Innocents* "A Story for Lovers," "a flagrant excursion, a tale for people who still read Dickens and clip out spring poetry and love old people and children." And with this brief notice, it may safely be passed over, as indeed an "innocent" and undistinguished tale. But *Free Air*, which concerns a banker's daughter who makes a cross-country trip in her big Gomez-Dep and falls in love, on the way, with a young engineering student in a cheap Teal roadster, is even worse. No one could possibly guess from reading this low-calibred yarn that in another year Lewis would be able to produce *Main Street*.

SWEET AUBURN   When *Main Street* appeared in 1920, it found the small town enshrined in popular fancy as the

[7] Lewis, Sinclair, *The Job* (1917), p. 47.

last home of virtue and benevolence. Such was the tradition we had inherited from Goldsmith's *Deserted Village* (1770), Mary Russell Mitford's *Our Village* (1819–1832), Mrs. Gaskell's *Cranford* (1853), and Washington Irving's *Sketch Book* (1819). More recently Booth Tarkington, in his *Gentleman from Indiana* (1899), had depicted the Hoosier hamlet of Plattesville as one big, happy, public-spirited family of "beautiful people." In *A Hoosier Chronicle* (1912) Meredith Nicholson had declared that "It's all pretty comfortable and cheerful and busy in Indiana, with lots of old-fashioned human kindness flowing round "; [8] and Zona Gale had pictured her *Friendship Village* (1908) as a haven of rest for the weary, whose inhabitants were always baking cookies, doing "good works," giving parties for one another, and repeating "Land sakes alive!"

Nicholson's essays in *The Valley of Democracy* (1918), which represented the high-water mark of "the friendly village" myth, looked upon small town "folks" as rich in

sturdy independence, hostility to capitalistic influence, and a proneness to social and political experiment. They are strong in the fundamental virtues, more or less sincerely averse to conventionality, and believe themselves possessed of a breadth of vision and a devotion to the common good at once beneficent and unique in the annals of mankind.[9]

But in 1783, not long after Goldsmith, another Englishman, George Crabbe, had brought in an entirely different verdict. His poem, *The Village*, betrayed the small town as a menagerie of ignoble creatures who bear malice, hate liberalism, thrive upon ugliness, and lack the rustic ideals usually attributed to them by bards. And exactly one hundred years later, E. W. Howe's *Story of a Country Town* (1883) fired the opening gun against the village in America, with its description of Twin Mounds, a numb, bleak,

[8] Nicholson, Meredith, *A Hoosier Chronicle* (1912), p. 606.
[9] Nicholson, Meredith, *The Valley of Democracy* (1919), p. 3.

prudish, ignorant, bigoted, stingy town in Kansas, whose citizens "walked in a stodgy round of orthodoxies." [10]

Howe's novel was followed by Harold Frederic's study, in *The Damnation of Theron Ware* (1896), of the mean, self-complacent, juiceless, secretive New York village of Octavius; and after *Main Street* came out:

The rather standardized small-town life on the flat plains, with its universal public-school system, its ubiquitous commercial clubs and secret societies, its competitive Protestant sects, its combination of Yankee business ruthlessness on week days with sentimental aspiration on Sundays and civic holidays, became the target for a score of literary archers. [11]

In *West of the Water Tower* (1923) and *R. F. D. No. 3* (1924), Homer Croy reconstructed the tobacco-stained, cackling, prying, hymn-singing burg of Junction City, Missouri. In *Arlie Gelston* (1923) Roger L. Sergel held up a trenchant mirror to Coon Falls, Iowa. In *Mitch Miller* (1920), *Skeeters Kirby* (1923), and *Kit O'Brien* (1927), Edgar Lee Masters exposed the rancid, falsely respectable town of Petersburg, Illinois (though his strictures contain a rich leaven of charity); and in *The Tattooed Countess* (1924), Carl Van Vechten portrayed Maple Valley, Iowa, as "a God-forsaken hole full of stupid fools."

Above this controversy stand *Country People* (1924), *The Odyssey of a Nice Girl* (1925), and *The Bonney Family* (1928), in which Ruth Suckow, with quiet vitality, has given us our best interpretation of the rural community. But it is Lewis's more sensational and less sensitive concept of the prairie town that reigns in the American novel today, and should continue to dominate literature for years, unless Phil Stong's recent *State Fair* (1932) and James Gould Cozzens' *The Last Adam* (1933) are indications that the pendulum is swinging back to "the friendly village" again.

[10] Van Doren, Carl, *Many Minds* (1924), p. 37.

[11] Slosson, Preston William, *The Great Crusade and After, 1914–1928* (1931), p. 417. By permission of The Macmillan Company, publishers.

THE HOME TOWN MIND   In *Main Street* Lewis has drawn his pen against "the ugliness of the American small town, the cultural poverty of its life, the tyranny of its mass prejudices, and the blatant vulgarity and insularity of the booster."[12]   "This is America," he says in his preface, "a town of a few thousand, in a region of wheat and corn and dairies and little groves."[13]

Main Street is the climax of civilization.   That this Ford car might stand in front of the Bon Ton Store, Hannibal invaded Rome and Erasmus wrote in the Oxford cloisters.   What Ole Jenson the grocer says to Ezra Stowbody the banker is the new law for London, Prague, and the unprofitable isles of the sea; whatsoever Ezra does not know and sanction, that thing is heresy, worthless for knowing and wicked to consider.[14]

As a student at Blodgett College, Carol Milford has decided to do something about the American village, to "get my hands on one of these prairie towns and make it beautiful.   Be an inspiration."[15]   But after she has married Dr. Will Kennicott and gone with him to live in Gopher Prairie, Minnesota, she finds the task harder than she had imagined.   Her husband proves to be a dolt with a rubber-stamp mind, good-natured and well meaning, but a smug, optimistic provincial.   The town itself, she discovers, is a fly-specked, drab, repressed, dusty hamlet, with its feet in the mud, a platitude in its mouth, and a secret desire to imitate the larger towns around it, a back-slapping, hypocritical, back-biting, guffawing "frontier camp," alive with prejudices and materialism, a terrifying receptacle for dead brains.   Into this blank wall of mediocrity Carol tries to inject "a seed of liberalism," to

[12] Allen, Frederick Lewis, *Only Yesterday* (1931), pp. 229–230.

[13] Lewis, Sinclair, Preface to *Main Street* (1921).

[14] *Ibid.* Good analyses of "the small town mind" may be found in Ruth Suckow's "Iowa," an article in *The American Mercury* for September, 1926, and in Albert Blumenthal's *Small-Town Stuff*, a sociological study published by The University of Chicago Press, 1932.

[15] Lewis, Sinclair, *Main Street* (1921), p. 5.

awaken Gopher Prairie's integrity, to wipe out its distrust of beauty, to remove its jealousies and its mean, low-flying hungers. But the "village virus" soon gets her, too, as it has already silenced Guy Pollack, the town lawyer; and so in the end, she learns to face her predicament with "unembittered laughter." For "though a Gopher Prairie," says Lewis,

regards itself as a part of the Great World, compares itself to Rome and Vienna, it will not acquire the scientific spirit, the international mind, which would make it great. It picks at information which will visibly procure money or social distinction. Its conception of a community ideal is not the grand manner, the noble aspiration, the fine aristocratic pride, but cheap labor for the kitchen and rapid increase in the price of land. It plays at cards on greasy oil-cloth in a shanty, and does not know that prophets are walking and talking on the terrace.[16]

IN PHILISTIA   By 1920 there were 1,800 Kiwanis Clubs in America, 1,200 Lions Clubs, and by 1930, 150,000 Rotary members, all singing "pep" songs, adoring Dr. Frank Crane, reading advertisements on "How to Develop Power at Home," doting on Efficiency, organizing social service campaigns, speaking often of "the redemptive and regenerative influence of business," quoting the Bible in directors' meetings, and building up, from the pages of Bruce Barton, a conception of Jesus as a "born executive," who had by sheer force of "personality" and salesmanship "put over" or "swung" Christianity.[17]   And it is to this group that Lewis's George F. Babbitt belongs.

Zenith, Minnesota, where Babbitt lives, is just a magnified edition of Gopher Prairie, a bright, standardized community of 361,000 inhabitants. Babbitt himself, forty-six, married, and father of three children, is what might be described, in simple terms, as a "philistine," or as the dic-

16 *Main Street*, p. 267.
17 See Bruce Barton's *The Man Nobody Knows* (1925).

tionary would put it: "A blind adherent to conventional ideas; an ignorant and narrow-minded person, especially one given to money-making; one devoid of culture, or indifferent to art." [18] He is that species of the *petite bourgeoisie* known as a "Solid Citizen," a successful realtor, a slave to current and popular ideas, a Republican, Presbyterian, Elk, hater of Bolsheviks, devotee of zeal, zest, and zowie, a worshiper of business acumen, a respecter of "bigness," and a member of the Zenith Athletic Club. Here is his own definition of the "Ideal Citizen."

I picture him first and foremost as being busier than a bird-dog, not wasting a lot of good time in day-dreaming or going to sassiety teas or kicking about things that are none of his business, but putting the zip into some store or profession or art. At night he lights up a good cigar, and climbs into the little old 'bus, and maybe cusses the carburetor, and shoots out home. He mows the lawn, or sneaks in some practice putting, and then he's ready for dinner. After dinner he tells the kiddies a story, or takes the family to the movies, or plays a few fists of bridge, or reads the evening paper, and a chapter or two of some good lively Western novel if he has a taste for literature, and maybe the folks next-door drop in and they sit and visit about their friends and the topics of the day. Then he goes happily to bed, his conscience clear, having contributed his mite to the prosperity of the city and to his own bank-account.[19]

That is to say, he is "a God-fearing, hustling, successful, two-fisted Regular Guy, who belongs to some church with pep and piety to it, who belongs to the Boosters or the Rotarians or the Kiwanis, to the Elks or Moose or Red Men or Knights of Columbus or any one of a score of organizations of good, jolly, kidding, laughing, sweating, upstanding, lend-a-handing Royal Good Fellows, who plays hard and works hard, and whose answers to his critics is a square-toed boot that'll teach the grouches and smart alecks to respect

[18] Funk and Wagnalls, *New Standard Dictionary of the English Language.*
[19] Lewis, Sinclair, *Babbitt* (1922), pp. 181–182.

the He-man and get out and root for Uncle Samuel, U. S. A.!" [20]

Babbitt, though, is not quite happy. " 'Kind of comes over me,' he says, 'here I've pretty much done all the things I ought to; supported my family, and got a good house and a six-cylinder car, and built up a nice little business, and I haven't any vices 'specially, except smoking — and I'm practically cutting that out by the way. And I belong to the church, and play enough golf to keep in trim, and I only associate with good decent fellows. And yet, even so, I don't know that I'm entirely satisfied.' " [21] Confused by this feeling that something is wrong, and dimly aware that Philistia has caught him in its toils, he tries feebly to kick over the traces, by refusing to join the Good Citizens League (a society to drive "undesirable elements out of Zenith") and by doing a bit of philandering on the side. A whispering campaign and a boycott by his fellow townsmen, however, soon bully him back into the fold. He joins the League, gives up his lady friend, closes his eyes to whatever disquiets him, and forever holds his peace. Yet when his son decides, against everyone's advice, to get married, leave college, and take a factory job, Babbitt upholds him. "I've never done a single thing I've wanted to in my whole life," he confesses, wearily,

I don't know 's I've accomplished anything except just get along. I figure out I've made about a quarter of an inch out of a possible hundred rods. Well, maybe you'll carry things on further. I don't know. But I do get a kind of sneaking pleasure out of the fact that you knew what you wanted to do and did it. . . . Tell 'em to go to the devil! I'll back you. Take your factory job, if you want to. Don't be scared of the family. No, nor all of Zenith. Nor of yourself, the way I've been. Go ahead, old man. The world is yours! [22]

[20] *Babbitt*, p. 188.
[21] *Ibid.*, pp. 60–61.
[22] *Ibid.*, p. 401.

The Truth Seeker. Carol Kennicott and Babbitt were unfortunately victims of their environment and "the village virus." The philistines finally cornered both of them. But *Arrowsmith* is the record of a victory. In it we are introduced to Martin Arrowsmith, son of a clothes merchant in a small midwestern town. His leisure as a boy is spent in watching the office for old Dock Vickerson, a gentle bibulous practitioner in Elk Mills, and in poring over Gray's *Anatomy*. For even at this early age, he has decided to become a·doctor. His parents die; and in a few years he enters medical school at the state university, where almost at once he conceives an overwhelming regard for Max Gottlieb, a sardonic professor of bacteriology, whose lonely and conscientious devotion to the ideals of pure science causes his colleagues on the faculty to look upon him as an impractical lunatic.

Arrowsmith soon realizes that the university is "a mill to turn out men and women who will lead moral lives, play bridge, drive good cars, be enterprising in business, and occasionally mention books, though they are not expected to have time to read them," that it is "a Ford Motor Factory" whose graduates "are beautifully standardized," [23] and that the medical college is very much the same sort of place, with professors whose only interest is to teach their acquiescent students a handful of staple prescriptions, the importance of "making money," "how to impress your patients," the proper choice in office furniture, and the essentials of "getting ahead." But to Martin this information, though it entirely satisfies his pestiferous classmates, does not seem adequate. What he wants is "to do big things," to become an honest laboratory worker, and to win the respect of men like Gottlieb, for whom professional integrity still retains a spark of meaning.

He joins a "frat," from which he resigns when he can no longer endure the sophomoric pranks and narrow ambitions

[23] Lewis, Sinclair, *Arrowsmith* (1925), p. 7.

of its other members; works as a line man on a telephone crew in Montana during one vacation; labors untiringly to imitate his hero, Gottlieb; gains the confidence of this nervous touchy genius; and at the same time, finds himself being lured away from the pursuit of knowledge by Madeline Fox, a frigid and possessive co-ed. From a disastrous marriage he is rescued by falling in love with Leora Tozer, a gay, courageous, and altogether charming nurse in a Zenith hospital. Gottlieb makes him his assistant, only to fire him in one of his testy moments. He leaves school and wanders around the country for a while, drinking steadily and riding in box cars. But at last, in sheer disgust at himself, he goes to Leora's home town in Wheatsylvania, North Dakota; elopes with her; and returns to the university, where he takes up his studies again and she enters business college. After graduating he takes a job as house physician in the Zenith Hospital, decides that he must give up his dream of becoming a pure scientist, and drifts out to Wheatsylvania to open up an office as a general practitioner.

The paths of Arrowsmith and Gottlieb cross again, but for a few years they diverge. Gottlieb loses his position at the university; pockets his principles in order to obtain a job with a large pharmaceutical firm in Pittsburgh; sickens of the commercialism there; and goes to New York, to work for the McGurk Institute of Biology, a privately endowed research organization.

Meanwhile, as a country doctor, Arrowsmith finds the gossip, jealousies, and moral desiccation of village life hard to bear, and transfers to the larger town of Nautilus, Iowa, where he becomes an assistant to Dr. Almus Pickerbaugh, the Director of Public Health. But Pickerbaugh turns out to be a bubbling, moronic Billy Sunday crusader against drinking and germs, whose chief delight is to spread his views by means of jingles and rousing addresses before clubs, on such themes as " Health First, Safety Second, and

Booze Nowhere A-tall." He has organized his eight daughters, Orchid, Verbena, Daisy, Jonquil, Hibisca, Narcissa, Arbuta, and Gladiola, into what he calls the Healthette Octette, and trained them to recite his doggerel verses and sing The Health Hymn (to the tune of The Battle Hymn of the Republic).

Oh, are you out for happiness or are you out for pelf?
You owe it to the grand old flag to cultivate yourself,
To train the mind, keep clean the streets, and ever guard your
    health,
            Then we'll all go marching on.

            A healthy mind in A clean body,
            A healthy mind in A clean body,
            A healthy mind in A clean body,
            The slogan for one and all.[24]

Pickerbaugh gets elected State Senator, goes to Washington, and leaves Martin in charge of the clinic. But his scruples and skepticism soon earn him his discharge; and like Gottlieb he goes over to the field of commercial research. From a Chicago post which he does not enjoy, he goes to join his old teacher at the McGurk Institute in New York. Gottlieb welcomes him, and for a time he is happy, until he finds that the Institute is nothing more than a social playground for Capitola McGurk, the rich and exasperating wife of its founder. Then he discovers a bacteriophage, and is sent by the Institute to the West Indies to use it in checking an epidemic that is raging there. Leora, who has insisted on going with him, falls a victim to the plague; but Arrowsmith succeeds in his mission, marries a wealthy and insidiously charming widow who tries to regularize his habits and thoughts, escapes her by running away to a shack in the Vermont hills with a sympathetic fellow scientist, and presumably spends the rest of his life in further experi-

[24] *Arrowsmith*, p. 203.

mentation, still clinging to his "religion of science," and to Gottlieb's conviction that

To be a scientist — it is not just a different job, so that a man should choose between being a scientist and being an explorer or a bond-salesman or a physician or a king or a farmer. It is a tangle of very obscure emotions, like mysticism, or wanting to write poetry; it makes its victim all different from the good normal man. The normal man, he does not care much what he does except that he should eat and sleep and make love. But the scientist is intensely religious — he is so religious that he will not accept quarter-truths, because they are an insult to his faith.

He wants that everything should be subject to inexorable laws. He is equal opposed to the capitalists who t'ink their silly money-grabbing is a system, and to liberals who t'ink man is not a fighting animal; he takes both the American booster and the European aristocrat, and he ignores all their blithering. Ignores it! All of it! He hates the preachers who talk their fables, but he iss not too kindly to the anthropologists and historians who can only make guesses, yet they have the nerf to call themselves scientists! Oh, yes, he is a man that all nice good-natured people should naturally hate!

He speaks no meaner of the ridiculous faith-healers and chiropractors than he does of the doctors that want to snatch our science before it is tested and rush around hoping they heal people, and spoiling all the clues with their footsteps; and worse than the men like hogs, worse than the imbeciles who have not even heard of science, he hates pseudo-scientists, guess-scientists — like these psycho-analysts; and worse than those comic dream-scientists he hates the men that are allowed in a clean kingdom like biology but know only one text-book and how to lecture to nincompoops all so popular! He is the only real revolutionary, the authentic scientist, because he alone knows how liddle he knows.[25]

Arrowsmith is Lewis's finest novel, and one of the masterpieces of recent fiction. In it we find a vertical depth, magnitude, purity of character, inventiveness, and mastery of form that Lewis has never since been able to duplicate.

[25] *Arrowsmith*, p. 279.

"It has more variety of pace and interest than *Main Street*, and its satire is quite as aggressive as in *Babbitt;* but it has that additional quality which belongs only to the higher levels of literature, the sense of facing the issues of life and creating, in the very face of defeat, an inner assurance." [26]

SCHMALTZ ON LIFE   *The Man Who Knew Coolidge* interprets "the soul of Lowell Schmaltz, constructive and Nordic citizen," Zenith business man, and friend of George Babbitt. A *tour de force*, it consists of six monologues on such topics as prohibition, Coolidge, office supplies, travel, radios, Service, golf, poker, "sorehead Bolsheviks," and women, all by Mr. Schmaltz himself, whose motto is "Read widely, think scientifically, speak briefly, and sell the goods!" [27]   Nowhere does Lewis's amazing gift of mimicry show to such advantage as in this book; and nowhere are we given a better chance to observe what one critic has termed his talent for catching "the lying overtones in all human speech," and his "printed dialogue that talks right into your brain." [28]   Yet *The Man Who Knew Coolidge* is a volume that many readers will find it impossible to complete, for the very reason that it is so successful in making us see its hero. Lowell Schmaltz, it should be noted, is the kind of a person one crosses the street to avoid, and 275 pages of him is more than enough.

SALESMAN OF SALVATION   The title rôle of *Elmer Gantry* (which Rebecca West, the English critic, has termed "a sequence of sermons and seductions") is played by a profligate clergyman, a ponderous monster, bleater of platitudes, ankle-snatcher, and arch hypocrite, whom we meet

---

[26] Mumford, Lewis, "The America of Sinclair Lewis," *Current History* (January, 1931), XXXIII, 531.

[27] Lewis, Sinclair, *The Man Who Knew Coolidge* (1928), p. 275.

[28] Casseres, Benjamin de, "Portraits en Brochette," *The Bookman* (July, 1931), LXXIII, 488.

first as an "eloquently drunk" student at Terwillinger College, in Cato, Missouri.

A huge young man, Elmer Gantry; six foot one, thick, broad, big handed; a large face, handsome as a Great Dane is handsome, and a swirl of black hair, worn rather long. His eyes were friendly, his smile was friendly — oh, he was always friendly enough; he was merely astonished when he found that you did not understand his importance and did not want to hand over anything he might desire. He was a barytone solo turned into portly flesh; he was a gladiator laughing at the comic distortion of his wounded opponent.

He could not understand men who shrank from blood, who liked poetry or roses, who did not casually endeavor to seduce every possibly seducible girl. In sonorous arguments with Jim [a friend of his] he asserted that "these fellows that study all the time are just letting on like they're so doggone high and mighty, to show off to these doggone profs that haven't got anything but lemonade in their veins." [29]

His earliest ambition is to become a lawyer; but as graduation approaches, he gives it up because preaching seems to offer him a better chance to earn applause, "sway audiences," and salve his egotism. Once this decision has been made, a big "snort" of corn whisky enables him to imagine that he has heard a "Call" from heaven to join the Baptist ministry. So off he hikes to Mizpah Theological Seminary in Babylon, Minnesota, where he is instantly turned into a sink of

flush florid polysyllables, with juicy sentiments about God, sunsets, the moral improvement inherent in a daily view of mountain scenery, angels, fishing for souls, fishing for fish, ideals, patriotism, democracy, purity, the error of Providence in creating the female leg, courage, humility, justice, the agricultural methods of Palestine *circ.* 4 A.D., the beauty of domesticity, and preachers' salaries.[30]

[29] Lewis, Sinclair, *Elmer Gantry* (1927), pp. 8–9.   [30] *Ibid.*, p. 58.

After his ordination, but while still in the seminary, he takes an appointment in a nearby village, seduces a farmer's daughter, and skins out of trouble by throwing the blame on an innocent bystander. Later he is fired out of Mizpah, and takes a job as traveling salesman for the Pequot Farm Implement Company, though he is still an ordained member of the clergy. However, while selling manure spreaders in Sautersville, Nebraska, he runs across Sharon Falconer, a famous woman evangelist then touring the country, and teams up with her. Together, two half-crazy mounte-banks, they set out to fleece the public. For a while all goes well. The evangelistic troupe, with musical directors, costumers, advertising managers, press agents, etc., moves from one triumph to another, while Elmer and Sharon trade kisses back stage, rake in the shekels, plan investments, and do faith healing. But their Waters of Jordan Tabernacle, which they have erected on the Jersey Coast, burns down on "opening night," and Sharon is killed. Elmer takes another job with a female swami, Mrs. Evans Riddle, proprietor of the Victory Thought-power Headquarters, New York, is kicked out for stealing from the collection plate, starts a "will power" institute of his own, and eventually makes his way into the Methodist pastorate of Banjo Crossing, Minnesota, intent on rising quickly to the post of bishop, and drawing in some "spondulix" again. Here is a sample from one of his first sermons there:

Oh, do you not sometimes hear, stealing o'er the plains at dawn, coming as it were from some distant secret place, a sound of mel-ody? When our dear sister here plays the offertory, do you not seem sometimes to catch the distant rustle of the wings of cheru-bim? And what is music, lovely, lovely music, what is fair melody? Ah, music, 'tis the voice of Love! Ah, 'tis the magi-cian that makes right royal kings out of plain folks like us! 'Tis the perfume of the wondrous flower, 'tis the strength of the athlete, strong and mighty to endure 'mid the heat and dust of the valorous conquest. Ah, Love, Love, Love! Without it, we are less than beasts; with it, earth is heaven and we are as the gods! [31]

But unfortunately he conceives an itch for "our dear sister here," marries her, becomes a fervent "salesman of salvation," preaches on such lively topics as "Would Jesus Play Poker," manages soon to grab a more lucrative appointment in the town of Rudd Center, joins all the lodges in sight, rants against booze, mixed bathing, and the fox trot, cultivates the friendship of rich members of his congregation, leads raids on vice dens, damns the Huns during the War, works his way up to be spiritual shepherd of a church in Zenith, joins the Rotary Club, conducts pulpit stunts, raids more vice dens, plays golf with bankers, takes a trip to Europe, visits London, and finds there that

Why say, we got a dozen streets in Zenith, say nothing of N' York, that got better stores. No git up and git to these foreigners. Certainly does make a fellow glad he's an American! [32]

He meets J. E. North "the renowned vice-slayer, executive secretary of the National Association for the Purification of Art and the Press," and in a short while takes over his post in this organization. A bit later he gets a bigger church in New York, caresses his stenographer on the sly (who pulls the old badger game on him to the tune of fifteen hundred dollars), turns the tables on his enemies, and emerges victorious on page 432, standing proudly before his cheering parishioners, and praying (with one eye cocked on the ankles of a girl in the choir):

Let me count this day, Lord, as the beginning of a new and more vigorous life, as the beginning of a crusade for complete morality and the domination of the Christian church through all the land. Dear Lord, thy work is but begun! We shall yet make these United States a moral nation! [33]

[31] *Elmer Gantry*, p. 275.   [32] *Ibid.*, p. 405.
[33] *Ibid.*, p. 432.

Sinclair Lewis's opinion of the church might be summed up in the words of Frank Shallard, an earnest minister in this book, honestly tormented by his doubts but fervent in his desire to find in religion a balm and truth, who says:

My objection to the church isn't that the preachers are cruel, hypocritical, actually wicked, though some of them are that, too — think of how many are arrested for selling false stock, for seducing fourteen-year-old girls in orphanages under their care, for arson, for murder. And it isn't so much that the church is in bondage to Big Business and doctrines as laid down by millionaires — though a lot of churches are that, too. My chief objection is that ninety-nine per cent of sermons and Sunday School teachings are so agonizingly *dull!* [34]

THE MAN WITHOUT A COUNTRY   *Dodsworth* is the story of an American "captain of industry," a rich automobile magnate, one step up in the social and business scale from Babbitt. Realizing at fifty that he has become "a human cash-register," he takes a trip to Europe with his gay, shallow wife, Fran, on the strength of her conviction that they can "make more passionate lives merely by running away to a more complex and graceful civilization." [35] But the experiment does not work. That Europe has its advantages he readily admits. He likes its freedom from optimism and oratory, high-pressure advertising, prohibition, and morality hounds. And yet he finds it impossible to adapt himself to the absence of these things; for he has overlooked the fact, in seeking to escape from them, that "wherever he traveled he must take his own familiar self along, and that that self would loom up between him and the new skies, however rosy." [36]   Fran, on the other hand, manages to give herself up entirely to European ways; and at last Dodsworth is forced to come home alone to America, which he now finds he cannot live either with, or without. He drifts back to

[34] *Ibid.*, p. 378.   [35] Lewis, Sinclair, *Dodsworth* (1931), p. 59.
[36] *Ibid.*

Europe to meet Fran again, a man without a country.   But when his wife deserts him for a German nobleman, he manages to break with his past to the extent of refusing to take her back; finds a measure of peace with Mrs. Cortright, the widow of a diplomat; and returns to America to carry out a scheme that he has for building a modernized and uniquely American suburb in Zenith.

The tragedy of Dodsworth is, in effect, that of Babbitt. Their perspectives have been irrevocably limited by the many years they have spent in a sterile pursuit of money. Spiritual and cultural impotence has descended upon them. Their souls have been murdered by business and conformity to the narrow views of Zenith.   They have been sucked dry of individuality.   Both want to escape from their emaciated philistinism; but Zenith will not let Babbitt, and Dodsworth's meager triumph is purchased at a heavy cost. Neither ever rises above himself; neither can ever change. Their wings have been clipped.   Both can make impressive speeches to their salesmen; but neither can ever hope to "love passionately, lose tragically, nor sit in contented idleness upon tropic shores." [37]

A WOMAN WHO DID   *Ann Vickers* traces the career of a neurotic Amazon, who starts out as a social worker and ends up as the mistress of a politician.   Just as the hero of *The Trail of the Hawk* received his first lesson in life from the lips of a "village Voltaire," so Ann is awakened to economic injustice in America by listening to Oscar Klebs, a Socialistic cobbler in the town of Waubanakee, Illinois, where she grows up as the daughter of the school superintendent. Says the shoemaker:

Did you ever stop to think, young lady, that the entire capitalist system is wrong?   That you and I should work all day, but Evans, the banker, who just takes in our money and lends it back to us again, should be rich?   I do not even know your name, young

[37] *Dodsworth*, p. 11.

lady, but you have luffly eyes — I t'ink intelligent. T'ink of it! A new world! From each so much as he can give, to each so much as he needs. The Socialist state! From Marx. Do you like that, young lady? *Hein?* A state in which all of us work for each other? [38]

But the cobbler's son, Adolph, a phlegmatic youth, is inclined to smile at his father's "ideas." For "He belonged not to the sedentary and loquacious generation of his father, but to a restless new age of machinery, of flashing cam-shafts, polished steel, pistons ramming gayly into a hell of exploding gas, dynamos humming too deep for words." [39] And so while Ann learned from Old Oscar "that all of life was to foresee Utopia, from Adolph she learned that to be hard, self-contained, and ready was all of life." [40]

The first half of her career is spent under the influence of Oscar's vision, but it is to Adolph's selfish philosophy that she returns in the end. She goes to Point Royal College for Women, a mutinous, spartan girl, whose ambition it is "to contribute, oh, one millionth of a degree to helping make this race of fat-heads and grouches something more like the angels." [41] Briskly intent upon carving out a man's place for herself in the world, she decides that men are to play no part in her life, repulses the overt advances of her history professor, Glenn Hargis, and to drown her doubts about the wisdom of her refusal, plunges into debating and socialistic activities in the school.

After graduating she spends the next ten years in welfare work. She takes nursing in a New York hospital and agitates for Woman's Rights in Ohio. Thrown into jail, she comes out with a revised view of the suffrage movement; teaches in a New York settlement house; lives with a soldier for ten days; has an abortion; leaves charity work; takes a trip to England; comes back to a job as educational director in the Green Valley Refuge for Women; studies criminol-

---

[38] Lewis, Sinclair, *Ann Vickers* (1933), p. 12.   [39] *Ibid.*, p. 14.
[40] *Ibid.*, p. 15.   [41] *Ibid.*, p. 49.

ogy; enters prison reform; works in a western penitentiary
until, nauseated by the "licensed sadism" there, she revolts,
is "framed," and resigns; goes back to New York to super-
intend a large reformatory; and in time becomes a Great
Woman, with honorary degrees and her name in the headlines. But renown, she finds, is empty. What she really
wants is love and a home and children.

She marries prosaic J. Russell Spaulding, a kind of grown
up Boy Scout; wearies of him; goes away for a week end
with Barney Dolphin, a Tammany judge; and has a child
by him. Then Dolphin is sent to prison on a graft charge;
but Ann, realizing now that she is just A Woman and not A
Great Woman, waits for him. And when after a year he
is pardoned, they retire to live in happy adultery, with
Ann released at last from "the prison of ambition, the prison
of desire for praise, the prison [as she puts it] of myself." [42]

There are three important things to be noted about the
Lewis of *Ann Vickers*. First, this is the only book in which he
has dealt copiously with social problems, in the sense that
Upton Sinclair deals with them. Heretofore he has been
chiefly interested in slaying the dragon Smugness and its
mate, Dullness. Yet in this book he strikes directly at
war, prisons, anti-abortion laws, graft, patriotism, "the
idle rich," and the tendency of settlement houses to
become mere "cultural comfort stations." Second, he
seems in this volume to have lost or discarded his genius
for satire. *Main Street*, *Babbitt*, *Arrowsmith*, and *Elmer
Gantry* contain whole galleries of genial idiots, whereas
Dodsworth verges upon tragedy rather than comedy, and
the only evidence in *Ann Vickers* of Lewis's extraordinary
ability to bait fools is that unspeakable person, J. Russell
Spaulding.

The third and most significant feature of his latest work,
however, is its lack of moral health, its swing from the mor-
dant to the morbid. Like most of Lewis's other characters,

[42] *Ann Vickers*, p. 562.

Ann Vickers is a rebel. But though we feel inclined to applaud Carol Kennicott and Arrowsmith, in their revolt against the philistines who seek to enslave them, we feel no such sympathy for Ann, whom Lewis treats as a heroine even in the hour when she lowers herself to the plane of a patently dishonest grafter. While Lewis is at war against Dullness and Smugness and provincial minds, we can follow him; and when in *Ann Vickers* he berates the anti-birth control forces, the whole idea of incarcerating criminals, and the weaknesses of our welfare system, many of us can still shout his praises. Yet when he adopts a selfish, naturalistic attitude of "Be hard" and condones political delinquencies, a puzzling loss of tone enters his work. That *Ann Vickers* should blur out in a sugary "happy ending" is not (bad as it is) surprising, inasmuch as Lewis is at bottom something of a sentimentalist. What is amazing is his loss of dynamic sanity.

If we omit Elmer Gantry, we see that all of Lewis's major characters try, at one time or another, to "free" themselves from provincialism, to free themselves from something they realize is not worthy of them in order to attain something that is worthy of them. All, that is, except Ann Vickers. She reverses the situation, and strives to be "free" in order to achieve, not Arrowsmith's noble dream or the cosmopolitanism that Dodsworth seeks in vain, but the opportunity to be selfish and carnal. She represents, in fact, a type of neurotic that in the past Lewis would have cauterized with high satire instead of glorifying, a melting away of his idealism. In *Ann Vickers* his occasional bitterness, his concern with the more nauseating aspects of certain American prisons and their mentally diseased officials, and his unwholesome heroine, all point to an increasing demoralization in Lewis's work and to the fact that the author of *Arrowsmith* is no more.

Work of Art (1934), his most recent book, chronicles the life of Myron Weagle, an American hotel-keeper, whose dream it is to create a perfect hostelry, a very poem of a hotel. Business, too, avers Lewis, has its unsung heroes, its romance, and its dreamers. And in writing of Myron Weagle he has sheathed his claws, and again betrayed his secret fondness for the Babbitts, a fondness that many readers must regret. For Lewis, in his more satiric moments, was a valuable prophylactic force, a sham-smasher, and a nemesis of little minds. Perhaps he has grown tired of insurrection; or perhaps, now that it has become almost a literary convention to scourge the philistines, he feels that it would be more rebellious to rebel against the rebels for a while. Yet for all his loss of power, we can hardly expect to see in our time another novelist with his general talent for scalping "the home town mind," that wasting sickness of culture, source of bigotry, and bane of liberal and humane spirits.

WHAT SHALL IT PROFIT A MAN   The plot of Lewis's novels is relatively constant. A boy (or a girl) grows up in a hidebound country village, catches a vision of something finer from someone, goes to college, discovers that "the home town mind" has invaded even our halls of learning, leaves school, travels to England (and often Panama), finds that marriage can also be a Babbitt trap, struggles to escape from Philistia, and either fails with Carol Kennicott and Babbitt, or achieves a degree of victory, as Hawk Ericson, Arrowsmith, Dodsworth, and Ann Vickers do.

Sinclair and Lewis both paint in black and white. The first plays the rich against the poor, in bold contrast; and the second plays idealist against philistine, Carol Kennicott vs. her husband, Paul Riesling vs. Babbitt, Gottlieb vs. Pickerbaugh, and Frank Shallard vs. Elmer Gantry. Sinclair and Lewis also resemble each other in their tendency to deepen these contrasts by exaggerating the virtues of their heroes and the vices of their villains. But there are some important differences between the two.

Sinclair, for instance, objects to the effect of plutocracy on the average man's stomach; Lewis objects to the effect of provincialism upon his soul. Sinclair believes that only the machinations of money tyrants keep America in pain; Lewis believes that it is "the mass of smug human stupidity which keeps the world uncivilized," [43] and that wars, gossip, malice, and vanity are due "not to inherent fiendishness but to lack of knowledge and lack of imagination." [44] "Know the truth," he contends, "and the truth shall make you free." Sinclair is more interested in problems; Lewis is more interested in people. Sinclair stands for revolt on the economic plane; Lewis stands for revolt on the cultural, and the key to his philosophy is, "What shall a man be profited, if he shall gain the whole world, and forfeit his soul?"

Lewis is in "revolt from the village," yet he finds that "provincialism is not confined to the small town; nor is it confined to the Middle West. The Middle Western village is simply a symbol of American provincialism, wherever found, whether in Gopher Prairie or Chicago." [45] He is representative of that uprising of intellectuals which followed the war and (until it began to wane about 1927) took up the cudgels against Methodists, defenders of censorship, hypocrites, prohibition, bourgeois foibles, evangelism in business and religion, Victorian standards of conduct, and regimentation of every kind. Along with Mencken, whom Walter Lippmann has termed "the most powerful personal influence on this whole generation of educated people," Lewis has led the fight against *Boobus americanus*, that amazingly prevalent individual who feeds on platitudes, supplies the *Mercury* with material for its "Americana" section each month, thinks all foreigners are "radicals," Keeps Kool with Koolidge, and cherishes a belief

[43] Lewis, Sinclair, "Self-Conscious America," *The American Mercury* (October, 1925), VI, 134.

[44] *Ann Vickers*, p. 256.

[45] Wann, Louis, "The 'Revolt from the Village' in American Fiction," *The Overland Monthly* (August, 1925), LXXXIII, 299.

That all male negroes can sing.

That if a woman about to become a mother plays the piano every day, her baby will be born a Victor Herbert.

That all great men have illegible signatures.

That it is bad luck to kill a spider.

That the accumulation of great wealth always brings with it great unhappiness.

That a workingman always eats what is in his dinnerpail with great relish.

That all men named Clarence, Claude, or Percy are sissies.

That a jury never convicts a pretty woman.

That a man always dislikes his mother-in-law, and goes half-crazy every time she visits him.[46]

Dullness, which he feels has its origin in conformity, is one of Lewis's "bêtes noires." To use Carl Van Doren's phrase, he would "rather be wrong than regimented." "Restraint, Repression, Respectability — those are the three Rs that make him see Red." [47] He believes that

About ten times as many people find their lives dull, and unnecessarily dull, as ever admit it; and I do believe that if we busted out and admitted it sometimes, instead of being nice and patient and loyal for sixty years, and nice and patient and dead for the rest of eternity, why, maybe, possibly, we might make life more fun.[48]

He has his gun loaded for *Smugness*, too, and the mental constipation that he finds in Rotarianism, "the village," some physicians, Elmer Gantry, American tourists, and our Academy of Arts and Letters.[49] As he says with one of his characters in *Arrowsmith*, "Ah, smugness! That is the

[46] Nathan, George Jean, and H. L. Mencken, *The American Credo* (1920), pp. 111, 109, 112, 115, 114, 136, 140, 179, and 190.

[47] Phelps, William Lyon, "As I Like It," *Scribner's* (April, 1933), XCIII, 256.

[48] *Babbitt*, p. 65.

[49] For his criticism of our Academy of Arts and Letters, see Lewis, Sinclair, *Addresses by Erik Axel Karlfeldt and Sinclair Lewis, on the Occasion of the Award of the Nobel Prize* (1931).

enemy!" [50]   He hates both the mob and the snob.   He ridicules those cheery merchants who

sing of four-wheel brakes as the Persian poets sang of rose leaves; their religion is road paving and their patriotism the relation of weather to Sunday motoring; and they discuss balloon tires with a quiet fervor such as the fifteenth century gave to the Immaculate Conception.[51]

He objects to the presumption that "all American men are tall, handsome, rich, honest, and powerful at golf; that all country towns are filled with neighbors who do nothing from day to day save go about being kind to one another; that although American girls may be wild, they change always into perfect wives and mothers; and that, geographically, America is composed solely of New York, which is inhabited entirely by millionaires; of the West, which keeps unchanged all the boisterous heroism of 1870; and of the South, where everyone lives on a plantation perpetually glossy with moonlight and scented with magnolias." [52]   He thinks that Americans are "incomparably the most interesting tribe living." [53]   But it makes him very angry to note that while we have advanced in material comforts we have gone back in spiritual vigor, and that the pioneers, with their "juice and jests," have

been replaced by people with bath-tubs and coupés and porch-furniture and speed-boats and lake-cottages, who are determined that their possession of these pretty things shall not be threatened by radicals, and that their comments on them shall not be interrupted by mere speculation on the soul of man.[54]

[50] *Arrowsmith*, p. 357.

[51] Lewis, Sinclair, "Main Street's Been Paved!" *The Nation* (September 10, 1924), CXIX, 260.

[52] *Addresses by Erik Axel Karlfeldt and Sinclair Lewis, on the Occasion of the Award of the Nobel Prize*, p. 11.

[53] Lewis, Sinclair, "Self-Conscious America," *The American Mercury* (October, 1925), VI, 135.

[54] Lewis, Sinclair, "Main Street's Been Paved!" *The Nation* (September 10, 1924), CXIX, 260.

Like Mencken, he is against "patrioteering, against fraud
and violence and tyranny disguised as freedom, against the
hand of the oppressor wrapped in the cap of liberty, against
words that are froth, against a crafty hypocrisy which is the
death of all originality in art, against uniformity, against
the dead level, against erecting the mediocre opinions of the
majority into the canons of art," and "against a mean
flattery of the mob and playing down to it." [55]

Lewis has described himself as "a rather nebulous
radical." In 1924 he supported La Follette for President;
and in his *Cheap and Contented Labor* (1929), a study of working conditions in the cotton mills of Marion, N. C., he has
spoken out in favor of a "most militant and universal and
immediate organization of trade unions." Business, he
argues,

must fail unless it becomes noble of heart. So long as capital
and labor are divided, so long as the making of munitions or
injurious food is regarded as business, so long as Big Business
believes that it exists merely to enrich a few of the lucky or the
well born or the nervously active, it will not be efficient, but
deficient.[56]

The thought of an entirely perfect world, however, leaves
him cold; for he too believes in Sinclair's "Communism
in material production, Anarchism in intellectual production." "I can imagine," says Lewis,

nothing more horrible than a world in which no one was hard-
boiled and mean; in which every one beamed like a Y.M.C.A.
secretary, insisted on helping all the brethren who damned well
wanted to be left alone, and conversed with mellifluous omnis-
cience about Keats, the quantum theory, S. Parkes Cadman,
four-wheel brakes, S. A., and Chateau Yquem.[57]

[55] O'Sulliven, Vincent, *H. L. Mencken* (1920), p. 20.
[56] *The Job*, p. 26.
[57] Lewis, Sinclair, "Mr. Lorimer and Me," *The Nation* (July 25, 1928),
CXXVII, 81.

But he would prescribe for his Babbitts at least three Utopian ideals, "that they should know a little more about history; that they should better comprehend the difference between Irish stew in America and fried mushrooms at Schoener's in Vienna; and that they should talk of the quest of God oftener than of the quest for the best carburetor." [58]

[58] *Ibid.*

*

THE ANARCHIST

*

SOLDIER AND ESTHETE   John Dos Passos, of whom V. F. Calverton has said, "No other left-wing writer in America at this time has won such sweeping approval from the public and press," [1] was born in Chicago, January 14, 1896. In 1916 he received his A. B. from Harvard, where he made a number of contributions to the school magazines, among them a *Harvard Monthly* article entitled "A Humble Protest," in which he denounced man's growing enslavement to "the machine" and industrialism.   After graduating he began to study architecture; but in 1917 he joined the Norton Harjes Volunteer Service, and left for France.   The next year found him in Italy, and later he served as a private in the U. S. Army Medical Corps.

The effect of the war on Dos Passos has been considerable; it influences most of his work, as it does the novels of Hemingway.   His first volume, *One Man's Initiation — 1917* (1920), records the experiences of Martin Howe, an ambulance driver.   And *Three Soldiers* (1921), another but weightier battlepiece, tells in a fierce, graphic, colloquial way the story of three American rookies, Andrews, Chrisfield, and Fuselli, while describing their reactions to the hysteria, fatigue, stinking horror, mockery, and de-individualization of war.

In his next book, however, Dos Passos seems to have tried

---

[1] Calverton, V. F., *The Liberation of American Literature* (1932), p. 463. Malcolm Cowley's article "The Poet and the World," in *The New Republic* (April 27, 1932), LXX, 303–305, is perhaps the best study of Dos Passos that we have, so far.

to forget the hydraheaded problems and diseases of our world by escaping from it into that estheticism which has always tempted him a great deal, in spite of his opposite inclination to face life and its questions of social injustice. *A Pushcart at the Curb* (1922) is a volume of poetry, scented and lighted up with rich phrases that appear to burst out of melting smoke, like the winking of an electric sign at dusk. Here, in a sample from this book, we may observe Dos Passos' extraordinary love of color, his anarchistic yearnings, and his staccato style:

> Shining spring rain
> O scud steaming up out of the deep sea
> full of portents of sundown and islands,
> beat upon my forehead
> beat upon my face and neck
> glisten on my outstretched hands,
> run bright lilac streams
> through the clogged channels of my brain
> corrode the clicking cogs the little angles
> the small mistrustful mirrors
> scatter the shrill tiny creaking
> of mustnot darenot cannot
> spatter the varnish off me
> that I may stand up
> my face to the wet wind
> and feel my body
> and drenched salty palpitant April
> reborn in my flesh.
>
> I would spit the dust out of my mouth
> burst out of these stiff wire webs
> supple incautious
> like the crocuses that spurt up too soon
> their saffron flames
> and die gloriously in late blizzards
> and leave no seed.[2]

[2] Dos Passos, John, *A Pushcart at the Curb* (1922), pp. 209–212.

Rosinante to the Road Again (1922) is ore from the same vein. It embraces a series of essays on Spanish art, culture, and social ferment, in which Dos Passos again gives free rein to hot intoxicating language and "the lyric cry," as he follows a character named Telemachus in his quest for the gesture that is Spain, or *lo flamenco*. "Something that is neither work nor getting ready to work, to make the road so significant that one needs no destination, that is *lo flamenco*," says the author,[3] in contrasting the organized repressions of America to the happy "life for life's sake" point of view of the Spaniard.

Streets of Night (1923) is the rather précieuse story of David Wendell, Fanshaw Macdougan, and Nancibel Taylor, two young men and a girl who, though they want to escape from the nightmare "streets" of youth and convention, are afraid to "live dangerously." Yet it does contain a few such jeweled bits of writing as:

They were cutting diagonally across the Common, under a hurrying sky lit by a last mustard-green flare from the west. The electric signs along Tremont Street bit icily through the lacy pattern of the stirring twigs of trees. The wind was getting steadier and colder, occasionally shot with a fine lash of snow.[4]

Manhattan Transfer, two years later, has been termed the "Rhapsody in Blue of Contemporary American fiction." It marked Dos Passos' literary coming of age, and a new departure in his style. Heretofore, his method had been definitely impressionistic, but with this book it became even more so, and reached beyond a mere kaleidoscopic use of words (in the manner of Crane) to a fragmentary treatment of characters, scenes, and events. *Manhattan Transfer* weaves together, into a "syncretic panorama," the lives of several New Yorkers, by a kind of patchwork technique, which reproduces for us in its swift interlocking parade of

[3] Dos Passos, John, *Rosinante to the Road Again* (1922), p. 46.
[4] Dos Passos, John, *Streets of Night* (1923), pp. 184–185.

sensations an excellent image of metropolitan life, perhaps the best that has ever been achieved by an American.[5] In it we catch glimpses of the city in most of its various aspects. This is Manhattan itself, with its tenement fires, racial conflicts, lunch rooms, dice games, people renting apartments, L stations, street scenes, peddlers, Broadway, telegraph offices, hotels, dyers and cleaners, taxis, Central Park, odors of gum, powder, sunshine, rain, and gasoline, Chinese restaurants, immigrants, ferries, Staten Island, burlesque shows, Washington Square, court rooms, newspapers, Brooklyn Bridge, warehouses, holdups, Wall Street, dance halls, ships, crowds, beggars, criminals, speakeasies, brownstone houses, pimps, and subways.   And here are the actors in its daily drama, Bud Korpenning, the farm boy who has run away from home after killing his father; Emile the waiter; Marco the anarchist; William C. Olafson, sanitary engineer, and his wife; Gus the milkman, who is injured at a railway crossing; George Baldwin, a young lawyer who handles Gus's suit for damages and falls in love with the wife of his client; Ed Thatcher, the indigent accountant; Nicky Schatz, a thief; Jimmie Herf, a reporter; Elaine Oglethorpe, the actress, and her husband; shop girls, crooked business men, and politicians. Of any continuous "story," there is almost no trace; the special achievement of *Manhattan Transfer* lies not in its "progression," or welded narrative, but in its sense of medley, "procession" of lights and shadows, human interest, that multifarious whispering which rises from a city's streets from dawn to dark, and Dos Passos' amazing talent for evoking such vignettes as this slightly luscious picture of twilight in New York:

Dusk gently smooths crispangled streets. Dark presses tight the steaming asphalt city, crushes the fretwork of windows and

[5] For a similar picture of Parisian life, see *Men of Good Will* (1933) by Jules Romain, who claims to be one of the earliest exponents, if not the originator, of that "flicker" technique used by Dos Passos in *Manhattan Transfer, 1919,* and *42nd Parallel.*

lettered signs and chimneys and watertanks and ventilators and fire-escapes and moldings and patterns and corrugations and eyes and hands and neckties into blue chunks, into black enormous blocks. Under the rolling heavier heavier pressure windows blurt light. Night crushes bright milk out of the arclights, squeezes the sullen blocks until they drip red, yellow, green into streets resounding with feet. All the asphalt oozes light. Light spurts from lettering on roofs, mills dizzily among wheels, stains rolling tons of sky.[6]

The Garbage Man (1926) and *Airways, Inc.* (1928) are plays, the first a story of two lovers who are almost relegated to the "dump heap" by the cold, plutocratic functioning of modern society, and the second a study of life among a group of mill workers during a strike. *Facing the Chair* (1927) is a pamphlet written by Dos Passos for the Sacco-Vanzetti Defense Committee, in an effort to save those two martyrs of labor from the death penalty. And *Orient Express* (1927), in which Dos Passos again toys with the idea of escape, is a luminiferous travel diary, whose background is the Near East, and whose tense, brilliantined word painting may be observed in:

Blue smokespirals uncoil crisply from the camp fires through the amethyst twilight. Camels stroll towards the camp in a densening herd, sniffing the air and nibbling at an occasional cluster of twigs, urged on by the long labial cry of the driver. The mollah is chanting the evening prayer. The men stand with bare feet in a long rank facing the southwest, make the prostrations slowly, out of unison. Gradually, the camels fill the great oval place between the camp fires, are hobbled and fold themselves up in rows, chewing and groaning. The stars impinge sharply like flaws in the luminous crystal-dark sky. My blankets smell of camel and are smoky from the fire. Once asleep, I am awakened by two shots that ring out in the night like on a bell. There's a sound of voices and pebbles scuttling under naked feet. Saleh sticks his head in the tent and says proudly, — Haremi, bang, bang, imshi,

[6] Dos Passos, John, *Manhattan Transfer* (1925), p. 112. Published by Harper & Brothers, copyright 1925, by John Dos Passos.

go away. And I'm asleep again rocked like by waves by the soft fuzzy grumbling noise of five hundred camels.[7]

CROSS SECTION   But in *42nd Parallel* (1930) and *1919* (1932), Dos Passos returned once more to the native material and tessellated method of *Manhattan Transfer*. In these two books he reached the top of his stride. Together they form the first and second units in a projected trilogy, and lay bare a cross section of American life from about 1900 to 1920, much as the "42nd parallel" geographically bisects the United States from east to west. No more than *Manhattan Transfer* do they represent a centralized plot. A few characters come and go among their pages, Benny Compton, the Jewish radical; Eveline Hutchins, a Red Cross worker; Joe Williams, a sailor; Richard Ellsworth Savage, Harvard student and ambulance driver; and others from every walk of society and almost every part of the world, harlots, pederasts, schoolboys, waiters, actresses, painters, anarchists, publicity agents, "wobblies," doctors, printers, Socialists, book salesmen, hoboes, and ranchers.[8] Yet only two or three of them appear in both volumes or interact. What Dos Passos has sought to do is to picture the vast and intricate design of America, its shifting forces, and its magnetic personalities. *42nd Parallel* and *1919* are, in effect, a pair of enlarged tabloid papers, two wide futuristic canvases in which the author has again employed his "flicker" technique to reproduce by suggestive excerpts a vista that is much too spacious to be captured entire.

[7] Dos Passos, John, *Orient Express* (1927), pp. 121–122. Published by Harper & Brothers, copyright 1922, 1927, by John Dos Passos. His latest book, *In All Countries* (1934), is another volume of edged impressions, dealing with the social scene at home and abroad.

[8] "Where Sinclair's people are wax dummies, Dos Passos' are alive and convincing. The contrast raises again the old problem of the propagandistic novel. Are '1919' and 'The 42nd Parallel' propagandistic? Certainly in *effect* they are so; yet their effectiveness both as fiction and as propaganda lies in the fact that their communistic sympathies are never more than *implicit*." Hazlitt, Henry, "Panorama," *The Nation* (March 23, 1932), CXXXIV, 344.

To his *Manhattan Transfer* method Dos Passos has added three new devices.   The first, termed "Newsreel," consists of speeches, bits of popular music, and typical newspaper headlines.

COLLEGE HEAD DENIES KISSES
JOFFRE ASKS TROOPS NOW
WOMAN TRAPS HUSBAND WITH GIRL IN HOTEL
8 YEAR OLD BOY SHOT BY LAD WITH RIFLE
DEBS IS GIVEN THIRTY YEARS IN PRISON
WILSON WILL TAKE ADVICE OF BUSINESS
FERTILIZER INDUSTRY STIMULATED BY WAR

These he strews through *42nd Parallel* and *1919* to "date" various incidents as they occur, to lend a further "sense of multiplicity" to his volumes, and to reflect an ironical light upon the crimes, prejudices, and follies of our present civilization.   The second comprises a number of interspersed thumbnail "Biographies" of noted "figures of the day," Joe Hill, labor organizer; Paxton Hibben, journalist; William Jennings Bryan, the Boy Orator of the Platte; Luther Burbank, the Plant Wizard; Bill Haywood, I. W. W. leader; Minor C. Keith, financier; Andrew Carnegie, Edison, Theodore Roosevelt, Eugene V. Debs, La Follette, and Steinmetz; Randolph Bourne, critic; Jack Reed, American radical; and The Unknown Soldier.   "The Camera Eye," his third device, might be written "The Camera I," for Dos Passos uses it as a *sotto voce* means of smuggling chunks out of his own "stream-of-consciousness" into these otherwise impersonal novels.   It is also in "The Camera Eye" that his suppressed estheticism breaks out; and in such passages as the following, he becomes an incipient "dadaist," with some of the typographical quirks and truncated rhythms of "e. e. cummings":

to hell with 'em   Patrick Henry in khaki submits to shortarm inspection and puts all his pennies in a Liberty Loan   or give me

Arrivés shrapnel twanging its harps out of tiny powderpuff clouds invites us delicately to glory we happy watching the careful movement of the snails in the afternoon sunlight talking in low voices about

La Libre Belgique The Junius papers Areopagitica Milton went blind for freedom of speech If you hit the words Democracy will understand even the bankers and the clergymen I you we must

When three men hold together
The kingdoms are less by three

we are happy talking in low voices in the afternoon sunlight about après la guerre that our fingers our blood our lungs our flesh under the dirty khaki feldgrau bleu horizon might go on sweeten grow until we fall from the tree ripe like the tooripe pears the arrivés know and singing éclats sizzling gas shells theirs is the power and the glory

or give me death [9]

These tricks of style and his tendency to "snatch at instants" have been deprecated by other reformists, who feel that his experiments in technique detract from the meaning and social value of his work.[10] However, it would seem that no criticism can ever change Dos Passos from what he is, a social novelist grafted upon an esthete. He is a merger of Sinclair and Hergesheimer, a poet over whose work there dwells a mood of sick dismay; and yet he has not flown from life. Even in *Orient Express*, *A Pushcart at the Curb*, and *Rosinante to the Road Again* he has managed to escape escapism; and in his other books he has frankly, if artfully, come to grips with the contemporary scene. So that, in the last analysis, he must be judged as a reformist.

Yet as a reformist, Dos Passos represents a curious and anomalic figure. In the first place, his art is more pano-

[9] Dos Passos, John, *1919* (1932), pp. 102–103.
[10] See *The Living Age* (October, 1932), CCCXLIII, 178–179, for a letter to Dos Passos from two Russian writers. This trait of style in his work has also been criticized by Upton Sinclair.

ramic than proletarian.   And in the second place, reformist though he surely is, his doctrines of social renewal are directly opposed to those of Lewis and Sinclair. For whereas they stand for Socialism, he stands for Anarchism.   All three, of course, recognize that the privilege of *laissez faire* (of doing as you please) at present extends only to the capitalist class, and that the working class lives under a rigid web of checks and balances imposed from above and enforced by the power of wealth.   But to repair this injustice, Sinclair and Lewis would enlarge the system of checks and balances to cover both classes, while Dos Passos would grant *laissez faire* to all.   Sinclair and Lewis would lay the hand of law upon both rich and poor; Dos Passos would remove law entirely, and trust to the inherent "goodness" of man's nature to restrain him from wrongdoing and selfishness.

THE MEANING OF LIBERTY   In Dos Passos' first book, *One Man's Initiation — 1917*, which contains the best statement of his social theories, there is a symposium held by six men in a French farmhouse; and one of the expressions voiced there might be construed as the point of view of Sinclair, Lewis, and Socialists in general.   It is Merrier, one of Martin Howe's comrades, speaking.   "We are very simple folk," he says,

who want to live quietly and have plenty to eat and have no one worry us or hurt us in the little span of sunlight before we die. All we have now is the same war between the classes: those that exploit and those that are exploited.   The cunning, unscrupulous people control the humane, kindly people.   This war that has smashed our little European world in which order was so painfully taking the place of chaos, seems to me merely a gigantic battle fought over the plunder of the world by the pirates who have grown fat to the point of madness on the work of their own people, on the work of the millions in Africa, in India, in America, who have come directly or indirectly under the yoke of the insane greed of the white races.   Well, our edifice is ruined.   Let's think no more of it.   Ours is now the duty of rebuilding, reorganising. I have not faith enough in human nature to be an anarchist. . . . We are too like sheep; we must go in flocks, and a flock to live must organise. There is plenty for everyone, even with the huge growth in population all over the world. What we want is organisation from the bottom, organisation by the ungreedy, by the humane, by the uncunning, socialism of the masses that shall spring from the natural need of men to help one another; not socialism from the top to the ends of the governors, that they may clamp us tighter in their fetters. We must stop the economic war, the war for existence of man against man. That will be the first step in the long climb to civilisation. They must co-operate, they must learn that it is saner and more advantageous to help one another than to hinder one another in the great war against nature. And the tyranny of the feudal money lords, the unspeakable misery of this war is driving men closer together into fraternity, co-operation.[11]

With this philosophy Lewis and Sinclair are in virtual accord. They realize that while our form of government needs to be radically changed, the idea of an organized state cannot be discarded, since (as Aristotle puts it) "Most men would rather live in a disorderly than in a sober manner." But in Dos Passos' opinion this concept of organization is hateful. He takes exception to the theory that men require to be governed by laws, and seems to feel, with Rousseau and Kropotkin, that if all restrictions were suddenly removed the world would subside into ethical harmony, and the laborer would lie down with the capitalist, in a dream of "mutual aid." "No," he objects, in the words of one Lully, another of Howe's friends,

It is better for man to worship God, his image on the clouds, the creation of his fancy, than to worship the vulgar apparatus of organised life, government. Better sacrifice his children to Moloch than to that society for the propagation and protection of commerce, the nation. Oh, think of the cost of government in all the ages since men stopped living in marauding tribes! Think of the great men martyred. Think of the thought trodden into

[11] Dos Passos, John, *One Man's Initiation — 1917* (1922), pp. 117–118.

the dust. . . . Give man a chance for once. Government should be purely utilitarian, like the electric light wires in a house. It is a method for attaining peace and comfort — a bad one, I think, at that; not a thing to be worshipped as God. The one reason for it is the protection of property. Why should we have property? That is the central evil of the world. . . . That is the cancer that has made life a hell of misery until now; the inflated greed of it has spurred our nations of the West to throw themselves back, for ever, perhaps, into the depths of savagery. . . . Oh, if people would only trust their own fundamental, kindliness, the fraternity, the love that is the strongest thing in life. Abolish property, and the disease of the desire for it, the desire to grasp and have, and you'll need no government to protect you. The vividness and resiliency of the life of man is being fast crushed under organisation, tabulation. Over-organisation is death. It is disorganisation, not organisation, that is the aim of life.[12]

Yet there will always be need for government, inasmuch as private property can never be entirely abolished. *Material possessions* may come to be held in common, but men will forever retain private *opinions*, out of which disputes will never cease to arise. Until men achieve individual control of self and selfishness, external regulations must be retained in some form to preserve order and proportion, and protect us from murderers, lunatics, and profiteers. With no government, bad men would have as much liberty as good men. Freedom cannot be extended to everybody, unless some people are rendered less free. To make this world safe for unselfish persons, it must be made dangerous for selfish ones. A radical modification of society, however, is urgently needed, in order to free those who might otherwise prove to be "men of good will" from the necessity of living at the expense of their neighbors. Some men will always behave in an unethical way; but under our present system of economics, there are many who would share the necessities of life with others if they were not

12 *One Man's Initiation — 1917*, pp. 119–120.

forced, against their better nature, to compete with their neighbors for existence, or stupefied by outworn habits of thought and capitalistic propaganda. Liberty does not imply the right of all men to "do as they please," as the anarchist urges. In its best sense, it means simply the "liberty to be rational and social," [13] a freedom that most of us today do not enjoy. Rather than freeing man from good as well as evil, liberty should free him from that tradition which now impedes the exercise of conscience and intelligence. What we require is an improved type of government, not an absence of government.

[13] Briffault, Robert, *Breakdown* (1932), p. 169. Or as Joubert, the French philosopher, once said, "Universal justice will be liberty enough."

* LAWS AS WINGS

Every inordinate cup is unblessed.
SHAKSPERE

*

THE GOLDEN MEAN

*

VIA MEDIA Humanism is a name that has often been
taken in vain; but it really answers to just one meaning, and
that is: moderation in all things, "nothing in excess."
Wherever found, it has always been the enemy of extremes.
It divides the universe into three levels. "On the lowest
level is the natural world, which is the plane of instinct,
appetite, animality, lust, the animal passions or affections;
on this level the regulation is by necessary or natural law.
On the middle level is the human world, which is regulated
and, in a sense, created by the will and knowledge of man;
working upon the natural world; but governed by reason,
the special human faculty; and illuminated more or less
from the level above. On the third level is the supernatural
world, which is the plane of spiritual beings, and the home
of eternal ideas." [1] The middle plane is the level of humanism, which conceives of man as a personage of rare dignity,
occupying a niche somewhere between the apes and the
angels, as a being who is neither "a puppet of God" nor
"a puppet of Nature," as a pilgrim whose road must be the
via media if he is to find happiness. His guide, in short, must
be The Golden Mean, of which Horace sang:

> Yes, there's a mean in morals.   Life has lines
> To north or south of which all virtue pines. [2]

The humanist is determined to be neither an animal nor a
religious hermit, but a normal man, interested only in what

[1] Sherman, Stuart P., *On Contemporary Literature* (1917), p. 294.
[2] Horace, *Satirae*, Bk. I, satire 1.

is distinguishingly human.   He believes that "The joy of
the game is in playing it within limits," [3] that "Man is a
creature who is foredoomed to one-sidedness, yet who becomes humane only in proportion as he triumphs over the
fatality of his nature, only as he arrives at that measure
which comes from tempering his virtues, each by its opposite." [4]   And he holds that

The aim of conduct is to acquire that golden mean which is
nothing other than a certain bound set to the inherent limitlessness of our impulsive or desiring nature.   The determination of
this bound in each case is the function of reason, which embraces
the whole existence of man as an organism in his environment and
says to each impulse as it arises, thus far shalt thou go and no
further.   But as the basis of practical life is the limitless sway of
unrelated impulses, reason, to establish its balance and measure,
to find, that is, its norm of unity, must look ultimately to some
point quite outside of the realm of impulse and nature.   Hence
the imposition of the theoretical life, as Aristotle calls it, upon the
practical — the contemplation of that absolute unity which is
unmoved amid all that moves.   This unity not of nature is the
infinite; it is the very opposite of that limitlessness which is the
attribute of nature itself; it is not a state of endless, indefinite
expansion, but is on the contrary that state of centralization which
has its goal in itself.[5]

CIVIL WAR IN THE CAVE   To aid him in walking this tight-
rope between an excess of worldliness and an excess of other-
worldliness, to guard him against all forms of irrational
impulse, and to enable him to pick out "the moderate,
sensible, and decent" from the torrent of Nature upon which
he is borne along, the humanist has recourse to a mingled
faculty of judgment and insight, which is peculiar to man
and marks him off from the beast.   This faculty, termed by
Socrates the "divine monitor" and by others "the ethical

[3] Sockman, Ralph W., *Morals of Tomorrow* (1931), p. 130.
[4] Babbitt, Irving, *Literature and the American College* (1908), p. 23.
[5] More, Paul Elmer, *The Drift of Romanticism* (1913), pp. 226–227.

will," "the inner check," "the law of measure," "the *frein vital*," and "the will to refrain," is "some element of man's being superior to instinct and reason, some power that acts as a stay upon the flowing impulses of nature, without whose authoritative check reason herself must in the end be swept away in the dissolution of the everlasting flux," [6] some psychic voice that declares, "I am a man with the power to control myself. I have the impulses of the brute, but I can direct and command these impulses." [7] "Besides the flux of life," notes the humanist, "there is also that within man which displays itself intermittently as an inhibition upon this or that impulse, preventing its prolongation in activity, and making a pause or eddy, so to speak, in the stream. This negation of the flux we call the inner check." [8] Man, in other words, is a duality, a cave in which the forces of temperance and intemperance clash in an eternal duel. In him two laws collide, a natural self of impulse and a human self that exercises a power of control over desire. For "if man is to become human, he must not let impulse and desire run wild, but must oppose to everything excessive in his ordinary self, whether in thought or deed or emotion, the law of measure," [9] though "the real humanist consents, like Aristotle, to limit his desires only in so far as this limitation can be shown to make for his own happiness." [10] Unless vetoed by this human law, man's passions operate under the law of Nature, which simply means that they continue to empty and restore themselves as fast as they can, without pause or direction. Like a team of wild horses, they must be reined in by some charioteer, and prudently disciplined, in order to preserve man's health, spirit, and social status. Thus, "A man of character is one in

[6] *Ibid.*, p. xiii.

[7] Boynton, Percy Holmes, *The Challenge of Modern Criticism* (1931), pp. 108–109.

[8] More, Paul Elmer, *op. cit.*, pp. 247–248.

[9] Babbitt, Irving, *Rousseau and Romanticism* (1919), p. 16.

[10] Foerster, Norman (ed.), *Humanism and America* (1930), p. 48.

whom a vigorous disposition is continuously controlled by the habit of attention, or the will to refrain. As character develops, the disposition takes on a more regular pattern; the impulses become harmonious as if arranged upon a centre, and display a kind of unity in multiplicity. The outcome in conduct is consistency, self-direction, balance of faculties, efficiency, moral health, happiness. At its highest development the will would appear to act automatically, as if the troublesome choice among heterogeneous impulses had been surmounted. The man would no longer be subject to the alternations of happiness and misery, but would rise to a state of equable activity in repose which we call peace." [11]   Says the humanist:

1. An adequate human standard calls for *completeness;* it demands the cultivation of every part of human nature, including "natural" human nature. It suppresses nothing.

2. But it also calls for proportion: it demands the harmony of the parts with the whole. Instead of "accepting life" indiscriminately, it imposes a scale of values.

3. This complete, proportionate standard may be said to consist of the *normally* or *typically human.* It is concerned with the central and the universal, not the eccentric and the idiosyncratic. It is concerned with a permanently valid ethos, not with any temporary code of conventional society.

4. Although such an ethos has never existed, it has been approximated in the great ages of *the past,* to which humanism accordingly looks for guidance. It looks chiefly toward Greece, where it still finds its best examples (in sculpture, in Homer and Sophocles, in Plato and Aristotle); also toward Rome (Virgil, Horace), toward the Christian tradition (Jesus, Paul, Augustine, Francis of Assisi), toward the Orient (Buddha, Confucius), toward moderns like Shakespeare, Milton, and Goethe. Selecting the "constants" that appear to be worthy of preservation, humanism seeks to transcend the specialism that limits all ages in the past as well as the present age.

[11] More, Paul Elmer, *op. cit.,* p. 275.

5. Unlike romanticism, which in its quest of a natural ethos repudiated the logical faculty, humanism is always true to its Hellenic origin in its faith in *reason*. It seeks to deal positively with the whole of experience, including those elements of experience that do not fall within the scope of what is termed science.

6. Unlike the conceptions of life that grow out of science, humanism seeks to press beyond reason by the use of *intuition* or *imagination*, following the example of the most poetical of Hellenic philosophers, who resorted again and again to symbol and myth, and the example of the foremost Christian poet when he forsook the guidance of Virgil in favor of that of Beatrice. Humanism holds that, after reason has brought us before the veil that shrouds truth, a power above the reason is needed to cope with what Goethe terms "the illusion of a higher reality." This power above the reason is the human or ethical imagination, as distinguished from the natural or pathetic imagination, which is below the reason.

7. The ultimate ethical principle is that of *restraint* or *control*, indicated alike by practical experience and by the light of reason and the ethical imagination. There is a law for man and a law for thing. That which is law in nature becomes anarchy when surrendered to by man — the anarchy of wandering desires and blind impulses, the morbid ebb and flow of unhindered temperament, the restless oscillations of expansive pride and expansive sympathy. This anarchy is the product of romanticism and naturalism in their pure state, that is, when they do not wittingly or unwittingly draw upon the humanistic or religious tradition. As Coleridge perceived,

> The Sensual and the Dark rebel in vain,
> Slaves by their own compulsion!

Freedom and power and happiness cannot be won by those who practice the modern philosophy of what is loosely termed " self-expression." They can be won only when the energies of the instinctive self have been harnessed by the ethical self:

> The winged Courser, like a gen'rous Horse
> Shows most true Mettle when you *check* his Course.

Humanism remembers, to be sure, that the Popean neo-classicists as well as the Puritans, instead of checking the steed, generally locked him in the stable, where he might indeed rebel in vain; it remembers always the need of freedom, which it defines as liberation from outer constraints and subjection to inner law. It asserts that this inner law of concentration, when it has eagerly expansive senses and emotional energies to command, is the true source of power, of character, of elevation, of happiness.

8. This center to which humanism refers everything, this centripetal energy which counteracts the multifarious centrifugal impulses, this magnetic will which draws the flux of our sensations toward it while itself remaining at rest, is the reality that gives rise to religion. Pure humanism is content to describe it thus in physical terms, as an observed fact of experience; it hesitates to pass beyond its experimental knowledge to the dogmatic affirmations of any of the great religions. It cannot bring itself to accept a formal theology (any more than it can accept a romantic idealism) that has been set up in defiance of reason, for it holds that the value of supernatural intuition must be tested by the intellect. Again, it fears the asceticism to which religion tends in consequence of a too harsh dualism of the flesh and the spirit, for, as we have said, humanism calls for completeness, wishing to use and not annihilate dangerous forces. Unlike religion, it assigns an important place to the instruments of both science and art. Nevertheless, it agrees with religion in its perception of the ethical will as a power above the ordinary self, an impersonal reality in which all men may share despite the diversity of personal temperament and toward which their attitude must be one of subjection.[12]

LITTERAE HUMANIORES   Humanism stands between science, which says "Man is entirely determined by Nature," and religion, which says "Man is completely subject to some outside, supernatural power." It touches both Nature and the Supernatural, and draws a quota of strength from each, but belongs to neither; it has man's own character to love and his equilibrium to perpetuate. And when either the subhuman or the suprahuman begins to drive out the human in man, and destroy his balance, it must be

[12] Foerster, Norman, *Toward Standards* (1930), pp. 165–171.

curbed. During the Renaissance (when the term "humanism" first came into general use), the humanist protested against the growing power of a medieval and "petrified ecclesiasticism" that had almost crowded science out of existence. But at present he is fighting against too much science; for science in dethroning religion from its tyrannical seat has climbed up to that eminence itself. Yesterday the menace of surfeit lay in supernaturalism; today it resides in naturalism.

The scientist, objects the humanist, "multiplies the points of contact between man and nature, but it is impossible for him to modify in any particular the essential character of the mutual relations between the two," [13] Hence,

To demand a system of morals from Science is to invite cruel disappointments. Men believed, three hundred years ago, that the earth was the centre of creation. Nowadays we know that it is only a coagulated drop of the sun. We know what gases burn at the surface of the most distant stars. We know that the universe, in which we are a wandering speck of dust, is for ever in labour, bringing to birth and devouring its offspring; we know that heavenly bodies are ceaselessly dying and being born. But wherein has our moral nature been altered by these prodigious discoveries? Have mothers come to love their little ones better or less ardently? Do we appreciate the beauty of women any more or any less in consequence? Does a hero's heart beat any differently within his bosom? No, no! Be the earth great or small, what matter is that to mankind? [14]

Indeed, far from endowing us with a system of morals, science has contributed much toward the destruction of those we had. It pictures man as a walking heap of protoplasm, with no power of control over his actions or thoughts, a complex automaton operated by natural instincts of greed, hunger, and sex, a large amoeba, whose highest deeds of kindness, mercy, and reason are merely the haphazard

[13] France, Anatole, *The Garden of Epicurus* (1923), p. 39.
[14] *Ibid.*, pp. 39–40.

reactions of a sensitized piece of matter to its environment. Man, according to the scientist, is no different from other animals, save in intricacy. He is governed by the same laws that guide the stars in their heavenly paths. Pain repels him; joy attracts him. He is a simple iron filing in the magnetic field of Nature, sucked here and there by changing circumstances or the pressure of bodily demands, a roving wolf, a perambulant tree. His only moral code is that of the wolf and tree, self-preservation, abandonment to the dictates of Nature, and an unrestrained discharge of his energies, except when external factors in the environment prevent him from doing so. Naturalism is founded on "the pleasure principle" of psychology (with Freud's qualifications), which holds that whatever is pleasant cannot be injurious or immoral, and whatever is painful cannot be beneficial or moral. This is its rudimentary rule of conduct, based on a scientific observation of animal behavior. The humanist, however, feels that there is a gap between man and Nature; that man is not a brother of the wolf; that love and honor are not just instincts in disguise; and that whereas "the pleasure principle" may serve as an adequate moral criterion for the wolf, man (who is civilized and possessed of complex sympathies) cannot be happy if he follows it. The animal can afford to be an egotist and a hedonist, since he does not, presumably, feel remorse, live in a conscious tradition, or understand the larger theories of justice; yet man inhabits a world in which excess of any kind has a spiritual backfire. To discharge himself into purely expansive activities, as poison ivy does, would only be proper if he were poison ivy, instead of a human being. Nature has one law, and man has another. As a matter of fact, the naturalist, who urges relativity in morals, should be the first to recognize that inasmuch as man lives in a different state from that of the wolf, his ethical discipline should be different. For man, whatever his simian antecedents, does not dwell in a "state of Nature" today. At base he may still retain traces of his animal origins, and on his instinctive side he may yet bear the mark of the beast; but if his loins remain below the dividing line of Nature, his head and heart have penetrated upward into a new realm of "the human." And it is upon this level that he must find his true destiny. "In harmony with Nature?" inquires humanism of the naturalist:

> Restless fool,
> Who with such heat dost preach what were to thee,
> When true, the last impossibility, —
> To be like Nature strong, like Nature cool!
>
> Know, man hath all which Nature hath, but more,
> And in that *more* lie all his hopes of good.
> Nature is cruel, man is sick of blood;
> Nature is stubborn, man would fain adore.
>
> Nature is fickle, man hath need of rest;
> Nature forgives no debt, and fears no grave;
> Man would be mild, and with safe conscience blest.
>
> Man must begin, know this, where nature ends;
> Nature and man can never be fast friends.
> Fool, if thou canst not pass her, rest her slave! [15]

The naturalist's painting of life has no more design than a futuristic canvas; he sees existence as a jumble or flood of unrelated objects, events, and impressions. But the humanist enforces an order and meaning upon his picture. The naturalist believes that Nature tamed is Nature spoiled; the humanist points to the apple tree, which produces more and better fruit when husbanded by man than when allowed to grow untended, and notes that "Even solid mahogany needs some dressing to show off its natural grain." [16] The naturalist is centrifugal, the humanist, centripetal. The first is expansive, the second, integrative.

[15] Arnold, Matthew, *Poetical Works* (1897), p. 5.
[16] Sockman, Ralph W., *op. cit.*, p. 94.

One does not believe in limits, except those set for him by the strength or weakness of his passions and his enemies. The other believes in conditioning the free play of his instincts at every moment. The naturalist declares that we are mere ephemera on the stream of Nature; the humanist asks, with Edwin Arlington Robinson:

> Are we no greater than the noise we make
> Along one blind atomic pilgrimage
> Whereon by crass chance billeted we go
> Because our brains and bones and cartilage
> Will have it so? [17]

The naturalist takes his values from Nature itself; the humanist refers all experience to a human scale of morals. The naturalist measures each situation by a new point of view; the humanist has one system of values for everything. The humanist is selective, the naturalist, non-selective. The naturalist reveres the "noble savage" and would emulate him; the humanist, however, does not make the error of supposing that man, in returning "back to Nature," would gain in liberty. Savages, he knows, are more bound round with tabus and tribal conventions than civilized men; and Caspar Hauser [18] warns him of what a true "child of Nature" might resemble. The naturalist is a monist, the humanist a dualist. That is to say, the first contends that man and Nature form one contiguous whole, that nothing exists which is not made of matter, that ideas are just spurts of electrical or chemical energy running along the nerve circuits of the brain, and that the soul is a myth; while the second avers that man and Nature, body and spirit, are different entities, with opposite responsibilities. In the term "human nature," the naturalist emphasizes the second

[17] Robinson, Edwin Arlington, *The Man Against the Sky* (1921), p. 143. By permission of The Macmillan Company, publishers.
[18] See Park, Robert E., and Ernest W. Burgess, *Introduction to the Science of Sociology* (1927), pp. 239–241.

word, and humanism the first. The naturalist would "naturize" man; the humanist would "denature" him.

The basis of all fiction is a conflict or crisis. In the naturalistic novel this struggle is usually between men, or man and his surroundings. In the humanistic novel it is chiefly between man's impulses and his "inner check." One is an exterior drama, the other an interior. The naturalist is at war with everything that tries to restrain the free play or "self-expression" of his instincts; the humanist is at war with these instincts themselves, seeking to control and guide them. The humanistic novel deals with moral problems, whereas the naturalistic, because it is non-moral, largely devotes itself to a denial of moral problems.

Naturalism says, "Imitate Nature," but humanism says, "Imitate man at his best." The naturalist believes in the *will to power*, the humanist in the *will to perfection*. The humanist stands for "what is normal and central in human experience," [19] the naturalist for the unique and abnormal. The naturalist believes in self-expression, the humanist, in self-control. Naturalism subscribes to Spingarn's theory that we should judge literary products by asking ourselves this question: "Has the author succeeded in doing what he set out to do?" But to this query the humanist would add: "Was what the author tried to do *worth* the effort?" For he realizes that while Spingarn's criterion may sound enticing as a theory, no one, not even the naturalist himself, would ever really think of using it in practice. If he did, the naturalist would be forced to rank Harold Bell Wright (whom he despises) as high as Sherwood Anderson, since both have accomplished their aims. No, objects the humanist, sincerity is not enough; there are many sincere people in insane asylums. Or as Sinclair Lewis has put it: "Sincere? Hell, so is a cockroach!" "To write at all without introducing explicit or implicit judgments of value in respect of conduct is wholly and

[19] Babbitt, Irving, *Rousseau and Romanticism* (1919), p. xxii.

forever impossible,"[20] argues Ludwig Lewisohn; and the same might be said of the critical act.

The naturalist is a romanticist, in the sense that romanticism stands for anarchy and the superiority of the part to the whole; the humanist is a classicist, in the sense that classicism stands for unity and the superiority of the whole to its parts. The naturalist favors energy, the humanist, will. The humanist praises mediocrity; the naturalist feels, with William Hazlitt, that the ideal "is always to be found in extremes." The naturalist thinks that restraint means less "freedom." But the humanist replies that

The athlete, by the disciplining of his body, creates for himself a new world of actions; he can now do things which before were prohibited to him; in consequence, he has enlarged the sphere of his freedom. The thinker and the artist by discipline of a different kind are rewarded in the same way. They are now more free, because they have now more capacity.[21]

Naturalism believes that life and sensations are valuable in and for themselves; the humanist sees them only as instruments of the soul's health. The naturalist feels that whatever is enjoyable is desirable; the humanist quotes Aristotle in describing human good as an "activity of the soul in accordance with virtue."[22] The naturalist bases his view of morality upon the *immediate* pleasure or pain afforded him by any act; but while the humanist also judges vice and virtue by the pleasure and pain of an act as they affect an individual, he refers to the *final* consequences, and means by "pleasure" not the easy relief of a desire, but a "harmonious increase of life." Naturalism is opposed to inhibitions, whereas the humanist understands (what a writer of Anderson's type does not) that it is often a man's "repressions that make him interesting." The naturalist is pleased by novelty; the humanist asks, with

[20] Lewisohn, Ludwig, *Expression in America* (1932), p. 60.
[21] Muir, Edwin, *We Moderns* (1918), p. 114.
[22] Aristotle, *Ethica Nicomachea* (1925), Bk. I, 7.

George Eliot: "What novelty is worth that sweet monotony where everything is known, and *loved* because it is known." The naturalist lives for "the bright immediacy" of the present, and draws his standards from the data of science; the humanists, in studying what man is,

> put more store by the observations of what the race did in Egypt and Palestine and Greece than by the observations of what a white rat does in some psychological clinic. They believe that the "proper study of mankind is man," and for this there must be the long perspective as well as the immediate introspection.[23]

Yet "In setting his standards the humanist of the best type is not content to acquiesce inertly in tradition. He is aware that there is always entering into life an element of vital novelty and that the wisdom of the past, invaluable though it is, cannot therefore be brought to bear too literally on the present. He knows that, though standards are necessary, they should be held flexibly."[24]

The naturalist believes that vitality must be indicated (as the slang phrase has it) by "throwing your weight around," while the humanist, who feels that even suspended motion or emotion can be dynamic, seeks to achieve an "energy in repose." Naturalism's only system of balance is that of matching one excess against another; or as Aldous Huxley has stated it, in his *Do What You Will* (1929):

> The aim of the life-worshipper is to combine the advantages of balanced moderation and excess. The moderate Aristotelian partially realizes part of his potentialities; the life-worshipper aims at fully realizing all — at living, fully and excessively living, with every one of his colony of souls. He aspires to balance excess of self-consciousness and intelligence by an excess of intuition, of instinctive and visceral living; to remedy the ill effects of too much contemplation by those of too much action, too much solitude by too much sociability, too much enjoyment by too much

[23] Sockman, Ralph W., *op. cit.*, p. 169.
[24] Foerster, Norman (ed.), *Humanism and America* (1930), p. 42.

asceticism.   He will be by turns excessively passionate and excessively chaste.   (For chastity, after all, is the proper, the natural complement of passion.   After satisfaction, desire reposes in a cool and lucid sleep.   Chastity enforced against desire is unquiet and life-destroying.   No less life-destroying are the fulfilments of desires which imagination has artificially stimulated in the teeth of natural indifference.   The life-worshipper practises those excesses of abstinence and fulfilment which chance and his unrestrained, unstimulated desire impose upon him.) [25]

But to this, the humanist would reply that it only requires one excess to carry a man into disaster, and that a much safer method would be to produce a balance by thoughtful moderation in all things, instead of by a series of violent compensations.

Humanism also objects to the escapist, who (in the words of Shelley) "looks before and after and pines for what is not"; to his view of life's conflict, not as a "war in the cave," but as a clash between his dream and reality; and to his use of the imagination as a means of producing an "illusion of unreality" rather than Goethe's "illusion of a higher reality."   It recognizes that "Man needs at times to relax, and one way of relaxing is to take refuge for a time in some land of chimeras, to follow the Arcadian gleam." [26]   But it adds that one should not allow himself to become the dupe of his dreams.   This pursuit of anodynes should never assume the proportion or character that it does, for instance, in Cabell.   It is wrong, he declares, to seek an escape from hardships and the duty of disciplining one's appetites. For "a virtuous life requires exertion," [27] and demands a constant exercise of the will to refrain.   "The good," he would have it, "is better when it is harder."

REFORM BEGINS AT HOME.   The spirit of modern reform, too, meets with the humanist's disapproval.   Re-

---

[25] Huxley, Aldous, *Do What You Will* (1929), p. 282.

[26] Babbitt, Irving, *Rousseau and Romanticism* (1919), p. 209.

[27] Aristotle, *op. cit.*, Bk. X, 6.

formists believe that before the world's misery can be noticeably reduced, there will have to be radical social adjustments made, probably in the direction of nationalizing industry. But humanism, for the most part, is convinced that reform should begin at home, that it is a personal rather than a public problem. Let every one mind his own business, insists the humanist, and "first show that he can act on himself; there will then be time enough for him to act on other men and on the world." [28]   He does not want to place governmental restrictions on the individual; he wants the individual to place restraints upon himself. He does not feel, so much, that there should be laws to prevent men from *offering* bribes; instead he thinks that each man should discipline himself not to *accept* them. He says, in effect: "We do not need the corset of social regulations to hold us upright. We prefer the human muscles of will power." He wants to change man rather than his environment, and wants to do it directly; whereas the reformist seeks to change man by revising his surroundings.

Reformists hold that man's conscience is a *product* of his background; hence, improve the background, and you improve the man. The humanist, however, believes that a man's conscience is the *source* of his moral standards, and not a product of anything. He is of the opinion that the conflict between good and evil in life should be fought out in every person's heart, rather than in a war between classes. He believes that happiness and misery, either social or individual, are after all less dependent upon outside conditions than on character. "A tree brings forth of its kind," he says. "Whatsoever a man soweth, that shall he also reap. For he that soweth to his flesh shall of the flesh reap corruption; but he that soweth to the spirit, shall of the spirit reap life everlasting." [29]   Moreover, he is not in

[28] Babbitt, Irving, *Literature and the American College* (1908), p. 70.
[29] Paul's *Epistle to the Galatians*, 6 : 7–8.

sympathy with the idea held by some reformists (who love mankind better than they know it) that the workingman is "naturally good" and would live in perfect harmony with his neighbors if a higher ruling class were not present to keep him in order, though he does believe that this higher class should be an aristocracy of character instead of money or birth. He does not think the proletariat capable of governing itself by "brotherly love," since he is convinced, with Aristotle, that "most men do evil when they have an opportunity." "A perfect government," he asserts,

would be neither a crushing despotism or an unrestrained license; its aim would be to bring the character of the few to bear in some effective way upon the impulses of the many; it would be an aristocracy of justice. The theory of absolute democracy might imply that the will to refrain would in the long run assert its inner potency in all men if they were freed from external checks. The generality of men, however, are so intermittently conscious of the inner check that practical democracy, whether it calls itself anarchy or socialism, proceeds on the theory that the dispositions of men tend of themselves to order and harmony.[30]

The reformist is a democrat, the humanist an aristocrat. The first would nationalize property; the second would keep it in private hands. The reformist would eliminate the specter of business profits and rivalry; the humanist would retain the principle of competition, keep it from turning into "a struggle for existence" by training "the nobler sort of natures not to desire more," and equalize the passions rather than the possessions of man. "Humanists are concerned with self-reform; the radicals are concerned with social reform. The humanists are conservative; their attitude toward man, toward government, toward labor, toward literature, is conservative. The

[30] More, Paul Elmer, *The Drift of Romanticism* (1913), pp. 282–283.

radicals are revolutionary. The humanists are individual-
istic; the radicals are collectivistic." [31]

THE FATE OF ANTAEUS   In his hostility to vague Utopias,
the humanist, with his "Physician, heal thyself," renders a
valuable service; because it cannot be repeated too often
that while individuals remain selfish, any permanent improvement of society as a whole is out of the question.   And
in his denial of certain naturalistic fallacies, the humanist
again performs a worthy task.   Yet this same opposition to
naturalism goes far to disprove humanism's own basic
theory of impartiality.   It is not a true "golden mean,"
but a dualistic philosophy which sees body and soul as
perpetual rivals, and throws its weight to whichever
chances to be the weaker at any given time, in order to
counteract the excesses of the stronger and restore balance.
During the Renaissance, the humanist favored science, as a
means of restraining a religion that threatened to become
despotic; and today he has begun to feel that "unless he
adds to his creed the faith and hope of religion," he may
"find himself at the last, despite his protests, dragged back
into the camp of the naturalist." [32]

But in thus aligning flesh against spirit, humanism risks
disablement of both.   The checkmate toward which it
aspires can never last.   Sooner or later this internal feud
must end in the defeat of one side or the other, with soul
dominating body or body tyrannizing over soul.   The object is co-operation, not an armed truce.   At present some
humanists tend to undervalue Nature; and in doing so, they
run the danger of Antaeus, who lost his strength when lifted
from the earth.   There is in modern humanism too much of
what Neitzsche called "immaculate perception," too much
of the transcendental and eclectic.   Only when we have

[31] Calverton, V. F., *American Literature at the Crossroads*, The University of
Washington Chapbooks (1931), No. 48, p. 36.
[32] More, Paul Elmer, "A Revival of Humanism," *The Bookman* (March,
1930), LXXI, 9.

realized that the enemy of man is not Nature, but man, and only when we have faced the fact that the body and soul are indispensable to each other, can we hope to achieve that "ripeness" which Shakspere said "is all."

> Let us not always say,
> "Spite of this flesh to-day
> I strove, made head, gained ground
>   upon the whole!"
> As the bird wings and sings,
> Let us cry, "All good things
> Are ours, nor soul helps flesh more,
>   now, than flesh helps soul!" [33]

[33] Browning, Robert, *Complete Poetic and Dramatic Works* (1895), p. 384.

*

SWEETNESS AND LIGHT

*

ARBITER ELEGANTIAE From the death of Lowell in 1891 to the rise of the "magazinelets" about 1912, William Dean Howells was "the Dean of American Literature." As editor of the *Atlantic* during the years 1872–1881, he won for himself a towering reputation, and consolidated it by over a hundred volumes of poetry, drama, biography, travel, autobiography, criticism, social essays, and fiction. Whenever a new book swam into the literary skies, thousands of readers awaited his verdict before expressing their own. And his was the testimonial eagerly sought by nascent authors, many of whom (like Madison Cawein, Henry James, Stephen Crane, Hamlin Garland, Paul Laurence Dunbar, Frank Norris, and Brand Whitlock) owed part of their acceptance to his avuncular O. K.

The second of eight children, Howells was born at Martin's Ferry, Ohio, March 1, 1837. His father, a country journalist of Welsh stock, was the author of two Swedenborgian tracts; and in this faith Howells was reared. In 1840 his parents moved to Hamilton, the scene of *A Boy's Town* (1890), and there Howells, whose regular schooling was meager, educated himself in the use of English by setting type in his father's printing office. He was only twelve when his family migrated to Dayton and bought the *Transcript*, which Howells helped to publish; but this venture soon failed, and his father retreated to a log cabin on the Little Miami River, took over some grist and saw mills, and tried in vain to convert them to the manufacture of paper.

At the age of fourteen Howells went to Columbus and found himself a compositor's job on the *Ohio State Journal*, at four dollars a week. By this time he had begun to read widely; to add to his discovery of Pope, Irving, Goldsmith, Poe, and Cervantes, a knowledge of Shakspere, Chaucer, Dickens, the critical works of Lowell, and Macaulay (whose prose style had a formative influence on his own); to teach himself four or five languages after working hours; and to try his hand at juvenile verses, plays in rhyme, and even a historical romance. During the next year his family purchased the Ashtabula *Sentinel* on credit, and later moved with it to Jefferson, where Howells studied law for a while, and received the offer of a Scotch farmer to help send him to Harvard, a proposition he was unable to accept because his earnings were sorely needed at home. In 1856 he was in Columbus again, serving as correspondent for the Cincinnati *Gazette*, and perusing De Quincey and Tennyson in the State Library. Three years later he became news editor of the *Ohio State Journal* (which printed his first poetry); made a number of acquaintances in Columbus; collaborated with one of them in writing *Poems of Two Friends* (1859); penned *Lives and Speeches of Abraham Lincoln and Hannibal Hamlin* for the crucial election of 1860; and took a trip East, to meet Lowell (who had just accepted some of his verses for the *Atlantic*, and who introduced him to "The New England Circle" of Longfellow, Emerson, Whittier, and Holmes. "I find this young man worthy," said grave Hawthorne, in passing him along to Emerson).

His Republican biography of Lincoln earned Howells the consularship at Venice, after he had previously rejected a similar position at Rome; and his next four years were spent in that quiet city, browsing among the great figures of Italian literature, especially Dante and Goldoni. On his return from abroad he re-entered journalism, wrote editorials for various papers, obtained a position with the *Nation*, in which he had been publishing a series of articles on Italy, assisted James T. Fields on the *Atlantic*, and with Field's retirement in 1872, took over the editorship, at the age of thirty-five. Meanwhile his *Venetian Life* (1866) had come out, and caught the eye of reviewers; and in 1872 appeared his first novel, *Their Wedding Journey*.

Nine years later he resigned from the *Atlantic*, in order to devote more of his time to writing, and in 1885 moved to New York. In 1886 he assumed charge of a department in *Harper's*, entitled "The Editor's Study," and following the expiration of his contract, edited *Cosmopolitan*. But he soon went back to *Harper's*, and from 1900 to his death in 1920, he superintended that magazine's "Easy Chair" section, wrote steadily, spent his summers in New England and his winters in Florida, and traveled in Europe.

Books on travel, in fact, comprised a good share of his printed work. They are *Venetian Life* (1866), *Italian Journeys* (1867), *Three Villages* (1884), *Tuscan Cities* (1886), *A Little Swiss Sojourn* (1892), *London Films* (1905), *Certain Delightful English Towns* (1906), *Roman Holidays* (1908), *Seven English Cities* (1909), *Familiar Spanish Travels* (1913), *The Seen and Unseen at Stratford-on-Avon* (1914) ("a fantasy of the reconciliation of Bacon and Shakespeare, returning as materializations for the August memorials of Shakespeare"), and *Hither and Thither in Germany* (1920). *Poems* (1873), a collection of his early verse, *Stops of Various Quills* (1895), and *The Mother and Father: Dramatic Passages* (1909) contain Howells' rather undistinguished poetry, the first examples of which are reminiscent of Heine and Longfellow, and the later ones of Tennyson. His plays, whimsical and dehydrated, are to be found in *The Parlor Car* (1876), *Evening Dress* (1893), *Room Forty-Five* (1900), *Bride Roses* (1900), *The Smoking Car* (1900), *An Indian Giver* (1900), *The Sleeping Car* (1883), *The Register* (1884), *The Elevator* (1885), *The Garroters* (1886), *A Sea-Change* (1888), *The Mouse Trap and Other Farces* (1889), *The Sleeping Car and Other Farces* (1883), *The Albany Depot* (1892), *A Letter of Introduction* (1892), *The Unexpected*

Guests (1893), *A Likely Story* (1894), *Five O'Clock Tea* (1894), *A Previous Engagement* (1897), *Parting Friends* (1911), *Out of the Question* (1877), and *A Counterfeit Presentment* (1877). And his tales and sketches include *Suburban Sketches* (1871), *A Day's Pleasure and Other Sketches* (1876), *A Fearful Responsibility and Other Stories* (1881), *Buying a Horse* (1881), *Christmas Every Day and Other Stories Told for Children* (1893), *A Parting and a Meeting* (1896), *Doorstep Acquaintance and Other Sketches* (1900), *A Pair of Patient Lovers* (1901), *The Flight of Pony Baker* (1902), *Questionable Shapes* (1903), *Between the Dark and the Daylight* (1907), and *The Daughter of the Storage* (1916).

My Mark Twain (1910) is an anecdotal account of his forty-five-year friendship with the author of *Huckleberry Finn*, in which, among other things, he sadly records Twain's proclivity for earthy epithets, and his own embarrassment when, on one famous occasion, Twain made innocent fun of Boston's literary gods, Emerson, Holmes, and Longfellow. *Years of My Youth* (1916) describes Howells' life up to his receipt of the Venetian consularship. *Modern Italian Poets* (1887) is composed of nineteen pale, shapely critiques on Manzoni, Aleardi, Vittoris Alfieri, etc. *Imaginary Interviews* (1910) consists of thirty-five neat, feathery essays on such topics as "The Practices and Precepts of Vaudeville," "The Superiority of Our Inferiors," "Some Moments with the Muse," "Reading for a Grandfather," "The Quality of Boston and the Quantity of New York," "Dressing for Hotel Dinner," "The Fickleness of Age," "The Advantages of Quotational Criticism," and "A Day at Bronx Park." *My Literary Passions* (1895) deals with those authors "I must call my masters," Goldsmith, Cervantes, Irving, Pope, Shakspere, Chaucer, Macaulay, Tennyson, Heine, Goethe, Dante, Turgeniev, George Eliot, Hardy, Tolstoy, and a few other European novelists. *My Year in a Log Cabin* (1893) records the Little Miami River experiment. *Criticism and Fiction* (1891) delivers a flurry of gentlemanly blows at the "bad manners" of critics, all departures from the normal, "original genius," Hawthorne, books in which passion outweighs principle, Dickens, and "art for art's sake." *Literary Friends and Acquaintance* (1900) covers his youthful visit to New England, his first impressions (some of them very shocked) of New York's "Bohemia," and his notes on contemporary authors. *Heroines of Fiction* (1901) discusses such characters as Hawthorne's Zenobia, Fanny Burney's Evelina, Kingsley's Hypatia, Bulwer's Nydia, James's Daisy Miller, George Eliot's Maggie Tulliver, Dickens' Nancy Sikes, and others, and states that the English novel "arrived at what is still almost an ideal perfection in the art of Jane Austen." And *Literature and Life* (1902) offers us a group of articles in support of Howells' thesis that fiction must be "true to life," among them "Worries of a Winter Walk," "At a Dime Museum," "Spanish Prisoners of War," "Some Anomalies of the Short Story," and "The Psychology of Plagiarism."

The lesser novels of Howells include *Their Wedding Journey* (1872), in which Basil and Isabel March, just married, take a jaunt around to New York, Niagara, Montreal, and Quebec; *A Chance Acquaintance* (1873), in which a young maiden, on another of Howells' sightseeing trips to Canada, meets one Mr. Miles Arbuton of Boston, and falls in love with him; *A Foregone Conclusion* (1875), in which a Venetian priest is captivated by a pretty American tourist, but finds that his priesthood outlaws him from romance; *The Lady of the Aroostook* (1879), in which a modest daughter of New England sails on the freighter *Aroostook* to visit a friend in Venice, and finds herself in the distressing position of the only woman on board; *An Undiscovered Country* (1880), in which Howells denies that mediums can really get in touch with that "undiscovered country from whose bourn no traveler returns"; *Dr. Breen's Practice* (1881), in which a young woman permits a morbid sense of duty to lead her into a career, in a day when careers for women were considered improper; *A Woman's Reason* (1883), in which the daughter of an old Boston family, impoverished by her father's death, tries to make a brave living by painting vases, and refuses the suit of an English lord in order to marry an American sailor; *Indian Summer* (1886), in which the editor of an Indiana paper retires, goes to Italy, makes the error of seeking to regain his lost youth by wooing a girl twenty years his junior, and when he is rebuffed, marries a widow nearer his own age; *The Minister's Charge* (1887), in which a Boston clergyman debates man's Christian responsibility for the welfare of his fellowmen; *April Hopes* (1888), in which Howells says he meant to show "That an engagement made from mere passion had better be broken, if it does not bear the strain of temperament";[1] *The Shadow of a Dream* (1890), in which a man is crushed by the weight of his "subconscious" vision; *An Imperative Duty* (1892), in which Howells wonders whether or not one should tell the truth or live a lie, if one discovers that he has Negro blood in him; *The Coast of Bohemia* (1893), in which a young woman from the West goes to New York to learn to paint, but gets married instead; *The Day of Their Wedding* (1896), in which two Shakerites try to run away from their religion and get married, only to find their training and faith too strong for them; *The Landlord at Lion's Head* (1897), in which the theme is "as ye sow, so shall ye reap"; *The Story of a Play* (1898), in which Howells details the struggle of a young playwright to conceive and produce his "brain child"; *Ragged Lady* (1899), in which a retired business man and his wife transform the daughter of a poor mill hand into a débutante; *Their Silver Wedding Journey* (1899), in which the Marches extend their travels to Europe; *The Kentons* (1902), in which a family moves to Europe to prevent its daughter from marrying an impudent young blackguard; *Letters Home* (1903), in which Howells tells a love story in the epistolary fashion; *The Son of Royal Langbrith* (1904), in

---

[1] Howells, Mildred (ed.), *Life in Letters of William Dean Howells* (1928), I, 410.

which a man's evil lives after him, and sets his son's teeth on edge; *Miss Bellard's Inspiration* (1905), in which we are presented with the lover's quarrels of a sweet capable school-mistress and her English suitor, through the eyes of her affectionate aunt and uncle; *Fennel and Rue* (1908), in which Howells builds a romance around an amusing incident in his own career (having to do with a girl who wrote to him asking for the advance sheets of one of his serials which, as she falsely pleaded, the doctors had told her she would not live to read in the ordinary course of its publication); *New Leaf Mills* (1913), in which he fictionizes his father's attempt to set up paper mills on the Little Miami River; *The Leather-wood God* (1916), in which "the bedevilment of a raw Ohio settlement in the eighteen-twenties by a religious mounte-bank" [2] is recorded; *The Vacation of the Kelwyns* (1920), in which a young lecturer on historical sociology, his wife, and their two boys rent an old farmhouse from a Shaker com-munity for their summer holidays, have servant trouble, and watch their visiting niece fall in love with a "scholar gipsy"; and *Mrs. Farrell* (1921), in which a handsome widow wreaks mild havoc among the guests at a New England summer boarding house.

For the most part, these minor novels establish no fact other than that "the course of true love never does run smooth," and have "no problems," as Howells himself once said of *A Foregone Conclusion*, "but the sweet old one of how they shall get married." They resemble, in fact, cheerful little plays that have been fattened with scraps of descrip-tion and exposition, and seem to be composed largely of dry dialogues on those drawing-room questions to which men and women of Howells' day and class devoted much of their "small talk": the menace of "tramps," Shakerism, the perils of liquor, Tolstoy's theories of brotherhood, mental telepa-thy, the power of dreams, careers for women, the possibility of inhabitants on Mars, the "younger generation," the

[2] Firkins, Oscar W., *William Dean Howells* (1924), p. 203.

lewdness of the French and the superiority of the Anglo-Saxon, atavism, the place of the church in social "uplift," travel, divorce, sectional differences in dialect among Americans, and international marriages. Usually they are set in some New England village or summer hotel, Boston, New York, Saratoga Springs, Italy, or Ohio, and peopled with Yankee farmers, small town lawyers, liberal ministers, doctors, adolescent novelists and painters, Harvard students, magazine editors, reporters, middle-aged couples who find their chief delight in playing "Cupid" to some young lady of their acquaintance, Bernhardtesque widows, smiling schoolma'ams, titled foreigners, Shakerites, and (Howells' favorite characters) winsome, radiant, high-minded daughters of Brahminical Boston, who fall in love with nice eligible young Americans, and after a terrific amount of "soul searching" and worrying about whether honor, modesty, and all the proprieties have been thoroughly observed, at last venture into matrimony. Not for nothing has Howells been termed the "delineator of young men and maidens, and a chronicler of all the fluctuations of love affairs." True, he did once declare, in *The Rise of Silas Lapham*, that this "whole business of love, and love-making and marrying, is painted by the novelists in a monstrous disproportion to the other relations of life." [3] But he seems not to have profited by his own advice in these "chronicles of very small beer." The only excuse for his constant occupation with the love motif, is that like most novelists of that day he wrote for a female public; and marriage is, or was then, the prime crisis of woman's life.

GEESE AMONG SWANS   A more significant theme, however, animates *A Hazard of New Fortunes* (1889) and *The Rise of Silas Lapham* (1885). Together they represent an impeachment of materialism in American life, and embody Howells' belief that while crude *nouveaux riches* may possess money,

[3] Howells, William Dean, *The Rise of Silas Lapham* (1928), p. 279.

they very often lack the manners of the true aristocrat. Breeding is breeding, Howells seems to aver, and wealth is wealth; and rarely the two shall meet. In *A Hazard of New Fortunes*, we encounter Basil and Isabel March again. Basil has left the insurance business in Boston, to become the editor in New York of a magazine whose "angel" (or backer) is a Mr. Dreyfoos, once a poor Indiana farmer and now a rich oil magnate. Dreyfoos has come to New York in order to buy his daughters into its old Knickerbocker society; but oil and blue blood do not mix, and the Dreyfooses find that their vulgar ignorance and gaucheries do not appeal to the sensitive ladies and gentlemen whose favor they have set themselves to court. Nor does the magazine prosper, because of its owner's desire to change it from an artistic venture into a commercial one; and after his son (whose ideals are much finer than his own) is slain while trying to aid a group of striking workmen, Dreyfoos suddenly realizes the emptiness of material success, sees also what fearful vengeance it has wrought upon his character, catches a final glimpse of the moral gap between his naturalistic love of quantity and that nobler, humanistic veneration of quality to which he can never attain, and departs sorrowfully for Europe and the haunts of "fortune-hunting" barons, in the hope that there his money may purchase him a welcome among the select, and gain titled husbands for his two plebeian daughters. Says March, as he watches Dreyfoos's failure to elbow himself and his family into New York's patrician world of culture and gentility:

I don't believe a man's any better for having made money so easily and rapidly as Dreyfoos has done, and I doubt if he's any wiser. I don't know just the point he's reached in his evolution from grub to beetle, but I do know that so far as it's gone the process must have involved a bewildering change of ideals and criterions. I guess he's come to despise a great many things that he once respected, and that intellectual ability is among them — what we call intellectual ability. He must have undergone a moral deterioration, an atrophy of the generous instincts, and I don't see why it shouldn't have reached his mental make-up. He has sharpened, but he has narrowed; his sagacity has turned into suspicion, his caution to meanness, his courage to ferocity. That's the way I philosophise a man of Dreyfoos's experience, and I'm not very proud when I realise that such a man and his experience are the ideal and ambition of most Americans.[4]

This same warning against the sacrifice of quality to quantity, which constitutes Howells' chief message to his readers, is touched upon again in many of his less important novels and in *The Rise of Silas Lapham*. The latter presents us with another capitalist, this time a Vermont manufacturer of paint, who tries to buy his wife and daughters an entrée into Boston society, and after a series of tragic and mortifying reversals, finds that money has its limitations, that it cannot buy taste or judgment. In *Silas Lapham* Howells' satire, usually implicit and impotent, becomes explicit and potent; and his grasp of realities takes on a new range and warmth. But quite equal to his humane portrayal of the characters in this book, with their breathing presence and moral implications, is his piquancy of style, and easy upright flow of language, which Mark Twain once likened to the quiet circulation of blood in the veins. Nor is his able construction of plot any less of a delight. His chapters move ahead with the intricate precision of a spider's legs; his symbolization of Lapham's ambitions in the fine mansion he builds, then loses as a result of his own ethical confusion, is in the Greek tradition of tragedy;[5] and his device of introducing us to Lapham, in the first chapter, by means of an interview with a reporter, is a unique inspiration. How to work in the "antecedent action" of a novel, without slowing up its progression, is usually one of the most difficult problems the author has to face. But by this stratagem of the interview, Howells has

[4] Howells, William Dean, *A Hazard of New Fortunes* (1891), p. 279.
[5] See p. 91.

been able to solve it with rare plausibility and smoothness. The only trouble is, that such a striking trick can never be used twice. And yet even *The Rise of Silas Lapham* is weakened by Howells' inevitable intrusion of a love affair and one of those lovers' problems he was so fond of posing to himself; in this case, whether a girl should marry a man if she knows her older sister loves him too. Howells' motto seems to have been, "In spite of hell and high water, every book must end with wedding bells," though in *A Modern Instance* he did, for once, set this principle aside.

A Modern Instance (1882), Howells' third major opus, is structurally inferior to *The Rise of Silas Lapham;* but it is far superior to the bulk of his work, and cuts nearer than any of his novels to the dark and fundamental marrow of life. It might be termed "the spectacle of a love affair in which the woman gives more of her heart than the man gives of his." Bartley Hubbard, its hero, is a rakish young egoist, " 'a poor, cheap sort of creature. Deplorably smart, and regrettably handsome. A fellow that assimilated everything to a certain extent, and nothing thoroughly. A fellow with no more moral nature than a base-ball. The sort of chap you'd expect to find, the next time you met him, in Congress or the house of correction.' " [6] While working as a country editor in the Maine village of Equity, he hypnotizes with his superficial charm the daughter of a local lawyer, Marcia Gaylord. They become engaged; then a scandal over another girl deprives him of his job, and almost alienates Marcia. But casting pride and propriety to the winds, she permits her helpless fascination to draw her into marriage at the last moment ; and they run away to Boston, where in a short while, by his native cunning and unscrupulousness, Bartley manages to climb up in the newspaper game. Success, however, releases his latent turpitude and her latent jealousy. He loses his position, deserts Marcia and their baby, tries to obtain a divorce

[6] Howells, William Dean, *A Modern Instance*, p. 243.

behind her back, and when he is balked in this, goes down to Arizona, starts a newspaper there, and is shot to death by some irate victim of his printed calumnies. With *A Modern Instance* Howells seems "to have relinquished the delicate tête-à-tête in the secluded bow-window commanding the rich terrace and the view of manors and steeples in the distance, and to have taken a turn that looked toward passion and power."[7]

The harpy of cosmic evil brushes this story with its wings, as it does none of Howells' other novels. Of the Hubbards, their creator says, "They chose misery for themselves,"[8] in failing to discipline their impulses, Marcia by her inordinate fondness for her husband, Bartley by his inordinate self-indulgence. Both of them, we might observe, as Howells did of another character in the same book, had everything they wished, save the training to know what they "ought to wish." And in departing from the golden mean of conduct, they sacrificed their peace, just as Lapham and Dreyfoos did, with their extreme acquisitiveness. "We make," declared Howells, "our own hell in this world and the next."[9] In Bartley Hubbard he ventured nearer than he ever did again to an essentially vicious character. Dreyfoos and Lapham were at bottom kindly men, corrupted by a point of view. But Bartley's misdemeanors spring from a temperamental sickness. Unlike most of Howells' heroes, he is a complex human being, and not just a mouthpiece for his creator's "Autocrat of the Breakfast Table" remarks. There is more "psychology" to this volume, and because Bartley is even less a master of his own debacle than Lapham or Dreyfoos, more fatality. Beside it, Howells' other stories resemble structures of painted tin. At times it seems to have the deep note of a buoy, marking the submerged presence of dangerous rocks. Here Howells has left his playing on the shores of "young love," and swum out to where the

[7] Firkins, Oscar W., *op. cit.*, p. 107.
[8] *A Modern Instance*, p. 473.   [9] *Ibid.*

water is deeper and the waves higher. There is in its pages, too, a richer sense of trees and snow and the earth upon which man treads out his drama, and something of Tolstoy, whose novels Howells so genuinely admired. Yet throughout *A Modern Instance*, the reader is conscious of its author's moral caution, which forever prevents him from assigning pure hues to sin and disaster. Almost does Howells manage to escape from his idolatry of the "moderate, sensible, and decent," but in the end he fails, and draws up short of that desperate hush which marks real tragedy of whatever brand. His grotesque abolition of all sexual references from a story that is based upon a violent relationship between a man and his wife is also a fault. Not one quiver or thought does either Marcia or Bartley devote to the other's sex, even on their wedding night. The place of sex in life, of course, may easily be overstressed, and frequently has been; but Howells errs in the opposite extreme. His heroines are all born without bodies (though once he does speak of some girls "wearing red jerseys, which accented every fact of their anatomy"),[10] and his heroes never seem to notice the omission. For passion is a thing Howells never mentions, except as he once referred to it in his title *My Literary Passions*.

DEAR COMMON LIFE To his philosophy of fiction Howells gave the adopted name "realism," which he seemed to hold meant "truth to life." But this is an inadequate definition, since it would exclude nothing, not even the wildest fairytales of the escapist. What, in the last analysis, is not "true to life"? Is not everything that exists, fact or fiction, a part of existence? And yet Howells apparently did not think so, for his conception of realism as "nothing more and nothing less than the faithful treatment of material" outlaws man's romantic dreams and prevarications. To be sure, as a youth he himself had fed on honey dew; but from what he considered his error he had been saved by an early reading

[10] Howells, William Dean, *An Imperative Duty* (1892), p. 3.

of Heine, who never ceased to be his favorite poet, and who taught him "once for all that the dialect and subjects of literature should be the dialect and facts of life." [11]   Until he met the German poet he had been trying with different models to "literarify" himself (his own word).   He had previously supposed "that the expression of literature must be different from the expression of life" (in which he was really correct).   "But Heine," he says, "at once showed me that this ideal of literature was false; that the life of literature was from the springs of the best common speech, and that the nearer it could be made to conform, in voice, look and gait, to graceful, easy, picturesque and humorous or impassioned talk, the better it was." [12]

Thereafter he gave no quarter in his war upon the bizarre in fiction; and in a paper on Henry James in the *Century* for November, 1882, he did not hesitate to score even Dickens and Thackeray for their caricatures.   At other times it was Scott and Hawthorne who suffered his criticism. But most of his displeasure was reserved for those "sickly romances, cloak-and-sword fantasies, and sentimental love stories" so popular in his day, which consisted of

a great, whirling splendor of peril and achievement, a wild scene of heroic adventure and of emotional ground and lofty tumbling, with a stage "picture" at the fall of the curtain, and all the good characters in a row, their left hands pressed upon their hearts, and kissing their right hands to the audience. [13]

Against this type of literature, Howells revolted.   He thought "that the fault in all this welter of worthless novel-writing lay in the fact that the novelist had utterly lost his grip on reality; that he was working in a realm of cheap and conventional fantasy.   Novels were no longer imitations of

---

[11] Van Doren, Carl, "William Dean Howells," *The Cambridge History of American Literature* (1927), III, 77.

[12] Howells, William Dean, *My Literary Passions* (1895), p. 172.

[13] Howells, William Dean, *Criticism and Fiction* (1891), p. 106.

life, but imitations of imitations of imitations. The remedy, according to him, was to turn away from models, to drop all conventions of art, and to reproduce life itself — pure, unadulterated life." [14]   However, by the end of the century, when the dying historical romance flared up in all its sunset glory, he knew that he had made no headway; and in 1911 he said, "I perceive now that the monstrous rag baby of romanticism is as firmly in the saddle as it was before the joust began, and that it always will be as long as the children of men are childish." [15]

Howells' "realism," then, embraced only the common-place, and not the extraordinary. By "real" he meant the "ordinary," "the divine average." To Howells a thing was "true" only to the extent that it was commonplace. If uncommon, it was "false." With Emerson he said, "I embrace the common; I sit at the feet of the familiar and the low," and with Robert Louis Stevenson, "the common-places are the great poetic truths." He felt (to quote John Keble) that "The trivial round, the common task, should furnish all we ought to ask." "Ah! poor Real Life, which I love," he wrote in *Their Wedding Journey*, "can I make others share the delight I find in thy foolish and insipid face?" [16]   He saw himself belonging to a new school of the novel, which as he declared,

studies human nature much more in its wonted aspects, and finds its ethical and dramatic examples in the operation of lighter but not less vital motives. The moving accident is certainly not its trade; and it prefers to avoid all manner of dire catastrophes. It is largely influenced by French fiction in form, but it is the realism of Daudet rather than the realism of Zola that prevails with it, and it has a soul of its own which is above recording the rather brutish

[14] De Mille, George E., "The Infallible Dean," *The Sewanee Review* (April, 1928), XXXVI, 153.

[15] Quoted in Phelps, William Lyon, "William Dean Howells," *The Yale Review* (October, 1920), X, 101.

[16] Howells, William Dean, *Their Wedding Journey* (1899), p. 67.

pursuit of a woman by a man, which seems to be the chief end of the French novelist.[17]

If we substitute the word "novel" for "newspaper" in the following excerpt from *A Modern Instance*, we have Howells' theory of literature, and, to an extent, another statement of the humanist's "three levels" concept of life.

There are several tones in every community, and it will keep any newspaper scratching to rise above the highest. But if it keeps out of the mud at all, it can't help rising above the lowest. And no community is full of vice and crime any more than it is full of virtue and good works. Why not let your model newspaper mirror these?[18]

"The commonplace," says Howells of authors in general, "is just that light, impalpable, aerial essence which they've never got into their confounded books yet. The novelist who could interpret the common feelings of commonplace people would have the answer to 'the riddle of the painful earth' on his tongue."[19]

A BOUQUET FOR MRS. GRUNDY   From his conception of "the commonplace," he ousted all things morbid or profane. Except for a period after the death of his daughter Winifred, in 1889, he never dealt with "otherworldly" topics; and most of his deaths, like his birth scenes, are carefully held off stage, instead of in the audience's view. He has, it is true, one suicide in his novels; but usually he manages to avert his characters' suicidal impulses at the last moment. And sex, for him, is entirely tabu. He seems to have had a very squeamish mind where this subject was concerned. In fact his abnegation of passion amounted almost to a passion in itself. He wanted to expurgate the classics, objected to Chaucer's "lewdness," and talked a great deal about erasing "the beast-man" from literature. Of bes-

[17] Quoted in Howells, Mildred (ed.), *op. cit.*, I, 327–328.
[18] *A Modern Instance*, p. 299.   [19] *The Rise of Silas Lapham*, pp. 284–285.

tialities in fiction, he said, "At the end of the ends such things do defile, they do corrupt." Though he admired Robert Herrick, he worried about the adulteries "potential or actual" in his novels. As much as he respected Maxim Gorky, the Russian, he could not stomach his coming to this country in 1906 with a woman not his wife. And when, in *An Imperative Duty*, he noted a few couples innocently holding hands on park benches, he could be so purblind as to term them "vulgar young people, who were publicly abusing the freedom our civilization gives their youth." [20]

There would seem to be some evidence for Frank Norris's remark that he was "as respectable as a church and proper as a deacon." Howells wrote about forty volumes of fiction, and in all of these books

Adultery is never pictured; seduction never; divorce once and sparingly ("A Modern Instance"); marriage discordant to the point of cleavage, only once and in the same novel with the divorce; crime only once with any fullness ("The Quality of Mercy"); politics never; religion passingly and superficially; science only in crepuscular psychology; mechanics, athletics, bodily exploits or collisions, very rarely. [21]

What remains, when these important constituents of life have been removed, is an interest in travel, pure love, literary gossip, and some watered sociology. How, then, is it possible for one critic to declare that "Howells produced in his fourscore books the most considerable transcript of American life yet made by one man"? [22] As another critic has noted, he has recorded "scarcely a crime in all his volumes: he has not in his voluminous gallery a woman who ever broke a law more serious than indiscretions at an afternoon tea. As a result there is no remorse, no problems of life in the face of broken law, no decisions that involve life and death and the agony that is sharper than death. In

[20] *An Imperative Duty*, p. 7.   [21] Firkins, Oscar W., *op. cit.*, p. 65.
[22] Van Doren, Carl, "William Dean Howells," *The Cambridge History of American Literature* (1927), III, 84.

his pages life is an endless comedy where highly conventional and very refined people meet day after day and talk, and dream of Europe, and make love in the leisurely, old-fashioned way, and marry happily in the end the lover of their choice." [23]   Partial exceptions to this criticism, of course, must be made in the case of *Silas Lapham* and *A Modern Instance*.   There we do find a touch of "the agony that is sharper than death."   But this is perhaps because they stray from "the commonplace," rather than adhere to it.   In these two books Howells disproved his own theory that only in the trivia of everyday life can be found the materials for profound literature, a theory, if he had but realized it, that had already been disproved by most of the great books of the world.

Howells, in his *Criticism and Fiction*, argued that the true "realist" must believe that "nothing that God has made is contemptible. He cannot look upon human life and declare this thing or that thing unworthy of notice, any more than the scientist can declare a fact of the material world beneath the dignity of his inquiry." [24]   Yet by all of his tabus and exclusions, Howells violated this very precept.   For while he may have conceived of "realism" as a "slice of life," he was pretty careful where he did the slicing.   Pessimism, for instance, was barred as definitely as profanity from his stories.   In *Literature and Life* he insisted that he "had seldom seen a sky without some bit of rainbow in it," [25] and went on to say that if others could not see likewise, "they have not had their eyes examined and fitted with glasses which would at least have helped their vision." [26]   But is this realism, or "truth to life" ?   Is it not, on the contrary, viewing life through rose-colored spectacles?   Some situations there surely are in which the rain-

[23] Pattee, Fred Lewis, *American Literature Since 1870* (1915), p. 212.
[24] *Criticism and Fiction*, p. 16.
[25] Howells, William Dean, *Literature and Life* (1902), p. iv.
[26] *Ibid.*

bow is conspicuous by its absence; yet these Howells strictly avoided. And in all but one or two of his numerous volumes, he clung to the "happy ending," even where it meant warping probability to do so. As Henry James once said of him, he was haunted by "a tendency to factitious glosses." [27]

UNDER GLASS   Part of Howells' constricted vision, to be sure, sprang from his sheltered habits of life; for he was "A Lover of the Chair." His days, from 1860 on, were lived mostly at a desk or in libraries, far away from the uglier and rawer aspects of our civilization. Even as a boy in Ohio, he spent most of his time indoors, reading in a "study" that he had rigged up for himself; and upon his return from Venice, where he resided while a civil war was raging in this country, he exiled himself from America by running away to the literary and social salons of Boston. Once, as a young man, he had tried to approach the more violent side of human experience by becoming a reporter. But he failed. "One night's round of the police stations with the other reporters," he confessed, "satisfied me that I was not meant for that work, and I attempted it no farther." To which he adds, "I have often been sorry since, for it would have made known to me many phases of life that I have always remained ignorant of." [28] As a novelist, intent upon recreating "real life" with power and insight, he might be compared to "a war correspondent who has never been in range of the bullets." [29]

Howells' work is replete with tender wisdom, charm, and grace of execution, but it lacks vitality (of either the overt or imaginative kind), and has nothing contagious about it. In his obsession with "the divine average" he is as dull as many naturalists in their mania for the spectacular. When

[27] Lubbock, Percy (ed.), *The Letters of Henry James* (1920), I, 105.
[28] *My Literary Passions*, p. 165.
[29] Macy, John, *The Spirit of American Literature* (1913), p. 289.

he reduced "truth" to the "commonplace," he seems to have gone on and reduced it to the "insignificant." His error was "to assume that the tea-table situations rule the world at large — that whether a man has his tie on straight and his shoes shined is just as significant, say, as his adjustment to the universe, as the clash of men in finance and industry or as the relation of the sexes." [30]   Consequently his books have (to steal one of his own phrases) "a blameless middling-ness" about them.   In general he illustrates one danger of humanism, which is to become immoderate in the use of moderation, and to forget that there is just as much "truth" in the abnormal as in the normal, and decidedly more interest.   The greatest humanists, as a matter of fact, have never scrupled to treat of extraordinary events and people. Milton, Homer, and Sophocles all dealt with situations that are more excessive and morbid than any in Dreiser, though toward these situations they retained an attitude of disapproval that is missing in the latter.   The "golden mean" may have an application in the sphere of actual life, but the giants of literature (whatever their philosophy) have rarely avoided the unusual in choosing their themes. In their books we find a candid recognition of the fact that sin is as normal as virtue, as "common," and as universal.

OF THEE I SING   Along with his provincialism in morals (and to a degree because of it), Howells betrayed a narrow point of view in regard to America as a whole that may be designated "nationalistic."   He was a loyal patriot, be-lieved that this country was "God's footstool" and Boston "the hub of the universe," and was reluctant to grant other nations superiority in anything, except perhaps certain kinds of scenery.   Most Europeans were to his mind de-praved, especially the French; and no doubt he was able to infect many of his readers and disciples with a like distrust

[30] Grattan, C. Hartley, "Howells: Ten Years After," *The American Mercury* (May, 1930), XX, 49.

of "the bad French morality," for Hamlin Garland, who looked upon Howells as a prophet, was also predisposed toward the idea of an exclusively Anglo-Saxon virtue. While in Venice, Howells wrote back to one of his sisters:

O Vic, Vic! prize America all you can. Try not to think of the Americans' faults — they are a people so much purer and nobler and truer than any other, that I think they will be pardoned the wrong they do. I'm getting disgusted with this stupid Europe, and am growing to hate it. What I have told you of society here in Italy, is true of society throughout the continent. Germany is socially rotten — and the Germans have a filthy frankness in their vice, which is unspeakably hideous and abominable to me. The less we know of Europe, the better for our civilization; and the fewer German customs that take root among us, the better for our decency. You will read the lies of many people who say that life in Europe is more cheerful and social than ours. Lies, I say — or stupidities, which are almost as bad. There is no life in the whole world so cheerful, so social, so beautiful as the American.[31]

But in this attitude it is only fair to add that Howells departed from the true spirit of humanism, which aims to be cosmopolitan rather than nationalistic, and to include in its scope the best parts of every civilization, past or present, American, European, or Asiatic.

A PARLOR SANSCULOTTE   As a matter of fact, it would seem that Howells' only liberal tendencies consisted of his social and economic opinions, though even this is open to doubt. With our expanding interest in reform today, these opinions have taken on a new value. Howells, in a measure, was a pioneer American socialist, at a time when socialism did not enjoy even the restricted popularity that it does now. However, this social consciousness was not a quality of his early work; it dates from his discovery of Tolstoy after he had "turned the corner" of his fiftieth year. In *My Literary Passions* he has said of the Russian, whose "heart-searching

---

[31] Howells, Mildred (ed.), *op. cit.*, I, 58–59.

books" (he avowed) were "worth all the other novels ever written," [32]

As much as one merely human being can help another I believe that he has helped me; he has not influenced me in aesthetics only, but in ethics, too, so that I can never again see life in the way I saw it before I knew him. Tolstoy awakens in his reader the will to be a man; not effectively, not spectacularly, but simply, really. . . . Tolstoy gave me heart to hope that the world may yet be made over in the image of Him who died for it, when all Caesar's things shall be finally rendered unto Caesar, and men shall come into their own, into the right to labor and the right to enjoy the fruits of their labor, each one master of himself and servant to every other.[33]

Boiled down, his socialism has a definitely religious cast. With Tolstoy he believed in a "brotherhood of man," based on "the life rather than the doctrine of Christ," and on the principle that "no one for good or for evil, for sorrow or joy, for sickness or health, stood apart from his fellows, but each was bound to the highest and the lowest by ties that centred in the hand of God." [34]

Though in most of his work Howells shows himself a convert to the aristocratic criteria of Boston and humanism, he had a charitable regard for "the under dog," and a wider curiosity about social conditions than many people of his day, or this. There are discussions of industrial conflict in *A Hazard of New Fortunes*. *The Quality of Mercy* (1892) deals with a Massachusetts capitalist who absconds with his company's money, and the consequences of his crime. *The World of Chance* (1893), in which a young man comes to New York to market his first novel, raises the question as to whether success is just a matter of "luck" (though Howells decides it is not), and states that "The people must vote themselves into possession of their own business." [35]   *A*

[32] Howells, Mildred (ed.), *op. cit.*, I, 405.
[33] *My Literary Passions*, pp. 250–251.
[34] Howells, William Dean, *The Minister's Charge* (1886), p. 458.
[35] Howells, William Dean, *The World of Chance* (1893), p. 91.

Traveler from Altruria (1894), "which was a whimsical extension of Looking Backward," [36] describes the impressions of a visitor to America from a mythical Perfect State, and contrasts the inequities of this country with the fairer civilization of his. *Through the Eye of the Needle* (1907), a sequel to this romance, enlarges upon Howells' conception of Arcadia. *Annie Kilburn* (1888) is "from first to last a cry for *justice*, not *alms*" in our efforts to improve the condition of the poor. *New Leaf Mills* touches upon the subject of communistic colonies; and in *The Son of Royal Langbrith*, Howells at least mentions profit-sharing. He stood out against the Spanish-American war, and felt we had no right to interfere in Cuba. After it had been rejected by four publishers, he persuaded Harper & Brothers to print Henry D. Lloyd's *Wealth Against Commonwealth* (1894), which antedated Miss Tarbell's attack on the Standard Oil Company. He also attended Socialist meetings, and declared that he would have joined a labor party had there been one "embodying any practical ideas." But most remarkable of all was his bravery in risking his reputation to say of the four Chicago "anarchists" who were jailed in the famous Haymarket Riots of 1886: "I have never believed them guilty of murder, or of anything but their opinions, and I do not think they were justly convicted." [37] To Garland he wrote in 1888:

You'll easily believe that I did not bring myself to the point of openly befriending those men who were civicly murdered in Chicago for their opinions without thinking and feeling much, and my horizons have been indefinitely widened by the process. Your land tenure idea is one of the good things which we must hope for and strive for by all the good means at our hands. But I don't know that it's the first step to be taken; and I can't yet bring myself to look upon confiscation in any direction as a good thing. The new commonwealth must be founded in justice even

[36] Calverton, V. F., *The Liberation of American Literature* (1932), p. 377.
[37] Howells, Mildred (ed.), *op. cit.*, I, 393.

to the unjust, in generosity to the unjust rather than anything less than justice. Besides, the land idea arrays against progress the vast farmer class who might favor national control of telegraphs, railways, and mines, postal savings-bank-and-life-insurance, a national labor bureau for bringing work and workmen together without cost to the workman, and other schemes by which it is hoped to lessen the sum of wrong in the world, and insure to every man the food and shelter which the gift of life implies the right to. Understand, I don't argue against you; I don't know yet what is best; but I am reading and thinking about questions that carry me beyond myself and my miserable literary idolatries of the past; perhaps you'll find that I've been writing about them. I am still the slave of selfishness, but I no longer am content to be so. That's as far as I can honestly say I've got.[38]

Howells' economics may be summarized as follows, "The system of competitive capitalism, with its accompanying ideal of individual success, is no longer satisfactory. It produces only a heartless struggle for survival, governed largely by chance, in which no life is secure; in which even invention, fruit of man's ingenuity, only adds to the misery of the unemployed. It produces, contrary to the equalitarian ideals of America, insuperable class distinctions between the rich and the poor. Competitive capitalism should therefore be replaced by socialism; the machinery of government should be employed to control production in the interest of all rather than in the interest of the exploiting few. This socialism should not be the effect or agent of class conflict, but should represent the will of the majority, peaceably expressed by suffrage." [39]

Yet his socialism must be qualified; even here he belongs on the conservative side. While he seemed to insist in *Annie Kilburn* that the upper and lower classes might be merged on an economic plane, he still retained the view that between them there must always be a cultural hiatus; that

[38] Howells, Mildred (ed.), *op. cit.*, I, 407–408.
[39] Taylor, Walter Fuller, "William Dean Howells and the Economic Novel," *American Literature* (May, 1932), IV, 113.

"workingmen *as* workingmen are no better or wiser than the rich *as* the rich"; [40] that "equality before the law and in politics was sacred, but that the principle could never govern society"; [41] and that "Decency transcends humanity." Though "chance" plays a major part in life, he is convinced that "whatsoever a man soweth, that shall he also reap," that "most things seem to turn out pretty well in the end," and that when (humanistically speaking) we "take man out of the clutches of Nature, and put Nature in the keeping of man, we shall have the millennium." [42]   In the last analysis, it is to "the inner check" that he returns. And for these reasons, and because his revolutionary utterances never exceeded the bounds of propriety, he has been termed a "parlor sansculotte." "Nevertheless, Howells must be credited with having advanced farther along social lines than any of the literati of his time, and even though he did retain a considerable part of the petty bourgeois ideology of his period," he helped prepare the way for "the coming of the muckraker's movement which was to precipitate in the person of Upton Sinclair the appearance of the first signs of radical culture in this country." [43]

Today, a decade after his death, Howells' fame has suffered an eclipse, due to the fact that humanism has been replaced as our philosophy of life by naturalism, and the fact that Boston is no longer America.   Had Howells stayed in the West, instead of going East, his work might have taken on, not a virtuous neutrality, but a real vitality.   The West was growing, the East was dying when he made his change.   And so he may be said, as one writer puts it, to have "left a christening to attend a funeral."   The same thing happened to him that happened to Garland; he went to Boston, accepted the urbane mores of its social

40 Howells, Mildred (ed.), *op. cit.*, I, 357–358.
41 Howells, William Dean, *Annie Kilburn* (1889), p. 64.
42 *The World of Chance*, p. 100.
43 Calverton, V. F., *op. cit.*, p. 381.

and literary arbiters, and wasted the rest of his career in "safe and sane" (and eminently tedious) works for "young ladies," books that dealt only "with the most smiling aspects of life." His reputation has withered, because he was the fireside raconteur of a vanishing audience, the happy bourgeoisie of 1890 who stood for "my country right or wrong," thought that nothing could shake our prosperity, and still voted for Lincoln, an optimistic, comfortable public, now touched by the first frosts of reality.

*

CAVIAR TO THE GENERAL

*

THE PASSIONATE PILGRIM   In 1866 Howells said of Henry
James, "He is a very earnest fellow, and I think extremely
gifted — gifted to do better than any one has yet done
toward making us a real American novel." [1]   But here the
tea leaves lied.   "Gifted" James surely was; a "real American novel" he never produced.   The greater share of his
life, as it turned out, was spent in Europe; and only two of
his many novels, *Washington Square* (1881) and *The Bostonians*
(1886), have an exclusively American background.   Despite
the fact that he was born in New York City, April 15, 1843,
James seems almost to have been an expatriate from birth.
While he was still a babe in arms, his parents carried him
and his older brother over to the Continent, to dip them,
as Rebecca West puts it, in the "holy well" of European
culture; and from this baptism he never recovered.
During the balance of his earthly span, his point of view
remained that of the Old World rather than that of the
New.

James's father, the grandson of an Albany millionaire,
was a theologian, and like Howells' father, author of several
treatises on the Swedenborgian religion.   His brother,
William, later became the most renowned of American
philosophers.   Both boys, after their very early trip abroad,
went to neighboring dame-schools in New York; but in
1855, their parents, who were anxious that they should
receive a liberal and cosmopolitan education, again sailed

[1] Howells, Mildred (ed.), *Life in Letters of William Dean Howells* (1928),
I, 116.

with them across the Atlantic and took up quarters in Geneva, where James studied at a boarding school until their return home to Newport for a year in 1858. By 1859 they were all back in Geneva, and James was imbibing French and German literature at the Academy. Trollope, Dickens, Meredith, George Eliot, Reade, Thackeray, and du Maurier he met in the pages of the *Cornhill Magazine* and *Once A Week*, two English periodicals; and a bit later, when the family had moved on to France and England, he whetted his esthetic sensibilities still further by many long walks through the art galleries of London and Paris.

In 1860 the Jameses once more returned to Newport, in order that William, who was artistically inclined, might study with the American painter, William Hunt. And James was left to while away his leisure in dreaming of Europe; visiting the studios of Hunt and John La Farge, reading Balzac, George Sand, de Musset, Browning, and the *Révue des Deux Mondes;* and translating one of Mérimée's sketches. William, however, soon deserted his art to take up science at Harvard; and there James followed him in 1862, to spend a year in the Law School, though by this time he really knew that what he "wanted to want" was a literary career. In Cambridge he formed an intimacy with Charles Eliot Norton, Howells, and the Boston intelligentsia, and from 1864 to 1869, wrote reviews for the *Nation* and *North American Review*, as well as tales for the *Atlantic* and *The Galaxy*. Then in 1869, convinced that England and Italy, with their many aids to life and pleasure, were the lands for peace and happiness, he went for another *Wanderjahr*.

By 1870 he was back in America, and in 1871 he tried the novel form with *Watch and Ward*, a weak love story, which he later disowned (leaving *Roderick Hudson*, 1876, as his first volume of fiction). England received him again in 1872, with a commission from the *Nation* for a series of pictorial essays, now included in his travel books, *Transatlantic Sketches*

(1875), *Portraits of Places* (1883), *A Little Tour in France* (1885), *English Hours* (1905), and *Italian Hours* (1909). Nine years later he made a brief visit to these shores, and another in 1904, when he returned to gather material for that shrewd estimate of our civilization, *The American Scene* (1907). But the rest of his days were spent abroad, writing, and making a host of friends, among them William Morris, Ruskin, Lowell, Turgeniev, Flaubert, Zola, Daudet, Edmond de Goncourt, Tennyson, Lord Houghton, Gladstone, Stevenson, John Addington Symonds, Burne-Jones, Arnold, and George Eliot.

In 1879 he achieved a measure of fame with the publication of *Daisy Miller*, in which he pictured a hoydenish young lady from Schenectady, New York, "a mixture of innocence and crudity," who travels on the Continent with her mother and brother, refuses to heed the voice of civilized society, and by one last indiscretion, loses her life. Misinterpreted as an attack on American girlhood, this story brought James a momentary audience. Yet the novels that followed it went largely unnoticed; so after *The Tragic Muse* (1890), he deliberately turned his hand to what he thought was the "vulgarest of the muses" in order to make money, and wrote a number of English drawing-room plays, which have been collected in *Theatricals* (1894–1895). To this period also belong many of his novelettes and sketches, now to be found reprinted in *A Passionate Pilgrim and Other Tales* (1875), *An International Episode* (1879), *The Madonna of the Future and Other Tales* (1879), *The Siege of London and Other Tales* (1883), *Tales of Three Cities* (1884), *Stories Revived* (1885), *The Aspern Papers* (1888), *The Reverberator* (1888), *A London Life* (1889), *The Lesson of the Master* (1892), *The Private Life* (1893), *The Wheel of Time* (1893), *The Real Thing and Other Tales* (1893), *Terminations* (1895), *Embarrassments* (1896), *The Two Magics* (1898), *In the Cage* (1898), *The Soft Side* (1900), *The Better Sort* (1903), *Julia Bride* (1909), *The Finer Grain* (1910), and *A Landscape Painter* (1919).

Breathing spaces between novels afforded James time to draft biographies of *Hawthorne* (1879) and *William Wetmore Story* (1903); and toward the end of his life he wrote three volumes of autobiography, *A Small Boy and Others* (1913), *Notes of a Son and Brother* (1914), and *The Middle Years* (published posthumously in 1917). His last complete novel, *The Golden Bowl*, appeared in 1904. In 1896 he bought a house at Rye, Sussex, and in 1915, as a protest against America's tardiness in throwing itself upon "the enemy," he became a naturalized British subject. His final years, broken by illness, were mainly given to revising his work for a definitive edition, and to writing war essays for various charitable purposes, which were later merged into *Within the Rim* (1918). He died in 1916, leaving two unfinished novels, *The Sense of the Past* (1917)[2] and *The Ivory Tower* (1917).

A REVERSE COLUMBUS   Though his father, as we have seen, entertained the hope that he might become a cosmopolite, James (in the strictest sense) never did. To be cosmopolitan means that one must be "at home" in any country and this James was not. Both he and Howells dealt with highly restricted areas of experience, space, and thought; and to this degree they were provincial, just as most people, authors or otherwise, must of necessity be. Howells loved America and mistrusted Europe; James loved Europe and disliked America. Each cared only to write about the cream of society, which James found in England and Howells in Boston. Both were converts to what they felt were mellower, more aristocratic worlds than the ones they were born into, even if in old age they gazed back with a little homesickness toward the lands they had repudiated, Howells toward Ohio and James toward the United States.

[2] *Berkeley Square*, a recent stage success by John L. Balderson and J. C. Squire, was based on this fragment.

For Howells, Boston represented the *ne plus ultra* of refinement; but James, who was at least more cosmopolitan than his friend, found Boston too prim. America as a whole, he felt, was a joyless country, whose inhabitants (especially of the New England variety) were all "undergoing martyrdom, not by fire, but by freezing." [3] It was a "bare, sterile, and uncivilized" locality, cursed with a "flagrant morality," inane, commercialized, vulgar, and more devoted to quantity than quality. As he points out in *Hawthorne*, his native land lacked all those things he most enjoyed, since it had

No State, in the European sense of the word, and indeed barely a specific national name. No sovereign, no court, no personal loyalty, no aristocracy, no church, no clergy, no army, no diplomatic service, no country gentlemen, no palaces, no castles, nor manors, nor old country-houses, nor parsonages, nor thatched cottages nor ivied ruins; no cathedrals, nor abbeys, nor little Norman churches; no great Universities nor public schools — no Oxford, nor Eton, nor Harrow; no literature, no novels, no museums, no pictures, no political society, no sporting class — no Epsom nor Ascot.[4]

On the other hand, Europe offered him these amenities in abundance. There he found a "world of hereditary quiet," where all "the echoes of the general life arrive but to falter and die," and where the very air seemed to be thick with "arrested voices" of the past. James, like his hero in "The Passionate Pilgrim," had a love of old objects and usages. And these he decided could be embraced nowhere save in England. He revered the "blunted outlines" there, the worn autumnal background, the atmosphere filled with sleeping history, the warm patina that lies on aged things, the decayed castles "old in story," the antiquity that "awakes and sings" in classic landscapes, the smoky tap-

[3] James, Henry, *The Europeans* (1884), p. 48.
[4] James, Henry, *Hawthorne* (1879), p. 43. By permission of The Macmillan Company, publishers.

estry of London life, the art treasures, the neat countrysides, and the hieratic spirit of English society. America was thin and new, with no depth or tradition; whereas England, France, and Italy fairly breathed of the hundreds of generations whose lives had gone into their making. Europe was polished and flavored with use, seasoned with time, ripe with associations, more hospitable to value, and more friendly to beauty. In a word, it was civilized; and this was the quality James admired.

Many critics seem to be much concerned about his desertion of America for England, but this must be chiefly a result of our habit of feeling "nationly." In reality there is nothing strange or distempered in James's choice of residence. Had he migrated from Redbird, Nebraska, to New York City, his move would scarcely have occasioned notice among patriotic historians; yet the disparity of environment would have been quite as great, if not greater, between village and city than between the United States and Europe. One cannot choose where he is to be born, and if when he grows up his birthplace does not suit him, he would appear to be justified in leaving it. We can only say, as in the case of Howells, that James's removal to England altered the future nature of his work. Of his right to make the change, or his wisdom in doing so, we can hardly judge. No doubt he and Howells both would have been unhappy in any milieu other than Europe and Boston; no doubt they reaped, in the end, the full fruit of their potentialities. And perhaps the changes they made were indispensable to this final harvest.

Nor can we allege that James was wrong in leaving the lower classes and the rawer aspects of life to be treated of by the naturalists, while he confined himself to the activities of the European *noblesse*, bibliophiles, artists, and the whole tranquil, sheltered, fastidious sphere of wealth and culture. For in the first place, if we termed him a snob, he might reply (with David Graham Phillips) that snobs are made not so much by those above as by those below. And in the second place, reflection should convince us that here his instinct was perfectly true. James, being himself a cultivated man, had to use cultivated characters to express his sentiments, to choose as his protagonists such people as might plausibly be expected to emit the things he had to say, in whose mouths his thoughts would not sound incongruous. Of what value, anyway, would any social novel that James might write be to the cause of reform, or any naturalistic novel of his be to naturalism? He was not suited, either by temperament or education, to write anything except what he did write. Moreover he seems to have had a legitimate theory that life can be read best in translation, that it should not be studied at its base but in its condition of highest growth. He prefers to walk in the daylight rather than "burrow in the dark" with the naturalists. He is a student of society's matured products, whose method is to trace down from the top, instead of up from the bottom, as the naturalist does. While Dreiser begins with origins and works toward their developed state, from causes toward effects, James begins with the fruit and works backward toward the roots; and which system is more revelatory must remain a matter of conjecture and private taste.

Vulgar, Vulgar, Vulgar The same cultural pros and cons that played tug of war with his life not surprisingly gave a pattern to James's fiction. He was a "reversed Christopher Columbus." So much of Europe did he get into his novels, in fact, that Ezra Pound has termed him the "Baedeker to a continent." His genre was the émigré novel. Using transplanted Americans as his pawns, he demonstrated how sadly (as products of a young, inferior culture) they lacked the taste and moral perspective for adjusting themselves to a richer European environment, or how, once they had realized the advantages of foreign society, they became "disamericanized." There was but one word he could find to describe Americans abroad, and that was

vulgar, vulgar, vulgar.   Their ignorance — their stingy, defiant, grudging attitude towards everything European — their perpetual reference of all things to some American standard or precedent which exists only in their own unscrupulous wind-bags — and then our unhappy poverty of voice, of speech and of physiognomy — these things glare at you hideously.   On the other hand, we seem a people of *character*, we seem to have energy, capacity and intellectual stuff in ample measure.   What I have pointed at as our vices are the elements of the modern man with *culture* quite left out.   It's the absolute and incredible lack of culture that strikes you in common travelling Americans.[5]

Daisy Miller presents us with James's favorite character, the "typical American girl," whom he sees as honest and high spirited, but imprudent, nervous rather than sensitive, clever rather than wise.   *Roderick Hudson* has for its hero a promising young sculptor who, removed from a lawyer's office in Northampton, Massachusetts, to a studio in Rome, goes to pieces in the relaxed moral climate of Italy, and failing to win the heart of Christina Light, an enigmatic beauty, tumbles over a precipice in the Alps.   In *The American* (1877) Christopher Newman, a retired American manufacturer, discovers he no longer cares for the mere piling up of wealth, and goes to Europe to drink of its culture.   He penetrates the circle of an old French family, the de Bellegardes, and falls in love with the widowed daughter of this proud house, Claire de Cintré.   But the mother, antagonized by Newman's air of confident energy, refuses to sanction the match; and Claire enters a convent.   Then fate places in Newman's hands a document containing information which, should he care to use it, might humble the mother and enable him to take a pleasant revenge.   Having by this time, however, absorbed a measure of taste and restraint from his contact with the de Bellegardes and

[5] Lubbock, Percy (ed.), *The Letters of Henry James* (1920), I, 22.

their civilization, he decides to do "the finer thing," and burns the paper.

The Europeans (1878) introduces Eugenia, a Baroness, and her brother Felix, who come to this country to look up some New England relatives. Felix marries his cousin, Gertrude Wentworth; but the Baroness, outraged by the low standards of civilization and pinched morality of America, returns home. *Confidence* (1880) hinges upon the love complications of three American expatriates. In *The Portrait of a Lady* (1881), an eccentric English woman, Mrs. Touchett, happens upon an American niece, Isabel Archer, and struck by her unusual mind, plans to take her on a trip to Italy. Isabel, bored with life in Albany, U. S. A., hungry for experience, and anxious to escape a phlegmatic suitor, Caspar Goodwood, consents; and the two stop over at the aunt's home in England, en route to Florence. There Isabel rejects the proposal of a rich nobleman, Lord Warburton, and meets Mrs. Touchett's invalid son Ralph, who persuades his dying father to leave her a handsome bequest. With her aunt she travels on to Italy; falls under the spell of an adventuress, Madame de Merle; and is by this mysterious lady introduced to Gilbert Osmond, a middle-aged widower, of graceful indolence and lean purse. Losing her self-control in this foreign environment, as Roderick Hudson did, she marries Osmond, only to realize too late that he is a selfish rogue. Lord Warburton shows up, ostensibly to court Osmond's fifteen-year-old daughter Pansy; and Isabel, enjoined by her mercenary husband, tries to further the union. Yet it soon becomes apparent that Warburton is only intent on being near Isabel, and Osmond's enmity toward her turns to open hatred. Learning that Pansy is the child of an old liaison between Madame de Merle and her husband, and that she has merely been roped in to secure Pansy's future with her fortune, she defies Osmond in order to pay a last visit to her cousin Ralph, now on his death bed in England, and while absent, again encounters Caspar, the resolute young man from Boston, who offers himself as a way out from her misery. But feeling that "one must accept one's deeds," she goes back to Italy.

In *The Outcry* (1911) a group of impoverished English lords and ladies, offered large sums of money for their art treasures by an American dealer, put temptation behind them, and thwart his sordid purposes. *The Ambassadors* (1903) acquaints us with Lambert Strether, a native of Woollett, Massachusetts, and *confidant* of that town's leading social light, Mrs. Newsome, a very prosperous woman whom it is expected he will some day marry. As the story opens, he has just been sent to Europe by Mrs. Newsome to ascertain why her son Chad is neglecting his inherited interests in America to linger in Paris. A "wicked woman" is suspected of being the cause for his delayed return. But under the liberalizing influence of Gallic life, Strether soon throws his harsh Woollett moral standards overboard, and after a short investigation convinces himself that Chad's affair with Madame de Vionnet, the "wicked woman," is entirely "virtuous." Guessing his apostasy, Mrs. Newsome dispatches another "ambassador" in the person of her glassy daughter, Mrs. Pocock, who instantly sees everything, and informs Strether that he has lost the hand and fortune of his patroness. A chance encounter betrays to him, a bit later, the true relationship between the lovers. Nevertheless he clings to the belief that Chad should remain loyal to Madame de Vionnet. As for himself, he feels that it is now too late for him to begin over again; and his sense of "duty" leads him back to Woollett.

The first pages of *The Golden Bowl* describe Amerigo, an indigent Roman prince, and his arrival in London, where he has come to be married to Maggie Verver, the daughter of an American capitalist. In London he meets Charlotte Stant, a former sweetheart (who happens also to be a friend of the bride's), and goes with her to buy a wedding present for Maggie. While debating the purchase of a certain golden bowl, they are so indiscreet as to behave like lovers in front of the shopkeeper, and leave without the gift when Amerigo discovers a flaw in it. After his marriage he finds life with the Ververs a rather tasteless dish, and when Charlotte pays them a visit at the Verver's estate in England, he permits himself, by his attentions to her, to arouse his wife's suspicions. Maggie, who has felt that in marrying she has perhaps left her father feeling deserted, goes to buy him a present, chances upon the golden bowl, and brings it home. But the shopkeeper, whose conscience has got the better of him, comes to tell her of the flaw, and in doing so, betrays the visit of Amerigo and Charlotte to his shop, as well as their behavior while there. The rest of the novel is concerned with Maggie's successful efforts to win her husband back, without letting him know that she is in possession of the truth. Though she holds his fate in her power, she does not expose her knowledge, but by tact and serenity finally brings Amerigo to the realization that he is, after all, in love with his wife. In welding their affection into a thing as complete and beautiful as "the original crystal of the broken bowl," however, she is aided by her discerning parent, who weds Charlotte to prevent Maggie from thinking him lonely, and who, when he learns that the latter's presence is an embarrassment to his daughter, carries his wife off to America, never to return.

The novels, though, in which this theme of the "international episode" is most central are those that precede *The Princess Casamassima* (1886). For by 1888, James had grown a trifle weary of the whole question. As he put it in that year, "I can't look at the English-American world, or feel about them, any more, save as a big Anglo-Saxon total, destined to such an amount of melting together that an insistence on their differences becomes more and more idle and pedantic." [6] During his "middle period" he limited

[6] Lubbock, Percy (ed.), *op. cit.*, I, 141.

himself to English scenes and subjects, and excluded all Daisy Millerism from *The Princess Casamassima*, *The Tragic Muse*, *The Other House* (1896), *The Spoils of Poynton* (1897), *What Maisie Knew* (1897), *The Awkward Age* (1899), and *The Sacred Fount* (1901). Yet in his last novels, *The Wings of the Dove* (1902), *The Ambassadors*, and *The Golden Bowl*, this old Anglo-American debate sneaks back again; so that, in a way, he can hardly be said ever to have abandoned it.

SPIRITUAL COURTESY   But far more important than his discussion of cultural variations is James's attitude toward the deeper problems of conscience, duty, and moral integrity. In spite of the surface obstacles he often puts in the way of our perceiving it, his ethical outlook is clear. Just as Howells did (to an extent), he saw in life a web of infinitely fragile relationships; and to him, good conduct meant a recognition and preservation of this intangible skein. His attitude toward others consisted in believing that, since there are always at least two parties to a relationship, one's activities should forever be conditioned by the knowledge that in satisfying some desire of his own, he may be impairing the peace of someone else. His, then, was not the naturalistic code of "every man for himself," but the humanistic standard of judicious restraint.

On the proletarian level of those people about whom London and Dreiser have written, man, of course, is often forced to be subversive of the social equilibrium in order to exist; among the poor, man's generous impulses are compromised by a lack of money. In this cramped position he cannot afford to indulge himself in the noblest human gestures. But among the independent members of that leisure class about whom James wrote, man has a larger freedom of choice, and a multiplicity of relations. And with this enlarged independence, James felt, with this privileged liberty of action, should come a greater respect for the rights of others. True, James never seemed to realize that this "respect" might be applied to the relationship between classes. In his opinion the proletariat ought to feel proud of the chance to support with its deprivations a leisure group, or aristocracy, whose presence would lend tone and beauty to society, and whose indolence would give it time to produce and appreciate the artistic fruits of our culture. As he interpreted it, the average reformist was a creature who would, at the first opportunity, "throw the baby out with the bath," and in the process of changing society destroy its accumulated treasures of art and learning; to his mind, our relationship to the past was just as valuable as any other. But aside from this important (and perhaps damning) exception, James does have a strong consciousness of duty, an awareness that amounts to more than a love of decorum. "There is always for James the check of moral decency, and to live abundantly implies with him always to live beautifully as well." [7]

The key to James is renunciation, the "renunciation of something immensely valuable for the sake of something quite without price." Yet this philosophy of sacrifice is altogether "remote from that of Christian dogma and on a different moral foundation. The Christian consciousness of guilt is replaced by the consciousness of worth; the soul renounces, not that it may be tempered and sensitized in suffering, but simply that it may live up to itself. It suffers not blindly, but with eyes open and intent, after all the questions have been asked and suffering has been proved the one thinkable answer. Renunciation in this view is obedience to an inner law of necessity, the immediate exercise of a highest privilege.

"The social sense of this view becomes intelligible if we remember that the highest privilege in the world of Henry James's characters is expressible only in terms of their relations to their fellows. There is nothing in the world except attitudes; a personality is the sum of its relations.

[7] Edgar, Pelham, *Henry James, Man and Author* (1927), p. 250.

One is happy just in proportion to the gift for surrounding one's self with intimate and flawless relationships; one must learn to think out of one's own point of view, think the thoughts of others, and in so doing partly cease to think of one's self. A social situation is a network of gossamer threads floating invisible, binding life to life in bonds fragile and perfect. A blunderer may tear all those threads from their contacts and leave half a dozen lives detached, shorn of half their meaning. The indispensable social grace is, then, to walk softly enough to feel the faintest brush of those intangible relations and to retreat, if need be, in time. The retreat is one's personal loss. But one must have seen far enough into the situation to apprehend the still greater loss of having one's way at the expense of muddling situations and spoiling lives and generally proving one's self an impenetrable brute." [8]

"Spiritual courtesy" is personified in many of James's best characters. In planning *The American*, for instance, he said to himself, of Newman: "stricken, smarting, sore, he would arrive at his just vindication and then would fail of all triumphantly and all vulgarly enjoying it. He would hold his revenge and cherish it and feel its sweetness, and then in the very act of forcing it home would sacrifice it in disgust. . . . All he would have at the end would be therefore just the moral convenience, indeed the moral necessity, of his practical, but quite unappreciated, magnanimity; and one's last view of him would be that of a strong man indifferent to his strength and too wrapped in fine, too wrapped above all in *other* and intenser, reflexions for the assertion of his rights." [9]

Another object lesson in "renunciation" is *The Princess Casamassima*. In the name rôle we meet again that *femme fatale*, Christina Light, who after Roderick Hudson's death

[8] Follett, Helen Thomas, and Wilson Follett, *Some Modern Novelists* (1919), pp. 94–95.
[9] James, Henry, *The American* (1907), p. vii.

married a Neopolitan prince, deserted him, and went on "to multiply wreckage along her path." [10] This time she pours her "baleful and beautiful" charms on Hyacinth Robinson, the bastard son of a certain Lord Frederick. Reared among the "lower tenth," Hyacinth has joined a dangerous revolutionary movement in London; and Christina, having tired of the social whirl, fastens upon him as a means of approaching new thrills. In a moment of enthusiasm, Hyacinth has taken an oath to "the cause," which binds him to the performance of any perilous duty that may be required of him. But in a short while, glimpses into the upper world of the Princess revive the aristocratic side of his nature, and persuade him that he is making a mistake in wishing to destroy a social edifice that has been built on centuries of toil and aspiration. Supplied with a few funds, he leaves for a European holiday, and from Venice writes back to Christina:

The monuments and treasures of art, the great palaces and properties, the conquests of learning and taste, the general fabric of civilisation as we know it, based if you will upon all the despotisms, the cruelties, the exclusions, the monopolies and the rapacities of the past, but thanks to which, all the same, the world is less of a bloody sell, and life more of a lark — our friend Hoffendahl seems to me to hold them too cheap and to wish to substitute for them something in which I can't somehow believe as I do in things with which the yearnings and tears of generations have been mixed. [11]

Therefore, when he returns to England, and the order comes for him to fulfill his oath by committing an assassination, he does not shoot the high personage designated, but himself.

The Tragic Muse records the predicament of Nick Dormer, scion of an old English family, who, in order to pursue an artistic career, gives up a seat in Parliament, disappoints his

[10] Edgar, Pelham, *op. cit.*, p. 275.
[11] James, Henry, *The Princess Casamassima* (1908), II, 145–146.

mother, estranges his friends, blasts his love affair with Julia Dallow, and forfeits sixty thousand pounds which he might otherwise have received from a rich patron. In *The Spoils of Poynton* Fleda Vetch refuses to marry the man she loves because he has already pledged himself to another. " 'The great thing,' " she cries, in turning him away, " 'is to keep faith. Where's a man if he doesn't? If he doesn't he may be so cruel. So cruel, so cruel, so cruel!' Fleda repeated. 'I couldn't have a hand in that, you know: that's my position — that's mine. You offered her marriage. It's a tremendous thing for her.' " [12] Verena Tarrant, in *The Bostonians*, torn between love and her devotion to the cause of "women's rights," resigns what James considered a pernicious crusade to marry Basil Ransom. In *The Sacred Fount*, a young man on a week-end party notices that one of the guests, Mrs. Brissenden, is remarkably more youthful looking than when he saw her last. The reason, he decides, is because she has mysteriously drained her husband of his wit, and added it unto herself; for the husband is now much less brilliant than he used to be. Another guest, Gilbert Long, is also rejuvenated in the same way; and the narrator begins to look about him for Long's "sacred fount." But when it appears that he will either have to sacrifice his "perfect palace of thought" or injure the good name of a third guest, he generously chooses the former. In *The Other House*, when Rose Armiger finds that her love is not reciprocated by Tony Bream, whose dead wife has made him promise not to remarry during their daughter's lifetime, she concludes that "the finer thing" would be for her to murder the child, so that Bream may wed her rival. Isabel Arden, in *The Portrait of a Lady*, realizing that "certain obligations were involved in the very fact of marriage, and were quite independent of the quantity of enjoyment extracted from it," [13] goes back to her living hell. And

[12] James, Henry, *The Spoils of Poynton* (1908), p. 197.
[13] James, Henry, *The Portrait of a Lady* (1908), II, 421.

Washington Square, the story of Catherine Sloper (who, out of loyalty to her father, sacrifices her only lover and embraces spinsterhood) provides us with another example of James's "beautiful not-doing" theory.

THE PURE IN HEART Life to James was a chess game, in which all relations between the pieces were held to be inviolate, indeed even more sacred than the pieces themselves. He felt that nothing had meaning *per se* but only in relation to something else; and in this he was right. Because nothing achieves a separate identity, except as we differentiate it from, compare it to, and measure it by other things. Every object in the world helps to explain its neighbor, and acquires meaning only as it becomes a symbol, reflects its opposite and the life around it, and gathers everything else up into itself.[14] It was in the relation between people, however, rather than objects, that James was engrossed. His books are a "meeting of minds," not bodies, a tension between human beings instead of a naturalistic clash between two or more wandering elements of Nature. He avoided collisions, and the dust and heat of gross events, but he did not skirt topics to the degree that Howells did. What delighted him most was "the friction of personality upon personality." [15]

Character was his consuming interest, "and character in its highest expression, which he took to be under the conditions of leisure-class life. His people are very special types, carefully trained, specially disciplined, having ideals of conduct and motives for their conduct far removed from those galvinating more ordinary mortals. They were controlled neither by social compulsions nor by unconscious psychological drives. Indeed, they were supremely self-conscious. Never for a moment did they lose an acute

[14] Or as Kipling said, "What should they know of England who only England know."
[15] Knight, Grant C., *American Literature and Culture* (1932), p. 383.

awareness of the freedom of their wills, and they are portrayed as acting according to the dictates of conscience controlled by taste and imagination. While their values might be based on traditional accumulations, they never acted without thought, but only after the most scrupulous examination of their motives. Correct conduct became with them the product of taste, conscience, and imagination, and in consequence high, fine, and above all beautiful." [16]

But in at least three books, *What Maisie Knew*, *The Awkward Age*, and *The Wings of the Dove*, the "correct conduct" of his protagonists resembles a kind of divine gift, or a natural product of their very innocence. In this trio of novels, we see three unworldly characters placed in contaminated environments which might be expected to pervert them. Surrounded by intrigues and evil, they shine like stars in darkness, and with their freedom from guile neutralize the guileful atmosphere. Almost James seems to be saying, "Blessed are the pure in heart, for the gods watch over them."

What Maisie Knew is the story of Maisie Farange, a child of divorced parents, who shuttle her back and forth between them, every six months, in order to transmit their spite. Later, both find her in the way when they plunge into fresh marital and extra-marital relations; yet in the end, despite her contact with an adult and infected world, Maisie retains her moral sense.

In *The Awkward Age* Mrs. Brookenham's salon is disrupted by the entrance into its "circle of free talk, of a new and innocent, a wholly unacclimatised presence," her daughter Nanda. When a leading member of this group, one Vanderbark, falls in love with Nanda, her mother, who wishes to preserve him for her drawing room, checks the marriage by a series of frantic devices. But in her desperate efforts to save her social empire, Mrs. Brookenham destroys

[16] Grattan, C. Hartley, "The Calm within the Cyclone," *The Nation* (February 17, 1932), CXXXIV, 202.

it. And Nanda, who has quietly and disingenuously protected her peace and happiness from the backwash of this disaster, sets about to sew her mother's life together again.

The Wings of the Dove, however, presents us with the finest of these fine souls. It begins with an affair between Kate Croy, a young woman in whom poverty and parental disgrace have bred a species of cynicism, and Merton Densher, a moral weakling. Kate has been taken over by a wealthy aunt, and Densher, who is a struggling journalist, does not now feel that he can properly ask her to marry him. Then Milly Theale, an American heiress whose days are numbered by poor health, wanders into the situation. Finding that the gentle Milly is in love with Densher, Kate persuades him to simulate a like passion for the girl, so they may enjoy the inheritance she is certain to leave him after her death. Milly, when the plot has revealed itself to her, silently turns her face to the wall, and dies of a broken heart. But Densher has by this time lost most of his taste for the scheme, and when the legacy arrives he refuses it. Though he did not care for Milly alive, her memory has become an object of worship to him; and realizing that they have both been touched by the passing "wings of the dove," and that they can never again be as they were, the two conspirators part.

Thus James's heroes and heroines are seen to be very different from those of the naturalists. His characters revert to the Christian saint, who by his innocence or iron strength of purpose found it easy to win victories over spiritual indolence or mundane temptations. In the Jamesian hero the conflict is between something cheap and something fine; and he never fails to recognize and achieve the higher motive, at the expense of amputated desires, just as Silas Lapham, when faced with an unethical opportunity to recoup his fortunes, chooses failure rather than dishonor. Natures like Milly Theale, indeed, walk through the vileness that springs up in their path even without any painful loss of desire, and win victories to which they are already equal. But the naturalist hero is usually a victim of his passion or of his environment, and when he does triumph, it is to gain material ease or exemption from social codes. In one case the hero secures a victory of soul over body; in the other his victory is most often that of body over soul. One expresses the old ethics of religion, which holds that man is a creature independent of his milieu, whose heroism must be an inner one; the other expresses the new ethics of science, which holds that man is not independent of his environment, and must prove his heroism by defying it in a clash that takes place outside him. The first triumphs in contracting his desires, the second in freeing and expanding them.

THE WELL-BUILT NOVEL As a rule, the naturalist holds form to be of much less importance than content. "First," he declares, "have something valuable to say; then say it in the most natural way you know how. Let your subject matter dictate your technique; let the novel grow as instinctively as a tree or plant. Be natural, and if letting Nature take its course does not make for symmetry, or even for intelligibility, don't worry. The book's form must 'express' its author's personality. 'Style is the man,' and the main thing is to avoid tampering with it. Don't cramp your thoughts into fixed receptacles; permit them to take their own shape. Whatever is restrained is ruined."

But the humanist believes in stamping the symbols, conventions, and harmonies of man upon the anarchic stream of Nature. He practices an artistic husbandry in the novel, as he practices an ethical husbandry in life. To let "the chips fall where they may," either in life or art, is wrong. Haphazard growth may serve for weeds and other products of Nature, which have no power of self control; yet art is not a product of Nature. It is a product of man's imagination, and in order for it to be grasped by other men's minds, it must be made to conform to human standards of proportion, clarity, and magnitude. Life in the raw is formless, a mere flow of events with no order, direction, or significance; and the duty of art is to synthesize it, to lend it form, to render it edible and edifying for human consumption. Too often the only way we have of knowing when we have reached the end of a naturalistic novel is by the sudden absence of any more pages. But the humanist, with Aristotle, contends that every piece of art must have "a beginning, a middle, and an end," that it must possess an "orderly arrangement of parts," and that the structural union of these parts must be such that, "if any one of them is displaced or removed, the whole will be disjointed and disturbed." "Form," he believes, "is the only passport to posterity." [17]

To this humanistic point of view James seems to have subscribed in his critical papers, which may be consulted in his *Letters*, recently edited by Percy Lubbock; in the Prefaces he wrote for the New York Edition of his works (and termed "a sort of plea for Criticism, for Discrimination, for Appreciation on other than infantile lines — as against the almost universal Anglo-Saxon absence of these things"); in *Partial Portraits* (1888), (which "swings from Emerson to Du Maurier, with spotlights on his idol Turgenieff," [18] and contains his celebrated " Art of Fiction"); in *Notes and Reviews* (1921), his early essays for the *Nation* and *North American Review;* in *French Poets and Novelists* (1878), (which includes critiques on De Musset, Gautier, Baudelaire, Balzac, George Sand, Turgeniev, Flaubert, and others); in *Essays in London and Elsewhere* (1893), a group of judgments on Lowell, Frances Anne Kemble, Flaubert, Loti, the brothers de Goncourt, Browning, Ibsen, and Mrs. Humphry Ward; in *Views and Reviews* (1908) of George Eliot, Browning, Arnold, Swinburne, William Morris, Dickens,

[17] Brownell, W. C., *American Prose Masters* (1909), p. 348.
[18] Chislett, William, *Moderns and Near-Moderns* (1928), p. 21.

Ruskin, John Burroughs, and Kipling; and in *Notes on Novelists* (1914), in which he calls Balzac "the foremost member of his craft," pays his tribute to Zola, Flaubert, Sand, Dumas the Younger, Charles Eliot Norton, and Matilde Serao, and discusses several of the "new" novelists, such as Wells, Compton Mackenzie, Edith Wharton, Walpole, Conrad, and D'Annunzio.

From these sources it is not hard to draw a picture of what James felt "the well-built novel" should be. He despised "the loose, the improvised, the cheap, and the easy," and that episodic and naturalistic type of novel, of which Dreiser's *Titan* is a good example. "A novel," he said, "is a living thing, all one and continuous, like any other organism, and in proportion as it lives will it be found, I think, that in each of the parts there is something of each of the other parts." [19]   To Hugh Walpole, he once wrote, "when you ask me if I don't feel Dostoieffsky's 'mad jumble, that flings things down in a heap,' nearer truth and beauty than the picking and composing that you instance in Stevenson, I reply with emphasis that I feel nothing of the sort, and that the older I grow and the more I *go* the more sacred to me do picking and composing become — though I naturally don't limit myself to Stevenson's *kind* of the same. Don't let any one persuade you — there are plenty of ignorant and fatuous duffers to try to do it — that strenuous selection and comparison are not the very essence of art, and that Form alone *takes*, and holds and preserves, substance — saves it from the welter of helpless verbiage that we swim in as in a sea of tasteless tepid pudding, and that makes one ashamed of an art capable of such degradations." [20]   For him art meant a dramatized selection of pertinent facts, not a wholesale, indiscriminate documentation of life, or "seated mass of information." Every great

[19] James, Henry, *Partial Portraits* (1899), p. 392. By permission of The Macmillan Company, publishers.

[20] Lubbock, Percy, *op. cit.*, II, 237.

novel had to be first of all "based on a profound sense of moral values ('importance of subject'), and then constructed with classical unity and economy of means." [21]   His own brand of novel might be represented as a miniature solar system, moving along while it revolves about a central pivot, or to use his figure, "a circle consisting of a number of small rounds disposed at equal distances about a central object," the central object to be the situation, "to which the thing would owe its title," and the small rounds to be "so many distinct lamps," "the function of each of which would be to light with all due intensity one of its aspects." [22]

He clearly saw through Howells' error in supposing that the expression of literature must be no different from the expression of life.   Life, in his view, was a "splendid waste," and art its corrective.   "Really, universally," he insisted, "relations stop nowhere, and the exquisite problem of the artist is eternally but to draw, by a geometry of his own, the circle within which they shall happily *appear* to do so." [23] That is to say, "precisely because life is an affair of broken arcs, art must get all its meaning and force by constructing the perfect round." [24]

In fine, art for James bore the same relation to the novel's shape that "the golden mean" bore to its contents.   There should be "nothing in excess."   Yet, strangely enough, it was this very precept that James himself disobeyed in his own novels.   There is a wide divergence between his theory and his practice.   His criticisms, to be sure, echo moderation.   But his fiction sins against it.   Or rather it might be charged that he obeyed the humanistic dictum of "moderation in all things" by *modifying* everything.   He seems to have believed, at least in his later novels, that "The more

---

[21] Wharton, Edith, "Henry James in His Letters," *The Quarterly Review* (July, 1920), CCXXXIV, 197.

[22] James, Henry, *The Awkward Age* (1908), p. xvi.

[23] James, Henry, *Roderick Hudson* (1907), p. vii.

[24] Follett, Wilson, "The Simplicity of Henry James," *American Review* (May–June, 1923), I, 321.

things are qualified, diverse, irreducible to one another, the more the artist feels at ease and breathes freely," [25] for with *The Sacred Fount* he began to "turn plot and action into a standing pool of analysis." [26]

James is interested "not in actions but in reactions." [27] Literary strategy and psychological tunneling came to mean more to him than clarity or progression. His work, never any too obvious, took on an enigmatic character; and as technique absorbed more and more of his attention, subject matter absorbed less and less, until by the end of his career, his novels assumed the appearance of mountains made out of mole hills. Every event in his stories he placed under the microscope and dissected into thin air, and the speeches of his protagonists were so barnacled with minute implications that they lost much of their significance. Story kernels that might have served as material for sketches he elaborated into long tales, and those that might have supported novelettes he pumped up into two-volume novels. Art became for him a game, and the novel a laboratory experiment in architectonics. To quote André Gide, "His work is like that of the spider, who ceaselessly widens her web by hanging new threads from one chosen support to another." [28] Though "economy of means" was constantly on his tongue, he paid it only lip service. Where Dreiser erred in a defect of technique, James erred in an excess.

His style, too, suffered a monstrous distention as time went on, due in part, perhaps, to the habit of dictating his novels which he adopted about 1895 or 1896. As one critic has remarked, "He often makes the sentence groan under a paragraph's burden." [29] His prose is choked with qualifying clauses and phrases, and in *The Golden Bowl*, his periods

[25] Fernandez, Ramon, *Messages* (1927), p. 5.

[26] Krans, Horatio S., "Henry James," *The New International Encyclopaedia* (1923), XII, 552.

[27] Knight, Grant C., *op. cit.*, p. 383.

[28] Gide, André, "Henry James," *The Yale Review* (March, 1930), XIX, 641.

[29] Edgar, Pelham, *op. cit.*, p. 208.

seem to possess such "an effect of rank vegetable growth that one feels that if one took cuttings of them one could raise a library in the garden." [30]   "It was in Rome," runs one of his omnibus sentences,

during the autumn of 1877; a friend then living there but settled now in a South less weighted with appeals and memories happened to mention — which she might perfectly not have done — some simple and uninformed American lady of the previous winter, whose young daughter, a child of nature and of freedom, accompanying her from hotel to hotel, had "picked up" by the wayside, with the best conscience in the world, a good-looking Roman, of vague identity, astonished at his luck, yet (so far as might be, by the pair) all innocently, all serenely exhibited and introduced: this at least till the occurrence of some small social check, some interrupting incident, of no great gravity or dignity, and which I forget.[31]

But not all of this inflation of plot and style, of course, was directly the result of his grotesque concentration upon virtuosity.   Most of it sprang from an extraordinary refinement, which caused him to sublimate experience until it no longer resembled experience. His personal shyness may also be reflected in this trend of his art; now and then he seems almost to be trying to hide himself under a fabric of words. His themes are subtilized and rarefied out of all proportion; and emotion is sacrificed to cerebration, explicitness to texture.   He forever evades direct expression; and he has an annoying trick of breaking off explanations in the middle, and of teasing us with statements that dive underground at the approach of strangers.   "Ah, but that — !"   "Who then has what?" and "I don't see how we could have fancied —!" are typical of his truncated remarks, which seem to mystify even his own characters.   And here is a sample of the empty and infertile dialogue that passes for witty conversation in his books:

[30] West, Rebecca, *Henry James* (1916), p. 110.
[31] James, Henry, *Daisy Miller* (1909), p. v.

The way I said this appeared to amuse him. "I see what it does for *you!*"

"No, you don't! Not at all yet. That's just the embarrassment."

"Just whose?" If I had thanked him for his patience he showed that he deserved it. "Just yours?"

"Well, say mine. But when you do —!" And I paused as for the rich promise of it.

"When I do see where you are, you mean?"

"The only difficulty is whether you *can* see. But we must try. You've set me whirling round, but we must go step by step. Oh, but it's all in your germ!" — I kept that up. "If she isn't now beastly unhappy —"

"She's beastly happy?" he broke in, getting firmer hold, if not of the real impression he had just been gathering under my eyes, then at least of something he had begun to make out that my argument required. "Well, that *is* the way I see her difference. Her difference, I mean," he added, in his evident wish to work with me, "her difference from her other difference! There!" He laughed as if, also, he had found himself fairly fantastic. "Isn't *that* clear for you?"

"Crystalline — for *me*. But that's because I know why."

I can see again now the long look that, on this, he gave me. I made out already much of what was in it. "So then do I!"

"But how in the world —? I know, for myself, *how* I know."

"So then do I," he after a moment repeated.

"And can you tell me?"

"Certainly. By what I've already named to you — the torch of your analogy." [32]

RIDDLE ME THIS Since James spent so much time and ingenuity upon the presentation of his material, and since method in fiction ordinarily has clarity for its object, we might expect his work to possess a model transparency. "But with all his scrupulousness, clearness never seems to be an object of his care." [33] His stories appear to own for their purpose the desire to disguise his meaning rather than

[32] James, Henry, *The Sacred Fount* (1901), pp. 217–218.
[33] Brownell, W. C., *op. cit.*, p. 397.

sponsor it.   They sink, in artistic virtue, to the plane of the detective novel, without the latter's two redeeming features: frankness of motive and an enlightening dénouement. James does not solve his cases for us even at the end.   The mystery increases, the complete implications of his dramas rarely emerge.   Some room, of course, should always be left for the reader's imagination.   Great fiction may suggest or inspire without thoroughly defining its theme; it can be something for its audience to "grow up to."   But James's sinuosities do not even "suggest."   Far from placing clues in our way, he removes them.   And once the reader has perceived that the cards are "stacked" against his understanding James (and that since it does not curdle into view anyplace his meaning must be pretty thin and ghostly), reading turns into research, and the problem of perusing James with any pleasure becomes a formidable one.   Even his brother William felt moved to write to him, "Say it *out*, for God's sake," [34] and frequently, as in *The Golden Bowl*, James had to create auxiliary characters to act as a kind of Greek chorus and explain the action to the reader in simple terms.

The humanist holds that art, to be of the highest quality, should be universal, and in tune with the experience and cognitive stature of the normal human being.   Yet James is a traitor to this standard.   He deals with the esoteric rather than the ecumenical.   For him art is a means of retreat from life, and not (as it should be) a metaphor for resolving the complexity of life into symbols that enrich and explain it.   With all his worrying about "technique," and his ingrown psychologizing, he made existence even more mysterious than it is.   Instead of employing the novel to unify, shape, and interpret life, he used it as a vehicle for obscurantism; and for this he deserves as much as criticism as the humanists have been wont to heap upon the more readable "self expressionism" of Anderson, the "interior monologist," and the Dadaists.

[34] *The Letters of William James*, edited by his son (1920), II, 278.

One reason why James's books are gathering dust on the shelves today is that, like Howells, he was a man born out of his time, an anachronism, a last survivor of the Hawthorne-Lowell-Emerson tradition, whose backbone was severed by the Civil War.   His habit, however, of taking thirty-two bites to every sentence or thought is an even more pertinent reason why many people feel (as Mark Twain did) that they would rather be damned than read *The Ambassadors*, and why his name has become a synonym for all that is tedious in literature.   That James's audience is a very meager one is not due to any incapacity on the part of our generation to appreciate fine writing; since by the very standards he voiced in his own critical articles, his is not fine writing. Four of his volumes, *The American*, *The Portrait of a Lady*, *The Wings of the Dove*, and *The Ambassadors*, do not merit the neglect to which they are at present being subjected. But as for the rest, time will take care of them.

VANITY FAIR

*

A Friend of James   The disciples of James, like his readers, have not been legion.   While his finical and clinical analyses of human behavior have perhaps influenced the psychological drift of recent fiction, the modern novelists whose counsels have been darkened by his shadow are few, and consist, for the most part, of such writers as Anne Douglas Sedgwick, author of *Tante* (1911) and *The Little French Girl* (1924).   James's afterglow has hardly been as bright as Millie Theale's.

Yet among those who have acknowledged him as "master," there is at least one important name.   In her life and work, Edith Wharton closely resembles James.   Both were born in New York City with "silver spoons" in their mouths, and reared in an atmosphere of wealth and ancestor worship; both were educated abroad, and became expatriates; and both dedicated their novels to the world of "polite society."   In 1866, at the age of four, Mrs. Wharton (*née* Jones) was taken on a tour of Europe, which lasted until 1871 or 1872, and left her more than a bit discontented with "The American Scene."   For as she has phrased it, "In the mean monotonous streets, without architecture, without churches or palaces, or any visible memorials of a historic past, what could New York offer to a child whose eyes had been filled from babyhood with shapes of immortal beauty and immemorial significance." [1]

[1] Wharton, Edith, "A Backward Glance," *Ladies' Home Journal* (October, 1933), L, 135.

The rest of her adolescence was devoted, she says, to learning three things, "the modern languages," "good manners," and "a reverence for the English language as spoken according to the best usage." [2]   Her training, on the worldly side, was limited, her youthful notion of "adultery" being, that those who practised it had to pay higher fares in traveling, a fact deduced from a ferry boat sign: "Adults, 50 cents; children, 25 cents." [3]   But her acquaintance with books was wide.   By seventeen she had sampled every volume in her father's library, and at eleven had even begun a novel of her own, with this opening, " 'Oh, how do you do, Mrs. Brown?' said Mrs. Tompkins. 'If only I had known you were going to call I should have tidied up the drawing-room.' " [4]   Later she took to verse, published a poem in the New York *World*, tried a five-act metrical tragedy, and wrote a few lyrics, some of which found their way to Longfellow, upon whose recommendation, notes Mrs. Wharton, "my babblings were actually printed in the Atlantic Monthly." [5]

After her "début" into New York society, her days were largely taken up with sojourns at Newport, "card leaving," opera parties, and trips to the Riviera, until her marriage in 1885 to Edward Wharton, a Boston banker.   By 1891, however, she had discovered that henceforth "The Land of Letters" was to be her country; and stories from her pen began to appear in *Scribner's*.   In 1891 a relative sent a batch of these apprentice pieces to Henry James, and precipitated a friendship that ended only with his death. Three years later, James visited the Whartons at their home in the Berkshires, went with them on a motor trip through France in 1907, and in 1908 introduced Mrs. Wharton "to his London on the precise parabola of his pompous arm." [6]

---

[2] Wharton, Edith, " A Backward Glance," *Ladies' Home Journal* (October, 1933), L, 135.

[3] *Ibid.*, p. 137.   [4] *Ibid.*   [5] *Ibid.*

[6] Flanner, Janet, "Dearest Edith," *The New Yorker* (March 2, 1929), V, 27.

Her admiration for James has, at times, been so intense that she has even named some of her characters after his. And when she dies, she hopes that her epitaph will be "She was a friend of Henry James." [7]

Since 1904 she has lived in Europe. During the War she engaged in various kinds of relief work and (like James) saw in the "Huns" a horde of savages, intent upon destroying her beloved France. With James, too, she deplored America's neutrality, and found occasion to voice her protest against our inaction in *Fighting France* (1915), a book of impressions, and *The Marne* (1918), a mediocre novel.

DÉCLASSÉ Mrs. Wharton's non-fiction includes *The Decoration of Houses* (written in 1897 with Ogden Codman), *Italian Villas and Their Gardens* (1904), *Italian Backgrounds* (1905), *A Motor-Flight Through France* (1908), *French Ways and Their Meaning* (1919), *In Morocco* (1920), and *The Writing of Fiction* (1925). Her short stories have been harvested in *The Greater Inclination* (1899), *Crucial Instances* (1901), *The Descent of Man* (1904), *The Hermit and the Wild Woman* (1908), *Tales of Men and Ghosts* (1910), *Xingu and Other Stories* (1916), *Here and Beyond* (1926), and *Certain People* (1930). *Artemis to Actaeon* (1909) and *Twelve Poems* (1926) are books of verse.

As for her novels, they contain two major theses. One is that New York's old *haut monde* of culture and dignity has been for years giving way before a new cheap aristocracy of money and fashion. The other is that whoever breaks a social commandment, no matter how unfair it may seem, must pay for his transgression in the end.

In *The Touchstone* (1900) a young man named Glennard markets a package of love letters which he has received from a dead "woman of genius," in order to marry Alexa Trent, and then repents of his ignoble act. *The Valley of Decision* (1902), a historical romance which "cashed in"

[7] *Ibid.*, p. 28.

on the vogue for novels of this type, acts out its drama in the late eighteenth century, when the anti-religious ideas of Rousseau and Voltaire were arousing Europe. Otho, the heir-presumptive to a north Italian duchy, and a political free thinker, plots to liberate his native land from the feudalism of the Church and give it a constitution. He rescues Fulvia Vivaldi, the daughter of an exiled philosopher, from a convent, and escapes with her to Switzerland, where he learns that a cousin's death has made him Duke of Pianura. He ascends the throne, marries the widow of his predecessor, and tries to put some of his enlightened theories of government into action. But the people are as yet too backward for these reforms. They revolt, and in the uprising Fulvia, who has returned to help the Duke, is slain by a bullet intended for him. After her death he abdicates; and when at last the people are ready to accept his innovations, he has relapsed (ironically enough) into the old tradition, and has to flee the country. *Sanctuary* (1903) is the story of Kate Orme, who weds Denis Peyton, though realizing that his morals are not of the best, and after the birth of their son Dick, lives in fear that he may have inherited some of his father's weaknesses. In the course of time, the boy is faced with the choice of losing the girl he loves or entering an architectural contest with drawings that are not his own. However, with his mother's aid, he triumphs over the temptation to be dishonest, and invites the consequences.

The House of Mirth (1905) deals with life among New York's "Four Hundred" in the days of the hansom cab (when that gilded set was already far corrupted by luxury and lucre) and with the problem of a society that reared its daughters in the single belief that their only duty was to marry a wealthy husband. Lily Bart, a young woman with expensive habits but no money of her own, is a victim of this class theory. She has three lovers, Selden, a poor lawyer, Rosedale, a prosperous Jew, and Trenor, who takes advantage of her innocence to supply her with funds in order to levy a claim on her affections. Of these three, she cares only for Selden; but unfortunately he is not "a good catch." A scandal in which she becomes involved causes her pharisaical friends to discard her, and in desperation she tries to earn a living as a milliner. Then reduced to her last cent, she offers herself to the repulsive Rosedale, finds that now he will not have her, and weary of the struggle, ends her career with an overdose of chloral.

In *Madame de Treymes* (1907), John Durham, an American in Paris, falls in love with Fanny de Malrive, a compatriot who has married into an old French family. Though she is separated from her husband, she cannot obtain a divorce to wed Durham, because her husband's relatives, with their *esprit de corps*, will not permit it. The most powerful member of this clan, Madame de Treymes, promises to facilitate the divorce if Durham will pay the gambling debts of her inamorato, Prince d' Armillac; but he refuses. Whereupon Madame de Treymes informs him that if Fanny wins her court action she will, by a quirk of French law, lose the custody of her child, and leaves Durham to decide whether he will warn her of this fact or not. If he tells her, he can be sure of her refusal to go ahead with the divorce. Yet in spite of this knowledge he determines to do so.

The Fruit of the Tree (1907) opens with the injury of a factory hand in a New England woolen mill. Efforts are made to "hush up" the accident; but John Amherst, an assistant manager, and a trained nurse, Justine Brent, thwart this plan, and are discharged for their pains. Amherst later marries Bessy Westmore, the absentee owner of this plant, and urges her to improve the working conditions of her employees. But she cannot understand why she should give up her gowns, carriages, automobiles, and excursions to Europe in order to provide club rooms, gymnasiums, and higher wages for the workmen. Following one of their disputes, she gallops off on a vicious horse that he has forbidden her to ride, and is badly hurt. Since

Amherst has departed for South America, and cannot be notified for several weeks, the doctors are forced to resort to a painful surgical device to keep her alive until his return. And Justine, whom she has known as a girl, is retained to care for her. But so great is her anguish that Justine, believing that she will die anyway, gives her a lethal hypodermic. In time Justine and Amherst wed, but their happiness is brief; for a doctor, who had seen Justine administer the fatal morphine, tries to blackmail her, and she is forced to tell Amherst what she has done. To spare his feelings, she exits from the scene, and he, misunderstanding her absence, decides that she no longer loves him. A reconciliation is finally effected, however, and the pair settle down together to institute his reforms in the mills, which Bessy has generously left him.

Ethan Frome (1911) is the tale of a poor Massachusetts farmer, chained to the bleak, shrunken village of Starkfield ("from which most of the smart ones get away") by his wife Zenobia, a whining creature, addicted to neurasthenia and patent medicines. Zenobia's cousin, wistful Mattie Silver, comes to keep house for them, and brings a new warmth into Frome's life. But his wife suspects their relationship, and sends the girl away. As he is driving her to the railway station, one winter's day, Mattie proposes that they both escape their despair by coasting down a dangerous hill, and guiding the sled into a huge elm near the foot of the slope. This they do, but instead of being killed, they are horribly crippled. Twenty-four years later, through the eyes of a visitor, we are given a glimpse of the trio, Mattie, Zenobia, and Frome, all huddled in the farmhouse at Starkfield, condemned to spend the rest of their days together, while they degenerate into gnarled, tragic shadows, scarcely recognizable as human beings. When she wrote *Ethan Frome* Edith Wharton was at the peak of her powers; yet she does not consider it her finest achievement, as most critics do. "I am far from thinking *Ethan Frome* my best novel," she says, "and am bored and even exasperated when I am told that it is."[8]   Perhaps the laurels should go to *The House of Mirth*.

In *The Reef* (1912) an American diplomat, George Darrow, meets in London his youthful sweetheart, Anna Leath, who has since married, but is now a widow living abroad. Later he is about to join her in France, when he receives a telegram asking him to postpone his visit. Piqued, he has an affair with Sophie Viner, a young lady who has just lost her job as companion to Mrs. Murrett, a testy English-woman. It is upon this amorous interlude that their lives soon go aground, as upon a "reef." For when Darrow does visit his beloved, he finds Sophie installed in the house-hold as governess to Anna's daughter and fiancée to her son. After their secret comes out, Anna manages to forgive them both. But she cannot forget. And so the three go their separate ways.

The Custom of the Country (1913), the story of a young woman "on the make," is another criticism of "the idle rich" who, in Mrs. Wharton's opinion, have replaced the genuine nobility in New York's *monde où l'on s'amuse*. Escorted by her *nouveaux riches* parents, Undine Spragg blows in from the western town of Apex City, to break down the portals of fashionable Fifth Avenue and Washington Square. A sulky beauty, she represents the same kind of feminine parasite that Lily Bart does, except that Lily was too sensitive to play the part demanded of her by her age, while Undine has no such scruples. With her pretty face, her fortune, and her bad manners, she drives like a ship with streamers into the most exclusive circles of the élite, and marries Ralph Marvell, the descendant of a once proud family. Then, during their honeymoon in Europe, and after their return to the United States, she walks with dainty feet over her husband's life. But in the end she

[8] Wharton, Edith, "Confessions of a Novelist," *The Atlantic Monthly* (April, 1933), CLI, 391.

decides that her customs are not the customs of the old gentility, and sinks back into the arms of one Elmer Moffat, a wealthy vulgarian who, as it turns out, had once been her husband back in the Apex City days, and who "talks her language."

Summer (1917), a novel whose locale is the hill country of Massachusetts, has for its heroine the pathetic daughter of a prostitute, Charity Royall. Driven frantic by the poverty and harsh conditions of life in West Dormer, "a weather-beaten sunburnt village," she tries to free herself by becoming the mistress of a young visiting architect, Lucius Harney. But Harney deserts her, and leaves her to be rescued from the consequences of her revolt by the town lawyer, a bibulous Samaritan, who having already adopted her as a child, and given her his name, now marries her to save her from ruin and disgrace.

The Age of Innocence (1920), which won the Pulitzer Prize in 1921, again pictures Manhattan's Mayfair of the Victorian period, with its mingling of decayed grandeur and upstart crows decked in peacock feathers, its prudery, its tribal codes, its passion for "barricading" itself against "the unpleasant," and its lack of pity for the woman who "stooped to folly." In it we meet Ellen Olenska, a daughter of this world, who as a young woman, went to Europe and married a Polish count. Returning to America to divorce her husband, she finds her cousin, May Welland, about to be wed to a young lawyer, Newland Archer, and falls in love with the latter. Because the arrogant society of her day did not countenance women who leave their husbands, she is on the verge of being "cut" by everybody, when Archer persuades his powerful relatives, the ancient and socially supreme van der Luydens, to save her by inviting her to one of their rare dinner parties. Her family, dreading the publicity of divorce, asks Archer to convince her that she ought to drop proceedings against the Count, and for his sake she does. Later, Archer's decision to leave his wife and go away with Ellen is nipped in the bud by May, and the Countess departs for Paris alone. Twenty-six years afterwards, Archer, now a widower, makes a trip to Europe with his grown son, and almost reaches the point of going to see her; but at the last moment he holds back, feeling that it would probably be wiser to keep her just as a beautiful memory.

In *The Glimpses of the Moon* (1922), Nick Lansing and Susy Branch, two American expatriates, decide to get married and support themselves by "sponging" on their rich idle friends in Europe; yet in trying to carry out their scheme they are estranged, and it is only after much grief that they are reunited in honesty at the end. *A Son at the Front* (1923) describes the quandary of John Compton, an American painter living in Montmartre in 1914, who finds himself torn between a sense of duty and the desire to save his son from conscription, though he finally makes the sacrifice, and gives the youth to France, "so that beauty shall not perish from the earth." In *The Mother's Recompense* (1925) Mrs. Wharton chronicles the tragedy of Kate Clephane, a woman of social standing in New York, who leaves her husband to seek more freedom abroad; comes back to America years later to find that her daughter Anne is engaged to marry Chris Fenno, a man she herself once lived with at a Norman inn; and rather than destroy Anne's happiness by exposing this fact, returns to Europe forever.

Twilight Sleep (1927) puts New York's "fast set" of today under the knife. The quiet Knickerbocker society of yesterday, once represented by the noble van der Luydens of *The Age of Innocence*, has been driven out by a new aristocracy of wealth, whose male members are interested only in making money, and whose female members are interested only in spending it. The husbands grub their lives away, and their wives and daughters go in for gay parties, "uplift," domestic scandals, "mental deep-breathing," fads, rest cures, inspirational healers, and eurythmic dancing. Only Arthur Wyant and his daughter Nona remain to pay tribute to the older ways of decency and reserve, and bemoan their pampered friends and relatives, who have all been drugged with the "twilight sleep" of luxury.

The Children (1928), which points a warning finger at the habit of promiscuous divorce in modern "high society" (where marriages have become "just like tents — folded up and thrown away when you've done with them"),[9] centers around the character of Judith Wheater, a precocious girl of sixteen, who plays mother to seven other abandoned children of these fly-by-night nuptials.

Old New York (1924) consists of four novelettes, each dealing with a decade of the nineteenth century, beginning with the 40's and ending with the 70's. In the first, "False Dawn," a wealthy art fancier sends his son Lewis to Europe on "The Grand Tour," and instructs him, while there, to purchase some Old Masters for his gallery. Lewis, however, runs into young John Ruskin in Switzerland, and upon his advice buys instead a group of Preraphaelite paintings by artists who were at that time not yet famous. The shock leads to his father's death, and Lewis's disinheritance. But years later, these same pictures net a descendant of the family five million dollars. The second, "The Old Maid," is the story of two cousins, Delia and Charlotte Lovell. Delia loves Clem Spender, a struggling artist, but gives him up to marry rich and socially prominent James Ralston. Deserted, Clem turns to Charlotte, who has a child by him outside of wedlock, a fearful thing in those days of "the double standard." Charlotte's fall from grace comes out on the eve of her wedding to Joe Ralston, a cousin of James's. Delia, who has discovered the secret, keeps it, breaks off the contemplated wedding, and after her husband's death, brings Charlotte and her child Tina to live with her. In time, though, Charlotte's maternal passion tempts her to accuse Delia of coming between her and Tina

---

[9] Wharton, Edith, *The Children* (1928), p. 23.

and of aiding them only because of her lingering affection for Clem Spender. And when Delia adopts the child in order to facilitate the latter's marriage to prosperous Lanning Halsey, Charlotte almost upsets the match and ruins Tina's future. But before it is too late she gives in, realizing that Delia is really the girl's mother, and that to her daughter she represents only an "old maid." The third story in this series, "The Spark," concerns Hayley Delane, a "queer" courtly gentleman, married to a philandering wife, but protected from the banalities of New York society in the 60's by his memory of a mysterious figure, "a sort of a big backwoodsman," who had been kind to him while he was in a Washington military hospital during the Civil War. Then one day a picture in a book reveals this friend and mentor to have been Walt Whitman. The fourth tale, "New Year's Day," introduces Lizzie Winter, a young woman rescued from becoming a pensioner on society by her marriage to Charles Hazeldean, a promising lawyer. All goes well for six years after their wedding, until her husband contracts heart disease, and Lizzie, the victim (like Lily Bart) of a "hot-house" education, has to sell herself to Henry Prest, a rich sportsman, in order to keep them in funds. On New Year's Day a fire in the Fifth Avenue Hotel drives Lizzie and Prest into the street, where she is recognized. Charles dies soon afterwards, and Lizzie goes off to Europe. When she returns, Prest proposes to her; but she explains to him her motives in accepting his earlier advances, and withdraws from life to expiate her sins, "a middle-aged woman, turning grey, with a mechanical smile and haunted eyes." [10]

In *Hudson River Bracketed* (1929), Vance Weston, a youthful poet, finds life a torture in Euphoria, Illinois, with its religion of business and starved horizon. To convalesce from a serious illness, he visits some relatives at Paul's Landing, a dreamy village on the Hudson which the new

[10] Wharton, Edith, *New Year's Day* (1924), pp. 148–149.

America of noise, bustle, Success, vitamin diets, and platform lectures has somehow missed. There he meets a neighbor, Halo Spear, who reads *Kubla Khan* to him; but after her marriage to another man, he weds his ailing cousin Laura Lou, and goes on to New York to write a novel. Following his wife's death, and his own failure as an author, he drifts into a new relationship with Halo. And in the end, finding that the world does not measure up to his poetical standards, he comes to a temporary halt, convinced that "the creator of imaginary beings must always feel alone among the real ones," [11] and sinks even further into himself.

Mrs. Wharton's latest novel, *The Gods Arrive* (1932), is a sequel to *Hudson River Bracketed*. As it opens, we find Halo and Vance on their way to Europe together, to take a flyer in "free love," though passion without marriage proves not to be enough, and Halo returns to America. On the Riviera Vance is captivated by Floss Delaney, a mercenary seductress. But soon realizing his mistake, he deserts Floss, to seek out Halo back at Paul's Landing and obtain her promise that she will marry him when he has done penance, invested himself with fresh dignity, and learned to respect himself again.

WITH EDGED TOOLS   In style and design Edith Wharton is a traditionalist. The technical experiments of the naturalists, the liberation of the novel from the classical rules of "unity, coherence, and emphasis," the echolalia of Gertrude Stein, the scientific method of Dreiser, the athletic prose of Hemingway, the mental soliloquies of Joyce, and dadaism seem to have touched her not in the least. And if she has recently learned anything from Proust, whom she greatly admires, it is not his manner of writing. In all of her work, she represents perfect control and restraint. Selection and clarity, which she lauds in *The Writing of*

[11] Wharton, Edith, *Hudson River Bracketed* (1929), p. 560.

Fiction, she really builds into her novels, as James did not; and she does not hesitate even to score her favorite author for his "tangled talk" in, for instance, *The Awkward Age.* She stands opposed to "original genius," to "expressionism," to tales "told by an idiot, signifying nothing," all "unsorted abundance," and every type of formlessness. Like James she does not esteem Dostoievsky's "'mad jumble, that flings things down in a heap.'"

Nor does she care for Croce's statement that literary criticism should consist only of asking whether the author has done what he set out to do. "There would seem to be," remarks Mrs. Wharton, "but two primary questions to ask in estimating any work of art: what has the author tried to represent, and how far has he succeeded? — and a third, which is dependent on them: Was the subject chosen worth representing — has it the quality of being what Balzac called 'vrai dans l'art'?" [12] The naturalist is satisfied with the first two of these inquiries; the humanist always demands that the third be included. For while the naturalist feels that everything is "worth representing," the humanist would exclude many kinds of material from fiction on the grounds of their ugliness, their violence, their *bizarrerie,* or their immorality. Naturalism holds that in this pluralistic universe of modern science, where life is a chaotic flow of discontinuous objects and events, there can be no scale of values. Everything is on a par, in the matter of importance, with everything else. But Edith Wharton believes with James and other humanists in the principle of selection, and (it might be added) with Plutarch, who said, "To obtain a good crop, you must sow with the hand, not pour out of the sack." Every theory, she says, "must begin by assuming the need of selection." [13] And on the title page of *The Writing of Fiction,* she has enthroned this maxim from

[12] Wharton, Edith, "The Criticism of Fiction," *The Living Age* (July 25, 1914), CCLXXXII, 210.
[13] Wharton, Edith, *The Writing of Fiction* (1925), p. 8.

Thomas Traherne, the English poet: "Order the beauty even of Beauty is."

Her own stories are delicately balanced, with faultless tone and movement; and her tonic style, rich in biting imagery, lends itself well to the ironic pitch of her mind. There is also a nice articulation of sound and sense in her work, and she has a deft (if sometimes too remarkable) gift for revealing character in sharp lightning flashes of language. Here, for example, is her incisive analysis of a personality in *Twilight Sleep:*

Poor Arthur — from the first he had been one of her failures. She had a little cemetery of them — a very small one — planted over with quick-growing things, so that you might have walked all through her life and not noticed there were any graves in it.[14]

She has, too, a rare talent for finding the *mot juste,* as evidenced in this short passage from *Ethan Frome:*

We came to an orchard of starved apple-trees writhing over a hill-side among outcroppings of slate that nuzzled up through the snow like animals pushing out their noses to breathe.[15]

In fact the only objections which might be urged against her technique are that in her latest novels the melodrama upon which her work is based shows through too clearly, that her winking jewels of style and epigram often draw more attention to themselves than they should, that her satire now and then edges over into "cattiness," and that her plots are made to hinge upon too many coincidences. Why, we ask, should Frome and Mattie find an abandoned sled awaiting them at the sliding place; why should there have been an adverse decision handed down by the French courts just in time to thwart Fanny de Malrive's divorce; why should it turn out that Justine Brent had been an old friend of Bessy Westmore's; why should a doctor burst into the room at the very moment Justine inserted the hypodermic; why should

[14] Wharton, Edith, *Twilight Sleep* (1927), p. 23.
[15] Wharton, Edith, *Ethan Frome* (1911), p. 21.

Sophie Viner pick out Anna Leath's home to become a governess in; why should Elmer Moffat cross Undine Spragg's path again; why should Chris Fenno choose the daughter of his quondam mistress for his wife; and why should Lizzie Hazeldean emerge from the hotel just in time to be recognized by some friends across the street?

Both Edith Wharton and Henry James deal, above all, in situations, artificially constructed to evoke certain reactions from their characters, as a chemist might adjust the background of a test for the purpose of producing a desired result, or as the writer of a "problem play" stacks the cards to bring out his thesis. In order to achieve their purpose, they have to warp the irregular outlines of reality into invented symmetries, and make use of frequent coincidences. Life, it is true, contains many coincidences, which we call chance, but when too many of them turn up in a short space of time between the covers of a novel, the element of chance disappears; and we begin to see the hand of the author peeping through.

THE ANCIEN RÉGIME   One text of Edith Wharton's work, as we have seen, is the "decline and fall" of New York's old patrician society before the invasion of rich barbarians. The American peerage, she says, went out when the Gilded Age came in, soon after the Civil War. Since that time its Tory charm, dignity, exclusiveness, and conscience have steadily grown more effete. The "Four Hundred" have increased to the "Four Thousand." And gold has come to weigh more in the balance than ancestry or breeding. The ruling clans of the metropolis, the social registerites, sheathed in a ritual of stern morals that brooked no vulgar or sinful lapses from grace and scorned to value money for itself alone, have been replaced by a new, pushing generation of *bon-vivants*, who care nothing for reserve or culture, whose women are mere parasites, and whose men are lacklustre kings of finance. Respect for conventions, once based on a pure sense of ethical decency, has turned into an impure fear of scandal; decorum and etiquette have given way to gin, bad manners, gambling, adulteries, and "the divorce evil"; and the aristocrats have been forced to make way for an army of hectic plutocrats, spoiled children of wealth. The Blue Book has now become the bank book. Only a few of the Olympians are left, such as the van der Luydens; modern society belongs to the Rosedales, the Trenors, and the Spraggs. It has degenerated into an unhealthy swamp of "fads and fetishes and frivolities," a blind, hypocritical caste.

The aristocracy that she satirizes in her novels is not her ideal. It is an empty, decadent form of society, caring only for a kind of "fatuous fashionableness," rather than for the virtues of urbanity, erudition, and good taste which marked the *ancien régime*. Today, in every direction, she sees that old aristocracy being despoiled from within and from without. Within the walls, luxury is working to destroy, while outside are the newly rich, an unfragrant herd of social climbers, throwing ladders up against the ramparts. "She sees that in America, against the need and power of money and the lure of sex, tribal instincts and customs, family pride and hereditary principles are bound to go down, and their upholders can at best fight a rear guard action. Hers is the same tale that Thackeray had told of the wasting away of an aristocracy." [16] As one character in *The Age of Innocence* puts it, the last survivors of our old aristocracy might be termed "Aborigines," and likened to "those vanishing denizens of the American continent doomed to rapid extinction with the advance of the invading race." [17]

Hence Mrs. Wharton "turns to the authentic aristocracy of Europe for satisfaction of her genteel tastes." [18] She

---

[16] Lovett, Robert Morss, *Edith Wharton* (1925), p. 47.

[17] Wharton, Edith, *The Custom of the Country* (1913), p. 74.

[18] Parrington, Vernon Louis, *Main Currents in American Thought* (1930), III, 381.

stands with James on the opposite shore of the Atlantic, and whispers across to America, "Where are your manners?" But Europe, she realizes, while it may serve as a refuge for her discouraged compatriots, cannot redeem our society from its threatened loss of distinction and integrity. That is a task for the artist. In her novels and her short stories, she pays tribute to art's power of "humanizing the landscape." Like James, it is in the artist with his sensitive love of beauty, his respect for the past, and his moral insight that she sees the promised savior of American culture.

CRIME AND PUNISHMENT   Though she seems to pity her Lily Barts and Ethan Fromes, and though she condemns the ugly conditions of which they are the victims, Edith Wharton cannot but look upon every break with convention as a crime that must be punished. Often, she admits, the convention is an unworthy one, which might be improved; yet the fact remains. Social rules, even when they are cruel and superficial, are essential to social order, and cannot be violated with impunity. The moral code of the world she writes about is one that has been debased, and the same people who sat in judgment on Lily Bart were also her seducers. But no discount for this fact can be made, no pardon extended. In her opinion, "the wages of social sin" are "social death." [19] The wicked in her novels are those who have rebelled against accepted prejudices; and these wicked do not flourish like the green bay tree. They pay for their insurgency; in some way they do penance for their perversity. It is a Christianity of the Old Testament. "I'm sorry," says Mrs. Wharton, "but we must enforce the law." And so for daring to fracture convention, Charlotte Lovell has to give up her child, Frome reaps misery, Justine Brent suffers estrangement from her husband, Lewis in "False Dawn" is disinherited, Undine Spragg can never become the wife of an ambassador (which she would like

[19] Flanner, Janet, *op. cit.*, p. 26.

to be), Charity Royall is forced to marry a man she does not love, the Duke in *The Valley of Decision* wins exile and loses Fulvia, Lizzie Hazeldean dies in loneliness, Glennard feels the teeth of remorse, John Durham is made to surrender Fanny de Malrive, and George Darrow has to sacrifice both Sophie Viner and Anna Leath. All must pay the price of their folly. Life, Justine Brent found to her sorrow, was

not a matter of abstract principles, but a succession of pitiful compromises with fate, of concessions to old tradition, old beliefs, old charities and frailties. That was what her act had taught her — that was the word of the gods to the mortal who had laid a hand on their bolts.[20]

Edith Wharton "leaves no doubt as to her ethical convictions. Taken by and large, man is surrounded by forces quite beyond his own powers to control or defy. If he is a little man in a little world, little forces can intimidate him; if he is a more primitive creature in a more natural world, forces as relentless as the elements can crush him. The most triumphant of human powers is therefore not the defiance of fate, but the control of self." [21] For her, as for James, "morality has ceased to be the assertion of external authority, and is a matter of fine perception of the responsibilities of men and women toward each other in their mutual bonds and contacts." [22] "A frame of convention," she believes, "is at once a restraint and a stimulus to the joy of living," [23] man's method of "defending himself from his own frivolity." [24] With Alice Meynell she would say: "Dear laws, be wings to me."

All this moralizing, however, leaves the advanced reader of today quite cold. To his mind the institutions of marriage and the home no longer exercise an authority that can-

[20] Wharton, Edith, *The Fruit of the Tree* (1907), p. 624.
[21] Boynton, Percy H., *Some Contemporary Americans* (1924), p. 101.
[22] Lovett, Robert Morss, *op. cit.*, p. 79.
[23] *Ibid.*, p. 45.
[24] Wharton, Edith, *The Gods Arrive* (1932), p. 117.

not be questioned or set aside if found wanting. In the words of the vaudeville comic, he says, "Institutions are all right, but who wants to live in an institution?" And he is apt to feel that, along with Howells and James, Mrs. Wharton could do with a little of Whitman's "barbaric yawp."

Like James and Howells she writes about a privileged set. As a group, her characters "would be puzzled to know why the Lord's Prayer should include such a homely clause as 'Give us this day our daily bread.' Except for an occasional rather vulgar exploiter or an occasional decayed aristocrat, they all have incomes which proceed from invisible sources. The men, not infrequently, disappear into a vague realm of business, but the business is no more real than the sheep-herding of the shepherds and shepherdesses in the Latin pastorals. The world of labor is but mentioned in but one of the novels, and in this for the sole purpose of supplying an added ground for a marital misunderstanding. These people, moreover, are not interested in social institutions of any kind. They ignore the market-place no more than the bench and the bar, the church and the school; and no more so (except for a chapter or two in *The Age of Innocence*) than the whole world of institutionalized art — the theater, the opera-house, the art gallery, and the library. To be sure, they dissent from the crowd at every turn, but that is because of their instinctive feeling not so much that they themselves are right as that the crowd is certain to be vulgarly wrong. They are full of refinements, and vigilantly aware of the dictates of propriety, which make them live in continual fear of one another's faint disapproval, faintly but damningly expressed." [25]

The soil Edith Wharton plows in is indeed a bit thin, as it was in James; and her problems are often those of a class rather than those of mankind, problems that would never arise outside of a drawing-room. When she attempts to deal with the world of art, as she frequently does, she is

[25] Boynton, Percy H., *op. cit.*, pp. 94–96.

amateurish, and in regard to class relationships, the vital issue of today, she appears to be quite uninformed. Says one critic, "she remains for us among the voices whispering the last enchantments of the Victorian age," [26] and she herself admits "that to the greener growths of her day, she must seem like a taffeta sofa under a gas-lit chandelier." [27]

[26] Lovett, Robert Morss, *op. cit.*, p. 87.
[27] Flanner, Janet, *op. cit.*, p. 28.

*

SIMPLICITY WITH GLORY

*

DAUGHTER OF THE FRONTIER   Willa Cather, ranked by a group of critics in 1929 as the nonpareil of American novelists,[1] was born on a farm near Winchester, Virginia, December 7, 1876.   But when she was about nine years old, her father moved to a ranch in Nebraska.

The West, by that time, was in transition from the sod-house stage to the electric-light era.   The old generation of the pioneer was giving way to the new generation of the merchant.   The prairie was flowering with Main Streets. The air was darkening with the smoke of factories.   Wire fences, prophetic of a tight, standardized day, were entwining the earth.   And rural Nebraska was being colonized by immigrants.   Yet these "foreigners" retained many of the free and fearless virtues of the pioneer.   Nostalgia, the reluctant soil, and the deflated frontier bred in them an iron spirit.   The mute grandeur of Gray's "Elegy" lay over their venture.   Tragedy edged their dreams; and epics slept in their lives, waiting for the kiss of art to awaken them.

To Miss Cather, even as a girl, their native simpatico, their daily heroisms, and the final desertion of their sons and daughters into Babbitry were sources of deep and permanent interest.   Though her nights were devoted to reading the classics aloud to her grandmothers, and studying Latin, her days were spent in riding to town to bring back the mail for these peasants, and in watching them at their work and play.   "Few of our neighbors," she says, "were Americans

[1] Stalnaker, John M., and Fred Eggan, "American Novelists Ranked," *The English Journal* (April, 1929), XVIII, 295–307.

— most of them were Danes, Swedes, Norwegians, and Bohemians. I grew fond of some of these immigrants — particularly the old women, who used to tell me of their home country. I used to think them under-rated, and wanted to explain them to their neighbors." [2] After she had finished high school at Red Cloud, and entered the state university at Lincoln, she did try to "explain" these friends of hers in a handful of clumsy sketches, printed in the college magazine. Not until her senior year, however, did she realize that writing might be a conscious thing; and then it was James who broke the news to her. "In those days," notes Miss Cather, "no one seemed so wonderful as Henry James." [3]

On graduating in 1895 she took a job with the Pittsburgh *Leader*, taught English for a while at Allegheny High School, wrote *April Twilights* (1903), a book of conventional verse, published a few early short stories in *The Troll Garden* (1905), joined the staff of *McClure's* in 1906, and rose to managing editor two years later. But journalism did not entirely satisfy her, and "I had a delightful sense of freedom," she admits, "when I'd saved up enough to take a house in Cherry Valley, and could begin work on my first novel 'Alexander's Bridge.'" [4]

A LA RECHERCHE DU TEMPS PERDU   In *Alexander's Bridge* (1912), Bartley Alexander, an American engineer, arrives at middle age with the feeling that marriage and minutiae have "buried him alive," and on a visit to London, encounters the actress Hilda Burgoyne, an old sweetheart, who represents to him the axiom "Live Dangerously," just as his wife stands for social restraint and domesticity. His Jamesian desire to do "the finer thing," and remain true to his wife, is compromised by a moral "weak spot." But he

---

[2] Quoted in Carroll, Latrobe, "Willa Sibert Cather," *The Bookman* (May, 1921), LIII, 212. An article based on an interview with the author.

[3] *Ibid.*, p. 214.   [4] *Ibid.*

never solves this "civil war in the cave." Another "weak spot" crops out in a bridge he is working on, and he is killed in the crash.

Having written this novel, Miss Cather must have decided that the Nebraska of her childhood would prove more sympathetic material for her pen than the Boston or Europe of James, and that Richard Wagner was right when he said that art should be "only a way of remembering youth." [5] For her next volume, *O Pioneers!* (1913), which derives its title from Whitman, has for its heroine the daughter of a Swedish homesteader. We meet Alexandra Bergson as a young girl, and watch her take charge of her father's land after his death, hang on to it through many hardships, prevent her two older brothers from leaving the farm to seek an easier life in town, ignore gossip to marry the lover of her choice, forgive the jealous husband who has murdered her younger brother, subdue the earth with the vitality, patience, and breadth of vision that she has drawn from her contact with it, and emerge victorious over every obstacle, into a new and tamer West of paved roads, telephone poles, and "the village virus." Yet quite as engaging as this portrait of a pioneer woman is the author's picture of the Nebraska countryside, with its foreign settlers, the mad Russian horse doctor, the Shabatas, and the Toveskys, its Czech weddings, its aromatic summers, its prairie dogs, sunflowers, bright windy mornings, and its frozen silences of winter. So graphic, and so vivid is this "landscape with figures," that one almost feels he could step into the book, walk around, and come out again.

The Song of the Lark, published in 1915, traces the career of a musical prodigy from her youth in Moonstone, Colorado, to her success as an opera singer in New York. The daughter of a Swedish minister, she is early discovered to be a talented pianist by a drunken music teacher, Professor Wunsch, and inspired to do great things by Dr. Archie, a

[5] Cather, Willa, *The Song of the Lark* (1932), p. 460.

fatherly physician who, like Wunsch, sees in her a genius that must be snatched from Moonstone and given to the world. Left six hundred dollars insurance by the death of her lover, Ray Kennedy, a railroad man, she goes to Chicago to study for a year, escorted by Dr. Archie. There a celebrated musician, Harsanyi, finds that her real forte is singing, and turns her over to a voice instructor. Back in Chicago after a brief trip home to Moonstone, where she scandalized the neighbors by visiting a colony of Mexicans on the outskirts of town to hear their folk songs, she meets Fred Ottenburg, a combination beer baron and art patron, who takes her under his wing, introduces her to society, and even sends her away for a rest to Panther Canyon, Arizona. In Chicago she had begun to feel a bit weary and discouraged; but after prowling among the old cliff dwellings of the Southwest, she recaptures her enthusiasm, extracts fresh strength from the earth and sky, and catches a sudden vision of art as a discipline, the imposition of a form and design upon life. Just as the Indians molded the leaping stream of experience into graceful pottery, she would have to shape her perceptions and desires into a voice.

She travels to Mexico City with Ottenburg, to become his wife, but on learning that he is already married, borrows some money from Dr. Archie, and sails for further training in Germany. Years pass, and then after an interval of vigorous and determined work abroad, she returns to New York and her first professional triumphs. *The Song of the Lark*, says Willa Cather, "attempts to deal only with the simple and concrete beginnings which color and accent an artist's work, and to give some account of how a Moonstone girl found her way out of a vague, easy-going world into a life of disciplined endeavor." [6] "Disciplined endeavor." There could hardly be a better statement of the humanistic principle.

[6] *The Song of the Lark*, p. 480.

My Ántonia (1918), thought by many to be its author's masterpiece, is laid in and about the town of Blackhawk, Nebraska, and has for its central figure a Bohemian girl, well known to Miss Cather in her youth. Ántonia Shimerda is the daughter of an immigrant family, brought over to this country by her dreamy father and crass, ambitious mother. Defeated by homesickness and poverty, her father blows out his brains; and Ántonia is forced to work in the fields, until American friends obtain a job for her as a hired girl in town. But the village dances prove to be her ruin. She eludes the caresses of her employer, only to be deceived by Larry Donovan, a gay railway conductor, who promises her a wedding ring if she will go away with him, and then deserts her in Denver, leaving her to return home, face the music, and go back to work. Twenty years later the narrator of this story, Jim Burden, a friend of her childhood, visits Blackhawk again and finds Ántonia happily married to a Bohemian farmer, and the mother of a large brood of youngsters. Worn she might be, he perceived, but still instinct with a deep, quiet zest. Her stubborn passion for beauty and goodness and her innate nobility had borne this strong woman of the prairie above every adversity, and enabled her to win through to at least a partial mastery of her fate, without once losing "the fire of life."

In 1920 Miss Cather published *Youth and the Bright Medusa*, another volume of brief narratives, containing four sketches from *The Troll Garden*. And these two books, together with *Obscure Destinies* (1932), make up her collected short stories, many of which, like the *contes* of James and Wharton, contrast the artist's healthy and ardent soul with that of the modern philistine.

One of Ours, which came out in 1922 and won the Pulitzer award for that year, is the story of Claude Wheeler, a sensitive youth, brought up on a Nebraska farm. With his hunger for life, and his high respect for truth and beauty, he early finds that he is "out of step" with the breezy bigotry

of his friends and family; and his unrest deepens when he enrolls at the state university, and catches a short glimpse there
of "people who know how to live." But his spiteful father
soon bars this way of escape by forcing him to return home
again. He tries to drown his troubles in work, discovers
that he cannot, and eventually makes the error of marrying
Enid Royce, a pale cramped spirit in a thin body, who seeks
to lure him into church activities, and failing, leaves to nurse
a missionary sister in China. Whereupon Claude, happy
in his conviction that here at last is an ideal he can devote
himself to, enlists with America's entrance into the War,
and dies in the Argonne.

A Lost Lady followed in 1923. It is the tragedy of Marian
Forrester who, in her degeneration, symbolizes the decline
of our West, from the land of the dreamer, the pioneer, the
builder, and the adventurer to the haunt of "shrewd young
men, trained to petty economies." [7] The first part of the
book presents Mrs. Forrester in her prime, as the lovely,
laughing wife of Captain Forrester, a railroad contractor,
entertaining his guests in their Sweet Water home, and
shedding on all the radiance of her charm and wit. Then
misfortune hits them; a bank fails, her husband suffers a
stroke that leaves him an invalid for life, and she becomes
the mistress of one of his friends. Left alone when the
Captain expires and her lover weds another, she tries to
forget the past in the company of those hard, gaudy young
men who make up the coming generation, and hands herself
over to the lust of Ivy Peters, a shyster lawyer. In the end
we see Peters in possession of the Forrester house, learn that
"the lost lady" has died in the Argentine as the wife of a
"rich cranky old Englishman," and realize with a pang
that "that which once was great is pass'd away." Rather
than "die with the pioneer period to which she belonged," [8]
Marian had remained behind to be tarnished by a new and
cheaper era. "Only the stage hands were left to listen to

her.   All those who had shared in fine undertakings and bright occasions were gone." [9]

The Professor's House, which came out in 1925, introduces us to Godfrey St. Peter, a Michigan professor, who has reached the "dead calm" of middle years.   Though hard work has brought him success and enough money to purchase a new house, his best days, he realizes, are over; his great scholarly history of the *Spanish Adventurers in North America* is finished; his only happiness lies in memories. There is nothing more to be done.   His wife and daughters have drifted away from him, into a modern concern for wealth and comfort, where he cannot follow them.   Tom Outland, his favorite student, has been killed in the War. And so he sits in the dim study of his old house (which he has refused to give up), living his life over again; remembering the struggles, the freedom, the enchantment of his youth; reading in Tom Outland's diary of the latter's boyhood discovery of a mysterious Blue Mesa in the Southwest, filled with relics of a lost civilization; and trying to adjust himself to a shoddy, commercial age of quick results, by learning "to live without delight."

My Mortal Enemy (1926) revolves about Myra Driscoll, another "lost lady" of the 80's, a perverse young woman, "bright and gay and carelessly kind." [10]   An orphan, brought up by a rich uncle in the town of Parthia, Illinois, she defies her guardian and sacrifices a fortune to elope with genial Oswald Henshawe, the secretary of a railroad president in New York.   But once in the metropolis, she makes her good husband's life miserable by her extravagance and jealousy.   The Henshawes fall upon evil days, and are reduced to "shabby-genteel poverty."   Oswald loses his job; and Myra comes to realize that all their misfortunes have been her fault, that we often (as Wilde said) kill the thing we love, and that each human being is his own worst enemy.   The victim of a spiritual and physical disease, she

[9] *Ibid.*, p. 167.   [10] Cather, Willa, *My Mortal Enemy* (1926), p. 12.

turns to religion and to dreams of the happy past for solace; and the book closes with her death.

Death Comes for the Archbishop (1927) is a chronicle dealing with the establishment of the Catholic church in the Southwest. Its title is taken from Durer's celebrated engraving, the "Dance of Death." The plot itself is simple, based as it is upon the adventures of Archbishop Lamy, the first Bishop of New Mexico, and his coadjutor, Father Joseph Machebeuf (Fathers Latour and Vaillant, in the story). In a strange vineyard of blazing sand, adobe towns, red mountains, Indian ceremonials, hieratic mystery, violent colors, fire and ice, these two intrepid missionaries labor for many years, "two men riding across the desert, braving storm, accident, hostility and drought, christening, marrying, forcing reluctant priests to obedience, reforming abuses, bringing everywhere through their immense, ill-defined diocese, to souls benighted, rude, yet not altogether oblivious of the true faith, the grace of culture, kind words and kind deeds." [11] That is the whole tale. In the end hearty Father Machebeuf dies, up in Colorado where he has gone to carry the Word of God; and the old Archbishop, tired but happy, comes to rest before the high altar of the Santa Fé cathedral that his zeal and industry have erected.

Shadows on the Rock (1931), Miss Cather's latest novel, tells the story of those French settlers who brought a kind of culture to Quebec in the seventeenth century, "and somehow kept it alive on that rock, sheltered it and tended it and on occasion died for it, as if it really were a sacred fire — and all this temperately and shrewdly, with emotion always tempered by good sense." [12] Things change slowly in this tiny universe of Euclid Auclair (the philosopher-apothecary), his daughter Cecile, Bishop Laval, the Count de Frontenac, Nicholas Pigeon the baker, Noel Pommier the

[11] Rapin, René, *Willa Cather* (1930), p. 83.

[12] Cather, Willa, "Shadows on the Rock: A Letter," *The Saturday Review of Literature* (October 17, 1931), VIII, 216.

cobbler, and Mother Juschereau de Saint-Ignace. Trappers and annual ships from France supply the only news from outside; and the years, with their seasons, come and go, almost without leaving a mark on the serene lives of the colonists, who find in their religion a means of anchoring themselves against the current of time.

"To me," states the author, in speaking of this volume, "the rock of Quebec is not only a stronghold on which many strange figures have for a little time cast a shadow in the sun; it is a curious endurance of a kind of culture, narrow but definite. There another age persists. There, among the country people and the nuns, I caught something new to me; a kind of feeling about life and human fate that I could not accept, wholly, but which I could not but admire. It is hard to state that feeling in language; it was more like an old song, incomplete but uncorrupted, than like a legend. The text was mainly anacoluthon, so to speak, but the meaning was clear. I took the incomplete air and tried to give it what would correspond to a sympathetic musical setting; tried to develop it into a prose composition not too conclusive, not too definite; a series of pictures remembered rather than experienced; a kind of thinking, a mental complexion inherited, left over from the past, lacking in robustness and full of pious resignation." [13]

THE NOVEL DÉMEUBLÉ Willa Cather's first novel, *Alexander's Bridge*, betrays the influence of James and Wharton, and *The Song of the Lark* seems to resemble, in its multiplicity of detail, one of Balzac's crowded volumes. But since 1915, her technique has moved steadily in the direction of simplicity, under the inspiration of Mérimée, Turgeniev, and Sarah Orne Jewett, who once advised her to "Write it as it is, don't try to make it like this or that." Indeed her mature philosophy of composition might be represented by these words of Louise Imogen Guiney, which form the key-

[13] *Ibid.*

note of Miss Cather's introduction to "The Mayflower Edition" of Sarah Orne Jewett's works:

> But give to thine own story
> Simplicity, with glory.

The principle of selection, so central in humanism and so foreign to naturalism, has been carried in her novels even farther than in Howells, James, or Wharton. Yet her art has never bound itself down to the careful symmetry that James urged and Edith Wharton practices. *O Pioneers!* is loosely built; *My Ántonia* is episodic; *One of Ours* cracks in the middle, when the scene shifts from Nebraska to France; *The Professor's House* dares to pause in its flow to insert Tom Outland's eighty page "story within a story"; and *The Song of the Lark* has much extraneous material in it that Miss Cather would now like to reduce by at least a third, and which, if it were removed, might leave this novel one of the finest in our language. Her plots are not, like those of James and Wharton, constructed around situations or problems which may be welded into intricate and balanced structures. Rather they have come, more and more, to base themselves on the biographies of her characters, and to lean toward the naturalistic method in their tendency to follow the lines of human growth.

With such naturalists as Anderson, Hemingway, and Faulkner, such escapists as Cabell and Hergesheimer, such reformists as Dos Passos, and even such humanists as James, style often becomes an end in itself, instead of a means to an end. But to Willa Cather it remains only an implement for conveying sense and significance. In her opinion it should be kept as clear and sharp as crystal, in order that the author's meaning (which she considers to be of the highest importance) may shine through. The novel should be reduced to its essentials, not packed with minute descriptions of clothes, dishes, houses, streets, finance, legal procedure, scientific lore, economics, sexual psychology, and all those other kinds of literary "furniture" so dear to Balzac, Norris, Dreiser, and Zola.

The scene, she holds, must be left bare "for the play of emotions." The "emotional penumbra" of life is her chief objective, not its physical setting, though she is in no wise inclined to underestimate this second factor. Art, explains Miss Cather,

should simplify. That, indeed, is very near the whole of the higher artistic process; finding what conventions of form and what detail one can do without and yet preserve the spirit of the whole — so that all that one has suppressed and cut away is there to the reader's consciousness as much as if it were in type on the page. Millet had done hundreds of sketches of peasants sowing grain, some of them very complicated and interesting, but when he came to paint the spirit of them all into one picture, "The Sower," the composition is so simple that it seems inevitable. All the discarded sketches that went before made the picture what it finally became, and the process was all the time one of simplifying, of sacrificing many conceptions good in themselves for one that was better and more universal.[14]

"What I have always wanted to do," she resumes, "is to make the writing count for less and less and the people for more and more. . . . I'm trying to cut out all analysis, observation, description, even the picture-making quality, in order to make things and people tell their own story simply by juxtaposition, without any persuasion or explanation on my part. . . . Mere cleverness must go. I'd like the writing to be so lost in the object that it doesn't exist for the reader." [15] In her last two books, she has almost realized this aim. *Death Comes for the Archbishop* and *Shadows on the Rock* might both be described as quiet murals in which the brush strokes do not show. Both seem to come to us out of the past, with their outlines softened and simplified by

[14] Cather, Willa, "On the Art of Fiction," *The Borzoi, 1920*, pp. 7–8.

[15] Quoted in Carroll, Latrobe, *op. cit.*, p. 216. See also Canby, Henry Seidel, "Too Much of the Truth," *The Saturday Review of Literature* (October 22, 1932), IX, 185–186.

distance and time.   In a phrase once used by André Gide, they have been written "half-aloud."

The real triumph of Willa Cather's fiction, however, does not lie in its simplicity, but in her ability to fuse soul and body into a symbol of cosmic importance, to raise the literal into the figurative, to blend Plato's One and Many, to identify the general and the specific, and to lend spiritual implications to such things as a potsherd in *The Song of the Lark*, the two houses in *The Professor's House*, a bunch of wilted flowers in *A Lost Lady*, or a plow silhouetted against the sun in *My Ántonia*.

OPTIMA DIES . . . PRIMA FUGIT   As the *leitmotiv* for her novels, Miss Cather has chosen the passing away of romance and adventure from the West, the liquidation of our pioneer era, the decay of the frontier spirit into the weedy materialism of a machine age.   "The old order changeth," runs the burden of her song, echoing Tennyson; and Virgil's "Optima dies . . . prima fugit" decorates the title page of *My Ántonia*.

Like Professor St. Peter she cares more for the old house than the new, more for the past than the present.   "For all the superb vitality of frontier, it faces — and she knows it faces — the degradation of its wild freedom and beauty by clumsy towns, obese vulgarity, the uniform of a monstrous standardization." [16]   "We must face the fact," she says, "that the splendid story of the pioneers is finished, and that no new story worthy to take its place has yet begun.   The generation that subdued the wild land and broke up the virgin prairie is passing, but it is still there, a group of rugged figures in the background which inspire respect, compel admiration.   With these old men and women the attainment of material prosperity was a moral victory, because it was wrung from hard conditions, was the result of

[16] Van Doren, Carl, *Contemporary American Novelists* (1931), p. 116.   By permission of The Macmillan Company, publishers.

a struggle that tested character. They can look out over those broad stretches of fertility and say: 'We made this, with our backs and hands.' The sons, the generation now in middle life, were reared amid hardships, and it is perhaps natural that they should be very much interested in material comfort, in buying whatever is expensive and ugly. Their fathers came into a wilderness and had to make everything, had to be as ingenious as shipwrecked sailors. The generation now in the driver's seat hates to make anything, wants to live and die in an automobile, scudding past those acres where the old men used to follow the long corn-rows up and down. They want to buy everything ready-made: clothes, food, education, music, pleasure. Will the third generation — the full-blooded, joyous one just coming over the hill — will it be fooled? Will it believe that to live easily is to live happily?" [17] "The Old West," notes the author,

had been settled by dreamers, great-hearted adventurers who were unpractical to the point of magnificence; a courteous brotherhood, strong in attack but weak in defence, who could conquer but could not hold. Now all the vast territory they had won was to be at the mercy of men like Ivy Peters, who had never dared anything, never risked anything. They would drink up the mirage, dispel the morning freshness, root out the great brooding spirit of freedom, the generous easy life of the great land-holders. The space, the colour, the princely carelessness of the pioneer they would destroy and cut up into profitable bits, as the match factory splinters the primeval forest.[18]

"Change is not always progress," remarks Miss Cather, in *Shadows on the Rock*. With Edith Wharton, she mourns the vanishing of a cultural heritage, the wasting away of something fine and rare under the pressure of paltry motives and short cuts to pleasure that ignore the sovereign worth of character and individual discipline. And with other

[17] Cather, Willa, "Nebraska: The End of the First Cycle," *The Nation* (September 5, 1923), CXVII, 238.

[18] *A Lost Lady*, p. 106.

humanists, she prefers to draw her scheme of values from man's "best moments" of the past, rather than found it as the naturalist does, upon the shifting sands of Nature, easy satisfactions, expediency, and the present. She desires to treat, not of the new and peculiar, but of those "immemorial human attitudes which we recognize as universal and true." Instead of allowing her characters to surrender to their environment, as Dreiser's do, she makes them triumph over it by force of will. Her stories are dramas of personality, not of action. Not content with the naturalist's "teeming, gleaming stream" of Nature, she wishes to fix a pattern upon the tides, "to subject what she has seen in the world around her to an imaginative reconstruction," [19] "to imprison for a moment the shining, elusive element which is life itself." [20]

"Miss Cather always tacitly champions the poetic temper and the life of realization against practicality. The quarrel between the two furnishes the theme of *The Song of the Lark* and *One of Ours*, and is prominent in *O Pioneers!* and *My Ántonia*, as well as in most of her short stories. All her chief characters have the poetic point of view, and are forced by their viewpoint into conflict with their families and neighbors," [21] as witness the tragic hero of her sketch "Paul's Case," Kitty Ayrshire, the singer, in "A Gold Slipper," the aunt in "A Wagner Matinée," dead Harvey Merrick in "The Sculptor's Funeral," Thea Kronberg, Claude Wheeler, Tom Outland, Ántonia Shimerda, and Godfrey St. Peter. "The American community, whether family or town or neighborhood, is always the villain of the piece. It is the foe of life; it is worse than sterile — deadly, poisonous, adverse to human growth, hostile to every humane quality. She shows us communities of people who are little and petty but withal complacent and self-satisfied, who are intolerant

---

[19] Morris, Lloyd, "Willa Cather," *The North American Review* (May, 1924), CCXIX, 652.

[20] *The Song of the Lark*, p. 304.

[21] Whipple, T. K., *Spokesmen* (1928), p. 156.

and contemptuous of what differs from themselves, who are tightly bound by conventionality — not the sort that springs from free, deliberate approval of convention, but the sort that has its source in cowardice, stupidity, or indolence — of people who hate whatever does not jibe with their two-penny ha' penny aims, who hate everything genuine and human — genuine thought, or religion, or righteousness, or beauty — everything that means being genuinely alive, everything that shows true mind or feeling or imagination." [22]

"Her favorite theme persists throughout: the conflict of the superior individual with an unworthy society. . . . Her view is that the pioneers in general were folk largely endowed with creative power and imagination, but that the second generation, except for a few artists who have inherited the spirit of the fathers, has degenerated and succumbed to the tyranny of ease and money and things." [23] It is to the artist, in fact, that she looks for America's redemption, just as James and Wharton do. He alone is left to understand and appreciate the saturated beauty of reality, to discriminate between the worthless and the valuable things heaped on man's plate, to wed the past to the present and project both into the future, to contest and defeat our "custom-made" prejudice, our sneaking moralities, our cowardices, and our modern life, "adulterated, sterilized, with the sting taken out." [24] He is the "Lark," to whom we may pause in our work to listen, like that peasant girl in Jules Breton's painting, "The Song of the Lark."

"Willa Cather's passion for artists, especially musical artists, has been second only to her passion for pioneers." [25] Both, in her judgment, "are practically

---

[22] *Ibid.*, p. 155.
[23] *Ibid.*, pp. 154–155.
[24] Cather, Willa, *Youth and the Bright Medusa* (1920), p. 162.
[25] Sergeant, Elizabeth S., *Fire Under the Andes* (1927), p. 272.

equals in single-mindedness; at least, they work much by themselves, contending with definite though ruthless obstacles, and looking forward, if they win, to a freedom which cannot be achieved in the routine of crowded communities. . . . Her heroic days endure but a brief period before extinction comes. Then her high-hearted pioneers survive half as curiosities in a new order; and their spirits, transmitted to the artists who are their legitimate successors, take up the old struggle in a new guise." [26]

[26] Van Doren, Carl, *op. cit.*, pp. 116–117. By permission of The Macmillan Company, publishers.

* **MULTUM IN UNUM**

The essential problem that lies before humanity is how to combine creatively, as distinct from balancing negatively, apparent opposites, how to harmonize the individual and the social, the fact and the desire, the natural and the human, the conscious and the unconscious, the idea and the thing.

HUGH I'ANSON FAUSSET

AMPERSAND

WILDER AND CANFIELD   Two other humanists deserve to be
mentioned.   The first is Thornton Wilder, author of three
short novels, *The Cabala* (1926), *The Bridge of San Luis Rey*
(1927), and *The Woman of Andros* (1930), in which he has
tried to restate the ethics of Christianity in tingling prose,
and "discover the spirit that is not unequal to the elevation
of the great religious themes, yet which does not fall into a
repellent didacticism." [1]   The second of these two humanists is Dorothy Canfield.   Born as the daughter of a college
president, her youth was spent largely in an intellectual atmosphere, in studying at Columbia and the Sorbonne, and
in travel.   For a time it appeared that her training would
lead her quite naturally into academic labor.   But in 1907
she married John Fisher, whom she had met at Columbia,
and settled down to write on a farm near Arlington, Vermont.   In 1916 her husband went to France as an ambulance driver;   and taking their two children along, she
followed, to do relief work.   After the War they returned
to Vermont, where she has since devoted most of her time to
national projects for the advancement of education, and to
writing novels that reflect her keen interest in marriage and
parental problems, life in Vermont, her experiences in
France, her "distaste for the capitalist system," her faith in
self-control as an antidote for adversity, and her "insistence
on the dignity of work, the beauty of primitive human
relationships, the desirability of a simple life and only a

[1] Wilder, Thornton, *The Angel that Troubled the Waters, and Other Plays*
(1928), p. xv.

small *quid pro quo* as a fair reward of effort." [2]   There is nothing negligible about her early novels, *The Squirrel Cage* (1912), *The Brimming Cup* (1921), *Rough-Hewn* (1922), *The Bent Twig* (1915), and *Her Son's Wife* (1926); yet it is only with the publication of *The Deepening Stream* (1930) and *Bonfire* (1933) that she has come to be taken seriously as a writer.   Until recently "a neglected best-seller," disqualified by her popularity as a contributor to women's magazines and her determined "wholesomeness," she seems destined to win at last the critical praise she has long merited.

But in spite of Wharton, Cather, and Canfield, the last two or three decades of the American novel have been dominantly naturalistic.   At present, to be sure, a strong tide of "proletarian" literature has set in; and there are signs of a classical reaction that might be termed humanistic.   Yet there would seem to be little chance that either, in the near future, can replace naturalism as the reigning philosophy of fiction.   The whole age is definitely naturalistic in temper, and to expect art to contradict its environment on any large scale would not be justified by the evidence of history.   Faulkner, however, does represent a kind of dead end; and naturalism, which follows science closely, will no doubt change, as it has been changing, with new developments in science.   So that if it continues to rule the novel, it will perhaps take the shape of a "new naturalism."   Just now it is being slain by its apostles, whose broncho excesses have redounded to its discredit.

A NEW NATURALISM   The next few years may endow it with a more judicious meaning, restore it to the prestige it deserves as a majestic *religio laici*, and adjust it to the exigencies of modern culture.   By allowing its reverence for the senses to conquer its respect for the spirit, it has merely reversed the dualism of humanism, instead of escaping from

[2] Wyckoff, Elizabeth, "Dorothy Canfield: A Neglected Best Seller," *The Bookman* (September, 1931), LXXIV, 41.

it. In essence it is not dualistic, but monistic; and this is the proper condition to which it should return. Like humanism it has failed "to recognize how urgent has grown man's hunger for a deeper mode of being, for a unity." [3] It needs to learn how to "orchestrate" the impulses of body and soul, how to render (as Amiel urged) the spiritual natural and the natural spiritual, how to strike them both at once and produce a harmonious chord that is more beautiful than either taken by itself, how to teach appetite and reason to complete rather than counteract each other, and how to make extremes touch. Dualism in any form "leads as surely in time to spiritual death as disease (itself a functional dualism) to physical death." [4] Divided, man falls; united, he stands. What he requires is a working synthesis, a condition of *multum in unum*, "an order not based on conflict which, however, exhilarating for a time, must eventually demoralize, but rising through conflict to informed co-operation, which must indefinitely enrich." [5] And perhaps it is to art, rather than religion or science, that he must turn for this marriage of body and soul.

These two elements are not indissoluble, not naturally one. Left to themselves, they grow apart, become enemies, fight until one subdues the other, and thereby force man to commit a partial suicide. But when brought together by art (the symbolization of experience), they become friends. For art, both in life and literature, is harmony; and those who are unable to achieve it in life may (and often do) achieve it in literature. Its peculiar value to the world is its service in merging contradictory facts and forces into a symbol, into a whole that is greater than the sum of its parts. It is the ampersand, the & that links flesh to spirit.

[3] Fausset, Hugh I'Anson, *The Proving of Psyche* (1929), p. 177.
[4] *Ibid.*, p. 23.   [5] *Ibid.*, p. 21.

*

ADDITIONAL REFERENCES

*

GENERAL

Ames, Van Meter, *Aesthetics of the Novel*, The University of Chicago Press, 1928.

Beach, Joseph Warren, *The Outlook for American Prose*, The University of Chicago Press, 1926.

Blankenship, Russell, *American Literature as an Expression of the National Mind*, Henry Holt & Company, 1931.

Boyd, Ernest, *Portraits: Real and Imaginary*, George H. Doran Company, 1924.

Boynton, Percy H., *Some Contemporary Americans*, The University of Chicago Press, 1924.

Boynton, Percy H., *More Contemporary Americans*, The University of Chicago Press, 1927.

Brownell, Baker, *The New Universe*, D. Van Nostrand Company, 1926.

Brownell, Baker (ed.), *Man and His World*, 12 vols., D. Van Nostrand Company, 1929.

Burke, Kenneth, "A Decade of American Fiction," *The Bookman* (August, 1929), LXIX, 561–567.

Calverton, V. F., *The Liberation of American Literature*, Charles Scribner's Sons, 1932.

Canby, Henry Seidel, *American Estimates*, Harcourt, Brace & Company, 1929.

Canby, Henry Seidel, *Definitions*, Harcourt, Brace & Company, 1922. Second Series, 1924.

Canby, Henry Seidel (and others), *Designed for Reading*, The Macmillan Company, 1934.

Coblentz, Stanton A., *The Literary Revolution*, Frank-Maurice, 1927.

Cowley, Malcolm, *Exile's Return*, W. W. Norton & Company, 1934.

Eastman, Max, *The Literary Mind*, Charles Scribner's Sons, 1931.

Edgar, Pelham, *The Art of the Novel*, The Macmillan Company, 1933.

Edman, Irwin, *The Contemporary and His Soul*, Jonathan Cape & Harrison Smith, 1931.

Eucken, Rudolf, *Main Currents of Modern Thought*, T. Fisher Unwin, London, 1912.

Farrar, John (ed.), *The Literary Spotlight*, George H. Doran Company, 1924.

Foerster, Norman (ed.), *The Reinterpretation of American Literature*, Harcourt, Brace & Company, 1928.

Forster, E. M., *Aspects of the Novel*, Harcourt, Brace & Company, 1927.

Friedell, Egon, *A Cultural History of the Modern Age* III, Alfred A. Knopf, 1932.

Gale, Zona, "The Novel and the Spirit," *The Yale Review* (October, 1922), XII, 41–55.

Garland, Hamlin, *Companions on the Trail*, The Macmillan Company, 1931.

Garland, Hamlin, *My Friendly Contemporaries*. The Macmillan Company, 1932.

Garland, Hamlin, *Roadside Meetings*, The Macmillan Company, 1930.

Graham, Bessie, *The Bookman's Manual*, R. R. Bowker Company, 1928.

Joad, C. E. M., *Guide to Modern Thought*, Faber & Faber, London, 1933.

Knight, Grant C., *American Literature and Culture*, Ray Long & Richard R. Smith, 1932.

Kunitz, Stanley J. (ed.), *Authors Today and Yesterday*, The H. W. Wilson Company, 1933.

Lewis, Wyndham, *Time and Western Man*, Harcourt, Brace & Company, 1928.

Lewisohn, Ludwig, "The Crisis of the Novel," *The Yale Review* (March, 1933), XX, 533–544.

Lewisohn, Ludwig, *Expression in America*, Harper & Brothers, 1932.

Lubbock, Percy, *The Craft of Fiction*, Jonathan Cape, London, 1921.

Macleish, Archibald, "The New Age and the New Writers," *The Yale Review* (January, 1923), XII, 314–321.

Macy, John (ed.), *American Writers on American Literature*, Horace Liveright, 1931.

Martin, Everett D., *Civilizing Ourselves*, W. W. Norton & Company, 1932.

Michaud, Régis, *The American Novel To-Day*, Little, Brown & Company, 1928.

More, Paul Elmer, *The Demon of the Absolute*, Princeton University Press, 1928, 53–76.

Morris, Lloyd (ed.), *The Young Idea*, Duffield & Green, 1917.

Muir, Edwin, *The Structure of the Novel*, The Hogarth Press, London, 1928.

Munson, Gorham B., *Destinations*, J. H. Sears & Company, 1928.

Munson, Gorham B., *Style and Form in American Prose*, Doubleday, Doran & Company, 1929.

Murry, John Middleton, "The Break-up of the Novel," *The Yale Review* (January, 1923), XII, 288–304.

Nathan, George Jean (and others), *American Spectator Year Book*, Frederick A. Stokes Company, 1934.

Parrington, Vernon Louis, *Main Currents in American Thought* III, Harcourt, Brace & Company, 1930.

Patrick, G. T. W., *The World and Its Meaning*, Houghton Mifflin Company, 1924.

Pattee, Fred Lewis, *The New American Literature*, The Century Company, 1930.

Randall, John Herman, *The Making of the Modern Mind*, Houghton Mifflin Company, 1926.

Rascoe, Burton, *A Bookman's Daybook*, Horace Liveright, 1929.

Schmalhausen, Samuel D. (ed.), *Behold America!* Farrar & Rinehart, 1931.

Several Authors, "Statements of Belief," *The Bookman* (September and October, 1928), LXVIII, 25–27 and 204–207.

Shaw, Charles Gray, *The Surge and Thunder*, The American Book Company, 1932.

Shipley, Joseph T., *The Literary Isms*, The University of Washington Chapbooks, No. 49, The University of Washington Bookstore, Seattle, 1931.

Squire, J. C. (and others), *Contemporary American Authors*, Henry Holt & Company, 1928.

Tante, Dilly (ed.), *Living Authors*, The H. W. Wilson Company, 1932.

Trent, William P., John Erskine, Stuart P. Sherman, and Carl Van Doren (eds.), *The Cambridge History of American Literature* III, G. P. Putnam's Sons, 1927.

Twelve American Novelists, *The Novel of Tomorrow and the Scope of Fiction*, The Bobbs-Merrill Company, 1922.

Van Doren, Carl, *The American Novel*, The Macmillan Company, 1931.

Van Doren, Carl, *Contemporary American Novelists*, The Macmillan Company, 1931.

Ward, A. C., *American Literature, 1880–1930*, Methuen & Company, London, 1932.

Whipple, T. K., *Spokesmen*, D. Appleton & Company, 1928.

WHAT'S O'CLOCK

Beer, Thomas, *The Mauve Decade*, Alfred A. Knopf, 1926.

Belgion, Montgomery, *Our Present Philosophy of Life*, Faber & Faber, London, 1929.

Brownell, Baker, *Earth Is Enough*, Harper & Brothers, 1933.

Burroughs, John, *Accepting the Universe*, Houghton Mifflin Company, 1920.

Burtt, Edwin Arthur, *The Metaphysical Foundations of Modern Physical Science*, Kegan Paul, Trench, Trubner & Company, London, 1925.

Dampier, Sir William, *A History of Science*, The Macmillan Company, 1932.

D'Arcy, Charles F. (and others), *God and the Struggle for Existence*, The Association Press, New York, 1919.

Drake, Durant, *The New Morality*, The Macmillan Company, 1929.

Ellis, Havelock, *Views and Reviews*, Houghton Mifflin Company, 1932.

Givler, Robert C., *The Ethics of Hercules*, Alfred A. Knopf, 1924.

Haldane, J. S., *The Sciences and Philosophy*, Doubleday, Doran & Company, 1929.

Hobhouse, L. T., *Morals in Evolution*, Chapman and Hall, London, 1923.

Jeans, Sir James, *The New Background of Science*, The Macmillan Company, 1933.

Joad, C. E. M., *Mind and Matter*, G. P. Putnam's Sons, 1925.

Lange, F. A., *History of Materialism*, Houghton, Osgood & Company, Boston, 1879.

Lippmann, Walter, *A Preface to Morals*, The Macmillan Company, 1929.

Loomis, Roger Sherman, "A Defense of Naturalism," *The International Journal of Ethics* (January, 1919), XXIX, 188–201.

Martin, Everett D., *The Conflict of the Individual and the Mass in the Modern World*, Henry Holt & Company, 1932, 65–93.

Marvin, F. S. (ed.), *Science and Civilization*, The Oxford University Press, London, 1923.

McDougall, William, *Body and Mind*, Methuen & Company, London, 1913.

Menninger, Karl A., *The Human Mind*, Alfred A. Knopf, 1930.

Merz, John Theodore, *History of European Thought in the Nineteenth Century*, 4 vols., William Blackwood & Sons, Edinburgh, 1896.

Meyer, Adolph E., "Advocatus Diaboli [William Brann]," *The American Mercury* (September, 1927), XII, 68–74.

Needham, Joseph, *Man a Machine*, W. W. Norton & Company, 1928.

Osborn, H. F., *The Origin and Evolution of Life*, Charles Scribner's Sons, 1918.

Riley, Woodbridge, *From Myth to Reason*, D. Appleton & Company, 1926.

Russell, Bertrand, *What I Believe*, E. P. Dutton & Company, 1925.

Russell, Dora, *The Right to Be Happy*, George Routledge & Sons, London, 1927.

Sedgwick, W. T., and H. W. Tyler, *A Short History of Science*, The Macmillan Company, 1923.

Smith, Lewis Worthington, "The Drift Toward Naturalism," *The South Atlantic Quarterly* (October, 1923), XXII, 355–369.

Thomson, Mehran K., *The Springs of Human Action*, D. Appleton & Company, 1927.

White, Andrew Dickson, *A History of the Warfare of Science with*

Theology in Christendom, 2 vols., D. Appleton & Company, 1896.

Whitehead, Alfred North, *Science and the Modern World*, The Macmillan Company, 1925.

THE RED BADGE OF NATURE

Beer, Thomas, "Mrs. Stephen Crane," *The American Mercury* (March, 1934), XXXI, 289–295.

Bohnenberger, Carl, and Norman Mitchell Hill (eds.), "The Letters of Joseph Conrad to Stephen and Cora Crane," *The Bookman* (May and June, 1929), LXIX, 225–235 and 367–374.

Cazamian, Louis, "The Method of Discontinuity in Modern Art and Literature," *Criticism in the Making*, The Macmillan Company, 1929, 63–80.

Crane, H. R., "My Uncle, Stephen Crane," *The American Mercury* (January, 1934), XXXI, 24–29.

Dell, Floyd, "Stephen Crane and the Genius Myth," *The Nation* (December 10, 1924), CXIX, 637–638.

Faust, Camille, *The French Impressionists*, E. P. Dutton & Company, 1911.

Follett, Wilson, "The Second Twenty-Eight Years," *The Bookman* (January, 1929), LXVIII, 532–537.

Hughes, Glenn, *Imagism and the Imagists*, Stanford University Press, 1931.

Monroe, Harriet, "Stephen Crane," *Poetry* (June, 1919), XIV, 148–152.

Raymond, Thomas L., *Stephen Crane*, The Carteret Book Club, Newark, 1923.

Starrett, Vincent, Introduction to Stephen Crane, *Men, Women and Boats*, The Modern Library, 1921.

Starrett, Vincent, *Stephen Crane, A Bibliography*, The Centaur Book Shop, Philadelphia, 1923.

Van Doren, Carl, "Stephen Crane," *The American Mercury* (January, 1924), I, 11–14.

Wells, H. G., "Stephen Crane," *The North American Review* (August, 1900), CLXXI, 233–242.

Wickham, Harvey, "Stephen Crane at College," *The American Mercury* (March, 1926), VII, 291–297.

Norris and the Brute

Barbusse, Henri, *Zola*, E. P. Dutton & Company, 1933.

Cooper, F. T., "Frank Norris, Realist," *The Bookman* (November, 1899), X, 234–238.

Dobie, Charles Caldwell, "Frank Norris, or Up From Culture," *The American Mercury* (April, 1928), XIII, 412–424.

Garland, Hamlin, "The Work of Frank Norris," *The Critic* (March, 1903), XLII, 216–218.

Grattan, C. Hartley, "Frank Norris," *The Bookman* (July, 1929), LXIX, 506–510.

Millard, Bailey, "A Significant Literary Life," *Out West* (January, 1903), XVIII, 49–55.

Norris, Frank, "The Novel with a 'Purpose.'" *The World's Work* (May, 1902), IV, 2117–2119.

Wright, H. M., "In Memoriam — Frank Norris," *The University of California Chronicle* (October, 1902), V, 240–245.

Men with the Bark On

Anonymous, "How the Literary Man is Misrepresenting Evolution," *Current Literature* (July, 1907), XLIII, 99–100.

Berg, Leo, *The Superman in Modern Literature*, Jarrold & Sons, London, 1916.

Cooper, F. T., "Primordialism and Some Recent Books," *The Bookman* (November, 1909), XXX, 278–282.

Lane, Rose Wilder, "Life and Jack London," *Sunset* (October, 1917), XXXIX, 17–20; (November, 1917), XXXIX, 29–32; (December, 1917), XXXIX, 21–23; (January, 1918), XL, 34–37; (February, 1918), XL, 30–34; (March, 1918), XL, 27–30; (April, 1918), XL, 21–25; and (May, 1918), XL, 28–32.

London, Charmian, *The Book of Jack London*, 2 vols., The Century Company, 1921.

James, George Wharton, "A Study of Jack London in His Prime," *The Overland Monthly* (May, 1917), LXIX, 361–399.

The Hindenburg of the Novel

Duffus, Robert L., "Dreiser," *The American Mercury* (January, 1926), VII, 71–76.

Fadiman, Clifton, "Dreiser and the American Dream," *The Nation* (October 19, 1932), CXXXV, 364–365.

Mencken, H. L., "The Dreiser Bugaboo," *The Seven Arts* (August, 1917), II, 507–517.

Mencken, H. L., *A Book of Prefaces*, Alfred A. Knopf, 1917.

Munson, Gorham B., *Destinations*, J. H. Sears & Company, 1928, 41–56.

Orton, Vrest, *Dreiserana*, The Chocorna Bibliographies, New York, 1929.

Search-Light (Waldo Frank), *Time Exposures*, Boni & Liveright, 1926, 159–164.

Sherman, Stuart P., *The Main Stream*, Charles Scribner's Sons, 1927, 134–144.

Smith, Edward H., "Dreiser — After Twenty Years," *The Bookman* (March, 1921), LIII, 27–39.

Waldman, Milton, "A German-American Insurgent," *The Living Age* (October 1, 1926), CCCXXXI, 43–50.

Walker, Charles R., "How Big Is Dreiser?" *The Bookman* (April, 1926), LXIII, 146–149.

Watson, John B., and William McDougall, *The Battle of Behaviorism*, Kegan Paul, Trench, Trubner & Company, London, 1928.

BROKEN FACE GARGOYLES

Anderson, Margaret, *My Thirty Years' War*, Covici, Friede, 1930.

Anderson, Sherwood, *The Modern Writer*, The Lantern Press, San Francisco, 1925.

Bourne, Randolph, *History of a Literary Radical*, B. W. Huebsch, 1920.

Brickell, Herschel, "The Literary Awakening in the South," *The Bookman* (October, 1927), LXVI, 138–143.

Brooks, Van Wyck, *Sketches in Criticism*, E. P. Dutton & Company, 1932.

Budgen, Frank, *James Joyce and the Making of Ulysses*, Harrison Smith & Robert Haas, 1934.

Calverton, V. F., "Sherwood Anderson," *The Modern Quarterly* (Fall, 1924), II, 82–118.

Chase, Cleveland B., *Sherwood Anderson*, Robert M. McBride & Company, 1927.

Chase, Cleveland B., "Sherwood Anderson," *The Saturday Review of Literature* (September 24, 1927), IV, 129–130.

Dewey, John, "Americanism and Localism," *The Dial* (June, 1920), LXVIII, 684–688.

Drake, William A., "The Life and Deeds of Dada," *Poet Lore* (Winter, 1922), XXXIII, 497–506.

Frank, Waldo, *Salvos*, Boni & Liveright, 1924, 31–40.

Freud, Sigmund, *Civilization and Its Discontents*, The Hogarth Press, London, 1930.

Gorman, Herbert S., *James Joyce*, The Viking Press, 1924.

Haldeman-Julius, E., *The First Hundred Million*, Simon & Schuster, 1928.

Hawkins, Ethel Wallace, "The Stream of Consciousness Novel," *The Atlantic Monthly* (September, 1926), CXXXVIII, 356–360.

Hubbell, Jay B., "The Decay of the Provinces," *The Sewanee Review* (October, 1927), XXXV, 473–487.

Jocelyn, John, "Getting at Waldo Frank," *The Sewanee Review* (October–December, 1932), XL, 405–414.

Jolas, Eugène, "Transition: An Epilogue," *The American Mercury* (June, 1931), XXIII, 185–192.

Muir, Edwin, *Transition*, The Viking Press, 1926.

Mumford, Lewis, *The Golden Day*, Boni & Liveright, 1926.

Murphy, Gardner (ed.), *An Outline of Abnormal Psychology*, The Modern Library, 1929.

Peterson, Houston, *The Melody of Chaos*, Longmans, Green & Company, 1931.

Ransom, John Crowe, "The Aesthetic of Regionalism," *The American Review* (January, 1934), II, 290–310.

Rosenfeld, Paul, "Sherwood Anderson," *The Dial* (January, 1922), LXXII, 29–42.

Salpeter, Harry, "Portrait of a Disciplined Artist [Evelyn Scott]," *The Bookman* (November, 1931), LXXIV, 281–286.

Spiegel, Leo A., "The New Jargon," *The Sewanee Review* (October–December, 1932), XL, 476–491.

Stein, Gertrude, *The Autobiography of Alice B. Toklas*, The Literary Guild, 1933.

Symposium, "Revolution of the Word," *The Modern Quarterly* (Fall, 1929), V, 273–323.

Van Doren, Carl, "Sinclair Lewis and Sherwood Anderson," *The Century* (July, 1925), CX, 362–369.

Van Teslaar, J. S. (ed.), *An Outline of Psychoanalysis*, The Modern Library, 1924.

Wescott, Glenway, *Elizabeth Madox Roberts*, The Viking Press, 1930.

West, Rebecca, *The Strange Necessity*, Doubleday, Doran & Company, 1928, 309–320.

Wilson, Edmund, *Axel's Castle*, Charles Scribner's Sons, 1931.

Woodworth, Robert S., *Contemporary Schools of Psychology*, The Ronald Press, New York, 1931.

GRACE UNDER PRESSURE

Cohn, Louis Henry, *A Bibliography of the Works of Ernest Hemingway*, Random House, 1931.

Dewing, Arthur, "The Mistake about Hemingway," *The North American Review* (October, 1931), CCXXXII, 364–371.

Wilson, Edmund, "The Sportsman's Tragedy," *The New Republic* (December 14, 1927), LIII, 102–103.

THE CULT OF CRUELTY

Canby, Henry Seidel, "The School of Cruelty," *The Saturday Review of Literature* (March 21, 1931), VII, 673–674.

Faulkner, William, Introduction to *Sanctuary*, The Modern Library, 1932.

Green, A. Wigfall, "William Faulkner at Home," *The Sewanee Review* (July, 1932), XL, 294–306.

Thompson, Alan Reynolds, "The Cult of Cruelty," *The Bookman* (January, 1932), LXXIV, 477–487.

SINGERS OF AN EMPTY DAY

Saltus, Marie, *Edgar Saltus, the Man*, Pascal Covici, 1925.

Temple, Jean, *Blue Ghost* [Lafcadio Hearn], Jonathan Cape & Harrison Smith, 1931.

Vaihinger, H., *The Philosophy of "As If,"* Harcourt, Brace & Company, 1925.

THE JOURNEYS OF JURGEN

Brussel, I. R., *A Bibliography of the Writings of James Branch Cabell*, The Centaur Book Shop, Philadelphia, 1932.

Fadiman, Clifton, "(James) Branch Cabell," *The Nation* (April 12, 1933), CXXXVI, 409–410.

Glasgow, Ellen, "The Biography of Manuel," *The Saturday Review of Literature* (June 7, 1930), VI, 1108–1109.

Hatcher, Harlan, "On Not Having Read James Branch Cabell," *The Bookman* (February, 1931), LXXII, 597–599.

Hergesheimer, Joseph, "James Branch Cabell," *The American Mercury* (January, 1928), XIII, 38–47.

Hooker, Edward Niles, "Something About Cabell," *The Sewanee Review* (April, 1929), XXXVII, 193–203.

McIntyre, Clara F., "Mr. Cabell's Cosmos," *The Sewanee Review* (July–September, 1930), XXXVIII, 278–285.

Mencken, H. L., *James Branch Cabell*, Robert M. McBride & Company, 1927.

Van Doren, Carl, *James Branch Cabell*, Robert M. McBride & Company, 1925.

COSTUMES BY HERGESHEIMER

Fadiman, Clifton, "The Best People's Best Novelist," *The Nation* (February 15, 1933), CXXXVI, 175–177.

Gray, Jerome B., "An Author and His Town," *The Bookman* (April, 1928), LXVII, 159–164.

Haardt, Sara, "Joseph Hergesheimer's Methods," *The Bookman* (June, 1929), LXIX, 398–403.

Hergesheimer, Joseph, "Art," *The American Mercury* (November, 1926), IX, 257–263.

Hergesheimer, Joseph, "The Profession of Novelist," *The New Republic* (April 12, 1922), XXX, supplement.

Hergesheimer, Joseph, "Some Veracious Paragraphs," *The Bookman* (September, 1918), XLVIII, 8–12.

Jones, Llewellyn, *Joseph Hergesheimer*, Alfred A. Knopf, 1920.

Swire, Herbert L., *A Bibliography of the Works of Joseph Hergesheimer*, The Centaur Book Shop, Philadelphia, 1922.

West, Geoffrey, "Joseph Hergesheimer," *The Virginia Quarterly Review* (January, 1932), VIII, 95–108.

LITERATURE INSURGENT

Adamic, Louis, *Dynamite, the Story of Class Violence in America*, The Viking Press, 1931.

Adams, James Truslow, *The March of Democracy* II, Charles Scribner's Sons, 1933.

Adams, James Truslow, *Our Business Civilization*, Albert & Charles Boni, 1929.

Allen, Frederick Lewis, *Only Yesterday*, Harper & Brothers, 1931.

Anonymous, "Socialism in Literature," *The Bookman* (April, 1908), XXVII, 119–124.

Arvin, Newton, "Literature and Social Change," *The Modern Quarterly* (Summer, 1932), VI, 20–25.

Barnes, Harry Elmer, *Can Man Be Civilized?* Brentano's, 1932.

Barnes, Harry Elmer, *Living in the Twentieth Century*, The Bobbs-Merrill Company, 1928.

Bates, Ernest Sutherland, *This Land of Liberty*, Harper & Brothers, 1930.

Bimba, Anthony, *The History of the American Working Class*, International Publishers, New York, 1927.

Boynton, Percy H., *The Rediscovery of the Frontier*, The University of Chicago Press, 1931.

Brameld, Theodore B. H., *A Philosophic Approach to Communism*, The University of Chicago Press, 1933.

Brooks, Obed, "The Problem of the Social Novel," *The Modern Quarterly* (Fall, 1932), VI, 77–82.

Bury, J. B., *The Idea of Progress*, The Macmillan Company, 1932.

Calverton, V. F., *The Newer Spirit*, Boni & Liveright, 1925.

Calverton, V. F., "Art and Social Change: the Radical Approach," *The Modern Quarterly* (Winter, 1931), VI, 16–27.

Calverton, V. F., "Can We Have a Proletarian Literature?" *The Modern Quarterly* (Fall, 1932), VI, 39–50.

Calverton, V. F., "Leftward Ho!" *The Modern Quarterly* (Summer, 1932), VI, 26–32.

Calverton, V. F., "Social Forces in American Literature," in Schmalhausen, Samuel D. (ed.), *Behold America!* Farrar & Rinehart, 1931, 673–703.

Carlton, Frank Tracy, *Organized Labor in American History*, D. Appleton & Company, 1920.

Chamberlain, John, *Farewell to Reform*, Liveright, 1932.

Chamberlain, John, "The Negro as Writer," *The Bookman* (February, 1930), LXX, 603–611.

Charques, R. D., *Contemporary Literature and Social Revolution*, Martin Secker, London, 1933.

Chase, Stuart, *Men and Machines*, The Macmillan Company, 1929.

Chase, Stuart, *Prosperity: Fact or Myth*, Charles Boni, 1929.

Chase, Stuart, *The Tragedy of Waste*, The Macmillan Company, 1929.

Chase, Stuart, and F. J. Schlink, *Your Money's Worth*, The Macmillan Company, 1927.

Davis, Jerome, *Contemporary Social Movements*, The Century Company, 1930.

Dewey, John (and others), *Creative Intelligence*, Henry Holt & Company, 1917.

Dondore, Dorothy A., *The Prairie and the Making of Middle America*, The Torch Press, Cedar Rapids (Iowa), 1926.

Du Breuil, Alice Jouveau, *The Novel of Democracy in America*, J. H. Furst Company, Baltimore, 1923.

Fine, Nathan, *Labor and Farmer Parties in the United States, 1828–1928*, The Rand School of Social Science, New York, 1928.

Foster, William Z., *Toward Soviet America*, Coward-McCann, 1932.

Frank, Glenn, *Thunder and Dawn*, The Macmillan Company, 1932.

Frank, Waldo, *The Re-discovery of America*, Charles Scribner's Sons, 1929.

Ghent, W. J., *Our Benevolent Feudalism*, The Macmillan Company, 1903.

Haldeman-Julius, E., *The Big American Parade*, The Stratford Company, 1929.

Harrison, Frederic, *The Creed of a Layman*, The Macmillan Company, 1907.

Hays, Arthur Garfield, *Let Freedom Ring*, Boni & Liveright, 1928.

Hazard, Lucy Lockwood, *The Frontier in American Literature*, Thomas Y. Crowell Company, 1927.

Hazlitt, Henry, "Art and Social Change: the Eclectic Approach," *The Modern Quarterly* (Winter, 1931), VI, 10–15.

Hertzler, Joyce O., *The History of Utopian Thought*, The Macmillan Company, 1926.

Hicks, Granville, *The Great Tradition*, The Macmillan Company, 1933.

Hicks, Granville, "Literary Criticism and the Marxian Method," *The Modern Quarterly* (Summer, 1932), VI, 44–47.

Hillquit, Morris, *History of Socialism in the United States*, Funk & Wagnalls Company, 1903.

Hillquit, Morris, *Loose Leaves from a Busy Life*, The Macmillan Company, 1934.

Josephson, Matthew, *The Robber Barons*, Harcourt, Brace & Company, 1934.

Kropotkin, P., *The Conquest of Bread*, G. P. Putnam's Sons, 1907.

Kropotkin, P., *Mutual Aid*, William Heinemann, London, 1902.

Laidler, Harry W., and Norman Thomas (eds.), *The Socialism of Our Times*, The Vanguard Press, 1929.

Martin, Everett D., *Liberty*, W. W. Norton & Company, 1930.

Marx, Karl, *Capital*, George Allen & Unwin, London, 1928.

Marx, Karl, and Friedrich Engels, *The Communist Manifesto*, International Publishers, New York, 1930.

Mumford, Lewis, *The Story of Utopias*, Boni & Liveright, 1922.

Mumford, Lewis, *Technics and Civilization*, Harcourt, Brace & Company, 1934.

Myers, Gustavus, *History of the Great American Fortunes*, C. H. Kerr & Company, Chicago, 1911.

Notch, Frank K., *King Mob*, Harcourt, Brace & Company, 1930.

Odum, Howard W., *Man's Quest for Social Guidance*, Henry Holt & Company, 1927.

Ortega y Gasset, José, *The Revolt of the Masses*, George Allen & Unwin, London, 1932.

Page, Kirby, *Individualism and Socialism*, Farrar & Rinehart, 1933.

Page, Kirby (ed.), *The New Economic Order*, Harcourt, Brace & Company, 1930.

Park, Robert E., and Ernest W. Burgess (eds.), *Introduction to the Science of Sociology*, The University of Chicago Press, 1927.

Paxson, F. L., *The History of the American Frontier, 1763–1893*, Houghton Mifflin Company, 1924.

Randall, John Herman, *Our Changing Civilization*, Frederick A. Stokes Company, 1929.

Ratner, Joseph (ed.), *The Philosophy of John Dewey*, Henry Holt & Company, 1928.

Rauschenbusch, Walter, *Christianizing the Social Order*, The Macmillan Company, 1913.

Regier, C. C., *The Era of the Muckrakers*, The University of North Carolina Press, 1932.

Rusk, R. L., *The Literature of the Middle Western Frontier*, The Columbia University Press, 1925.

Samson, Leon, "A Proletarian Philosophy of Art," *The Modern Quarterly* (Spring, 1929), V, 235–239.

Schlesinger, Arthur M., *Political and Social History of the United States*, The Macmillan Company, 1930.

Schlesinger, Arthur M., "Social History in American Literature," *The Yale Review* (September, 1928), XVIII, 135–147.

Schmalhausen, Samuel D. (ed.), *Recovery Through Revolution*, Covici, Friede, 1933.

Sinclair, Upton (ed.), *The Cry for Justice: An Anthology of the Literature of Social Protest*, The John C. Winston Company, Philadelphia, 1915.

Slossen, Preston William, *The Great Crusade and After, 1914–1928*, The Macmillan Company, 1931.

Socialist National Campaign Committee, *The Intelligent Voter's Guide*, New York, 1928.

Soule, George, *A Planned Society*, The Macmillan Company, 1932.

Steffens, Lincoln, *The Autobiography of Lincoln Steffens*, Harcourt, Brace & Company, 1931.

Strachey, John, *The Coming Struggle for Power*, Covici, Friede, 1933.

Symes, Lillian, and Travers, Clement, *Rebel America*, Harper & Brothers, 1934.

Thomas, Norman, *America's Way Out*, The Macmillan Company, 1931.

Trotsky, Leon, *Literature and Revolution*, George Allen & Unwin, London, 1925.

Turner, F. J., *The Frontier in America History*, Henry Holt & Company, 1920.

Underwood, John Curtis, *Literature and Insurgency*, Mitchell Kennerley, New York, 1914.

Veblen, Thorstein, *Absentee Ownership and Business Enterprise in Recent Times*, B. W. Huebsch, 1923.

Veblen, Thorstein, *The Theory of the Leisure Class*, The Macmillan Company, 1911.

Wilkinson, Hazel, "Social Thought in American Fiction, 1910–

1917," *University of Southern California Studies in Sociology* III, No. 2, December, 1918.

Wilson, Edmund, "Literary Class War," *The New Republic* (May 4, 1932), LXX, 319–323.

PLAIN TALK

Grattan, C. Hartley, "Upton Sinclair on Current Literature," *The Bookman* (April, 1932), LXXV, 61–64.

Harris, Mrs. L. H., "Upton Sinclair and Helicon Hall," *The Independent* (March 28, 1907), LXII, 711–713.

Lippmann, Walter, "Upton Sinclair," *The Saturday Review of Literature* (March 3, 1928), IV, 641–643.

Morris, Lawrence S., "Upton Sinclair," *The New Republic* (March 7, 1928), LIV, 90–93.

Sinclair, Upton, *Books of Upton Sinclair in Translations and Foreign Editions*, published by the author, Pasadena, 1930.

THE VILLAGE VIRUS

Binsse, Harry Lorin, and John J. Trounstine, "Europe Looks at Sinclair Lewis," *The Bookman* (January, 1931), LXXII, 453–457.

Cabell, James Branch, "A Note as to Sinclair Lewis," *The American Mercury* (August, 1930), XX, 394–397.

Canby, Henry Seidel, "Schmaltz, Babbitt & Co.," *The Saturday Review of Literature* (March 24, 1928), IV, 697–698.

De Voto, Bernard, "Sinclair Lewis," *The Saturday Review of Literature* (January 28, 1933), IX, 397–398.

Gauss, Christian, "Sinclair Lewis *vs.* His Education," *The Saturday Evening Post* (December 26, 1931), CCIV, p. 20.

Harrison, Oliver, *Sinclair Lewis*, Harcourt, Brace & Company, 1925.

McNally, William J., "Mr. Babbitt, Meet Sinclair Lewis," *The Nation* (September 21, 1927), CXXV, 278–281.

Search-Light (Waldo Frank), *Time Exposures*, Boni & Liveright, 1926, 131–137.

Sherman, Stuart P., *The Significance of Sinclair Lewis*, Harcourt, Brace & Company, 1922.

Van Doren, Carl, *Sinclair Lewis*, Doubleday, Doran & Company, 1933.

Van Doren, Carl, "Sinclair Lewis and Sherwood Anderson," *The Century* (July, 1925), CX, 362–369.

THE ANARCHIST

Calmer, Alan, "John Dos Passos," *The Sewanee Review* (July–September, 1932), XL, 341–349.

Dos Passos, John, "A Communication," *The New Republic* (August 13, 1930), LXIII, 371–372.

Hicks, Granville, "Dos Passos' Gifts," *The New Republic* (June 24, 1931), LXVII, 157–158.

Hicks, Granville, "John Dos Passos," *The Bookman* (April, 1932), LXXV, 32–42.

THE GOLDEN MEAN

Arnold, Matthew, *Culture and Anarchy*, The Macmillan Company, 1875.

Ayres, C. E., *Science, the False Messiah*, The Bobbs-Merrill Company, 1927.

Babbitt, Irving, *Democracy and Leadership*, Houghton Mifflin Company, 1924.

Babbitt, Irving, *The New Laokoon*, Houghton Mifflin Company, 1910.

Brownell, W. C., *The Genius of Style*, Charles Scribner's Sons, 1924.

Brownell, W. C., *Standards*, Charles Scribner's Sons, 1917.

Frye, Prosser Hall, *Romance & Tragedy*, Marshall Jones Company, 1922.

Gass, Sherlock B., *A Lover of the Chair*, Marshall Jones Company, 1919.

Goodsell, Willystine, *The Conflict of Naturalism and Humanism*, Contributions to Education, No. 33, Columbia University Teachers College, 1910.

Grattan, C. Hartley (ed.), *The Critique of Humanism*, Brewer & Warren, 1930.

Hyde, Lawrence, *The Prospects of Humanism*, Gerald Howe, London, 1931.

Mercier, Louis J. A., *The Challenge of Humanism*, The Oxford University Press, 1933.

More, Louis Trenchard, *The Limitations of Science*, Henry Holt & Company, 1915.

Shafer, Robert, *Progress and Science*, The Yale University Press, 1922.

Shafer, Robert, "What Is Humanism?" *The Virginia Quarterly Review* (April, 1930), VI, 198–209.

Thompson, Alan Reynolds, "Back from Nature," *The University of California Chronicle* (April, 1930), XXXII, 211–225.

SWEETNESS AND LIGHT

Atherton, Gertrude, "Why Is American Literature Bourgeois?" *The North American Review* (May, 1904), CLXXVIII, 771–781.

Bass, Altha Leah, "The Social Consciousness of William Dean Howells," *The New Republic* (April 13, 1921), XXVI, 192–194.

Cooke, Delmar G., *William Dean Howells*, E. P. Dutton & Company, 1922.

Erskine, John, "William Dean Howells," *The Bookman* (June, 1920), LI, 385–389.

Hackett, Francis, *Horizons*, B. W. Huebsch, 1918, 21–30.

Mencken, H. L., *Prejudices*, First Series, Alfred A. Knopf, 1919, 52–58.

Tomlinson, May, "Fiction and Mr. Howells," *The South Atlantic Quarterly* (October, 1921), XX, 360–367.

Twain, Mark, *What Is Man?* Harper & Brothers, 1917, 228–239.

CAVIAR FOR THE GENERAL

Beach, Joseph Warren, *The Method of Henry James*, The Yale University Press, 1918.

Bethurum, Dorothy, "Morality and Henry James," *The Sewanee Review* (July, 1923), XXXI, 324–330.

Bosanquet, Theodora, "Henry James," *The Bookman* (August, 1917), XLV, 571–581.

Bosanquet, Theodora, "The Record of Henry James," *The Yale Review* (October, 1920), X, 143–156.

Brooks, Van Wyck, *The Pilgrimage of Henry James*, E. P. Dutton & Company, 1925.

Burr, Anna Robeson (ed.), *Alice James: Her Brothers*, Duffield & Green, 1934.

Cary, Elisabeth Luther, *The Novels of Henry James*, G. P. Putnam's Sons, 1905.

Cornelius, Roberta D., "The Clearness of Henry James," *The Sewanee Review* (January, 1919), XXVII, 1–8.

Elton, Oliver, "The Novels of Mr. Henry James," *The Quarterly Review* (October, 1903), CXCVIII, 358–379.

Ford, Ford Madox, *Henry James*, Martin Secker, London, 1913.

Freeman, John, *The Moderns*, Robert Scott, London, 1916, 219–241.

Garland, Hamlin, *Roadside Meetings*, The Macmillan Company, 1930, 454–465.

Grattan, C. Hartley, *The Three Jameses*, Longmans, Green & Company, 1932.

Herrick, Robert, "A Visit to Henry James," *The Yale Review* (July, 1923), XII, 724–741.

Hound & Horn (April–June, 1934).   This entire number is devoted to James.

Hughes, Herbert L., *Theory and Practice in Henry James*, Edwards Brothers, Ann Arbor, 1926.

Josephson, Matthew, *Portrait of the Artist as American*, Harcourt, Brace & Company, 1930, 70–138.

Kelley, Cornelia P., *The Early Development of Henry James*, The University of Illinois, 1930.

MacCarthy, Desmond, "The World of Henry James," *The Saturday Review of Literature* (August 29, 1931), VIII, 81–83.

Phillips, Le Roy, *A Bibliography of the Writings of Henry James*, Coward-McCann, 1930.

Read, Herbert, *The Sense of Glory*, The Cambridge University Press, 1929, 205–228.

Roberts, Morris, *Henry James's Criticism*, Harvard University Press, 1929.

Seldes, Gilbert V., "Henry James: An Appreciation," *The Harvard Monthly* (December, 1911), LIII, 92–100.

Sherman, Stuart P., *On Contemporary Literature*, Henry Holt & Company, 1917, 226–255.

Troy, William, "Henry James and the Young Writers," *The Bookman* (June, 1931), LXXIII, 351–358.

Wilson, Edmund, "The Exploration of James," *The New Republic* (March 16, 1927), L, 112–113.

Vanity Fair

Cross, Wilbur L., "Edith Wharton," *The Bookman* (August, 1926), LXIII, 641–646.

Hackett, Francis, *Horizons*, B. W. Huebsch, 1918, 31–42.

Herrick, Robert, "Mrs. Wharton's World," *The New Republic* (February 13, 1915), II, 40–42.

Lubbock, Percy, "The Novels of Edith Wharton," *The Quarterly Review* (January, 1915), CCXXIII, 182–201.

Melish, Lawson McClung, *A Bibliography of the Collected Writings of Edith Wharton*, The Brick Row Book Shop, New York, 1927.

Russell, Frances Theresa, "Melodramatic Mrs. Wharton," *The Sewanee Review* (October–December, 1932), XL, 425–437.

Sencourt, Robert, "The Poetry of Edith Wharton," *The Bookman* (July, 1931), LXXIII, 478–486.

Sherman, Stuart P., *The Main Stream*, Charles Scribner's Sons, 1927, 204–212.

Trueblood, Charles K., "Edith Wharton," *The Dial* (January, 1920), LXVIII, 80–91.

Wharton, Edith, *Backward Glance*, D. Appleton-Century Company, 1934. Reprinted from the *Ladies' Home Journal*.

Wharton, Edith, "The Great American Novel," *The Yale Review* (July, 1927), XVI, 646–656.

Winter, Calvin, "Edith Wharton," *The Bookman* (May, 1911), XXXIII, 302–309.

Simplicity with Glory

Boynton, Percy H., "Willa Cather," *The English Journal* (June, 1924), XIII, 373–380.

Cather, Willa, "A Letter from Willa Cather," *The Commonweal* (November 23, 1927), VII, 713–714.

Cather, Willa, "The Novel Démeuble," *The New Republic* (April 12, 1922), XXX, supplement.

Fadiman, Clifton, "The Past Recaptured," *The Nation* (December 7, 1932), CXXXV, 563–565.

Fisher, Dorothy Canfield, "Daughter of the Frontier," The New York *Herald Tribune* Magazine Section (Sunday, May 28, 1933), 7.

Hale, Edward E., "Willa Cather," *Union College Bulletin*, Faculty Papers Number (January, 1933), XXVI, No. 2, 5–17.

Kronenberger, Louis, "Willa Cather," *The Bookman* (October, 1931), LXXIV, 134–140.

McNamara, Robert, "Phases of American Religion in Thornton Wilder and Willa Cather," *The Catholic World* (September, 1932), CXXXV, 641–649.

Myers, Walter L., "The Novel Dedicate," *The Virginia Quarterly Review* (July, 1932), VIII, 410–418.

Sherman, Stuart P., *Critical Woodcuts*, Charles Scribner's Sons, 1926, 32–48.

West, Rebecca, *The Strange Necessity*, Doubleday, Doran & Company, 1928, 233–248.

Winsten, Archer, "A Defense of Willa Cather," *The Bookman* (March, 1932), LXXIV, 634–640.

AMPERSAND

Humphrey, Zephine, "Dorothy Canfield," *The Woman Citizen* (January, 1926), X, 13–14.

Mann, Dorothea Lawrence, "Dorothy Canfield: The Little Vermonter," *The Bookman* (August, 1927), LXV, 695–701.

Phelps, William Lyon, "Dorothy Canfield, Novelist," *The Saturday Review of Literature* (October 11, 1930), VII, 199.

Twitchett, E. G., "Mr. Thornton Wilder," *The London Mercury* (May, 1930), XXII, 32–39.

431